CAUGHT OUT

CAUGHT OUT

CRICKET MATCH-FIXING INVESTIGATED

LAURIE A CLAASE

UMUZI

To my father, a man of faith, who became a different kind of believer, and to Lee, my partner, who has always believed in me.

Published by Umuzi, P.O. Box 6810, Roggebaai 8012
umuzi@randomhouse.co.za
an imprint of Random House (Pty) Ltd,
Isle of Houghton, Corner Boundary Road & Carse O'Gowrie,
Houghton 2198, South Africa

First edition, first printing 2007
ISBN 978-1-4152-0043-8

Cover design by Sally Swart
Cover photograph courtesy of Gallo Images/Getty Images
Design and layout by Pete Bosman
Set in Minion Pro 10.3 on 13
Printed and bound by Paarl Print,
Oosterland Street, Paarl, South Africa

Contents

1

Too close to the sun

Cronjé and cricket's fall from grace

Many men and women enjoy popular esteem, not because they are known but because they are not known.

– Sebastien-Roch Nicolas Chamfort,
French journalist and playwright (1741–1794)

Like Hansie, I have a confession to make. When I first heard the news, at second hand, from a friend on that fateful weekend early in April 2000, I dismissed it out of hand. I didn't even bother to follow the feeding frenzy in the papers and when I got to work on Monday, I announced, loudly and with self-righteous authority, that the whole thing was a set-up. It would be like accusing Mother Theresa of embezzling church funds and everyone knew the Indians were a bunch of crooks, anyway. A friend ventured to suggest that perhaps I was not best qualified to judge the man's innocence or guilt as I had never met him. Such a timely warning, however, did not serve to stem the tide of my indignation.

I found myself in good company. Over the weekend that followed the New Delhi police filing charges against Hansie Cronjé, Herschelle Gibbs, Pieter Strydom and Nicky Boje for criminal conspiracy, a flurry of newspaper editorials called for apologies from the Indian government. Durban's *Sunday Tribune* on 9 April trumpeted, 'It's not our Hansie.' *The Mercury* ran with the front page lead, 'Nothing to hide, says Cronjé.' The Afrikaans newspaper *Beeld* insisted that the Indians must produce proof. Media reports couldn't agree whether the Delhi police had stumbled upon the match-fixing conspiracy by accident or acted on a tip-off and bugged Cronjé's cellphone. Whatever the facts of the matter, after apprising the Indian government of their discoveries, the Delhi police made their allegations public at a media conference, which was televised on Star TV on 7 April 2000. To back up their case, attached to the press release was a transcript of telephone dialogue between Cronjé and alleged London-based bookie, Sanjeev Chawla who, Delhi police claimed, had stayed at the same hotel as Cronjé during the first one-day international (ODI) against India in Kochi the previous month.

Non-cricketing nations would have been bewildered by the furore created by Hansiegate. The story pushed all else off the front pages in South Africa, even in white-collar publications such as the *Financial Mail*, which devoted its editorial of 14 April to the subject. 'The way the Indian police went about things hardly inspires confidence ... And if staying in a hotel at the same time as a crook is evidence of guilt, we must all be guilty of something.' In the same edition of the *Financial Mail*, the cover story is, not surprisingly, devoted to cricket. Barney Mthombothi, in an article entitled 'The end of our innocence' cuts straight to the chase in his opening sentence: 'Hansie's disgrace is an opportunity for South Africans to heal this sick country.' The author lays the moral degeneracy of South Africa at the WHITES ONLY door of apartheid, which reshaped the world to reflect the delusion that worth can be measured by the colour of one's skin. However, there is more to this contemporary tragedy than merely a black and white morality tale. Cronjé's fall from grace casts a long shadow. As an Indian fan pointed out in the aftermath of Cronjé's confession, '... if a man like Cronjé can be involved in these type of things then anyone may be corrupt.'[1] That conclusion would seem to be inescapable.

Reminiscent of Mark Anthony's insidious refrain that Brutus was an 'honourable man', the South African government, the United Cricket Board of South Africa (UCBSA, hereafter the UCB), team management, the media and the church rallied round their man. On the Saturday of that turbulent weekend, Aziz Pahad, Deputy Foreign Minister and long-standing friend of the UCB's Managing Director, Dr Ali Bacher, assured the UCB that the South African government would be looking into the Indians' breach of protocol in not contacting any cricket official in South Africa before publicising their charges. Pahad promised that the government would also be investigating the tapping of South African cricketers' phones while they were on tour in India.[2] 'I have spoken to Hansie Cronjé and he says it is absolute rubbish. There is nothing at all in it,' Bacher told AFP on the day the story broke. 'The United Cricket Board of South Africa is certain that no South African cricket player has ever been involved in match-fixing.'[3] The following day, 8 April, in a UCB press release, Bacher committed this sentiment to paper: 'South African captain, Hansie Cronjé, is a man of enormous integrity and honesty.'[4]

On 10 April, the acting UCB President at the time, Advocate Percy Sonn, drawing on his extensive legal experience, made it quite clear that there was no chance of Cronjé travelling to India to stand trial and no prospect of a South African inquiry into the Indian allegations:

> We have no treaties with India ... The Indian police are an agency of the Indian government. If they do certain things which affect any of our nationals – or

national assets as the South African team is – then obviously it's something for our own government to handle. It's not the Indian cricket board who approached us with anything. It's not a cricket matter, it's something for the governments to work out. Why should we institute an inquiry, especially as they don't want to surrender the tape to enable it to be assessed for veracity.[5]

Trevor Chesterfield, senior cricket writer and contributor to *cricinfo.com*, the official cricket website in South Africa, and one of Cronjé's closest media friends, was the only South African at the time to have heard the phone tapes, while waiting to be interviewed on an Indian radio station. He concluded that the whole thing was a hoax. 'It is felt that the tactics used (by the Delhi Police) were of a similar paranoid nature to those used by the South African secret police to trap a "suspect" at any cost.' He observed that, had the accusation been made a week earlier, it would have been '... a very poor April Fools joke'.[6]

Unconsciously echoing Chesterfield, Bob Woolmer, former South African coach, declared: 'My initial thoughts are that this is a bad April Fool's joke. I am convinced that Hansie Cronjé is not guilty and that he would not even contemplate such actions. These allegations are absolute garbage. He is not the type of person to get involved in anything like this.'[7] In spite of this vehement vote of confidence, it would turn out that Woolmer knew of a match-fixing offer put to the entire South African team by its captain in India in 1996. And he had been approached himself while coach of the South African team.[8]

Cronjé, himself, in the same UCB press statement, gave credence to such support: 'The allegations are completely without substance ... I have been privileged to play for South Africa since 1992 and I want to assure every South African that I have made a hundred per cent effort to win every match that I have played. It has been an honour to play for South Africa and I would never do anything to let my country down.' He reiterated his innocence, in person, the following day at a press conference in Durban on 9 April, in his first public appearance since the story had broken two days earlier: 'I was stunned when I heard the allegations. I told Dr Bacher it was absolute rubbish. I want to make it 100% clear that I never received any sum of money during the one-day international series. I want to make it clear that I have never spoken to any member of the team about throwing a game.'

Subsequent revelations give these words a hollow ring.

Ray McCauley, Cronjé's spiritual advisor, head of the charismatic Rhema Church and unofficial chaplain to the South African cricket, rugby and soccer teams, also vouched for his black sheep: 'Because I know Hansie as a person of integrity I cannot believe he would be party to any such allegation.'[9] Like the captaincy he inherited from Kepler Wessels, Cronjé was also bequeathed Pastor

Ray McCauley. The former bodybuilder-turned-preacher was first invited on tour with the South African team by then-skipper, Wessels, to lead bible study with some of the players. Once Cronjé became captain, McCauley became a regular team fixture and had spent the previous ten years travelling the world as the '...unofficial chaplain to the South African cricket, rugby and soccer teams'. He told writer Deon Gouws, 'I do it because it's a calling; no sports body has ever paid for a plane ticket or hotel room of mine'.[10] Coincidentally, McCauley's father was a professional bookmaker and it was Pastor Ray that Cronjé called in the middle of the night to confess his association with the bookmaking fraternity.

So much for the weekend's sound and fury. By Tuesday I, along with many others, was applying myself to eating crow. In the early hours of 11 April, Cronjé confessed to not having told the whole truth: '... in a moment of stupidity and weakness, I allowed Satan and the world to dictate terms to me, rather than the Lord'.[11]

The newspaper banners heralded the sea-change:

Cape Argus: 'I lied'
The Star: 'Hansie: A nation betrayed'
The Citizen: 'If Hansie can be bought who cannot?'

The Citizen's political cartoon was suitably elegiac. 'Too close to the sun' was the caption, appropriating the Greek myth of Icarus who challenged the natural order and built himself wings to knock upon the very gates of heaven. He flew too close to the sun and the wax binding his wings melted, plummeting him into the sea. Raymond White, former president of the South African cricket board, in an interview with the UK's *Independent* on 4 June 2000 drew the parallels: 'A flawed hero has been brought down by a weakness for money that gave in under the enormous pressure that goes with the job of modern cricket captain. Few men in modern times have been able to handle it for long.'

And I, after wiping the last crow-feather from my mouth, cast about for the author of the myth of Hansie Cronjé.

Hansie Wessels Cronjé was earmarked for greatness early on, attracting sponsorships since the age of 17. Long the crown-prince-in-waiting, he officially assumed the mantle of South African captain from Kepler Wessels in November 1994, six months after the country's first democratic elections.

At the age of 25 he was the youngest member of the team and for the next five years was to epitomise the fresh face of cricket in the newly branded Rainbow Nation. Throughout the suburbs and the squatter camps, the factories and the farms, the high-rises and the hinterland of South Africa, the team flickered green and gold on TV screens and came to life in hard-fought backyard World Cup games. Well-known South African journalists Andrew Donaldson and Adam Levin summed it up: 'Cricket has become the sport of national unity, putting paid to that soccer/rugby, black/white thing.'[12] It was a message tailor-made for media marketing campaigns. The setting: A dusty township road at twilight. An impromptu cricket game is about to get underway. The dusky ten-year-old participants are wrangling over who gets to be the skipper, 'You can be Jonty and I'll be Hansie'. Negotiations are disturbed by Mom, calling them in for supper because it's getting dark. Comes the plaintive refrain, 'But Ma, it's a day/night game!' as the floodlights come on courtesy of one-day international cricket sponsors, Standard Bank.

Cronjé was the personification of the English public school boy captain: upright, clean, God-fearing – with a Pentecostal twist. On TV, he was often shown wearing his WWJD (What Would Jesus Do?) bracelet. Veteran sports writer and contributor to the *Mail and Guardian*, Andy Capostagno, summed it up: 'A Cronjé behaving boorishly in public is about as likely as a volkstaat in Soweto.'[13] Then, a new side to the South African captain was glimpsed at the end of the final Test against Australia in Adelaide in February 1998 when Cronjé speared a stump through the door of the umpires' room. There was more controversy during a limited-overs game on this tour when TV replays showed Cronjé rolling the ball underfoot. No official action was forthcoming and the United Cricket Board of South Africa refused to sanction its captain.

Matthew Pearce, editor of *SA Sports Illustrated*, underwent some collective soul-searching in his editorial of July 2000:

> I realise that many people would question why we never documented those incidents in Cronjé's career before, the simple answer is that no-one was ever prepared to speak out about them and jeopardise their relationship with the then captain for fear of compromising their livelihood. That in itself gives one an indication of the kind of autonomy and power afforded to Cronjé in his running of the national team. As a reader pointed out, we as a magazine, have lauded Cronjé's efforts as a player and a captain for almost a decade, very seldom, if ever, finding fault with his demeanour and dedication to his sport and his country. Imagine, then, how difficult it is for us to put our hand up and say "Sorry, we got it so very wrong. We believed as much as all of you did." It is a tribute to the quality of a superb public relations effort.

By the end of 1998, the Colin Bryden report on a South African team meeting called in 1996 to discuss the possible fixing of a match was published in the *Sunday Times*. Headlined 'Proud South Africans hit match-fixers for six', the incident is passed off as an example of the South African team's moral mettle in rejecting the offer. After revelations in the King Commission, it seems that up to three meetings were required to muster the necessary mettle – if, in fact, the mettle was mustered at all. Coach Woolmer claimed that he knew of only one meeting and that he found out about it later. 'My stance,' he said, 'was that anyone who even thought about taking the money should be thrown out.' As Owen Slot pointed out in the *Electronic Telegraph*, 'Along those guidelines, his team would have been seriously depleted.'[14]

Despite such omens, the Cronjé myth persisted. Adrian Hadland, the then political editor of the *Sunday Independent*, explained: 'So much rested on Hansie Cronjé; more perhaps than we realised. Like Francois Pienaar, [captain of South Africa's victorious World Cup rugby team in 1995] he personified what we thought the new South Africa was about. Like our rainbow nation he persevered in the face of adversity and triumphed when those all around him had given up hope.'[15]

However, less than six years after becoming captain, the carefully constructed illusion was shattered. June 2000 saw '... the cricketing equivalent of Nelson Mandela'[16] exposing the underbelly of international cricket before the King Commission of Inquiry into Match-fixing in South African cricket. Cronjé's ten hours of testimony cast suspicion on a bewildering array of matches under his captaincy, including the first and last series in which he played. Both ODIs and five-day Tests, the games cover a period of time that stretched, ironically, from the Mandela Cup played in South Africa in January 1995 to Cronjé's last game in the final of the Sharjah Cup in March 2000.

On the concluding day of the King Commission before adjournment on Monday 26 June 2000, the cross-examination of Hamid Cassim, self-proclaimed cricket enthusiast, sweet-shop owner and suspected middleman in Cronjé's illicit earnings, was interrupted just before lunch as journalists flocked from the room to investigate a disturbance outside the Centre for the Book. A beefy chorus line of red and white track-suited Rand Afrikaans University students was giving a stirring rendition on Queen Victoria Street. Arms locked, they bellowed, 'We want the naked truth'. There could have been no doubt about the earnestness of their appeal. Their pants were around their ankles as they sang '*Gee Hansie nog 'n kansie*'. [Give Hansie another chance.] One feels that Queen Victoria would not have been amused.

Such displays of support for Hansie Cronjé reflected perhaps something of the South African psyche, battered and bruised as it has been by the revelations of dirty dealings in a sport that has done much to unite a divided country. If Cronjé was the face of the new South Africa, then the country was now being forced to hold up the mirror to itself. Denial was an understandable response to the revelations unfolding in our living rooms day after day, but as with the OJ Simpson case, reactions throughout the cricket world were coloured by ugly instincts.

Michael Henderson, writing for the online version of the English *Daily Telegraph* the day after the Delhi police publicised their charges, was of the opinion that, when discussing the subject of match-fixing, Pakistan cricket is '...always the best place to start'. He did, however, quickly move on to the Australians and the belated confessions of Mark Waugh and Shane Warne that they had taken money from a bookmaker. He continued:

> Nobody who studied the evidence could honestly say that the Australians were guilty of anything more damning than stupidity. It is not necessarily seen like that in India and Pakistan, where some people view the world of cricket as an Anglocentric conspiracy, and where the C word is never far away. As we have seen more seriously in Zimbabwe recently, the colonial past lives on in the popular imagination ... Now the torch of criticism is trained on the South Africans.[17]

Four days later, after Cronjé confessed to his extra-curricular dealings, Henderson was back. In an *Electronic Telegraph* article of the 12 April, peppered with Shakespearean quotes, righteous indignation and nationalistic fervour, Henderson declared, 'According to a Bombay police investigator, with the exception of Australia and England, some sides can be purchased.' There is no mention of the disclosures made by English players, Adam Hollioake, Dougie Brown and Chris Lewis, that they too had been approached by bookmakers and that, according to Lewis, three 'household names' in English cricket were on the take. Henderson called for the English and Welsh cricket boards to '... make a stand on moral grounds' and advised them to boycott one-day internationals with Pakistan and India until they brought the offenders to book. No mention was made of boycotting Australian matches because of Mark Waugh and Shane Warne, who continued to play for the national side. He maintained, 'If necessary, England should stand alone'.[18]

As for the Australians, a report on the Australian cricket website *The Pavilion* pleaded, 'Let's not cast the sinner adrift'. Quoting 1 Corinthians 10:12: 'Let him that thinks he stands take care lest he fall' alongside Kerry Packer's 'There's a bit of a whore in all of us, don't you think?' the article argues for Cronjé's return to cricket.

> Poachers make the best gamekeepers and he could be put in charge of a body appointed to root out corruption. Such a body could begin by cross-examining captains past and present and could seek help from those unaffected, espe-

cially Zimbabwe and England and, in recent times, Australia. Australia could play a part in Cronjé's rehabilitation. He could coach at an academy or a state, should a position fall vacant … Cronjé must not be turned away. Followers should be disappointed rather than outraged. Eventually cricket will be called upon to prove its stature by welcoming back the fallen hero.[19]

Shafiek Abrahams, a South African provincial cricketer and contemporary of Cronjé's, summed up his feelings on Cronjé's fall from grace:

He made a mistake. We should carry on with life because there's more serious crimes that are being committed and we should just live with it like we live with all those other crimes, and as a person or as a cricketer, I think he deserves every accolade he ever received. What he's done, I'm not saying it's right what he's done, but it's a mistake that he made, he's owned up to it, he's been punished for it and now life must go on.

Africa has long been used to endemic corruption, rooted in the colonial inheritance and brought to fruition throughout the post-independent continent. The popular South African cartoonist, Zapiro, linked the cricketing scandal to a megalomaniac African ruler running his country into the ground as fast as his Italian brogues allow. The context of his cartoon was the Zimbabwe election of 2000 which was marred by land invasions and widespread intimidation. Zapiro penned a shifty-eyed Mugabe in cricket whites, standing hand-on-hip at the wicket and tossing up a cricket ball while the opposition lies trussed in front of the stumps and the UN Monitors umpire runs off the field shouting 'Match-fixing!'[20]

Zapiro may well have been inspired by a piece of irony so exquisite that fiction must bow once more to the enduring strangeness of truth. Ten days before the publication of his cartoon, *The Star* newspaper on 13 June 2000 quoted cricket fan Robert Mugabe's sentiments on Cronjé's misfortunes: 'I'm heartbroken by what the chap is going through. I never thought he would be lost to cricket so early in his career.' Speaking as the mission-school boy he once was, Mugabe empathised, 'He used to be very good but, as he said, Satan got the better of him.'[21]

In India, too, it seems, corruption is taken for granted. In a guest column on the website *Rediff*, Ramesh Venkat described a visit to Bangalore which prompted the conclusion that 'Corruption in India is a given thing … Wherever I turned, I saw apathy … people have grown to accepting corruption as a way of life.'[22] Politicians and government officials, however, are not regarded as super-human. Contemporary cricketers, on the other hand, are all but deified in countries like India where role-models, in general, are in short supply, and as Venkat explains, '… heroes are literally worshipped'. Fans committing suicide when their team loses a match is a common phenomenon on the subcontinent. Disgraced physiotherapist to the Indian team, Dr Ali Irani, summed it up for an Indian judicial commission in 1997: 'Cricket is not a sport but a religion.' The clatter of falling gods reverberates long after in the vacant shrines they leave behind.

The life and times of Kapil Dev, captain of the Indian team that won the 1983 World Cup and former coach of the Indian team, was once on the high school reading list in two Indian states. Resigning under the match-fixing cloud that threatened to carry away many of Indian cricket's idols in the downpour, his biography was removed from the school syllabus.

It remained to be seen whether Cronjé's legacy to South Africa would be as easy to erase. Children who once idolised cricket's super-heroes now made fun of them on national TV. On the SABC 2 show *Small Talk*, presenter Martin Bailie encouraged six-year-old Jaycee-Lee to tell a joke. Jaycee-Lee obliged, pulling out this gem from his repertoire. Q: Why has the South African cricket team stopped smoking? A: Because they lost all their matches.

Out of the mouths of babes.

2

Passage to India

South Africa's return to international cricket

It's like apartheid you know. It's such a powerful thing. But if you analyse it, it was really driven by just a handful of politicians who felt strongly enough about the concept and for a long time they had enough power that they could institutionalise it ... So, yes, this match-fixing issue is like apartheid: it's a big thing and it's a terrible thing, but I honestly think in the end it's only a small number of individuals.

– Imtiaz Patel, former Director of Professional Cricket at the UCB[23]

A fact not often remarked upon is that there is a long history of Xhosa cricket in South Africa. The 'gentleman's game' came first to the southern tip of the 'dark continent' with the British, who took over the Cape in 1806 and promptly resumed playing cricket. As British influence extended northwards into the interior, the soldiers of the Empire took the game with them. Then came a wave of British settlement to the Eastern Cape in 1820. Back in England, cricket was engulfed in suspicion, the extent of the corruption confirmed by the banishment from Lords of William Lambert, one of England's greatest cricketing stars, in 1817. But in South Africa, by the mid-1880s, the game was entrenched with the help of popular village cricket tournaments known as *amacala egusha* – 'sides of the sheep'. The first African Cricket Club was established in Port Elizabeth in 1869 and by 1884 interracial matches were being played between town sides. In the British colony of Natal, however, the Zulu never took to the sport and it was the Indians and traders of Durban that padded up enthusiastically.

By 1913 all the major centres were playing cricket. Mining houses and mission schools encouraged the sport. Gold mines in Kimberley and the Witwatersrand attracted migrant workers from the rural areas who came into contact with horse racing, boxing and cricket; the mining houses built sports facilities, realising the advantages of having a healthy labour force. The fires were kept burning by mission schools such as Lovedale in the Eastern Cape and Zonnebloem in Cape Town, the latter a school for the sons of Xhosa chiefs started by Sir George Grey, the Cape Governor, with the aim of 'civilising' them. According to the Cape

Town Mayor in 1910, Zonnebloem had '… the best cricket team in the whole of the Peninsula'.[24]

However, those early Xhosa cricket stars from Zonnebloem missed the boat by almost half a century. South Africa fielded a black cricket team for a foreign tour for the first time in 1958. The country had almost had its first national black player in 1894. Fast bowler Krom Hendricks from Cape Town was included in South Africa's first tour to England before pressure from the Cape Colony administration forced his omission. The apartheid government of the National Party came to power in 1948 and continued the tradition.

Wicketkeeper/batsman Ben Malamba, also from Cape Town, had played for a Western Province black XI in 1947. Eleven years later, Malamba was selected to represent the black South African Cricket Board of Control on the first black international tour, to Kenya, in 1958. Little did he know that this was to be black cricket's swan-song for the next half-century. Segregation was in full swing, with the Group Areas Act, passed in 1950, forbidding blacks and whites to live in the same residential areas and the Separate Amenities Act of 1953 prohibiting different races from sharing recreational areas. 'After 1958, black cricket declined to the point of extinction.'[25]

South African cricket's international isolation began after the 1969/70 tour in which Ali Bacher captained a rampant home side to victory. Hansie Cronjé was born on 25 September 1969, three months before Bill Lawry's Australians arrived on what was to be the final official international tour of South Africa for the next two decades. India was instrumental in welcoming the South Africans back and a young Cronjé would travel with the team that played the first officially sanctioned matches of post-isolation in 1991. But first, the crown prince would have to learn his trade.

Like Zonnebloem in Cape Town, Grey College in Bloemfontein was also funded by the Cape Governor, Sir George Grey. Founded in 1855, it is the third oldest school in the country. Today, it continues the boys-only, English public school tradition, but in the singular medium of Afrikaans. Bloemfontein remains the Afrikaner heartland of the country where the traditional sport has long been rugby rather than cricket, which was regarded as an Englishman's game despite the fact that rugby too was a game inherited from the English. It was an Afrikaner who introduced cricket to Grey College and helped produce two of South Africa's Afrikaner cricket captains, Kepler Wessels and Hansie Cronjé, and its most famous pace bowler, Allan Donald. The three cricketers went back a long way together.

John Volsteedt, headmaster of Grey College like his father before him, started his thirty-seven-year association with the school as an Afrikaans teacher in 1971. A cricket enthusiast, he recognised the fledgling talent of young Kepler

Wessels right away and took him under his wing as cricket coach. Wessels went on to play sixteen Tests as South African captain. In Kepler's wake came Hansie Cronjé. Cronjé's mother had been Kepler's tennis coach at nursery school, yet despite the twelve-year age gap between them, Edward Griffiths, in his biography of Wessels, describes the two homeboys as 'Tweedledum and Tweedledee'.[26] Their careers were to overlap at several points over the years, with Wessels captaining Eastern Province when Cronjé made his debut with Orange Free State in January 1988 before going on to captain his province at the tender age of 20. Cronjé was to be South Africa's vice captain to skipper Wessels before taking over the mantle from him in November 1994, aged just 25. Allan Donald has been a family friend since his friendship with Hansie's older brother Frans in their primary school days. South Africa's best-loved fast bowler spent two years at Grey and eleven years in the national squad, from South Africa's international comeback in 1991 until early 2003. As for Volsteedt, before becoming headmaster of Grey in 1993, he served a stint as provincial coach from 1989, shortly after Cronjé was selected for the Orange Free State. At that time, the Free State team comprised no less than eight Grey Old Boys, including captain Joubert Strydom.[27]

While cricket has covered Grey College in glory, the events of 2000 marred a glittering record. Two of the four South African players named by the Delhi police in their charges of cricket corruption attended Grey. Nicky Boje followed in Hansie Cronjé's footsteps in Bloemfontein and is another long-standing family friend. In a much-publicised three-part interview on pay-per-view TV channel M-Net, in late August 2000, while still under the cloud of the King Commission, Cronjé described how '... the Boje and Cronjé family played in the back yard'.[28]

'Like father, like son,' the old saying goes. Cronjé's father Ewie was once a teacher at Grey College. He too played for the Orange Free State, from 1960–1971, and was captain in the 1960s. He was director of Sport at the University of the Orange Free State before extending his cricketing career by becoming the President of the Orange Free State Cricket Union. Ewie's ties with that other player-turned-administrator, Ali Bacher, go back many years. A much younger Ali captained a rampant South African side against Australia in 1970, convincingly winning the last international Test series before isolation. Thirty years later, the 58-year-old Bacher described his relationship with the Cronjés to the King Commission of Inquiry in 2000, with Ewie Cronjé in attendance. 'I have known the Cronjé family for decades. His father, Ewie here, is a wonderful man and has done wonderful work for sport in the Free State. He is synonymous very much with not only cricket and tennis and all other sports, not only in Bloemfontein but also at the university.' Of his father's relationship with the

Managing Director of the UCB, Cronjé said in the same M-Net interview, 'They spent a lot of time together.'[29] In the course of the King Commission hearings, Dr Bacher also shed some light on the long-standing friendship between Hansie Cronjé and that other stalwart of the South African side, Jonty Rhodes.

'During the 1980s, it emerged very quickly that there were two rising stars in South African cricket, Hansie Cronjé and Jonty Rhodes. In the latter part of the 1980s, a South African school team was chosen and had as their captain Hansie Cronjé and Jonty Rhodes as vice captain.'

In December 1987, the SA Schools team squared up for a match against the Orange Free State side in Bloemfontein. Cronjé and Rhodes took to the crease as opening batsmen and prepared to face the pace of Free State's Allan Donald and Corrie van Zyl, who would also play for South Africa before becoming assistant coach to the South African team. At the King Commission, Bacher's testimony turned to 1987: 'My memories go back to 1987 when for the very first time, we took cricket to the township of Rocklands in Bloemfontein. It was mid-winter, it was a very cold wintry day ... Ewie was there with Hansie and Corrie van Zyl to start the process of taking cricket to the disadvantaged people of South Africa in that particular area.' Back then, as fresh-faced boys with wealth and glory beckoning, who could have predicted the dizzy heights from which Cronjé would plummet, fifteen years and a lifetime later. The Cronjé and Rhodes families remained close and celebrated the millennium together at a party hosted by Sea Point bookie Henry Mansell, at Erinvale Golf Estate.[30] In February 2001, the Cronjés attended the christening of Jonty and Kate's daughter.[31] Donald and Cronjé still kept in touch. When, at the end of South African cricket's *annus horribilis*, Allan Donald became the fifteenth cricketer in the world to take 300 wickets, serendipitously in Bloemfontein, the home town he shared with his friend and former captain, he told the *Citizen* newspaper in South Africa, 'As it happened, my mind went straight to Hansie ... Whenever we've reached milestones, broken partnerships and taken great wickets, he was always the first one there to congratulate me. I will certainly give him a ring.'[32]

But all that still lay in the future. Up until 1977, South African cricket was racially segregated and separately governed. On 18 September 1977, white, Asian, coloured and black cricketers came together under one administrative umbrella – the South African Cricket Union (SACU). There were now high hopes for South Africa's recall from the wilderness, but the road back was no primrose path. A dissident breakaway group from the formerly non-white cricket organisations established a rival body, the South African Cricket Board (SACB), which insisted on political change before sporting co-operation. Thus the fractured nature of South African cricket continued and the gates of international participation remained closed.

When Ali Bacher masterminded the era of rebel tours, the battle lines were drawn and the liberation struggle moved onto the cricket pitch. The mass demonstrations that took place during England's second rebel tour under Mike Gatting forced the series to a premature end and brought about negotiations between the SACB and the SACU. The men who headed these organisations were Krish Mackerdhuj, who became President of SACB in 1984, and Ali Bacher, the South African Cricket Union's first Managing Director. That first tentative meeting between Bacher and Mackerdhuj, at a Durban hotel on 8 September 1990, was chaired by Steve Tshwete, who would go on to become South Africa's Minister of Sport and then Minister of Safety and Security.

Mackerdhuj had attended the University of Fort Hare in the Eastern Cape, that breeding ground of Africa's new leaders, between 1958 and 1963. Mission institutions such as Fort Hare had instilled an appreciation of cricket in many of Africa's leaders who passed through these halls of learning – Kenneth Kaunda and Robert Mugabe, Oliver Tambo, Nelson Mandela and Thabo Mbeki, to name some of the most prominent. Both South African Presidents, Mandela and Mbeki, played a role in facilitating South African cricket's return from exile.

In April 1991, three years before the apartheid government finally surrendered the reins of power, Ali Bacher met with top officials of the newly unbanned ANC in the Johannesburg suburb of Mayfair. Representatives included Thabo Mbeki, who was the foreign affairs spokesperson for the ANC at that time, and Joe Modise, who would become the Minister of Defence in the new South Africa and who would also later be implicated in the probe into the ANC government's multi-billion rand arms tender. Following that meeting in 1991, Steve Tshwete joined Ali Bacher in his crusade to the world's cricket-playing nations. They carried with them a letter from Mbeki encouraging South Africa's readmission to world cricket. Just two months later, on the 29 June 1991, all the racially segregated cricket bodies came together in the United Cricket Board of South Africa (UCBSA), led by Dr Ali Bacher. A week later, UCB President Geoff Dakin, Vice-President Mackerdhuj, Managing Director Ali Bacher and Steve Tshwete represented South African cricket at the annual meeting of the ICC in London. On 10 July 1991, South Africa was officially welcomed back into the fold of Test-playing nations, after almost twenty-two years of international isolation.

Jagmohan Dalmiya, President of the Bengal Cricket Association, helped bring about the South African tour of India that heralded South African cricket's return from the wilderness. India had supported South Africa's appeal for readmission and, fittingly, it would be on Indian soil that South Africa made its long-delayed international comeback. However, this came about by accident rather than design.

The UCB delegation continued on their scheduled goodwill visits to the Indian subcontinent and Kenya, now in celebratory mood. In India, Pakistan had pulled out of a tour to India '… for security reasons' and the Board of Control of Cricket in India (BCCI) was facing major financial losses. Ten days before the scheduled start of the tournament, on 10 November 1991, the South Africans found themselves in the right place at the right time. They agreed, on short notice, to step in and bring a team to India, despite the fact that South Africa did not, as yet, have an international squad. Banking on the previous domestic season's statistics to yield a team and the experience of Clive Rice as captain, despite his demotion from the captaincy and then the side for Gatting's rebel tour two years previously, the team was announced. Dave Richardson, captain of Eastern Province, would be wickie and vice captain to Rice and together they would lead some of the old and some of the new greats of South African cricket. Only Kepler Wessels, who had played for Australia during the dark years of South Africa's banishment, had been previously capped. Jimmy Cook, Allan Donald, Andrew Hudson, Peter Kirsten, Adrian Kuiper, Brian McMillan, Clive Rice, Dave Richardson, Tim Shaw and Richard Snell all earned their first international colours.

Three nights before the squad left on its historic tour, Hansie Cronjé, now studying for a BCom at the University of the Orange Free State, received a phone call from Ali Bacher. 'Pack your bags. You're going to India.' Along with Faiek Davids from Western Province, Hussein Manack from Transvaal and Derek Crookes from Natal, whose cricketing career was to overlap with Cronjé's once again nine years later in less auspicious circumstances, Cronjé and his fellow acolytes followed the team to India, to watch and learn.

South Africa's first international one-day game in twenty-two years was played at Eden Gardens in Calcutta on 10 November 1991. All 90 452 seats were taken, the enthusiastic spectators out in full force to witness the rare spectacle of the international debut of almost an entire team. Mohammad Azharuddin who, like Clive Rice, had been absent from his squad for two years, returned to captain his side and Indian wicketkeeper Kieran More, another good friend of Cronjé's, was vice captain. Consummate batsman Azharuddin was Wisden's Cricketer of the Year for 1991.

India won the toss and sent South Africa in to bat. Andrew Hudson, at number 2, faced just 3 balls before succumbing to Kapil Dev and wicketkeeper More to depart for a duck. Kirsten went for 7 and Cook for 17 with South Africa's top order having left the team on 49/3. While Kepler Wessels made his 50, Wisden suggests that it was too slow and at the end of the allotted 47 overs, South Africa yielded the wicket on 177/8.

In what was almost a replay of the South Africans' opening innings the

Indians lost their top order to Donald in his first 4 overs. Like Hudson, opener Ravi Shastri was taken out by Donald and wicketkeeper Richardson for a duck. Numbers 2 and 3, NS Sidhu and S Manjrekar, added 6 and 1 respectively to the tally before bowing to the rampant Donald and India was on 20/3. Azharuddin, batting in his accustomed skipper's berth, number 5, managed only 16 before being bowled by Shaw and stumped by Richardson. Sachin Tendulkar, the 18-year-old boy wonder, helped right the listing ship with a fine 62 and India easily overtook South Africa in just 40.4 overs to win the first historic contest between the two countries. Wisden's Almanack for 1993 observed that 'The cricket was a disappointment and India's victory was easier than the margin suggested'. Despite the Indian win, in a foreshadowing of greatness to come, Allan Donald was Man of the Match.

The home side went on to take the three-match series. However, the national jubilation was not shared by all. Apparently, one of India's biggest bookmakers committed suicide following South Africa's surprise win over India in the third and final ODI of the South African tour of India in November 1991.[33] In his book, *Hansie and the Boys,* Rodney Hartman describes an excited Cronjé telling his brother Frans, after returning from India, 'We even got to see Mother Teresa … We were in the room when Ricey met her. She didn't shake hands with all of us but she handed out her cards.'[34]

By now the participating countries and fixture lists had already been announced for the upcoming World Cup early in 1992. However, the dream of staging South Africa's comeback in the World Cup arena drove a UCB delegation to a special meeting of the International Cricket Council (ICC) in Sharjah in October 1991. The little-known Emirates city of Sharjah was to spring to infamous prominence during the match-fixing scandals of 2000. Displaying the new face of South African cricket, Dakin, Mackerdhuj and Bacher presented their trump card to the ICC – a letter of endorsement from Nelson Mandela, pleading for South Africa's inclusion in the World Cup. While this same strategy would not work for Cape Town's Olympic bid, it worked for cricket. South Africa was going to Australia.

On 26 February 1992, South Africa returned to the international stage at Sydney's cricket ground and beat cup-holding hosts and favourites Australia, on home ground this time, by 9 wickets, bringing history full circle. Hansie Cronjé, Jonty Rhodes and Meyrick Pringle made their ODI debuts in this, the sixth match of the tournament. One of the lasting images of that triumph, prefiguring Nelson Mandela in Francois Pienaar's No 6 rugby jersey, was an emotional Steve Tshwete embracing Kepler Wessels at the 1992 World Cup. South African cricket had finally caught up with the promise of its past. Or had it?

3

A shining light?

South African cricket development

One of the problems I do have with development in the country is so much of it is for the purposes of window-dressing. I'm not just talking here about the white administrators, I'm talking about black politicians every bit as much … I think there's a lot of window-dressing.

– Martin Gillingham, Sports Editor, *Cape Talk* Radio

Six years after South Africa's readmission to world cricket, Dr Ali Bacher, acknowledging the fractured history of South African cricket and the omissions of the past, wrote in a UCB brochure put out in April 1997 that development has been a priority since the inception of the UCBSA. Steve Tshwete, by then South Africa's Minister of Sport, delivered the brochure's introduction: 'The United Cricket Board's development programme is, indeed, a shining light and an example of what can be achieved with initiative, commitment and a sense of purpose.'

Belying such self-congratulation, however, early in 1997 there had been rumblings of discontent within South Africa's cricket community in the Western and Eastern Cape. Articles appeared in regional and national newspapers observing that there was a good representation of black players at junior level, but they were not making the jump into the provincial or national teams. Club cricket in the Western and Eastern Cape provinces of Border, Western Province and Boland was pinpointed as the problem and the almost exclusively white clubs were seen as the surviving strongholds of social privilege. There was a perception too that Dr Ali Bacher single-handedly ruled the roost and that the Board was '… little more than a means to an end.'[35] What that end might have been was not spelt out, but calls were made for a quota system in provincial cricket.

Ironically, Minister of Sport Steve Tshwete and his fellow Robben Island prisoner, Mluleki George, found themselves in different dressing rooms on the cricket issue. George, then President of the National Sports Council, was outspokenly critical of the UCB's development policy. He was quoted in a contentious report in the *Cape Times* on 24 April 1997 as saying: 'They [the UCB] can talk a lot about development, but right now it looks more like a PR exercise than anything else and we're not seeing results.'[36]

In July of this fractious year, the UCB called together all stakeholders in South African cricket to assess the achievements and failures of the past and to plot the way forward in the 1997 Cricket Vision Seminar. However, the team announced by Peter Pollock and his team of selectors for the Pakistan tour in September and October 1997 did not help matters. Apparently, George was incensed that Herschelle Gibbs had not been included in the squad. But Gibbs could hardly be classified as 'under-privileged', having attended the Diocesan College (Bishops), one of the most elite schools in Cape Town. The only non-white member of the squad was Paul Adams.

Ten years on, despite the long tradition of black cricket in the country and a development programme that had been described by the South African cricket board as 'a shining light', the South African team still does not reflect the country's demographics or the rapidly expanding cross-racial appeal of the game. Of the fourteen players contracted to Cricket South Africa (CSA) for 2007/8, only four were players of colour.

In search of answers when the Hansie story broke, I interviewed three people well-placed to tell me why this should be so. John Young, sports writer, cricket-lover and friend of Langa Cricket Club; Craig Matthews, former South African vice captain and then Marketing Manager for Western Province cricket; and John Commins, ex-captain of Western Province and capped Test batsman.

Sitting in the dining room at Newlands Cricket Ground with Craig Matthews, the past South African fast/medium seam bowler, I asked him where were the grandchildren of those great black cricketers of the 1950s and 1960s. Matthews admitted, 'They're not there.'

> Now the thing that worries me about that … I used to have that theory from a development point of view that it was always going to be the second generation who really came on as cricket people because you need to be brought up in a cricket household and your father needs to have played and all that. We used to have that naive feeling about them, the development players, which wasn't strictly true because, if you talk to them and read the history and whatever, they had a great passion for cricket. So that destroys that theory. So there were people being brought up in cricket homes as such, so that theory I'm not sure is justified. I understand the problems with facilities and I also understand the difficulty of coming out of that type of scenario and coming to a place like this. Psychologically it's difficult to handle. The problems and challenges we have are not cricket. They're social, political.

It was John Young, former schoolteacher and cricket coach, that introduced me to the notion that cricket was a 'heritage game', one inherited from one's forebears, polished at a traditional cricket school and displayed at the right club with the right connections. 'Very few players make it. Of any sort. But the odds are hugely stacked in favour of traditional schools.' Young outlined his reasons. Established cricket schools have better facilities and coaching expertise and encourage expectations of success, confident in the belief that they know the game best. Prejudice rears its ugly head. The mindset of past selectors, according to Young, was that '... a Grey boy is more likely to handle pressure than a Plumstead boy or a Belhar boy or a Langa boy' – all Cape Town suburbs on the wrong side of the tracks. Presumably acting on this hypothesis, an assessment of the 1996/97 achievements of the UCB revealed that 55 young disadvantaged players were given bursaries to traditional cricketing schools. By 2000, this figure had risen to 180. Commented Matthews:

> If we really genuinely, honestly want to grow the game in this country we need a sustainable, preferably a group, but particularly one, sustainable black cricketer who becomes a hero in his own township. We still haven't done that. I understand the hard work and the money that has driven cricket development in this country but we still haven't created one black cricketer, even in our domestic competition, who comes from an historically township-type school. We don't let them do that. Hence, Ntini, all these guys ... Even a guy like Thami Tsolekile went to Pinelands. It's not a township or development-type school. Now, I'll only believe that we've actually got there when a guy matriculates from a township school and then goes to play for South Africa. Then it's the genuine article. Until we can do that and have a production line of that, it doesn't work. It's not only cricket. Rugby's in the same boat.

The softly spoken John Commins agreed with Craig Matthews, his former Western Province team-mate. We were sipping coffee in his suburban restaurant, all his ties with cricket now severed, it would appear. 'Gibbs, we're still calling Gibbs a development player.' Commins also mentioned Thami Tsolekile and added Paul Adams to the list of pseudo-development players. Paul Adams of the loopy wrist action came from Grassy Park, a lower-middle-class coloured area, but transferred across the tracks to Plumstead High School for the sake of his cricketing future, while hot prospect Thami Tsolekile attended Pinelands High, Craig Matthews' old school. 'All traditional schools,' pronounced Commins.

> We're pulling the wool over our eyes here ... Their development programme is all about taking it to the masses, which is great, I've got nothing against

it, but traditional schools is where you're going to produce the next cricketing stars. They're sitting there waiting, their parents were great cricketers, they're sitting waiting for someone to grab them and bring them through and we mustn't forget about them. Because they're not disadvantaged, whether they're disadvantaged enough or not, I don't care, there's talent sitting there that needs to come through … you can't ignore them and I think the parents are starting to get frustrated now because they can see their youngster has talent but no one is doing anything about it.

INTERVIEWER: What about undiscovered talent in the townships?

COMMINS: I've got nothing against us going out there but let's not focus completely on that. Let's make sure we still focus on traditional schools. We want to become a nation that wins Test matches. We can't try and find eleven disadvantaged players, we've got to make sure that the main core is just on talent, on natural talent and ja, if one or two guys come through from townships, great, that's fantastic but we can't be pushing towards ten or fourteen disadvantaged players for the sake of the community.

INTERVIEWER: But what about all the potential talent that is going untapped in the townships and the rural areas?

COMMINS: There's a lot of talent around the world that's going untapped. If you're born into a certain society, sometimes it's just unfortunate. For example, in the States, there must be plenty of tall basketball players out there who couldn't go to college, their parents couldn't afford it; they also get lost. It happens. Life is tough.

Much like South Africa, where there is a history of black cricket yet sparse representation in the national side, contemporary Australian Test cricket has never produced an aboriginal player. In 2001, the incumbent Australian Cricket Board Chairman, Denis Rogers, remarked on this fact:

> There is no doubt cricket is seen as a white man's game but the irony is that, in 1868, an aboriginal team was the first to go to England … I don't know that we have been capable of getting the aboriginal people to understand the culture of the game nor good at understanding their culture. But we think that somewhere out there, in the aboriginal community, are people who can play Test cricket for Australia and the sooner we find them the better.[37]

Surmounting the class barrier and shortage of first-class facilities over the intervening 133 years, a historic encounter between a Prime Minister's XI and the Aboriginal and Torres Strait Islander Commission (ATSIC) Chairman's XI was won by the Aboriginals on 19 April 2001. Coach of the ATSIC team, Geoff Sloane, the day after his team's victory, was mindful of the obstacles black cricketers still face:

> Cricket is a more elitist sort of sport. Coming from England you'll find that it was always the class system, you played for the school and it was a big thing … You'll find that people who try to break into that culture were subjugated to lesser people within the cricket hierarchy. People get entrenched within cricket. They think that they own the clubs. If you're not a local or a brother or cousin within that cycle, they make you feel you're not part of that process.[38]

In South Africa, over the years since cricket's racial integration, there have been a number of promising disadvantaged prospects who have made their debuts only to slip back into the relative obscurity of provincial cricket. A young black fast bowler from Cronjé's home town of Bloemfontein and a fellow old boy of Grey College, Victor Mpitsang was the only name on the national Plascon Cricket Academy's Hall of Fame in 1998. Part of the U/19 World Cup Team, Mpitsang made his debut for South Africa the same season, at his home ground of Bloemfontein. With the series against the West Indies done and dusted, he was included in the squad for the sixth ODI in February 1999. Later the same year, he went on tour to New Zealand – as an apprentice to Allan Donald, some media reports suggested. Be that as it may, Mpitsang didn't get to play any official games on this tour.

Victor Mpitsang proved to be a tall, insouciant young man who discussed his humble background and subsequent success with disarming frankness. Over a Coke at a Cape Town bar, Victor recalled his trip to the Antipodes following his 1999 debut.

> I toured New Zealand with them after the debut. I only played warm-up games. When we were here we played two or three games but when you're over there you learn a couple of things and you work with the guys and everything, so it's not like, basically, you're not doing anything but at a certain stage it actually gets frustrating 'cos you're not playing all the time … I probably played three warm-up games in the space of two months. It's terrible.

Despite this lack of opportunity to prove himself at a national level, by the end of the year, senior cricket correspondent Trevor Chesterfield, in an article on 18 November 1999, hailed Victor Mpitsang as a hot contender to secure a permanent position in the South African team.[39] With England visiting South

Africa at the end of 1999 on a tour that would end with the controversial Centurion Test-turned-ODI in January of 2000, Chesterfield unfavourably compared Makhaya Ntini, South Africa's black fast bowler of choice, with Victor Mpitsang, who had slipped back to South Africa A. In Chesterfield's opinion, Mpitsang should have carved himself a niche in the national squad by the Sri Lankan tour in mid-2000. This was the away tour that followed the Hansiegate revelations in April. By July, the South African team that went to Sri Lanka was missing its long-time captain as well as development darling Herschelle Gibbs. Despite the Indian police charges, Nicky Boje went to Sri Lanka, although apparently reassurance had had to be sought from the authorities that he would not be arrested upon his arrival. Ntini was there, Mpitsang was not. When asked why, Mpitsang replied, 'I've got no idea. I think ... Mackie went through a bad patch and he got picked. I don't know. When he played in the first-class season he played well. When he played against Australia, he did well. Since then he's been in. I think he deserves to play there. Ever since he came back into the scene, he's been doing well and if a guy's doing well you can't just drop him'.

In John Commins' opinion, it was not quite as simple as that. 'The selection policy is very interesting. The core of the side picks itself, but the bits and pieces that they pick around just change from series to series. I don't know what they're doing. Surely, you've got to throw Mpitsang in there and say you've got this ODI series and the next one as well.'

Instead, Robin Peterson was the new black kid on the block, flown over to Sri Lanka after the start of the tour in July 2000 as a cover for Paul Adams, who had picked up a groin strain. Peter Robinson wrote: 'The selection of Peterson ... may raise some eyebrows.'[40] Having established himself in the Eastern Province team only the previous season, the 20-year-old bowler was still attending the national coaching academy at the time of his selection. With Gibbs unavailable because of his six-month ban and Adams under the threat of injury, it seems the South African team faced the problem of finding a left-arm spinner of colour to replace Adams.

Commins remarked on Peterson's call-up:

> Peterson, we send to Sri Lanka, he's hardly taken a wicket in first-class cricket here, we send him to Sri Lanka, he sits on the bench, he comes back and he's nowhere. We've kitted him out, given him a Springbok opportunity, he comes back and he's not even played. Tours are not good for guys who don't play in the Test matches because they sit and do nothing week after week, then play in those mid-week games, which are a complete farce, where they could be playing provincial cricket back home. You just ruin players like that, you

> know. Sure, we can expose these guys to international cricket, but we don't expose them; all we expose them to is touring different countries.

With Eastern Province in to bat at the Boland cricket ground, the young bowler Peterson, at the threshold of his professional career, discussed his selection for Sri Lanka while waiting his turn on the field. He unconsciously echoed Commins' observations:

> For me, when I went to Sri Lanka, I was 20 years old; I'd only played one full season. It's kind of difficult just to be thrown into the deep end and you can see why a lot of young players that just come through the system very quickly just fall by the wayside. It's best to like learn your trade and once you've played a few more seasons and become a bit more experienced probably then you graduate to play for the national team.

Robin Peterson finally made his ODI debut in 2002 against India in Colombo. He bowled 10 overs and, although he didn't take a wicket, he was the second most economical bowler in the side with an average of 4.7. The following year he made his Test debut against Bangladesh, picking up 5 wickets and scoring 61 with the bat. Despite this Test success, he continued to feature sporadically only in the ODIs. He was nevertheless called up for World Cup duty in 2007 along with fellow non-white and non-contract players Loots Bosman and Roger Telemachus. The South African public was less than enthusiastic about the players' inclusion. Their previous form had been patchy and their national appearances irregular, and general consensus was that they were there purely to fill the requisite quota of seven non-white players in the side. Their fellow non-white team-mates, Langeveldt, Ntini and Prince, were players contracted to Cricket South Africa. Nonetheless the coach and selectors defended their choice. Coach Mickey Arthur was happy that Peterson and Telemachus brought variation to the bowling attack and thus he had '... the best possible bowling combination'. Selection convener Haroon Lorgat backed opening bat Loots Bosman to help South Africa with quick starts.[41]

At the conclusion of the 2007 World Cup, with South Africa bowing out of the semi-final with a whimper, newspaper reports analysed all the players' contributions to the South African team's disappointing showing. Said Stuart Hess, writing for the *Weekend Argus* on 28 April: 'Robin Peterson was okay when given a surprise outing against the Sri Lankans and then hit the winning runs as part of the stunning climax to that Super Eight match. Why they never allowed him the chance to build on the confidence gained in the match in subsequent games against Ireland and Bangladesh is a mystery.' While the South Africans, who went into the tournament ranked number 1, managed to trounce Ireland by 7 wickets without the aid of Peterson's spin, they could have done with him in the Bangladesh match. The minnows took on the mighty and beat the South Africans by 67 runs. Loots Bosman was picked for just one game, against the West Indies, but didn't get a chance to bat while Roger Telemachus '... just carried drinks for the entire tour'.[42]

Martin Gillingham, then sports editor of Cape Town radio station *Cape Talk*, drew attention to a similar fast-tracking process in rugby whereby youngsters go on international tours only to slip back into obscurity.

> Please, this does not mean that fast-tracking affirmative action in sport is wrong because, of course, it's not wrong but what I'm saying is it's also fraught with dangers, dangers that can have a negative impact on players. It buggers up their minds. Again, people do often forget that these young black sports stars, all they've ever wanted to be is sportsmen; all they've ever wanted to be is the best. They play sport because they enjoy it and they understand the rules. One of the most basic rules of sport, when it's working properly, is that everything is fair and equal. They do not want to be political pawns. That's very sad because many of them become that ...

John Commins didn't have any easy answers either.

COMMINS: I don't know what the solution is because you have to take sixteen players but we have to be careful about who we take. You can't take some young guy who is actually going to benefit more from playing domestic cricket than sitting on the sidelines and watching the main guys.

INTERVIEWER: What's the thinking behind that? The selectors choose someone who they think is good enough for the team and then don't use them, or use them once or twice like Mpitsang. Presumably it's good for cricket's image to have black players in the team and we have them it seems, but...

COMMINS: And then we leave them out. It's crazy. I can't quite work it out.

Like Victor Mpitsang, off-spinner Shafiek Abrahams also made his national debut in a sixth and final ODI at his home ground, in this case against New Zealand in Cape Town on 4 November 2000. With the first match of the series rained out and South Africa the victor in the next four, the series was effectively over bar the shouting. Abrahams, who had sat on the bench for the entire series, would finally be given a go. To a packed house, Abrahams bowled a tight 10 overs for 40 runs. John Commins described Abrahams' contribution to the match. 'Klusener won the game but he [Abrahams] did a great job, holding down the innings with Klusener. We won the series 4-0 up with one match to go. Pick someone who we know we're really going to continue with. Don't just throw someone a game ... This guy Abrahams. I'm convinced it will be the end of him.'

The player in question, however, was more optimistic about his prospects of getting another crack at the national squad. Shafiek Abrahams, Robin Peterson's Eastern Province team-mate, spoke of his national debut:

> I was going to play earlier and then the wickets didn't suit my game ... it's all about the conditions, the situation. I think at Newlands, we'd won the series so then they could take the chance and play me. I don't know if it's wrong but if you select a squad you shouldn't worry about whoever you play in that squad to get you through the games and I thought I had a fair game – 10 overs, 40 runs. That is how I see it. If you select a squad, everyone should be good enough to play and I think when they selected the squad, I thought I was good enough and I still think I'm good enough to play, so I'm just keeping working hard on my game and see how I go.

John Commins concurred with Abrahams' assessment of his ability, however he predicted, 'Now, Abrahams is a good enough cricketer to play, but he won't play in these Test matches [at home against New Zealand at the end of 2000], and then the next ODI series we go away, I bet you he won't even be in the squad'.

Sure enough, Abrahams did not play in the Tests that followed the one-day series against New Zealand. In pre-selection speculation, Abrahams' name came up in the magazine, *SA Cricket Action*, as a candidate for the next tour, away to the West Indies in March 2001. However, when the touring team was announced in February, Abrahams' name was absent from the list. Despite a listless provincial season, Paul Adams was back in the international arena.

Such instances add weight to Commins' assessment: 'We're just throwing Springbok caps at people and then not looking after them.' When I put this thorny issue to Abrahams, he attempted a diplomatic response but couldn't hide his bemusement at the selection process:

> I wouldn't like to look at it that way – they can probably state the reasons why you're not playing but no one's spoken to me about it. The convener was here yesterday. But no one's communicated anything to me as to why I'm not going or why this guy's going but it's all about telling people. If they told me, 'No, you're not good enough, go and work on this or that,' then I'd go and do it but ... Robin [Peterson] never even played a game. I don't want to go and compare him to players selected but he also had a fair season and I don't

know ... If I knew how they select, then I wouldn't be worrying about all this. It is a bit strange.

Commins elaborated on his view of the selection process's shortcomings:

> I'm not saying they don't deserve their caps, but if you're going to pick someone then make sure we're going to now look after them. Abrahams plays in the ODI but doesn't get a contract with South Africa. He gets his match fee, goes back to provincial cricket, puts his Springbok stuff in the cupboard and you never see him again. Poor guy. It's supposed to be the start of something and it's never a start.

John Commins has some personal experience of this 'tracksuit and tour' syndrome, although disadvantaged he was not. A product of the 'heritage game', he was schooled at Rondebosch Boys' High, another traditional boys-only school in Cape Town, and then followed in his father Kevin's footsteps. Commins senior played for the provinces of Border and Western Province between 1951 and 1960. Son John went on to captain Western Province. 'In my day, when I first captained Province, my dad was CEO of Western Province. People say that was one of the reasons why they didn't want to give me an extended run, because it looked like it was favouritism.'

Described as 'consistent', 'reliable' and an 'elegant batsman' in a UCBSA profile of 26 December 1996, John Commins' cricketing career looked rosy. Nonetheless, Commins struggled to hold down a regular place in the Western Province team despite his undisputed talent. The West Indian cricketer, Desmond Haynes, maintained that 'John Commins could be in the South African side at any time.'[43] Craig Matthews went even further: 'Commins is a better batter than Cronjé.' However, he only earned three Test caps for his country and never got to play in a one-day international, to his lasting regret. Commins attributed his less-than-glorious international career to 'poor selection'.

INTERVIEWER: Why do some make it and others not?

COMMINS: That's a difficult one. Maybe you don't fit the character. Maybe your personality doesn't fit in with the present selectors or maybe they don't like your attitude; you're too laid back or you look like you're not trying.

INTERVIEWER: What about you?

COMMINS: It's difficult to talk about your own selection. I got a chance. In the third Test I injured myself. I would have gone to New Zealand and I injured myself and then when I came right, I just never got picked and then I eventually got picked to go to India to replace Jonty Rhodes.

Commins' Test debut was against the touring New Zealanders in the second Test in Durban from 26-30 December 1994. He knocked off a fine 30 in the first innings and upped that to 45 in his second. Included in the third Test at Newlands, he managed 27 in the first innings and 10 not out in the next. Subsequently selected for the home Tests against Pakistan in January 1995, Commins found himself out for just 13 in the first innings and was run out in the second innings for a duck, injuring himself in the process. Thus he missed the return New Zealand tour in February/March 1995 and the hiatus continued for almost two years until the close of 1996, which proved to be a busy year-end for the South Africans on the subcontinent.

Early in November 1996, after winning all their games in the Titan Cup one-day international series in India, the touring South Africans lost the final to their hosts. This triangular tournament, involving South Africa, India and Australia, gave rise to stories of fixing and counter-fixing, police tapes of Indian cricketers talking to bookies and massive illicit gains and losses. The Indian bookie Mukesh Gupta (MK) and his partner Anil Steel reportedly lost heavily on the final ODI and MK was looking to Indian captain, Mohammad Azharuddin, to help him make up his losses in the ensuing three Tests against the South Africans.

India won the first Test at Ahmedabad and, according to MK's subsequent revelations to Indian investigators, he recouped 30% of his losses. With the visitors needing 170 runs in their second innings, the scorecard shows no less than 6 ducks – Hudson, Cullinan, Rhodes, De Villiers, Symcox and Adams all failed to score. Hudson went on 1/0 with Cullinan following the opening batsman with the score on 2/0. The rest of the team added only another 103, leaving the Indians 64 runs and one Test ahead.

After this disappointing performance, Ali Bacher approached the ICC for their Match Referee John Reid's report on the first Test as the South Africans were unhappy with the standard of pitch and practice facilities provided by the Indians. Rhodes picked up a hamstring injury and was declared unfit to play in the second Test in Calcutta.

Commins picks up the story:

> They flew me over on an urgent flight as the second Test match was starting in Calcutta the following day [27 November 1996]. I arrived there and I wasn't in the side. There are some great players who played in my place so I'll never ever say that I should have played, but it seems strange that you get sent over there and then you sit there and at the same time you're losing out on provincial cricket. OK, they have to have spare batters there if someone breaks a finger just before the game – have to have replacements. Sure, when

you are on the brink of selection, you do sometimes get the wrong end of the stick.

India lost the second Test, even without Commins' contribution, and MK reportedly made up 60% of his losses.

The third Test was played from the 8 December in Kanpur where MK Gupta paid Hansie Cronjé for ensuring a South African defeat in the match and with it the Test series. Commins related his part in events:

> By the start of the third Test, in Kanpur, I'd had enough. I'd thought, 'Well, maybe I'll get a game in the third Test and they picked the side and I wasn't in it.' Then I said I want to go home. Strangely, Hansie was quite good in the way that he handled it but also a little bit naughty in that he said to me the only way to organise that would be for me to play in the first Test in Durban [scheduled for 26–30 December 1996].

The Indians were to return the South Africans' visit almost immediately. Commins went home to await his recall to the national team after Christmas. Commins left behind him a sick and depleted South African squad facing the final game of a long tour – the Mohinder Armanath benefit match – in which the South African skipper put a match-fixing offer to the entire team. After losing both the one-day and the Test series, the South Africans ended their 1996 tour of the subcontinent 74 runs shy of the target set in the upgraded ODI and came home to the prospect of facing the Indians again in the New Year. But this time it would be on home ground.

According to Cronjé's testimony to the King Commission, MK was in South Africa for the first Test in Durban and the second Test in Cape Town, where he stayed at the cricketers' hotel, the Cape Sun. Two deposits totalling US$80 000 made their way into Cronjé's bank account before the third Test in Johannesburg. Cronjé admitted to the King Commission that the money could have come from MK, as he was giving the New Delhi bookie and punter 'daily forecasts' during this series, which included a prediction about the first Test. Cronjé confessed that he told MK, 'I think South Africa has a very good chance of beating India handsomely'. The home side did indeed win – by 328 runs. South Africa went on to take the series 2–1. Commins mused on his absence from the South African team to play in the first Test in Durban.

> Who played in that Test – Jonty or a new player? Usually, you play six batters at Kingsmead. If there's six batters and one of them wasn't on that tour, then there's something wrong. First of all, if they send me up as a replace-

> ment and they don't play me and then the sixth batter is actually some guy who was in South Africa at that time, then they should really have sent him up because if I was the next in, then I should have been the next in for the Test match in Durban. I wonder who that guy was? Maybe somebody who made his debut?

Ali Bacher's nephew, Adam Bacher, won his first Test cap for South Africa against the Indians at Kingsmead. Commins did not play for his country and never would again. 'The big thing to look at when not selected is who plays in your place. Who plays in your place? If Hansie Cronjé is batting three in your place then there's something wrong because he hasn't got the technique to face fast bowlers, which has been proven over time. He's had a fantastic career but on middle order runs. Don't waste him up the order … Selectors can change their mind. It did seem strange.'

The public got a glimpse of what goes on behind in the scenes in the selection process in February 1999 when, in a well-publicised fall-out with Ali Bacher, Cronjé stormed out of a meeting about an affirmative action selection policy and came very close to resigning his captaincy over what he saw as 'government interference' in the selection of the team. In the M-Net TV interview after his sacking from the South African team, he reiterated his views: 'I'm against affirmative action … You've got to have your best side out there and it doesn't matter if that means fielding seven, eight or nine players of colour or a totally all-white side.'[44]

Ray White, former President of the UCB, *did* resign over the same issue – the controversy sparked by his comments about 'discriminatory' selection. He maintained in an article in the English newspaper *The Independent* on 4 June 2000 that Ali Bacher carried some of the responsibility for Cronjé's downfall since, after the departure of coach Bob Woolmer, the UCB's Managing Director endowed the South African captain with extensive powers. Woolmer himself claimed that Cronjé had tried to have him replaced as coach back in 1997.[45] This is something that has been commented upon many times in the media. Cricket writer Peter Robinson stated: 'It is quite clear, with the benefit of the Indian police investigation and now the King Commission, that the UCB, and Ali Bacher in particular, placed too much trust in Cronjé and allowed him far too much power. This cannot be allowed to happen again.'[46] Radio commentator Martin Gillingham put it more succinctly on the regional radio station *Cape Talk*: 'Cronjé had so much power.'[47] Sports Science Professor Tim Noakes, who was involved in the health and fitness side of South African cricket, concluded that Cronjé became '… the captain, the coach and the selector'.

Cronjé was not the only world captain to be wielding such influence over the national team. Former Pakistani captain Javed Miandad, in testimony to Pakistan's Qayyum Commission of Inquiry into match-fixing, stated that the modus operandi of the Pakistani team's senior players was to influence the younger players and those who did not agree to come on board were put out of the team.[48] The same accusation was made to Judge Qayyum by Pakistani cricketer Aaqib Javed, who related that he had received an indirect message from Wasim Akram to the effect that '... as he was not part of the game he would never play cricket while Wasim Akram was captain.' Rashid Latif, the one-time Pakistani vice captain, who prematurely resigned from international cricket after match-fixing allegations against his captain, Salim Malik, during Pakistan's tour to southern Africa in 1995, echoed this allegation: 'An Indian player told me this. "Apparently, one of the reasons that captains are interested in a team of their choice is to have players who toe the line." Akram now has the players he wants.'[49]

Did Cronjé?

Kumaran Pillay thinks so. A cricket supporter from Natal who was set upon by fellow cricket fans and policemen for supporting the opposition during the tainted triangular series between Zimbabwe, England and South Africa early in 2000, he told Paddy Harper in Durban that 'Cricket is one of the last bastions of white supremacy. Perhaps the way in which black cricketers have been kept out of the side has as much to do with the financial gains made by the Old Boys Club as with race.'[50]

4

Cronjé and his cronies

The case against Cronjé and his co-accused

Put a rogue in the limelight and he will act like an honest man.

– Napoleon Bonaparte, French general and politician (1769–1821)

The Delhi Crime Branch issued an official press release on 7 April 2000:

> The Crime Branch of the Delhi Police has been able to unearth an international racket in cricket match-fixing and betting. Based on available information, a case FIR No. 111 of cheating, fraud and criminal conspiracy has been registered at PS Chankaya Puri on 6 April 2000 and one Rajesh Kalra, r/o Greater Kailash II, New Delhi, has been arrested. Available information with Anti-Extortion Cell of Crime Branch Inspector Ishwar Singh and ACP Rishi Pal, revealed that some businessmen of India were in contact with certain South African players for match-fixing in the recently held Pepsi Cup one-day international cricket series between India and South Africa. As such, as per provisions of laws, requisite permission for monitoring the telephone/cellphone was obtained. The South African cricket player participating in the conspiracy to fix the matches in consideration for money was identified as Hansie Cronjé. One of the conspirators was identified as Sanjeev alias Sanjay, r/o Jungpura, New Delhi. The meeting between the South African cricket captain and Sanjeev had taken place in Room No 346 of Hotel Taj Palace, New Delhi on 14 March 2000.
>
> From the conversation between Sanjeev aka Sanjay and Hansie Cronjé it emerges that the one-day international cricket matches between India and South Africa played recently in India, in March 2000, were fixed for exchange consideration of money. Those involved in such fixing have illegally amassed huge sums of money both in Indian and foreign currencies and made huge gains by wrongful means and by clearly deceiving the cricket fans and general public.
>
> When such matches are organised at the international level amongst the respective national teams, they represent their respective countries and national

> pride is attached with them. The people at large go to see these matches, under the belief that the matches will be played honestly and fairly and there would be no dishonest dealings compromising the result of the match or any part of it. General public had purchased the entry tickets to witness the match and many others had also travelled from distant places to witness the same. Since the fact that some people have conspired to alter the normal course of these matches by use of big money, they have dishonestly concealed the fact that there would be no honest and fair game and have thereby caused deception on the people. People had parted with their money property by way of purchase of tickets amounting to wrongful loss to them. By engaging in such activities these people have put the general public to a wrongful loss and have illegally increased large sums of money and made wrongful gain to themselves thereby committing the offence of criminal conspiracy and cheating.
>
> From the recorded conservation, it has transpired that between the people large amount of foreign exchange has also changed hands through *hawala* [undocumented money transfers] dealings for onwards payment to the South African team members who were part of the criminal conspiracy. These foreign exchange violations are being brought to the notice of the Enforcement Directorate separately.

It was in India that South Africa made its triumphant return to international cricket in 1991. Ironically, it was also in India that the greatest crisis of the post-apartheid game had its genesis.

On the face of it, the telephone transcripts that the Delhi police released conveyed damning proof of their case against Hansie Cronjé, Nicky Boje, Herschelle Gibbs and Pieter Strydom for cheating, fraud and criminal conspiracy in the five-match, ODI series played in India in March 2000. Other South African team members also cropped up in the snippets of dialogue between Hansie Cronjé and suspected match-fixer Sanjeev Chawla, such as Boland cricketer Henry Williams, Easterns off-spinner Derek Crookes and 1999 World Cup hero Lance Klusener. Add to the growing list of names that of Mornantau Hayward, which Cronjé mentioned in testimony to the King Commission about the first ODI in Kochi and tack on the testimonies of Jacques Kallis, Mark Boucher and Lance Klusener on Cronjé's approach to them before the second Test in Bangalore prior to the ODI series and you have one man short of a South African XI. All, however, repeatedly denied any knowledge of unseemly goings-on in the team and, for his part, Cronjé, in a press statement on 13 April 2000, came to the defence of his men: 'Some of my team-mates have come under the spotlight as a result of the police enquiries in India. I know of no member of any side that I have led who has done anything reprehensible or wrong. Speculation and criticism directed against other members of the team is wrong and unjustified.'

It is fair to point out that the phone transcripts were never authenticated by anyone in South Africa. However, in his disclosures to the King Commission, Cronjé admitted telling the UCB's Security Consultant Rory Steyn, on the night of his confession, that it was his voice on the tapes. As the investigating officer into Hansiegate received death threats, it is safe to assume that dense clouds of evil-smelling smoke probably spell fire.

An excerpt from Cronjé's seven-page confession handed to Rory Steyn on 11 April 2000 reads as follows (original interpolations in round brackets):

> On my way to the nets (before the first one-day international against Zimbabwe in January 2000) I was stopped by Hamid (Cassim), a bloke who has been hanging around the team for a few years now, always handing out biltong (dried meat) to the guys in return for some tickets. He told me that if only he knew I was going to declare (in the fifth Test against England at Centurion Park) he could have made himself some good money and my reply was, 'Why don't you ask?'
>
> Since that day, in a moment of stupidity and weakness, I allowed Satan and the world to dictate terms to me, rather than the Lord. Hamid called me almost four times a day from then on. He later introduced me to a friend called Sanjay during the one-day international series with England and Zimbabwe. Together, they told me that I could also make some cash if we could maybe cook a match. I told them that I was not prepared to do this unless we were assured of a place in the final. Of course, we only narrowly got through to the final and the opportunity never came. I had in my possession at that stage 10 000 to 15 000 US dollars that Sanjay gave me, just in case I had a change of mind. I told him that maybe (in) the first one-day international in India I could see what could be done, thinking that if we could get the match out of the way, we'd get rid of them and could then focus purely on cricket. My idea was never to involve other players.
>
> I would like to make it absolutely clear to any member of the South African team, whether player or management, about this: I lied to him (Sanjay) by saying certain players were involved when in fact I had never spoken to any of them. I couldn't face asking them to do it. I can't recall all the names that I mentioned and I can't remember the figures that were mentioned. I ignored him the night before the (opening India) match but, early the next morning, Hamid phoned me again and urged me to go ahead with the plan. I phoned him up and suggested we go for it. All this time, I had in the back of my mind pride to play for South Africa and my team-mates, whom I all respect. It was a

> difficult period for me before the match and I then decided I won't not try, I'll give it my best shot and see what happens.
>
> As it happened, we got 301 for 3. I got 19 off 20 balls and India knocked it off quite comfortably after (Mornantau) Hayward got injured. I can honestly say that I tried to win the match, even at that stage.
>
> When I got back to the hotel, Sanjay was upset because we got too many runs and I blamed the Indian keeper for three chances that he missed. I did not accept any money for that match.

A day or two before South Africa was due to face Zimbabwe in the sixth ODI of the Standard Bank triangular tournament between England, Zimbabwe and the hosts in Durban, Cronjé was introduced to an Indian man named Sanjay in the team's Beverly Hills hotel. According to Cronjé, their discussion revolved around losing the upcoming match and gaining his team-mates' co-operation to do so. An unspecified sum of money changed hands. Zimbabwe, the underdogs, won the Durban ODI by 2 wickets.

The two men were introduced by Hamid Cassim. A Johannesburg sweet-shop owner who goes by the cheery nickname of Banjo, Cassim has impressive connections. In England, Peter Robinson, the CEO of Liverpool in 1991, entertained Cassim in the Directors' Box at Old Trafford. In India, former cricket captains Kapil Dev and Mohammad Azharuddin are numbered among his personal friends, as are members of the Indian and Pakistani cricket sides. In South Africa, Hamid described his relationship with former Minister of Transport Mac Maharaj: 'I used to look after him, we used to go out for meals and we had a lot of things in common ...' Maharaj, though never charged, was under investigation for receiving off-shore payments while Transport Minister, in return for the awarding of several lucrative contracts to Schabir Shaik's company, Nkobi Investments. Schabir Shaik is currently serving a 15-year prison sentence for corruption.

Phone records show Cassim to have been in contact with several members of the South African cricket team. Cronjé described him as a 'hanger-on' who supplied team members with biltong and cut-price electrical equipment in exchange for match tickets. Banjo outlined to the King Commission a relationship with the cricketers that was somewhat more intimate.

> In or about 1993, Kapil Dev invited me to attend a game in India which I did, and it was there that I met and was introduced to the Indian players and I also met the South African players. I had a very good relationship with all the South African players as well as a large number of the overseas players. I formed a very good relationship, in particular with South African players like

> Fanie de Villiers, Brian McMillan and Daryll Cullinan … With the players such as Fanie de Villiers, Brian McMillan and Daryll Cullinan, and most of the other players, it was just not tickets. We used to go out for meals. I used to eat a lot with Fanie de Villiers, Brian McMillan, Daryll. I used to go and visit him at home sometimes. He used to come around with me.

On behalf of Kapil Dev, Cassim became involved in arranging for South African cricketers to play in benefit matches in India. Explaining the many calls to the South African players, Cassim told the King Commission on 26 June 2000: 'I would practically phone the players, I think, 20 to 30 times a day sometimes, just to find out if they will be available to play.' While Jonty Rhodes, it appears, was never available, other cricketers had availed themselves of the opportunity throughout the years, including: 'Clive Rice, Fanie de Villiers, Meyrick Pringle, Errol Stuart, Mike Rindell, Derek Crookes, HD Ackerman, Dave Callaghan, Andrew Hudson, Adrian Kuiper'. In his testimony to the King Commission, Cassim referred to one particular benefit match for Madan Lal, the Indian cricketer. There was indeed a benefit match for Madan Lal, played between a World XI and an Indian XI in India in March 1995. Cassim recollected: '… that particular match Clive Rice went down; Fanie de Villiers, Mike Rindell; Fanie took his dad along, Braam, and I was given a free ticket by Mr Kapil Dev, via Air India, to attend the matches.' When questioned by Advocate Shamila Batohi, the King Commission's Leader of Evidence, as to why these approaches did not go through official channels and what remuneration he received, Cassim explained that he '… merely did it out of the goodness of my heart'.

Phone records produced by Shamila Batohi showed a cross-hatch of calls between Cassim and most members of the South African cricket team as well as members of management including team manager Goolam Rajah. Featured on the list were Paul Adams, Darryl Cullinan, Jonty Rhodes, Herschelle Gibbs, Jacques Kallis, Shaun Pollock and Lance Klusener who, it seems, was particularly fond of Banjo's biltong. The team apparently had biltong delivered to them, before departing on tours, by Goolam Rajah's wife. Cassim's cellphone records showed 180 calls to Cronjé, 33 to Daryll Cullinan, 30 to Paul Adams and 28 to Lance Klusener, among others.[51] Banjo's cricketing ties apparently extended beyond the players and team management. Testifying before the King Commission, Hansie Cronjé recalled having dinner with Cassim and certain unnamed South African administrators: 'I may have had dinner with Mr Cassim on an occasion with certain administrators in the South African side. I may be corrected but that's my recollection.'

Confirming the fact that even Masters games are objects of the match-fixers' attentions, Clive Rice, who captained South Africa's first official tour to India in 1991, revealed that he had been approached during just such a veterans' match subsequent to his retirement from international cricket. On the day that it was made public that Rice had depositions of his own to make to the King Commission, breaking news in South Africa was the fact that both Clive Rice and Kepler Wessels would no longer be up for re-election as South African selectors. That same week, the media reported that Rice had been negotiating a book deal for Cronjé in England. Echoing Hansie Cronjé, Rice maintained that he had always given 100% for his country. When interviewed on the regional radio station *Cape Talk* on 24 July 2000, Rice talked also of earlier games in which he played, that now, with the benefit of hindsight, he regarded as suspicious. He referred in particular to a World XI match played in Delhi and was of the opinion that even benefit and Masters games are subject to tampering, as is any game that is televised.

Apparently, it is no secret that these exhibition matches are run purely for the benefit of the bookmakers. According to one knowledgeable South African sports writer, 'They have been fixed for the last 100 years.' One such World XI v India XI match is mentioned in the Australian O'Regan Report and features too in its confidential chapter where names are named and identities protected. Interestingly, the last cricket game that Cronjé played was a single-wicket competition at Newlands in Cape Town just before the scandal broke in April 2000. According to the same sports writer, who was the commentator for this match which was screened in its entirety by ETV, Herschelle Gibbs threw his first-round match against Cronjé. 'It was a fix blatant to everybody' bar a trusting public.

Hansie Cronjé, too, had had a sideline in arranging appearances for benefit and charity matches. Before he was exposed in early April, Cronjé had put together a South African XI for a limited-overs series involving South Africa and India. The tournament was for the benefit of a number of former Indian cricketing stars and was scheduled to be played in India from 24 April to 3 May 2000. South African players slated to appear were veterans Gibbs, Boje, Strydom, Klusener and Boucher and rookies Steve Elworthy, Louis Koen, Justin Kemp, Denis Carlstein, Mornantau Hayward and then SA (A) captain Dale Benkenstein. The captain of the opposing Indian side was to be Cronjé's old friend, Mohammad Azharuddin. Cronjé's 'good friendship' with Azharuddin went back to 1992 when India toured South Africa. Cronjé was the captain of the Under-23 President's XI that played at Centurion and Azhar led the Indian team at that time.

The 5 matches were to have sported a new format of 4 innings made up of 20 5-ball overs. The event was to be broadcast by a new TV channel, Sony SET Max, an offshoot of Sony TV in India, and organised by an Indian-based company identified only as PCM International. According to testimony heard during the King Commission, a representative of that organisation visited Cronjé in Bloemfontein in February 2000 and handed over US$25 000 in cash that had evaded normal foreign exchange controls. No receipt or voucher documented the transaction. Cronjé didn't find this way of doing business either surprising or unwise. While acknowledging that perhaps it wasn't the most appropriate way, he didn't think it was wrong because he needed cash to pay the players their appearance fees, prize money and subsistence allowances. In his initial statement to the King Commission, Cronjé had claimed that the money was an advance to cover a deposit, the players' signing-on fees and travel costs. That US$25 000 was going to have to go a long way. The event was subsequently cancelled after Cronjé's dismissal as South African captain.

Cronjé's final tour as South Africa's captain was to the subcontinent, where South Africa won an historic series victory against India in March 2000. It was the first time in over thirteen years that India had been defeated in a Test series on home ground. Cronjé testified that in the build-up to the two Tests in India, he received regular calls from Sanjeev Chawla and Banjo Cassim. South African bookie Marlon Aronstam, who had proposed the Centurion Test-turned-limited-overs match against England in January, phoned during the first and second Tests. During this tour, Cronjé also spoke to Sunil, another shadowy figure he had met years earlier in Dubai. Cronjé admitted telling Chawla that he had spoken to Gibbs, Strydom and Boje during the Indian Test series: 'I told Sanjay that I had spoken to Strydom and Gibbs and Boje, and that they were pretty much on our side, but he said that you need more players on your side to have a definite.' Cronjé insisted, however, that he never approached Gibbs and Boje. He was just leading Sanjay along.

Despite Cronjé's repeated denials that he had implicated any of his team-mates, six players testified to overtures made to them by Cronjé: Lance Klusener, Jacques Kallis, Mark Boucher, Herschelle Gibbs, Henry Williams and Pieter Strydom.

Border captain Pieter Strydom confirmed an offer of R70 000 (US$10 000) to help ensure that South Africa didn't get more than 250 in the first Test against India from 24–28 February 2000. Strydom claimed he turned down the offer even after the figure was upped to R140 000 (US$20 000). South Africa went on to win this first Test by 4 wickets and with 2 days to spare after scoring 176 in their first innings and 164 in their second. Of the noteworthy coincidence, Strydom said he'd observed, 'Shit, Hansie, we could have made a lot of bucks here.'

Indian cricket writer Prem Panicker, in his *Rediff* online match report for the first Test, summed up Strydom's batting performance: 'Strydom played with all the assurance of a man marooned on a minefield.'[52] Of his performance in the second ODI at Jamshedpur, the *Rediff* commentator was frankly nonplussed:

'Strydom keeps getting picked as a batsman, and every time he is in the side, he gets pushed as low down the order as it is possible for him to get. That strikes you as a bit strange, and a sign that the Proteas really don't have much confidence in his batting, which in turn begs the question somewhat, of what he is doing in the side.'[53]

In addition to the criminal charges laid against him in India, Strydom faced disciplinary hearings by the UCB for attempting to place a bet of R50 for Cronjé on South Africa during the controversial fifth Test against the English at Centurion in January 2000. This was the Test in which Strydom made his South African debut, aged 30. By his own admission to the King Commission, Strydom played Tests once a year despite a cricketing history that went back to South African Schools in 1987 when Cronjé was captain. According to Strydom, Cronjé wondered '… what odds could be obtained on a bet that the game would produce a result'. The waterlogged Test was, in fact, resurrected as an ODI during the fifth day's play – the first time in 123 years of Test cricket history that either side had forfeited an innings. England won. According to Cronjé and Strydom, the bet was not placed as they could not get odds. Strydom was acquitted by the UCB. Much as with fellow miscreants Gibbs and Williams' defence that his was preparation for an attempt rather than an attempt, the committee considered Strydom's story well-founded.

As Klusener, Kallis and Boucher all testified, they were approached by Cronjé during the second Test in India and all declined, thinking the ten-second conversation a joke. Cronjé was unable to explain why, if he was stringing Sanjay along, he did actually approach these players if he had no intention of getting anyone else involved. He also conceded that there was no reasonable explanation for his choosing the names of Strydom, Gibbs and Boje to mention to Sanjay. Of Strydom, he said, 'He was just the unlucky one and he's been named'. Strydom, in his testimony, speculated that his name came up because Cronjé was throwing names around under pressure from Sanjay. If this was the case, why would Cronjé mention the name of Boje?

Nicky Boje, like Cronjé, attended Grey College in Bloemfontein, where Cronjé was his cricket captain, and subsequently played provincial cricket for Orange Free State, once again under the captaincy of Hansie Cronjé, this time for ten years, before being selected for South Africa in 1995. The 1996 tour to India, which ended with the infamous team meeting [or three] to discuss the throwing of the final game of the tour, was his first main outing with the South African team. He made his Test debut for South Africa during the tainted first Test against India in February 2000. Of their relationship Cronjé announced, Boje is 'more than family'.

Despite the mounting evidence to the contrary, Cronjé maintained of his conversations with Sanjay in India that 'I told him I had players on my side, and the intention initially was never to involve other players. I tried faint attempts at Strydom, Klusener, Kallis and Boucher and as I said, their rebuffs were quite immediate, and then unfortunately I pushed it too far with Gibbs and Williams.' Cronjé insisted that such conversations were elaborate lies to lead Sanjay on, taking his money for effectively doing nothing. Judge King, begged to differ. The facts '... are not reconcilable with the notion of Cronjé spinning Sanjay along,' he affirmed in his interim report after reiterating those facts once again. According to further testimony from Cronjé, Sanjay showed up in Sharjah, during the ODI triangular tournament that followed the tour of India in March 2000, wanting to resume contact '... along the same lines as India.' King commented wryly: 'One must assume that Sanjay did not realize that Cronjé had been spinning him along.'

The contentious ODI series was scheduled to begin on 9 March 2000 in the southern Indian city of Kochi, in Kerala state. On the eve of the opening match, Cronjé ended his online column on a somewhat weary note: 'This is the first of the 13 consecutive matches to be played in 40 days in 3 different countries and in 9 different states. Buckle up for action and for travelling. No point in unpacking bags as tomorrow you pack again.' Michael Henderson, writing for the *Telegraph*, reminded us of the prophetic words of the *Wisden Cricket Almanac* of 1999: 'The South African Board, so enlightened in many ways, seems incapable of turning down an invitation. Rare is the triangular or quadrangular tournament that does not include South Africa. Probably the only person who has done more touring than Cronjé in the past few years is Bob Dylan. How many roads must a man walk down, before you give him a break?'[54]

For the first time, according to Cronjé, South Africa opted for a different one-day and Test squad on tour in India in early 2000. Dale Benkenstein, Derek Crookes, Neil McKenzie, Henry Williams and Steve Elworthy were brought on as one-day specialists. Williams and Crookes are the only two from this ODI specialist list to play in the first ODI, about which there have been as many revelations as insinuations. They were also the controversial opening bowling attack in the fifth and final match at Nagpur, which Cronjé, at the end of his lengthy first innings against the King Commission, admitted to attempting to fix.

Boland cricketer Henry Williams was first selected for South Africa during the 1998/1999 season for the West Indies tour at home, making his ODI debut nearing the watershed age of thirty, much like Pieter Strydom. He failed to find himself a regular place in the side, but reappeared for the one-day internationals of the Indian tour, in this, his benefit season. He played in the first ODI, injured his right shoulder the following day at practice and did not play again until the final game at Nagpur.

The morning of the opening game in Kochi, Cronjé confirmed to the King Commission that Sanjay and Hamid Cassim had phoned and urged him to go ahead. He returned Sanjay's call and agreed that South Africa would keep the score below 220, or so Cronjé maintained. Five or six names were mentioned. These included Gibbs, Boje, Williams and Hayward, Cronjé revealed. It seems that the London-based Chawla and his South African sidekick, Hamid Cassim, were not the only people offering money on the first ODI. According to the Jo'burg bookie Marlon Aronstam's testimony to the King Commission, he and Cronjé had, prior to the Indian series, discussed the fixing of the first ODI in Kochi and Gibbs, Strydom and Boje were mentioned at some stage. While Cronjé acknowledged discussing the fixing of Kochi, he denied naming any other players to Aronstam, saying that these were the names he misleadingly mentioned to Sanjay. Although this is a detail that did not appear in his affidavit, Aronstam was adamant under examination, remembering '... for definite sure' the names of Boje, Strydom and Gibbs.

Both Cronjé and Aronstam agreed that when the Jo'burg bookie contacted Cronjé in India before the limited-overs series began, the deal was off. Aronstam added that after Kochi, Cronjé's attitude towards him seemed to cool. When Shamila Batohi put it to Cronjé that 'Mr Aronstam seems to think now that the reason why you had actually cooled off was because you had Sanjay now whose money obviously, who was offering a lot more money than he could possibly give you,' he replied, 'I don't think that is the case, I cannot speak for Mr Aronstam, but that certainly wasn't the case from my side'.

The South African innings did not match Cronjé's version of his arrangement with Sanjay. The Kochi match proved to be a high-scoring game on a traditionally high-scoring ground that went down to the wire. The South African captain won the toss and elected to bat. By the end of 35 overs, South Africa were coasting at 206 for no wicket, belying Cronjé's alleged assurance to Sanjay that they'd be looking for around 220. Gibbs was involved in a record-breaking 235-run partnership with Kirsten for the first wicket. He stuttered to his 111 after surviving a number of missed opportunities by the Indian wicketkeeper, Sameer Dighe. The first wobble came when Gibbs, on 37, was stranded out of his crease off Joshi's bowling and Dighe made a mess of the stumping. Just free of fielding restrictions and Gibbs escaped again; this time Tendulkar pitched a ball that hit the South African batsman on the toe and Dighe failed to hold the deflection. Robin 'Usually Reliable' Singh also dropped Gibbs off a sitter in the outfield. The South African batsman finally bowed out in the fortieth over on 111, surrendering to triple Nelson jitters, perhaps?

The *Rediff* match correspondent had the details. Apparently, wicketkeeper Dighe was selected for the preceding ODIs in Australia and was not a popular choice. It was rumoured that he had been selected solely because he was Tendulkar's team-mate but made the squad again for the South African series, although Ganguly had replaced Tendulkar as captain for the ODIs after India's defeat by South Africa in the preceding Tests. Dighe's performance in the first match of the series did little to endear him to Indian supporters. According to Prem Panicker, 'He gets a shocker of a game in Kochi and the calls for his axing are loud and prolonged'. The Indians were not alone in their fumbling as, according to various match reports, Crookes also missed two or three viable chances. 'When you see that, you pause and wonder, do you not, whether there was anything more to Dighe's muffs than mere incompetence?' Panicker wondered aloud.[55]

Kirsten followed Gibbs's departure less than 2 overs later on 115 and, despite the loss of both openers and the firm foundation they had laid for the innings, it was big-hitter Klusener that was sent on at number 4. Three balls later, he was gone, caught and bowled Dravid for a duck. After this flurry of wickets, Kallis and Cronjé pushed the score to 301, but this total reflected a drop in the run rate at the end of the innings when, at one stage, the projected target was looking like 335/340. With 7 wickets in hand, Cronjé opted for the singles and failed to score a boundary, getting 19 not out off 20 balls.

Of the 7 bowlers Cronjé fielded in this game, Williams' bowling figures of 0/40 in 9 were the best, although he failed to pick up a wicket and all but cancelled out his single maiden with 4 no-balls. He was injured at practice the following day and did not play again until the last ODI at Nagpur. Crookes, who would also be embroiled in the Nagpur controversy, had the worst bowling figures for the day, ending this outing with more than 7 runs an over. Hayward earned the nickname 'Wayward' with 2 no-balls and 5 wides strewn among his 0/35 in 6 before retiring injured. Boje bowled 6 overs for 34, conceded 2 wides and didn't claim a wicket. Their captain pipped them to the post with his 8 overs going for 48 runs although he did pick up the wicket of Ajay Jadeja, who was subsequently dropped from the Indian team. In all, the South Africans gave away four-and-a-half overs in extras.

Nonetheless, a total of 301 was on the board and victory seemed assured. South Africa, however, incredibly, lost to India after Ganguly and Tendulkar put on the runs to put India ahead 1–0 ahead in the series. Robin Singh, in the Indian lower order, hit the winning runs with two balls to spare. It was the first time in cricketing history that India had scored more than 300 runs to win the game and the first time that South Africa had been beaten when 300 runs to the good. Those punters wagering on the long odds would have gone home happy that night. However, Sanjay, according to Cronjé, wasn't one of them. Of this game, Cronjé said in his statement to the King Commission:

> When I got back to the hotel Sanjay was upset because we scored too many runs. I blamed the Indian wicketkeeper for three chances that he missed,

> obviously not revealing that the South African players concerned had not been involved and, in fact, none of them knew anything about the matter. I did not receive any money for that match, I believe Sanjay lost money.

Could the first game in a series tainted by charges of corruption have been double-bookied?

Concluding his mammoth ten-hour slog before the King Commission, Cronjé acknowledged that he had had a lot of conversations with Sanjay and that he had mentioned a lot of players. He moved on to the second ODI at Jamshedpur:

> During the following game at Jamshedpur, he phoned me again and not only wanting to get information, but wanting to actually influence the result and the excuse that I used in this instance was that I won't be able to get to any of the players because they are upset with me because they have not been financially paid, using that as an excuse to keep him away from me.

Why the players should have been paid if they hadn't fulfilled their obligations is unexplained. An excerpt from the unverified police transcripts seems to corroborate this conversation:

HANSIE: No, no. They were saying that they were already doing Cochin [Kochi]. The other guys are already angry with me because I have not received their money, you know.

SANJAY: No. But I told you, I have already given him altogether 60.

HANSIE: Okay.

SANJAY: And tomorrow, I can deposit the money in your account. It is not a problem because of the time difference. Tomorrow itself I can deposit the money.

HANSIE: Okay.

South Africa lost this match by 6 wickets after opener Gary Kirsten set the tone with a duck, a feat matched by tail-ender Crookes. Gibbs, Kallis, Klusener and Boje were all caught behind by wicketkeeper Dighe. Strydom's bowling figures of 57 in 10 overs were the most expensive of the 7 bowlers used in the game although Cronjé, in his 7 balls bowled, managed to collect the wicket of Tendulkar and concede 4 runs.

The media statement issued by the Delhi police on 7 April 2000, referred to a meeting between the South African captain and Sanjeev Chawla in Room 346 of the Taj Palace Hotel in Delhi on 14 March. This was the day before the third ODI was to be played at Faridabad. At the King Commission, Cronjé described events prior to this match: 'Sanjay was on his way back to London. We were now 2–0 in the ODI series and staying in Delhi. Sanjay phoned, wanting to influence the third ODI.' Cronjé maintained that he was still stringing Sanjay along, despite telling him that Boje, Strydom and Gibbs were 'playing'. One phone excerpt clearly refers to this encounter.

SANJAY: Hello.
HANSIE: Hello.
SANJAY: Hello, hi Hansie.
HANSIE: Hello, hi Sanjay.
SANJAY: Yeah, I am in the lobby at the moment. Is it possible I can drop in for a few minutes?
HANSIE: Where are you? In the lobby?
SANJAY: Yeah.
HANSIE: You can come in.
SANJAY: I can come in.
HANSIE: Yeah, I am in 346.
SANJAY: All right, no more. Okay bye, see you in two minutes.
HANSIE: Yeah, okay.

Further conversation excerpts attached to the police's media release seem to refer to the imminent third ODI although Cronjé and his alleged conspirators implied that the script plotted for the Nagpur game was that outlined in the partial transcript released by the Delhi police. In fact, Gibbs and Williams would later identify the fifth ODI at Nagpur as the game in which they agreed to perform according to Cronjé's script. The conversation in the transcripts, however, relates more closely to the events of the third ODI, at Faridabad.

CRONJÉ: OK. OK, I have spoken. Yes, everything is fine. Spoken to Gibbs and to Williams and Strydom. Everything is fine.
SANJAY: Already OK. And how many runs for Gibbs?
CRONJÉ: Less than 20.
SANJAY: Less than 20?
CRONJÉ: Yeah.
SANJAY: OK. So everything is according to plan. They have to score at least 250?
CRONJÉ: Yeah.
SANJAY: And if you score 270, it is off?
CRONJÉ: OK. And financially the guys want 25. They want 25 each.
SANJAY: All right, OK.
CRONJÉ: So that's 75 for those three and ... what can you pay me? I do not know how much you pay me.

SANJAY: You say.

CRONJÉ: If you give me … 140 for everybody.

SANJAY: 140 altogether?

CRONJÉ: Yeah.

SANJAY: OK, that's fine.

CRONJÉ: OK.

SANJAY: And we will sort something out for the previous one as well.

CRONJÉ: OK, sure.

SANJAY: Yeah?

CRONJÉ: All right. So we definitely are on.

SANJAY: OK and one last thing I want to ask you … you know, just in case India bat first and if they get out for less than 250 and when you come in to bat for the second innings, is it possible that you could ask Gibbs to … his wicket … we will score him out and try and score slowly and not so fast so that, you know … Maybe we can get out of it.

CRONJÉ: OK.

SANJAY: And just in case India is out for less than 250 if they bat first.

CRONJÉ: OK, I will tell him.

SANJAY: Yeah?

CRONJÉ: I will tell him.

SANJAY: And because if he starts scoring so early then we won't be able to get out of it.

CRONJÉ: OK. Not so early for the first five or six in the Indian innings.

SANJAY: Yeah.

CRONJÉ: OK.

Prior to the third ODI in Faridabad, Cronjé concluded his pre-match online column by saying, 'I can assure the Indian public that we will be going flat out to turn things around'.

On a cracked pitch that *rediff.com* cricket writer Prem Panicker expected would favour batting first, Cronjé won the toss and put India in to bat. According to Panicker, had India won the toss the Indian captain Ganguly would have elected to bat first himself. Of the South African bowling attack mentioned in the transcripts, Klusener, Strydom and Boje bowled 2, 3 and 4 overs respectively, and all went for 5 runs and more, Strydom serving up 4 wides in the process. Benkenstein, one of Cronjé's ODI specialists, gave away 9 runs in his only over. Their captain, however, outdid them all with his figures of 1/69 in a full 10 overs. He did, however, pick up the wicket of Ajay Jadeja, who would later that year be slapped with a five-year ban for match-fixing. In total, 17 extras were conceded. India was all out for 248 and

South Africa found itself chasing 249 in 49 overs after being fined for a slow over rate. Once again, the game seemed to be following the script outlined in the transcript.

Sachin Tendulkar, who had handed over the captaincy to Ganguly after the Indians' Test series defeat, was involved in the dismissals of openers Kirsten, Gibbs, Boje, skipper Cronjé and Klusener. Gibbs and Boje were the first 2 wickets to fall. Gibbs was caught Tendulkar bowled Kumble in the eighth over for 19 – less than 20, just as the transcripts had said. Boje was sent in at number three to pinch-hit although he hadn't batted in the first ODI. For the second, third and fourth ODIs he slid up and down the order, coming in at number 6, then number 5 and at Faridabad appearing at number 3. He added 14 to his previous score of 28 before being dispatched by Tendulkar in the eleventh over. Kallis put on 10 before being bowled by Joshi. India had reduced South Africa to 91 for 3 inside 18 overs before Cronjé, the middle man at number 5, in partnership with surviving opener Kirsten, steadied the innings. Cronjé, in turn, was dismissed leg before wicket (lbw) off Tendulkar but his 66 was enough to earn him Man of the Match. Klusener, pinch-hitting again at number 7, failed to recapture the form that had earned him Man of the Series in the 1999 World Cup and was caught Ganguly and bowled Tendulkar for 6. Strydom, at last man in, was 1 not out. South Africa went on to win this match with 2 wickets in hand and an over to spare, an indication perhaps that matches do not have to be lost to be manipulated.

That night Sanjay, who had not left for London yet, stopped by Cronjé's room at the Taj Palace Hotel in Delhi to congratulate him on the win. The following day, Cronjé ended his rather unsubstantial *Rediff* match report on this game with a message to all Indian spectators to '... continue their unbelievable support and love for the game'.

By the fourth ODI Chawla was back in London but was in telephonic conversation with Cronjé for the remaining two matches, in Baroda (Vadodara) and Nagpur.

SANJAY: Hello, hi Hansie.
HANSIE: Hello, hi Sanjay ... You back in London?
SANJAY: Yeah, I am in London
HANSIE: I had a look at pitch today. It can turn big.
SANJAY: It can turn big?

Both the fourth and the fifth ODIs delivered high-scoring games.

Lawyers at the King Commission dated the following conversation excerpt to the 16 March, the day before the fourth ODI at Baroda.

SANJAY: Is Strydom playing?
CRONJÉ: Yes, he is playing, yeah.
SANJAY: Boje?
CRONJÉ: Boje is playing.
SANJAY: Yeah, Boje is playing … and who is playing? Gibbs?
CRONJÉ: Gibbs and myself.
SANJAY: Ya, what about anybody else?
CRONJÉ: No, I won't be able to get more.
SANJAY: You won't be able to get more.
CRONJÉ: No.

As the game played out, South Africa won the toss and elected to bat. Opener Gibbs put on 37 before being bowled lbw by Joshi. Captain Cronjé added 26 before Joshi got him too and Boje followed up with 9, bowled Kumble and caught Joshi. Strydom didn't get to bat as the South Africans posted a sizeable total of 282/5 although this reflected a drop-off in the run rate in the middle overs. In the bowling stakes, Strydom picked up the captain's wicket of Ganguly and gave away 48 runs in his 9 overs. Boje snagged Dravid in his 10 overs for 43 runs while Cronjé was empty-handed after 6 overs for 33 runs. The Indians made heavy weather of the last 5 overs despite having 8 wickets in hand and, according to the Indian correspondent Prem Panicker's match report, '… came perilously close to losing the game thanks to faulty thinking and mindless batting.'[56] However, in a nail-biting finish, the home side reached the target with one ball to spare.

It was the final ODI in Nagpur that would return to haunt certain members of the South African squad on this Indian tour.

In his statement to the King Commission, Cronjé admitted: 'A discussion with Sanjay took place the night before the fifth one-day international during which we discussed Gibbs' score, a total of 270 runs, and Williams' bowling figures. If the results were as agreed, Sanjay was to pay US$140 000 into my NatWest bank account.' Cronjé maintained, however, that 'no money changed hands in respect of any of the matches in India, all of which were a true result'.

Herschelle Gibbs and Henry Williams admitted to accepting an offer from Cronjé to influence the outcome of the fifth ODI in Nagpur although they both maintained that, for their respective reasons, neither fulfilled the arrangement. However, Gibbs would later reportedly admit to the Indian police that it was the third ODI in Faridabad for which he agreed to score less than 20 runs, not this fifth and final match. Of the principals of the so-called Nagpur conspiracy, Gibbs had the following to say:

It was quite early in the morning, the morning of the last one-day game because I distinctly remember it was the 19th of March, which is my mother's birthday, and Hansie came into my room, I was sharing a room with Henry Williams. He had this huge grin on his face. He came to me and Henry had just finished showering, whatever, and he was coming out of the bathroom when Hansie said to me that somebody had – he'd been on the phone with somebody, or somebody had phoned him and they were prepared to offer myself US$15 000 if I made less than 20. At which I said 'yes'.

Williams told a similar story, down to the detail of Cronjé's beaming countenance.

On the morning of the 19th I was busy preparing and finishing in the bathroom, and I came from the bathroom into my room. I saw Mr Cronjé in our room with a big smile on his face. He was busy talking to Gibbs. I joined the conversation and Mr Cronjé said that somebody phoned him, he did not mention any name. There's a certain amount of money that they will give to us if we throw the game.

MR FITZGERALD: What was the amount in question?
WILLIAMS: US$15 000.
MR FITZGERALD: Was that amount offered both to you and to Mr Gibbs?
WILLIAMS: That's correct.
MR FITZGERALD: And what was required of you? What did you have to do?
WILLIAMS: I had to do less than – more than 50 runs in my 10 overs. And Mr Gibbs had to do less than 20 runs ... We were not supposed to get more than 270 runs.
MR FITZGERALD: What was your response to this suggestion?
WILLIAMS: I was at first very nervous, but because Herschelle agreed, I also agreed because I had a lot of respect for the captain, Hansie Cronjé. If he can do something like this, why couldn't I do it. That's the reason.

When questioned about the discrepancy between the money mentioned by Sanjay, '25', and the US$15 000 claimed by his accomplices, Cronjé finally conceded, 'Maybe I was trying to cut something for myself.'

Derek Crookes's contribution to the Nagpur match was also under scrutiny by the King Commission as his name too had come up in the evocative excerpts. So had Lance Klusener's, and not for the first time.

SANJAY: OK, just tell me. But you have only four with you and not anybody else?

CRONJÉ: No.
SANJAY: Klusener and no one?
CRONJÉ: No. No. Impossible. Impossible.

In another uncontextualised phone call excerpt Sanjay and Cronjé discussed the South African bowling order. A fragment of conversation reflects the untoward events of the fifth ODI at Nagpur in which Crookes and Williams opened the South African bowling attack for the first time.

SANJAY: Who will bowl the first overs?
HANSIE: Crookes and Williams
SANJAY: Who will bowl first change?
HANSIE: Klusener ... Don't worry, we will be bowling with non-regular bowlers.

With the limited-overs series already lost 3-1 and nothing to play for but the prize money in the last game, Pollock, Hayward, Kallis and Boje were rested. Klusener, another of the regular bowlers, had only bowled 2 overs (third ODI – 0/11) for the duration of the tournament. The reason given was that he had been held back due to injury and was being rested in preparation for Sharjah. However, he had batted in all 5 of the games, shuffled around the order from number 4 to number 8. He failed to display the form that had made him the hero of the 1999 World Cup and was caught and bowled Dravid, for a duck, in the first ODI, bowled Tendulkar for 19 in the second and for 6 in the third. He improved upon his 14 not out in the fourth ODI to end with an unbeaten 75 in the final game. Calcutta journalist LP Sahi of the Indian *Telegraph* had told an Indian board of inquiry in 1997 that 'Public memory is very short and if a key player makes a century or takes some wickets, his immediate poor past performance is forgotten by the public'. Klusener's bowling figures in the Nagpur match, while somewhat expensive at more than 6 an over, captured 3 wickets for 59 runs in 9 overs and, along with his unbeaten 75, earned him Man of the Match.

One of a number of startling captaining decisions during this game was the appearance of Crookes, known for his bowling rather than his batting, at number 4. He had had little match practice in this series, didn't bat in the first ODI and did not play at all in the third and fourth matches. In the second ODI at Jamshedpur he came in at number 9 and was promptly caught and bowled by Joshi for a duck. At Nagpur, in the fifth and final game, he was sent on after rookie Neil McKenzie at 3 and, after an opening boundary and 10 minutes at the wicket, was promptly dispatched by Kumble with 14 runs on the board.

Despite losing 4 wickets in the first 15 overs, including opener Gary Kirsten run out by Tendulkar for a single in the second over, South Africa set a cracking pace, emerging from fielding restrictions on 126/4 – an average of over 8 runs an over in the first 15. At this rate, the 270 runs referred to would have been reached by the thirty-fifth over. Fellow opener Gibbs escaped his doom twice, courtesy of bowler Kumble's failure to hold on to a catch hit straight back at him and capitalised further on a missed opportunity by Tendulkar, who had managed to get both hands to the ball only to drop it. Gibbs would repay the favour, allowing Tendulkar to escape early in the Indian innings, but he would have his revenge on Kumble, running him out for just 5. Gibbs himself was finally run out with the help of his own team-mate, wicketkeeper Boucher; his tally of 74 a far cry from the 20 he had mentioned to the King Commission. Gibbs explained this discrepancy by saying,. 'I'd forgotten what was even spoken about before the match in the hotel and I just kept on going'.

Of the top four of the South African batting line-up, three batsmen, Kirsten, McKenzie and Crookes, managed to put on a combined total of 28 runs. Cronjé, occupying his usual kingpin slot of number 5, was getting into his stride when he cut a ball to slip only to be caught by Dravid for 38 off 31 balls. It was up to the lower order to steer the ship home with Boucher at number 6 and Klusener at number 7 putting together a rearguard action that took South African's final score to a massive 320/7. India found themselves chasing a world record. Once again, this total was way off the 270 Williams had mentioned.

By lunchtime the deal was off, according to Williams, and no money was forthcoming. 'Yes, we had lunch, he [Cronjé] came to sit with me and he said, "Hi, the deal is off. We scored 320. We must now win the game for South Africa."'

Unusually, Crookes opened the bowling for the South African innings. Crookes denied anything untoward about his captain's unorthodox decision to use himself and Williams to open the bowling. Although often used as an opening bowler for his province, Gauteng, Derek Crookes had never before done the job for South Africa. Apparently, he had been told at the beginning of the tour by coach Graham Ford and Cronjé that he would not be considered for the opening spell. Then, at a selectors' meeting the day before the Nagpur game, attended by Graham Ford, assistant coach Corrie van Zyl, team manager Goolam Rajah, physiotherapist Craig Smith, Shaun Pollock and Hansie Cronjé, he was told that he was to open with Henry Williams.

Williams lasted only 11 balls, before retiring with a shoulder injury. However, in his brief stint with the ball he gave away 11 runs, delivered 6 wides and took the captain and opening batsman's wicket of Ganguly. In his initial 6 overs, bowling against former captain Sachin Tendulkar, new captain Saurav Ganguly and batsman Raoul Dravid, Derek Crookes conceded 56 runs and averaged over 9 runs an over. Despite a disastrous fourth and fifth over, he was kept on for another and was then later brought back to finish off his remaining 4 overs, ending with the wicket of Tendulkar and figures of 1/69 in 10 overs with 1 maiden, 2 no-balls and a wide.

With the help of the 31 extras conceded by the South African bowling attack, India came within 10 runs of the massive 321 required for victory. Sachin Tendulkar and Rahul Dravid both scored 79, with Dravid's run of form coming to an end in a run-out courtesy of Crookes and Strydom.

The South Africans won the match with their highest ever one-day score against India. Under the spotlight of the King Commission, Crookes conceded that all of this, taken together with the rumoured police tapes, 'I still find it, well, it makes you think'.

When Hansiegate was thrown wide open on the 7 April with Cronjé, Gibbs, Boje and Strydom facing criminal charges in India, Gibbs and Boje disclaimed any knowledge of events to the UCB's Managing Director, Ali Bacher. Later that day, Strydom too asserted his innocence. The players lied repeatedly to the UCB and their own lawyers up until a week before the King Commission got underway on 7 June 2000.

There was a meeting on 9 April between Bacher, media liason Bronwyn Wilkinson, team manager Goolam Rajah, UCB lawyer and Cronjé's commercial agent Clifford Green, and players Gibbs, Boje and Cronjé. All denied complicity once again. Cronjé maintained his innocence and all present confirmed their support for him. No mention was made by any of the cricketers of the offers put to them by Cronjé during the Indian tour. In the press conference that followed the meeting, the three repeated their denials, apparently on the instructions of their captain. According to the King interim report, Cronjé had said to Gibbs that he should '… just deny that I ever approached you and we ever accepted an offer'.

This week before Easter was a busy one for South African cricket. Amidst the flurry of partial confessions and half-truths, the UCB drew up contracts binding the South African team to informing the authorities of any match-fixing approaches. Following the South Africans' lead, the ICC's Code of Conduct Commission put forward recommendations that suggested it must be '… an obligation on the part of the players to report to the team manager or captain any approach made to them by bookmakers or knowledge of such approach to any other player'. As an article in the magazine *India Today* pointed out, 'It is for the players to help keep their sport unblemished, for a tainted game means even the honest will be under scrutiny'.[57] Given that allegations of match-fixing internationally dated back to the 1970s such measures could well be seen as a case of too little, too late.

Lance Klusener returned to Durban only on 10 April from a World XI game played in Bangladesh and there was a meeting of the team and management on this day. 'The first time I heard about the allegations against Hansie was when we arrived back here in South Africa,' said Klusener.[58] This may not have been the case. An article that appeared in the Dubai newspaper *The Gulf News* on the day after Cronjé's confession quoted senior New Delhi police sources and suggested that Klusener and Cronjé had had a row in the foyer of the Taj Palace hotel in Delhi after the third ODI at Faridabad and that it was Klusener who had shopped his captain to the Indian police.[59] South African sports journalist Neil Manthorp described how he had confronted Klusener about the Dubai report and how he was disquieted by the low-key response from the cricketer. Explaining his unease, the reporter said, 'If you're being accused of fixing games in cricket, it's the equivalent of a primary school teacher being accused of child-molesting. If somebody accuses you of that you've got to be stirred, surely, if not badly shaken. You've got to want retribution. You know, sue them. Anything to protect your reputation'. Klusener however, tersely denied the report. Further muddying still waters, Cronjé, in his opening statement to the King Commission, told of an approach he had received the night before the Sharjah final from an unnamed man about doing a promotion. The man also wanted Klusener's services. He offered Cronjé US$100 000 now and US$100 000 later to fix the final. According to Cronjé, Klusener was never informed about that offer.

In Klusener's own words to the King Commission: 'Hindsight is a wonderful thing.' In hindsight, then, from the Delhi charges of 7 April until Cronjé's surprise confession on the 11 April, there were deafening public denials of any knowledge of match-fixing within the South African team. Gibbs, in fact, denied his complicity to the UCB seven times, twice because Cronjé asked him to. He lied also at a press conference, in an interview with the *Cape Argus* and in meetings with his own lawyers until a week before the King Commission was due to begin public hearings.

It was Cronjé that finally broke down. On 11 April, a second team meeting was necessitated by Cronjé's midnight confession that he had indeed taken money from a bookmaker. At two o'clock in the morning Rory Steyn, the UCB's Security Co-ordinator, received a call from Cronjé requesting him to come to his room where he handed over the now famous seven-page confession. In his testimony to the King Commission Rory Steyn described Cronjé's emotional state at the time: 'His eyes were wide open and he was on the verge of tears while he was speaking to me, and he must have broken down into tears on two or three occasions. And I felt nothing but great sadness and great pity for him.' Steyn suggested that Hansie contact Percy Sonn, the Acting

President of the United Cricket Board, because he was a senior law officer and an advocate.

Steyn's advice was sound, as the late Percy Sonn was in a unique position to advise Cronjé. Sonn's long career had been built on two pillars – the law and cricket. He worked as an attorney and an advocate, was the Deputy Director of Public Prosecutions and a legal advisor to the South African Police Service. He also helped to establish and then lead the Directorate of Special Operations, known as the Scorpions, an elite South African crime unit that investigates organised crime. He played a leading role in the unification of black and white cricket in 1991 and worked his way through the ranks of cricket administrators before becoming the first African President of the ICC, world cricket's governing body, in June 2006. As Sonn's profile on the ICC website points out: '... his input has been invaluable in all legal matters affecting the UCBSA. This background has also made him a respected member of the ICC'. Sonn would go on to represent the UCBSA at the ICC in the match-fixing furore that would engulf world cricket following the events of 11 April 2000.

At the time, the UCB's Managing Director Ali Bacher and President Percy Sonn were at Phinda Game Reserve in Northern KwaZulu-Natal entertaining Australian cricketing dignitaries. Acting on Steyn's advice, Cronjé phoned Bacher and Sonn in the early hours of that fateful Tuesday morning and came clean. One media report described Bacher as being 'incandescent with rage' upon hearing the news, whether because of all the lies or because of the new-found truth is not clear.[60]

The South African cricket team was apprised of the unfolding events of that night by their manager Goolam Rajah in the dressing room at Kingsmead before a practice session for the long-awaited clash between Australia and South Africa on 12 April. Nobody, it seems, contributed any insights of their own into the match-rigging accusations levelled at their captain. After the practice, there was a second meeting, described as 'emotional' by some players, at the team's Durban hotel. At this second stand-up-and-be-counted gathering, UCB manager Ali Bacher, Bronwyn Wilkinson, Percy Sonn and other members of the board were present, as was the entire team. They were asked if they had ever been party to match-fixing or had ever been approached to get involved. Once again, no one came forward with their tales of Cronjé's conspiratorial sense of humour during the latest Indian tour, despite the fact that Gary Kirsten, Daryll Cullinan, Herschelle Gibbs, Lance Klusener and Nicky Boje had all been present at a meeting on tour in India in 1996 where Cronjé put a fixing offer to the entire team. It was left to Jonty Rhodes, who had not been present at the 1996 meeting, to mention the incident to Ali Bacher, who maintained that this was the first he had heard of it despite media reports in the *Sunday Times* in December 1998.

At a UCBSA press conference that same day, Ali Bacher announced the withdrawal of Cronjé for the following day's ODI with Australia and the appointment of Shaun Pollock.

> Shaun Pollock has been made captain. He's a player with an immense future ahead of him, he has a very good cricketing brain on him, his feet on the ground, and we have every confidence in the team, the country will rally behind Shaun Pollock and make the next three one-dayers against Australia an outstanding climax to what has been a very difficult season for many of us in South African cricket.

The outcome of the first ODI between South Africa and the Australians lived up to Bacher's highest expectations. In the wake of Cronjé's midnight confession, support for Hansie remained widespread amongst the public, the press and the players – so much so that Sadha Govender, the chairman of KwaZulu-Natal's cricket development programme, was assaulted at the Kingsmead ground by South African fans angry at the Indian police for bringing down Cronjé.[61] Shaun Pollock dedicated the team's 6-wicket win to their disgraced former captain and there was record crowd attendance at the game. Cronjé responded emotionally:

> The only light that I have seen in these last few, dark days has been the magnificent victory of Shaun and his team against Australia last night. I cannot begin to express the emotion I felt when that side emerged victorious and it must be indicative of the morale and commitment of that side to have won so high-profile a game under the circumstances in which they found themselves. I am truly proud to have been associated with this side one and all and wish Shaun and the rest of the team nothing but success in the future.[62]

Putting somewhat of a damper upon the celebrations, former South African coach Bob Woolmer chose the following day, 13 April, and the *Daily Sport* newspaper in London, to resurrect the story of the offer of US$250 000 that Cronjé had put to the entire team before an ODI game in India in 1996.

Herschelle Gibbs broke his week-long media silence to speak to the Saturday *Cape Argus* of 15 April: 'I felt bad, but I knew I was innocent. Nothing would ever make me do something so irresponsible … I think somebody who would become involved in anything like this would have let their country down, and themselves and the team and it is terribly unprofessional … Nobody approached us. When we were told about it we were terribly shocked.' Of Cronjé he said, 'He is a great man and one of the greatest captains who has ever played the game. I've known him for a good few years and I've still got the utmost respect for him. He will always be a great friend of mine'. Lending credence to his sincerity, Gibbs was spotted playing golf with Cronjé at Fancourt just weeks after confirming his former captain's match-fixing approach to the King Commission.

Then, on 16 April, Cronjé was in touch with Gibbs and told him to go ahead and admit the approach but to claim that no sums of money were discussed and that Gibbs had turned down the offer. Cronjé also asked Gibbs to tell Williams to relate the same story. Accordingly, this was the revised tale Gibbs told team manager Rajah when he phoned some time later and Gibbs confirmed the tale to Bacher when he phoned on 19 April. Strydom too admitted an approach and Williams all of a sudden was singing the same tune. According to the King Report's summary of Williams' evidence: 'On about 16 April 2000, Williams received Cronjé's instructions from Gibbs – that he must say that he had not accepted any offer from Cronjé, that he should say that it was all a big joke. At the meeting of 22 May 2000 with his legal representatives, Williams stuck to this story.'

On 20 April, Gibbs and Strydom met with the UCB and confirmed approaches by Cronjé. Wicketkeeper Mark Boucher and top-order batsman Jacques Kallis were also approached. Bacher phoned Boucher, who admitted that Kallis and himself, as well as Klusener, were sounded out by Cronjé. However, all denied accepting the offer and no figures were mentioned. Gibbs maintained this 'half-truth' to the UCB and to his own lawyers right up until 31 May, a week before the opening of the King Commission hearings, when Boucher finally persuaded him to come clean. Williams followed suit the next day. Boje continues to this day to protest his complete ignorance of any match-tampering. Of the three names, then, mentioned in the Delhi transcripts and in the separate testimonies of Cronjé and Aronstam, Strydom admitted to receiving an offer but denied accepting it. Gibbs admitted to accepting an offer but claimed that he had failed to act on the deal. Boje remained silent.

By the time of the King Commission, Cronjé's seven-page confession had become a six-page confession. The missing page mysteriously reappeared during the hearings, ostensibly handed over by Cronjé's team to UCB counsel Jeremy Gauntlett, during his cross-examination of Rory Steyn. In the first of the elusive points 5 to 9 contained on this page, Cronjé wrote: 'The team and management has been great in their support as they obviously never suspected anything. I would like to apologise in particular to Boje, Gibbs and Strydom, whose names were mentioned in the media. They were absolutely 100% innocent.'

Less than four months later, Gibbs and Boland cricketer Henry Williams found themselves facing charges that Michael Kuper, a member of the UCB's disciplinary committee, described as '... amongst the most serious that can be made of any cricketer' that they '... secretly and corruptly promised to play poorly' in the fifth and final ODI against India in Nagpur in March 2000.[63] The disciplinary committee would have had had their disposal a considerable amount of evidence about the Nagpur game, having waited as it did for the release of the King Interim Report.

Gibbs and Williams had been in contact with each other right up until the King Commission of Inquiry got underway. Williams told the Commission: 'I got all my information from Herschelle because Hansie never called me personally. Hansie, [sic] according to the information I got from Herschelle, was that we should stick to the plan. We must never say that we were approached together and that he also never asked us to do badly for South Africa.' Despite this distance from the man who had embroiled him in all this trouble, Williams declaimed on the witness stand: 'I had great respect for Hansie as a captain. I cannot say we were good or close friends, I played only seven matches under his captaincy. The manner in which he deals with matches, I can say he's one of the best captains in the world.'

During the King Commission, Cronjé admitted to accepting some US$130 000 from bookies to influence matches and performances. Subsequent forensic investigations would reveal 27 bank accounts held by Cronjé in South Africa and more than 70 accounts in the Cayman Islands, all undisclosed to the South African Revenue Service. However, before the amount of money in the accounts could be established, the investigation was terminated. With the World Cup coming to South Africa in 2003, the South African government was reportedly reluctant to reveal the full extent of Cronjé's corruption.

July 2000 saw the South African cricket team leave for Sri Lanka, minus Gibbs, Williams, Strydom and, of course, Cronjé. Boje was the only player to go on the South African tour of Sri Lanka in July, although there were reports that the UCB had had to get diplomatic assurance that Boje would not be arrested by Indian police while out of the country. Before departure, another declaration of integrity was signed. The venue of this ceremonial oath-swearing was the Sandton Sun, scene of dirty dealings between Hansie Cronjé and Jo'burg bookie Marlon Aronstam before the fifth Test against England at Centurion in January 2000.

By August 2000, former Judge Mervyn King, head of the triumvirate of legal eagles presiding over the cricketing fate of Herschelle Gibbs, Henry Williams and Pieter Strydom, was not present at the 28 August press conference to announce the findings of the UCB-appointed disciplinary committee into match-fixing allegations. Michael Kuper SC relayed the committee's findings. Kuper pointed out early on that the disciplinary committee was not bound by the published rulings of the International Cricket Council with regard to the penalty for match-fixing. While the ICC had not set any minimum punishments, the maximum life ban proposed by the ICC was agreed upon in October 1999 but only reached the South African cricket board on 20 April 2000, following the Cronjé revelations. Because of this, the committee declared itself independent of retroactive rulings and Gibbs and Williams '… beneficiaries of that lapse'.

Based on the testimony of Williams and Gibbs to the King Commission, which the UCB's disciplinary committee accepted was 'correct' and 'could be relied upon' it concurred that their offence amounted to, in the end, a 'still-born conspiracy' that never got off the ground. Another extenuating factor for the committee was the fact that the 'malign influence' of their captain corrupted them or '… they would not otherwise have been corrupt'. Although Gibbs had never adequately explained the reasons for his not following through with the arrangement, the disciplinary committee was of the opinion that he '… closed his mind to the corrupt agreement … and simply played to the best of his ability'. They found both Gibbs and Williams guilty of conspiracy but not of match-fixing. In justification of sentencing, the committee contended that a life ban would '… go beyond what is fair and proper …' while a suspended life ban would be a '… poor precedent for the proper discipline of cricketing offences'. Gibbs was therefore banned from taking part in any form of international cricket for a period of six months – from 30 June to 31 December 2000 – and was fined R60 000 (US$8 500). Likewise, Williams was banned from international cricket for the same period but his fine amounted to only R10 000 (US$1 400). The bans did not apply to domestic cricket and both cricketers were still able to participate in any form of the game, be it playing, writing or commentating. The disciplinary committee explained its reasoning: In addition to the loss of income already sustained by Gibbs, the cricketer '… would be prevented from earning a living if he couldn't play domestic cricket'. Describing Williams as a '… self-made man who fought his way to the top from humble beginnings' and as he was approaching the end of his career, the committee decided that such benefits as he could reap from the domestic season were due to him. Pieter Strydom was acquitted of conspiring to place a bet on the Centurion Test.

The committee confirmed that should new facts or new offences come to light, the trio would be tried again. However, it was emphasised that they couldn't be tried again for the same offence: '[We] can't sentence them on top of a sentence for the same offence … It's finished. Finito.'

Or was it?

Gibbs soon bounced back. Just over a month after the disciplinary findings, Gibbs returned to domestic cricket in a limited-overs match on 1 October 2000. His international come-back was announced on 1 January 2001, the very first day of the expiry of his six-month international ban. His selection was finalised, in fact, two days before the ban was up. Gibbs was included, some said with 'shameless haste',[64] in the squad to play Sri Lanka in the second Test at Newlands over the New Year weekend. Gainsaying such observations, Rushdi Magiet, Chairman of Selectors, said that Gibbs had served his time and was the best man for the job. The UCB obviously agreed as there was no protest at his quicksilver reinstatement. Gibbs won back his place over rising young star Boeta Dippenaar, who had made his Test debut in Sri Lanka in July and continued to show his form. *Argus* sports writer Michael Doman noted that Dippenaar had been unlucky to have had to make way for Gibbs. Doman, however, was phlegmatic: '... the issue of what kind of moral message is being sent by the apparent welcoming of Gibbs the transgressor with open arms at the earliest opportunity, loses impact in the modern dog-eat-dog world, where business and money rule.'[65]

Despite Gibbs' return to international cricket, he did not travel with the South African team on their two subsequent tours to India for fear of being detained by the Indian police. Nor did Nicky Boje. Finally, in October 2006, both Boje and Gibbs returned to India for the first time in six years for the ICC Champions Trophy. But first, Indian police questioned Gibbs on 12 October in an interview that had been long-delayed. According to the Indian newspaper *The Telegraph*, these are the questions that were put to Gibbs in a two-and-a-half hour interrogation. The abbreviated answers are based on what police sources present at the interview chose to reveal. (Original interpolations are in round brackets.)

POLICE: What is your present and permanent address?

GIBBS: The same as on my passport.

POLICE: Were you a member of the South African team which toured India in March–April 2000?

GIBBS: Yes.

POLICE: Had you brought any mobile phone or any other communications instrument with you from South Africa during your visit? If not, how did you communicate with your family members? What was the number of your mobile?

GIBBS: Yes. (He gave the mobile number but the source didn't reveal it.)

POLICE: Do you recognise to whom these phone numbers belong? (Gibbs had been sent the numbers of Sanjeev Chawla, Mukesh Gupta, Manoj Khattar and Hamid Cassim 'Banjo', the bookies implicated in the case.)

GIBBS: No.

POLICE: Do you know someone by the name of Sanjeev Chawla or Sanjay? Have you ever met him? Do you recognise him?

GIBBS: No.

POLICE: Do you know Hamid Cassim Banjo? Have you ever met him or spoken to him while in India or South Africa?

GIBBS: Yes, I have spoken to him.

POLICE: In which game of the Indian tour (in 2000) did the late Hansie Cronjé approach you?

GIBBS: Before the Faridabad match. [Note that Gibbs says the third ODI not the fifth game at Nagpur.]

POLICE: Who were the other players he had approached with the offer?

GIBBS: Nicky Boje, Derek Crookes, Peter Strydom, Henry Williams.

POLICE: Did Hansie Cronjé speak to you to give away the game in lieu of some consideration in the match in Faridabad. What was the amount offered?

GIBBS: Yes. The amount was not clear to me.

POLICE: As per the conversation between Hansie and Sanjeev Chawla, Hansie asked Sanjeev Chawla for US$25 000 for each player. Did Hansie Cronjé offer you this amount?

GIBBS: As I said, I was not clear about the amount to be paid.

POLICE: How many times were you approached to influence the outcome of the (Faridabad) match?

GIBBS: Once.

POLICE: Did you agree to accept the money and how much?

GIBBS: Yes, I accepted the offer. The amount was not clear.

POLICE: Can you explain the move to open the bowling with Derek Crookes?

GIBBS: It was Cronjé's decision.

POLICE: Is it true that your captain had approached you personally and offered you large amounts of money for giving away the game?

GIBBS: Yes.

POLICE: Have you earlier given any statement to any agency or commission regarding the above-discussed matter?

GIBBS: The King Commission in South Africa.

POLICE: Do you accept that Hansie largely fixed cricket matches played in India during the year 2000 tour and you were party to it?

GIBBS: I am not aware.

POLICE: What was your deposition before the King Commission of Inquiry? Did you confess to any wrongdoing? Please specify the amount paid by Hansie Cronjé and also disclose the advice given by him not to reveal the entire truth.

GIBBS: I told them I was approached by Hansie Cronjé on the tour. The amount was not clear. I have already told the King Commission I was advised (by Cronjé) to keep mum.

POLICE: Have you gone to London since 2000, and have you had any contact with Sanjeev Chawla?

GIBBS: No.

POLICE: Were you or any other player you know approached at any point other than that particular match? What happened in that/those cases?

GIBBS: The entire South African team was approached for under-performing in 1996. Two players out of the team of eleven refused, so we had to turn down the offer.

POLICE: Were you one of the two?

GIBBS: No.

POLICE: Do you know of any Indian cricketers approached by the bookies for the matches that you were approached for?

GIBBS: No.[66]

In reaction to the news that Gibbs had mentioned his name to the Indian police, Derek Crookes 'strongly protested his innocence'.[67] Similarly, according to the former Chief Executive of the UCB, Ali Bacher, 'Nicky Boje was innocent. I know that for a fact. When it [the scandal] all broke, Herschelle Gibbs's body language was not good. Boje was fine. I can read people. He was innocent.'[68]

Like Gibbs, Nicky Boje too went from strength to strength after the furore, in the estimation of cricket's commentators. Dave Richardson, former vice captain to Cronjé, writing for the *Supersport* website, drew attention to Boje's meteoric rise in the batting order. Peter Robinson, writing in the 26 January edition of the weekly *Mail and Guardian,* observed that Boje's 'remarkable run of form' started on that fateful tour of India in early 2000. Elevated suddenly from his customary bottom-order batting position to number 3 in the second Test at Bangalore, he responded with an 85 and took 5 wickets in the second innings, earning himself Man of the Match. Despite such success in the higher batting echelons, he returned to number 9 during the 3 Tests against Sri Lanka in July 2000, following the Cronjé scandal. His Test form was unprepossessing apart from a five-wicket haul in the third Test. By the end of the year, he had won Man of the Series against New Zealand in November 2000 for his two world-class centuries and followed that up with a hundred and a half-century in his first domestic game of the 2001 season. However, on tour to the West Indies early in 2001, Boje was back in the lower batting ranks once more and failed to fire.

With Gibbs and Boje firmly reinstated in the national side, Martin Gillingham, regional radio station *Cape Talk*'s then sports editor, was sceptical of the declarations of integrity signed by the South African team.

GILLINGHAM: I read another glorious editorial in the *Cape Times* this morning talking about how we should credit our cricket team, how they appear to have rejuvenated themselves and put behind them all that happened last year.

INTERVIEWER: And have they?

GILLINGHAM: Well, I think our cricket team does well and there's probably, on the whole, ten out of eleven very decent young men there and there may well be an eleventh but if we look at the evidence presented by the Indians, which has been shown in every case when it's been examined to be good and solid, the one person they've still got a warrant of arrest out on, I understand, is Nicky Boje … There was a warrant out for those four players. Now three have been examined and have been exposed as having stories to tell and they've told at least some of them. Now, the one person who has yet to be properly examined was Nicky Boje and Nicky Boje was just in and out of the witness box at the King Commission without any meaningful cross-examination. It still seems to me that he has not been … you know, he may well be innocent. As far as I'm concerned, I'd like to be generous; he's not been given the opportunity to clear his name, is my thought.

While Boje retained his place in the national side he refused to play in India and never would again. Named in the Test side for the 2006 end-of-year tour of India, he retired from international cricket two days before the start of the first Test.

As for Hansie Cronjé, whose midnight confession had illuminated this shadowy world of conspiracies and lies, he was banned for life from all forms of cricket on 2 November 2000. Percy Sonn delivered the judgment in a statement on behalf of the United Cricket Board:

> In terms of the evidence presented to the King Commission of Inquiry, Hansie Cronjé acknowledged accepting money from bookmakers as well as attempting to induce others in his team to under-perform. At the time of those actions, Mr Cronjé was the captain of the South African national cricket team – a position of importance and trust. The actions he admitted to cut across the foundation of trust placed in a person in such a position of integrity. In our opinion, his actions have harmed the good name of cricket in South Africa, not only from the Council's perspective, but also in the eyes of the public. Accordingly in pursuant to our resolution on October 4 and with immediate effect: WJ Cronjé is banned for life from membership or participation in the UCB, its structures or activities.

However, there was a glimmer of hope. 'We acknowledge that, with effort, people are able to rehabilitate themselves over time and there may be an opportunity for the UCB to take cognisance of this possibility in the future.'[69]

That future might have come sooner than expected, had fate not intervened. At the beginning of 2002, just over a year since the UCB's pronouncement, and his own assertion that under his presidency, 'Cronjé would not even be allowed to play beach cricket', Percy Sonn told the Australian Broadcasting Corporation: 'Who are we to damn people forever? Our board is not God in terms of determining what rehabilitation is sufficient. Hansie deserves to enjoy all the freedom of South African society. He is a child of the United Cricket Board.'[70]

Cast out from the game that had been his life, Cronjé took a job as account manager for a company that manufactured earth-moving equipment. Bell Equipment was based in Johannesburg, but Cronjé's home was in George, some 1 100 kilometres away. On Friday 30 May 2002, Hansie missed his scheduled flight home. The SA Express flight to George that Hansie was booked on was cancelled for 'operational reasons'.[71] Pam Jooste, Hansie's secretary at the time, was quoted in *The Observer* newspaper: 'When he missed the flight, it was cold and hailing in Jo'burg. It was late in the afternoon; most of the staff had gone home. It was freezing cold outside and Hansie asked whether anyone wanted coffee. He seemed anxious, a little uneasy.'[72] Cronjé, relying on a standing arrangement, hitched a free ride home with a small air cargo company, AirQuarius. The plane lost its bearings in bad weather in the early hours of Saturday morning and crashed into a mountainside just outside George. No one survived.

Like a modern-day Greek tragedy, the hero who had once flown so high, literally fell out of the sky. A commission of inquiry in 2006 declared the aeroplane crash accidental. However, at least one person would disagree. Former South African cricketer Clive Rice, in several interviews on *Cape Talk* radio, voiced his doubts: 'I will question Cronjé's death to the day I die. From the minute it happened, they needed him out because he knew too much.'[73]

In the aftermath of the tragedy, the world paid tribute to the fallen hero. In the opinion of sports correspondent Michael Owen-Smith, 'It would have been only a matter of time before Cronjé would have been welcomed back into the official cricket fold'.[74] Allan Donald and Jonty Rhodes dedicated the South African team's performance in the 2003 World Cup to their former captain, and former coach Bob Woolmer said, 'He was the best captain I have had the pleasure of working with. The team would have walked off Table Mountain for him.'[75]

5

The whole truth and nothing but the truth?

The media in the dock

You can fool all the people all of the time if the advertising is right and the budget is big enough.

– Joseph E Levine, American film producer (1905–1987)

South Africans and cricket fans around the world were bewildered by the sudden reversal of all they had once believed of the South African cricket team and its handsome young captain. How had we got it so wrong? Patrick Symcox, long-time stalwart of the South African team throughout all of Cronjé's tenure as captain, is one of many international cricketers who made the transition from the cricket pitch to the commentary box. Writing in an online guest column entitled 'Whom do we trust' for the magazine *India Today*, in the wake of Hansie's midnight confession, Symcox spoke for the country and the team:

> Yes, South Africa is in total disbelief at what has happened. But what about us, as fellow cricketers who have toured the world with Hansie, know him as our leader and role model? The hardest thing to absorb is that he is the last guy we would expect to make an elementary mistake by getting involved in something that could harm not only himself and his team, but also the entire game world-wide ... The problem I guess we all face at the moment is who do we believe now.[76]

In the light of Cronjé's revelations to the King Commission two months later, one must presume that Symcox would be in agreement with Mae West: 'Don't ever make the same mistake twice – unless it pays.'

As early as three months into his captaincy, Cronjé was approached by a match-fixer to influence the outcome of the first-leg final of the Mandela Cup between Pakistan and South Africa in January 1995. He told the King Commission that it was senior player Patrick Symcox that he turned to for advice on how to deal with the proposition. According to Cronjé, Symcox said the US$10 000 offer was too low and it was rejected. Symcox too was present at the team meeting (or three) in December 1996 before the final upgraded ODI game of the South African tour to India. Under cross-examination, Symcox admitted that he did not reject out of hand the offer of US$250 000 to throw the game and did initially take it seriously.

Veteran Pakistani cricket writer Qamar Ahmed explained that 'The system works through the agents of the bookmakers. With some masquerading as journalists, the agents are present in nearly every Test series, no matter where it is played or who is playing.'[77] Cronjé's 'first' encounter with a bookmaker followed Ahmed's script. Explaining why he allowed 'John,' the match-fixer posing as a journalist, up to his room in the Cape Sun, Cronjé told the King Commission: 'It is common practice in the South African cricket side to try to be as much as you can, friendly and open to journalists and particularly during that time of just coming back into international sport, I was trying my best to build up a good relationship with the media and in particular, the foreign media from the subcontinent.' The Indian report on cricket match-fixing released in November 2000 identified 'John' as an alias of Delhi-based bookie MK Gupta.

Ironically, then, it was the foreign media from the subcontinent, and in particular India, that helped to shed further light on the extent of the match-fixing epidemic. In the aftermath of Hansiegate, cricketing nations hastened to appear transparent and a rash of hitherto unpublicised official reports were released. The Board of Control for Cricket in India's Chandrachud Inquiry in 1997 was one such document. In addition to a host of India's past and present cricket players, Justice Chandrachud interviewed a number of experienced sports journalists representing an array of Indian media sources. Despite claims of never having heard of match-fixing in the Indian team, some of the journalists were most enlightening about the media's role in the state of play.

SK Shyam was an experienced Indian cricket correspondent who gave evidence at the Chandrachud Inquiry. While insisting that '… no player would risk his career by being directly involved in an illegal activity like betting on cricket', he told Chandrachud of people 'masquerading' as journalists, touring with the team and having access to the press box where, he alleged '… they chat on the phone all day and hardly write a line on the cricket of the day'. This observation was repeated by Shri Pradeep Magazine, then sports editor of *The Pioneer* in Delhi. He too had seen '… people on the phone in the press box giving information about the state of the wicket and the likely result of a match'.

Nor is the players' enclosure safe from illicit infiltration it seems – the Indian magazine *Outlook* reported in their cover story of 11 June 1997 that the Indian team would get 75 passes for every match and word had it that these were for sale.[78] Why these strangers in the players' enclosure are not picked up by the roaming TV cameras and remarked upon by commentators at the ground remains unanswered. Apparently, some intrepid reporters did try to record documentary evidence of bookies in the boxes. LP Sahi of Calcutta's *Telegraph* newspaper reported that Indian batsman Ajay Jadeja had brought a bookie to meet Mohammad Azharuddin in the players' dressing room during a competition in Sharjah, thought to be the Asia Cup in April 1995. When journalists tried to photograph the encounter, the bookie was hurried away by Jadeja and Azharuddin.[79] A similar plot unfolded during the same tournament, according to an article in *Outlook* online on 24 April 2000 that named Dawood Ibrahim's D-Company as being one of the kingpins of the betting syndicates. During a match between India and Pakistan in the 1995 Asia Cup, known members of D-Company were reportedly seen entering the press box.[80] South African sports journalist Neil Manthorp confirmed the frequency of such unauthorised visitors in the press box, players' enclosure and dressing room: 'Throughout the '90s, the dressing room was a thoroughfare for people.' According to Manthorp, the South African players ran the risk of offending any visiting dignitaries if they tried to clear the room.

Cricket journalists and media commentators, many of them ex-players and former coaches themselves, travel with the touring cricket team, stay in the same hotels and socialise in the same circles. Their expert knowledge and insider status is coveted by bookies, most of whom are not cricket experts but who have a financial interest in the outcome of matches. One Indian media source, Sabyasachi Sarkar of *Ananda Bazar Patrika,* told *Outlook* reporters that '... calls from Dubai and Mumbai come to certain journalists on a regular basis during the toss. The same journalists interact with the players in the dressing room.' For these admittedly untaxing endeavours, the journalists reportedly receive plane tickets, a contracted sum per match or a betting tab of their own with the bookie paying for the loss and the journo keeping the win.[81] In the same article, *Outlook* named R Mohan, the then sports editor of *The Hindu*, as a journalist who '... punts from the pressbox ... ' conveying insider information to bookies and punters. The journalist in question appeared before Justice Chandrachud in 1997, giving the inquiry the benefit of his long experience as a cricket correspondent:

> I consider it impossible that an international match can be fixed ... But during my eighteen years as a cricket correspondent with *The Hindu*, I do not know a single instance when I heard before the match or during the match that some particular player or players are going to play badly ... I have no personal knowledge, but it is widely believed that a large amount of betting takes place on cricket in India ... I have gone about five times out of India

> with the Indian touring team from 1979 to 1997. Not once did I suspect that any match was fixed or that any player had placed a bet for losing the match.

In contrast to Mohan's ingenuous self-portrayal, South African sports writer Neil Manthorp confirmed receiving such calls '... in Zimbabwe and in South Africa'. He recalled that, particularly in Zimbabwe:

> The Bombay [Mumbai] bookmakers were phenomenal. Calls would come through all the time. India played Zimbabwe's inaugural Test match and they needed a direct line. These lines were just installed by the Zimbabwe telephone company and there were calls within ten minutes. I didn't know what they were. India's most famous journalist, who's also their most famous gambler, R Mohan, he was on that tour as well and I remember him smiling at me, he'd chat away. Then the calls would come through to me. He introduced me and spoke to me about the whole thing. I was aware of it then. He explained to me, 'They're bookmakers.' I thought nothing of it. He was laying bets of Rs200 000 or Rs300 000 (US$5 000–US$7 000) at various stages and he made a lot of money on that Test match. I remember him asking me for information like 'What does this pitch, the Harare Sports Club, normally play like?' I thought then and still do that betting's fun and gambling's legitimate, isn't it?

Pradeep Magazine, then *Pioneer* sports editor, continued his testimony to Justice Chandrachud with a summarised account of his own, more direct dealings with the hidden side of cricket. In a controversial article written from Georgetown while he was covering the Indian tour to the West Indies and published on 19 April 1997, Magazine told of meeting a '... thin, short man ...' from Delhi at the Jamaica airport after the first Test in Kingston in March 1997. In his book *Not Quite Cricket,* Magazine refers to this man as 'Anil'. The two became friendly and during the course of two evenings spent together, the man revealed himself to be a '... businessman, a punter and a bookie-agent all rolled into one'. He travelled the world following cricket tournaments and told Magazine that he had been to South Africa six times because he found the country conducive to men of his business persuasion. 'And,' he added, 'it is always important to get all the information about match conditions first-hand until you find a trustworthy man.'[82] It would appear that 'Anil' passed on the information thus gathered to a contact in India. It is worth remembering here that Delhi bookie MK Gupta's partner at the time was Anil Steel.

By his own admission, Mr Magazine was close to a number of players on the Indian team, including the captain. Showing spontaneous confidence in this newly forged friendship, 'Anil' offered Pradeep Rs40 lakh (US$98 000) to set him up with some top Indian players and threw in the lure of a house in a posh Delhi suburb if he managed to get Indian captain Sachin Tendulkar on board. Magazine agreed. In the meantime, he arranged to supply the man, upon his return to Delhi after the second Test, with weather and pitch information and his informed opinion on the prospects of victory during each day of the subsequent Test matches and ODIs. Magazine admitted to Chandrachud that phone calls did come from Delhi, the information was passed on and the prearranged Rs15 000 (US$370) for each forecast did reach his home. He also approached Sachin Tendulkar as agreed, but according to Magazine, the former Indian captain was furious when the offer was mentioned and regarded it as 'beneath his dignity' to even discuss it. Justice Chandrachud in his commentary on this part of Magazine's testimony is '… inclined to hold that Sachin's reaction is representative of the reaction of the Indian players, by and large'. Magazine concluded: 'I knew that I had established one truth in my mind: bookies depend on people close to the team, in this case journalists like me, for information.'[83]

Sachin Tendulkar, in his statement to the Chandrachud Inquiry, was silent on this encounter and blissfully unaware of match-fixing: 'I do not believe that matches are fixed or can be fixed … Within my knowledge, no match has ever been fixed.' Three years later, in the wake of Hansiegate, Tendulkar, in an exclusive interview with *Outlook's* Manu Joseph, vehemently denied the presence of four top Mumbai bookies reportedly captured on revenue intelligence video footage at his wedding.[84] One of these bookies was said to be the alleged racketeering ringleader Shobhan Mehta, whom Indian investigators identified as one of India's nine biggest punters. Mehta has been linked in media reports to former international cricketers like Mohammad Azharuddin, Nayan Mongia, Ajay Jadeja, Mark Waugh and Hansie Cronjé.[85]

Based on his West Indian experience, Mr Magazine asserted that he would not be surprised if some matches were fixed but he had 'no evidence' of this. Justice Chandrachud concurred: 'Shri Magazine has rightly said that the bookies, on their own part, believe that matches can be fixed. Fortunately, the belief of bookies does not determine the rules and regulations of an orderly life.' Chandrachud's conclusion: 'In so far as the involvement of journalists in betting or match-fixing, there is equally no credible evidence to justify their implication.'

In South Africa, three years and a number of international match-fixing inquiries later, the *Cape Argus* editorial of 22 June 2000 applauded the previous day's High Court judgment allowing public broadcasts of the King Commission, as a '… triumph of our constitution … and a major advance in the interests of press freedom.' It concluded: 'There have been fears that the Commission may be something of a cover-up. Those are groundless, of course, but South Africa has become a sceptical nation and live broadcast along with print reporting can only enhance Judge King's attempts to get to the bottom of a very shady business.'

However, despite the fact that the proceedings were being televised live and broadcast in full on the radio, it was difficult to make sense of the evidence given, much of it disjointed and some of it conflicting. In fact, there was little meaningful analysis of the King Commission in the South African print media and no more than sound-bite chunks of testimony on the national TV broadcaster. The real implications of the evidence heard were not conveyed to the public. There were a lot of 'ducks to get in a row' to borrow an expression used by Jo'burg bookie Marlon Aronstom in evidence to the King Commission. The media did not seem to be helping line them up.

The weekly *Mail and Guardian* is not part of the *Naspers* and *Independent Newspapers* monopoly and is thus one of the last 'independent' newspapers in South Africa. It prides itself on its investigative reporting. During Cronjé's three days and ten hours of testimony to the King Commission when new twists and turns in the lurid tale were coming thick and fast, the *Mail and Guardian* of 23–29 June devoted most of a page to the architecture of the Centre for the Book (the venue for the Commission) and deliberated upon the irony of the statue of Sir Donald Currie in the entrance hall. The premier provincial rugby and cricket tournaments once bore his name. A column was ceded to the South African women's cricket team playing in England and another half a page was devoted to a retrospective of the Chicago White Sox scandal over the alleged throwing of the baseball World Series of 1919. Referring to this incident, the one pertinent comment on the biggest scandal to sweep South African sport belonged to F Scott Fitzgerald from *The Great Gatsby*: 'It never occurred to me that one man could start to play with the faith of 50 million people, with the single-mindedness of a burglar blowing a safe.'

The week the Commission ended, the *Mail and Guardian* edition (30 June–6 July) did not have any meaningful analysis of the Commission or the implications of the evidence heard, including the sensational revelations of itemised phone lists showing extensive communications between suspected money-launderer Hamid Cassim and most of the South African team. Instead, the newspaper had a quarter-page on Cassim the candy man, whose biltong sales had apparently soared since his appearance on the Commission. According to the article, 'He is also planning a flashy new package sporting the label "Cricketers Choice – Biltong by Banjo – Trialled and Tested by the South African Cricket Team."'[86]

I approached Martin Gillingham, then sports editor of the regional radio station *Cape Talk*, for an insider's perspective on South Africa's fourth estate. A Yorkshireman who represented Britain in the track and field at the 1984 Olympics on the same team as expatriate South African runner Zola Budd, Gillingham came to South Africa in 1992, where he worked in print media and radio before returning to the UK. In the cool, airy interior of a fashionable cafe on one of Cape Town's trendiest streets, I put my questions to the straight-talking Gillingham.

INTERVIEWER: Does the media help to create sports stars?

GILLINGHAM: Yeah, it does.

INTERVIEWER: How?

GILLINGHAM: Well, we always like to talk about role models, don't we? That's one of the most flawed concepts there is because what makes Herschelle Gibbs a good cricketer is clearly his talent to play cricket. With all respect to Herschelle Gibbs, were he not a talented cricketer he'd probably be like many others, I'm afraid. Well, he's a multi-talented lad, if you take his sporting talents away, you know, there's no shame in this, but you know he's not a rocket scientist, he comes from the wrong side of the tracks, that's where he'd still be. Does just because he happens to be exceedingly talented at cricket therefore make him a role model? Not necessarily. It makes him a role model if you want to learn how to bat properly but it has got nothing to do with how else you should run your life. But role models are held up as models that you should follow in every way. This is how someone like Hansie Cronjé became, you know a lot of people were saying, 'Well, Hansie, you let us down because you were a role model.' Now, who created that role model? Partly, we do ourselves, with a bit of help from the media, and particularly cricket, because also in this country ... Broadly, I don't think this country is being particularly well served by the media.

INTERVIEWER: What is your assessment of the quality of sports reporting in this country?

GILLINGHAM: In general? There are some exceptions but generally not good.

INTERVIEWER: And the reason for that?

GILLINGHAM: The culture of South African journalism ... I look at the *Sunday Times*, at what they did at the weekend on Tony Yengeni.[87] [This story, entitled 'Tony Yengeni, the 4x4 and the R43bn arms probe' ultimately led to the conviction and imprisonment of the ANC's Chief Whip for corruption.] Very good. All too rare I'm afraid ... There are some very good journalists in this country but I don't think the industry encourages enough of them ... You're dealing with a very depressed industry. I don't think a newsroom is a very nice place to work for journalists for a whole variety of reasons. I wasn't here before but there was a degree of political correctness that was hammered in with an iron fist in previous days, wasn't there? There is a very strong political correctness now, which is rather more subtle, but it still exists. It is not, in journalistic terms, the competitive environment that it is in other countries. In other countries, a journalist is judged on how many scoops he's produced in the last six months. It's not the case here. Journalists can adequately get through an entire year without writing a news story.

INTERVIEWER: Is that partly to do with public expectations. We don't expect more from our journalists, therefore we don't get it?

GILLINGHAM: I think in South African life, in many respects, we have an inbred inferiority complex ... The country was let down by its specialist media in the immediate aftermath of the Cronjé story. I don't think there are many cricket journalists, in fact, any journalists in this country who can look back on the Cronjé affair and say I'm proud of what I did. I did a good job.

INTERVIEWER: What did they do wrong or what did they omit to do?

GILLINGHAM: They never questioned. There were some editorials written, by both the *Argus* and the *Cape Times* here, which editors must now look back on and read and think well, that's actually the worst work I've ever done.

INTERVIEWER: Are you talking about the assumption that Hansie could never have done it?

GILLINGHAM: Ja, exactly in simple terms – with no basis other than their blind faith in Cronjé – the only basis that they had to make those judgements. You know, we now sit back and have a bit of a laugh to be honest and even they, I hope, can still afford themselves a bit of a chuckle, but the issue is that there are newspaper editors, certainly the *Cape Times* and *Argus*, that at some time last year wrote editorials that were based on nothing other than blind faith. They could not have been more wrong if they tried.

INTERVIEWER: Was it blind faith or was it the party line?

GILLINGHAM: It was both. Both. The party line as well, unquestionably. I sometimes wonder whether there are some journalists who if Ali Bacher told them the moon was made of green cheese they'd write it ... Cricket in this country has been run by Ali Bacher for a long time and he has had a vice-like grip on the sport. Some of the methods he adopts, certainly to get the media on his side, are not methods that I entirely approve of.

INTERVIEWER: Explain what you mean.

GILLINGHAM: I think he's been very astute, if I was in his position I would seek to have almost control of sport and the media in the sport that Ali has had, so in that respect it's a compliment to him but I think he has, the expression would be, 'in his pocket' – I think he's got several leading journalists in this country in his pocket, figuratively speaking. I'm not suggesting any impropriety here but what I'm suggesting is that there are not many journalists in this country that have the bottle to criticise Ali Bacher, not many at all.

INTERVIEWER: Because they owe him their jobs?

GILLINGHAM: Because they owe him their allegiance. They owe allegiance in some respects.

INTERVIEWER: How is that done?

GILLINGHAM: Fear. Journalists have to be able to do their jobs, if journalists can't speak to people or people won't speak to them it's difficult for a journalist to do his job. There are examples in other sports. Soccer, for instance, where football managers have not liked what journalists have written and have closed the doors to them, prevented them from watching soccer matches, which makes them unable to do their job. Now, I'm not saying things are quite as extreme in cricket but we have a similar principle that I think is the sort of pressure that journalists in cricket in South Africa have felt themselves under and it's a very small environment … This is the case in South Africa with almost all sports. It's a very small environment. Sport is a small environment; the journalistic fraternity is a small environment. In those sorts of environments quality is often compromised. Getting on with people, I think, in our business, has too high a premium placed on it. Because you know, it's desperately, desperately simple but I've always worked on the basic tenet that a popular journalist is not necessarily a journalist who is doing his job.

Echoing Gillingham's words, a man who has made himself unpopular several times with players and administrators alike for his forthright approach is sports writer Neil Manthorp: 'The pond is not big enough really. In other countries there are more newspapers, magazines, other outlets. You can play the controversial game all the time. You can't in South Africa.' This view was propounded also by sports scientist Tim Noakes: 'Cricket is a clique, there's no question. If you're part of that clique, you're restrained by that. You can't speak out and say what you want to say, else your future is in doubt.' It seems that such strong-arm tactics are not confined to South Africa alone. One of Indian cricket's former key administrators, Jagmohan Dalmiya, is said to have had a diary that went back to 1985 in which he recorded all the complimentary tickets and other favours he had bestowed upon journalists. When a reporter fell out of favour, those indulgences were leaked to the media.[88] More seriously, in South Africa, journalists have found that bucking the party line can result in lost contracts and sudden job dismissals.

Thus, the true face of Hansie Cronjé was never exposed. Subsequent insights into his character by those who knew him reveal a Jekyll-and-Hyde character with unpredictable moods who was given to excesses in the pursuit of both pleasure and physical exercise. By many accounts he wielded an enormous amount of power and protected it jealously. He was an inveterate deal-maker and, by his own confession, loved money to the point of greed. He was self-absorbed and manipulative, say some who knew him. Yet the public never saw that side of Cronjé. Acknowledging that fact, Neil Manthorp explained why, by using another cricketing icon as an example. Australia's Sir Donald Bradman had his own character flaws. However, the museum that commemorates the hero in Sydney is all oil painting and no warts. Manthorp pointed this out to the Australian journalist accompanying him, who summed up the reality succinctly, if not elegantly, 'Don't piss on statues, Manners, don't piss on statues'.

When the unexpected confession came on Tuesday 11 April, the only person to venture a negative opinion was Dr Tim Noakes of the Sports Science Institute. Respected physician, physiologist, athlete and author, Noakes had become involved in South African cricket at the behest of former coach Bob Woolmer, whose aim was to use scientific methods such as game analysis, fitness programmes and ball tracking to help South Africa win the 1999 World Cup. That didn't happen, the scientific approach was not taken up and Noakes was under no illusion why.

NOAKES: The leadership failed completely in the World Cup. When the story broke I said Cronjé was the captain, the coach and the selector and to some extent that was the position that he had got for himself. I think it was that he wanted to be in complete control and he didn't want any other influences outside of his own direct control to be involved.

INTERVIEWER: From whom had he acquired such power?

NOAKES: From whoever ran SA cricket at the time. [That man was, of course, Ali Bacher.] Hansie was a very powerful, charismatic person and unfortunately his flaws weren't noticed and I saw his flaws and that's why he had to sideline us.

INTERVIEWER: Those flaws were just never publicised.

NOAKES: Ja, and they weren't publicised because the team was doing well. All great con artists, I learnt, require three things: they have to have people who are gullible, people who are greedy and people who want to be controlled. If you look at the South African public, they were greedy for success, they were gullible and the third component was they wanted to be controlled. So that's why he could con the nation because the nation was willing to be conned.

INTERVIEWER: And remains so, I think.

NOAKES: Absolutely. But then that tells you something about the South African character, which is very sad: the gullibility, the greed and the wanting to be controlled. That may be a complication of the nature of the country …

> It's interesting that that is a South African syndrome, this phenomenon of these people who are desperately flawed but because they're good sportsmen they come to the higher echelons of SA society. If you're good at sport, and Cronjé was very good, all these other things get swept aside. If South Africa still accepts him as a hero, then what do they have to ignore? They have to ignore that he betrayed his nation. In war, you used to shoot people who did that. But now, he's still a hero which is paradoxical ... So that's what we came up against and, tragically, we lost the World Cup. There's no question in my mind that that was because Bob was not allowed to do what he could have done.

Noakes gave voice to his frustration in an interview with the *Cape Times* newspaper that Tuesday morning and in a talk show on the regional radio station *Cape Talk* that momentous Tuesday night. For the first time, a shocked South African public was exposed to criticism of Cronjé. Noakes recalled the radio interview:

> I said that the South African public had been misled and he'd been made this public image that he really wasn't. I said that we'd gone to the World Cup with the best team and the best coach and we lost because of poor leadership. And then I said that the UCB would forever regret having given him all power. So that was my position and I was the only person in Cape Town to have said anything negative so of course the whole focus came on that. It was so bad that people thought I'd brought the Institute into disrepute and so there were some nasty letters and phone calls. What made me angry on *Cape Talk* was that the South Africans were making it a racial issue and it became and it still is a racial issue. They were saying, 'These stupid Indians! How can you trust an Indian?' Now, I'd been in India and I have great respect for Indian people and I didn't like that. All I said was that in science we teach that you think according to a model and there are two models in conflict here. One is that Cronjé is an honest South African, and if that is true, then what you are saying is that the police are dishonest in India and I said, 'Which evidence do you have for both?' And I said, 'You don't really know the man or the police so you're making a judgement on those grounds'. I had watched this man over the years and I felt that there were moments that made me doubt his strength and his honesty. That's all I said. Then they asked if this was the limit of it and I said, 'No, I'm sure it's much deeper than that'. Then they asked about the relationship between Hansie and Bob and I said then that I felt that he had undermined Bob, as he had undermined us. They played it again five weeks later and by then, everything I'd said had come true so ... but until Gibbs

went before the Commission and said this is what happened, it was Cronjé or me, one of us was going to go, at least in the public's mind.

Subsequent events justified Noakes's stand. Cronjé was banned from the game for life, along with other cricketers in Pakistan and India.

INTERVIEWER: You've been vindicated now. Has anyone apologised to you?

NOAKES: No, no one's ever apologised. No, no. No one's asked me why I thought like that. Because the public is still not prepared to accept, they're still in denial. I'm reluctant to say the full story …

INTERVIEWER: I understand, but surely it's a case of don't shoot the messenger.

NOAKES: Ja, exactly.

INTERVIEWER: What was your opinion of the quality of reporting in the South African media during the Cronjé scandal and King Commission hearings?

NOAKES: I've been disappointed. I think they still really haven't got to the basics. No one has gone back and looked at Cronjé as a person except in a positive way. It's *volk* and *vaderland* is what they're writing. If you criticise him, you're criticising the *volk* [people] and the *vaderland* [homeland]. So no one's prepared to do it. I've spoken to a lot of black journalists and they've said that's classic racist writing. Because he was white, he couldn't have done anything wrong. That's how some black people in this country see it. There's a guy on the fourth floor here that runs a small business coaching young South Africans in previously disadvantaged communities. He said that the Cronjé affair cost his business R100 000. Now this guy is an absolutely committed cricketer, cricket is his life. I said to him, 'Why?' He said people just didn't want to come to cricket coaching any more. It's had a huge impact. So there are people who have suffered directly as a result of Cronjé's actions. He took something terrible away from us but then the public say, 'Well, everyone's doing it, so what?' That's not my view.

On the heels of Cronjé's confession, the Johannesburg newspaper *The Star* published the results of a readers' survey which had asked the question: 'Should the former South African captain be allowed to play for his country again?' Of the 7 220 responses, 94% said 'Yes'.[89]

6

The fix

According to the players, the media, and the bookies

It's more than a game. It's an institution.

– THOMAS HUGHES, BRITISH NOVELIST (1822–1896), IN *TOM BROWN'S SCHOOLDAYS*

In contrast to its predecessor, the 1997 Chandrachud Inquiry in India, which failed to interview any members of the bookmaking fraternity, it was a bookmaker that opened South Africa's King Commission on 7 June 2000. At that time, Neill Andrews had been involved in the gaming industry in South Africa for the previous fifteen years, starting out in horse racing and going on to work for South African media giant M-Net, the country's main sports broadcaster. Their International Gaming Network '... was looking at ... the introduction of a corporate sports-betting entity'. Andrews was involved in setting up the spread-betting enterprise Superbet, introduced into South Africa in 1998. Superbet closed a little over a year later, leaving behind two successors to the fledgling industry: Atlantic Sportsbet, created out of the management buy-out of Superbet and based in Cape Town, and the Johannesburg-based National Sporting Index or NSI, the company part-owned, at the time, by Marlon Aronstam, the bookie linked to Hansie Cronjé and the controversial fifth Test against England at Centurion in January 2000. As Andrews explained to the King Commission: 'With the increased television coverage of all forms of sport, obviously the interest in betting on sport has taken off over the last decade or so and now we are in a situation where basically any sport that is televised has a betting market.' According to Andrews, sports betting was in its infancy in South Africa in 2000 and far more money was traded on international markets, '... particularly those in the subcontinent.' He observed that '... the natural South African is not a gambler, or possibly not to the extent of the Australian market and, in particular, the Indian market. Plus of course, if you just look at population volumes, they do have a significant advantage in terms of purely numbers of people who possibly could bet, as opposed to South Africa, who, in comparative terms, we're a smaller population and, it would appear, less keen to bet.' The Australians enjoy legal betting. In 2003/4, Australians spent more than

A$150 million on sports betting, an increase of 92% over the previous year.[90] In India, where sports betting is illegal, punters wager well over US$5 billion a year, according to police estimates.[91]

The international popularity of sports betting has fuelled the innovation of spread betting. In contrast to the more traditional fixed-odds betting on the ultimate outcome of a contest between two parties, spread betting allows the bookmakers to revive betting interest in no-contest games, so that punters bet on the points spread of the win rather than on a predictable result. Andrews told the King Commission that in comparison to India, where more betting spreads are offered, the three most popular spreads on cricket in South Africa are on total runs scored, runs scored in the first 15 overs of an innings and individual performances.

Ironically, it is the complex minutiae of cricket statistics best loved by cricket fans that renders the gentleman's game most subject to spread betting. In cricket, punters can bet on practically anything. Therefore, even seemingly innocuous information is valuable to a bookie who is seeking to separate a punter from his money. In cricket, betting can take place on the total runs scored, which in a one-day can be anywhere between 100 and 300 runs an innings, in comparison to the single-figure goals of soccer. Pitch conditions, history of results at that ground, the weather and the team selection are factored in by the bookies to come up with a points spread for a total run bet. In this regard, insider information is useful despite the fact that such statistics are usually freely available but, as Andrews explained, it's a case of the early bird catching the worm. Thus, journalists and team captains are targeted for their insight and experience. In this way insider information helps the bookies to ensure that they limit their losses. The Indian Central Bureau of Investigation (CBI) Report cautioned that '... bookies generally manipulate the 'odds' in such a manner that they seldom incur huge losses. It is generally the punter who risks losing his money'. The unsuspecting Pakistani captain, Salim Malik, in conversation with undercover tabloid reporters in April 2000, explained that the bookies pay a percentage to the match-fixer for his efforts because there is an obvious advantage in knowing the outcome of a match when their punters don't.[92] But as Indian journalist Aniruddha Bahal told the Chandrachud Commission of Inquiry in 1997: 'The match can be fixed not merely by bookies; even punters can fix a match.'

Secondly, money could be placed on the runs scored in the first 15 overs, which, in a one-day game, were subject to fielding restrictions that meant that only 2 fielders were allowed outside the 30-yard circle. This changed in July 2005 when the ICC brought in the concept of powerplays. Fielding restrictions were increased from 15 to 20 overs and now apply during the first 10 overs of every innings. There are also two additional 5-over blocks, which the fielding captain can implement at any time. These innovations add to the scope of what punters can bet on.

The opening partnership is also imperative for the bookies to set a spread, which is determined partly by the aggressiveness or otherwise of the selected openers. The batting line-up is in itself an object of financial speculation, as are any withdrawals from the team playing on the day. Bets can be taken on partnerships and on which of the two batsmen will lose their wicket first. In addition, wagers can be made on individual performances, be they match-winning centuries or ducks, and the ability to quantify these performances in terms of runs and overs and wickets and averages offers fertile fodder for games of chance.

An added spin to the spreads outlined above is betting in running where bookies adjust the spread as the game progresses, allowing the punter to reap his profits or cut his losses before the final ball is bowled. A report in *The Independent* quoted a Bangalore bookie: 'The essential difference between betting on the race course and cricket betting is that if the horse has lost you lose your money. But in cricket you have a chance of recovering your money until the last ball.'[93] In a one-day game, bets are placed over three 'sessions'. The first session encompasses the first to the fifteenth over; the second session runs from the sixteenth to the thirtieth or the thirty-fifth over and the third session takes up the remaining overs of the 50. The second session of the match is the most significant (and the bets sizeable) because it is easier for the punter to predict the outcome of the match at this stage.[94] So betting often goes down to the wire on closely contested games.

A host of India's past and present cricket players and an array of members of the press gave statements to the Indian Chandrachud Inquiry into match-fixing in 1997. Despite claims of never having heard of match-fixing in the Indian team, some of the journalists and players were most enlightening about 'The Fix.'

On the subcontinent, according to an Indian correspondent, Krishna Prasad, 'Betting can be on the toss, runs scored by players, catches taken and dropped, the total runs scored by the team.' Andrews' testimony to the South African inquiry echoed this observation, by explaining that spread betting has enabled bookies to 'set a spread on anything'. This was confirmed in the first report published by the ICC's Anti-Corruption Unit (ACU) in May 2001. It included a laundry list of 'occurrence fixing' compiled from the intelligence it had gleaned from within the international cricketing fraternity. This included:

- outcome of toss
- selection of bowling end
- number of wides/no-balls in a specific over
- players in unusual/uncharacteristic fielding positions

- batsmen scoring fewer runs than their opposite number in an opening innings
- batsmen going out at a specific point
- total runs declaration
- timing of declaration
- total runs in innings (especially in the first innings of an ODI)
- at which end a particular umpire will stand at start of play.

'Fancy fixing', according to former Pakistani cricket captain and wicketkeeper Rashid Latif, involves taking bets on every ball of the match.[95] The ICC's Annual Report for 2005/6 described 'micro-betting' or spot fixing as 'small, sometimes incidental events' such as who will open the bowling or how many runs or wides there will be in a particular over. In an interview broadcast on BBC Radio Five Live, former Pakistan Cricket Board chairman Shahrayar Khan said that, in his opinion, '... spot-fixing is very much prevalent and really something you cannot prevent. This is opposed to match-fixing, which requires the entire team.'[96] This seemed to come as news to the ECB's incumbent chairman, David Morgan, who is in line to become the next President of the ICC. Responding to Khan's comments Morgan said:

> I was very surprised to hear Shaharyar say spot fixing is a fact of life ... Spot betting is a fact of life. Spot fixing – question mark. We don't know all we'd like to know but we're not aware of spot fixing ... I sit at the ICC and listen to annual reports from Lord Condon and it's very clear that the Anti-Corruption Unit are ever-vigilant, as are the member boards. It's never talked about as something that is prevalent in the game. Cricket is a lot cleaner than it was and I hope it's as clean as it can be.[97]

Tempering Morgan's optimism somewhat, the ICC's 2005/6 Annual Report cautioned that '...the risk of a player accepting substantial sums to under-perform during a particular phase of a match cannot be ignored'.

Back at the King Commission, Neill Andrews conceded that he had heard that in India it is possible to place a bet on who opens the bowling. He went on to explain that this, however, would be a fixed-odds bet rather than a spread bet as the permutations of opening bowlers are limited. Such bets are not as volatile as spread betting and spread betting on cricket is the most volatile game of all. 'There are a myriad of things that can happen during a game, individual performances, team performances, that change the outcome of a cricket match' even without 'deliberate human involvement' as Andrews pointed out. DV Subba Rao was the manager of the Indian team that toured the West Indies from February to May 1997. His testimony before Chandrachud was illuminating on this point. 'Cricket is a game of uncertainty. Situations of sudden collapse of a team arise quite often. In a one-day match in West Indies, we had a target of 267 runs to achieve. We were 230 for 3 wickets down. We lost 7 wickets for 30 runs and lost the match by 16 runs. In the Barbados Test, we wanted 121 runs to win but we were all out for 80 runs. All the players uniformly complained that the wicket was too bad to play ...' The Test referred to here is the third Test between the West Indies and India in Bridgetown from 27–31 March 1997.

The Indian *Daily Telegraph's* sports editor at the time of the Chandrachud Inquiry was Lokendra Pratap Sahi. In his 15 years of working for the newspaper he had toured with India 20 times and painted a picture of inexplicable run-outs, 2 to 3 people going out one after the other, shots which shouldn't have been played in those particular circumstances and bowlers conceding as many as 40–50 runs in 3 overs. According to his testimony in 1997, it is '... possible to fix an international cricket match involving any team'. He maintained the bookies target players in important matches such as those involving Pakistan, the West Indies, Australia, Sri Lanka and South Africa. India was noticeably absent from his list despite the huge illegal betting trade in the country.

Sahi explained that the bookies invest in a player who has cemented his place in the team. It is obviously not worth their while to approach the up-and-coming players who may still be fighting for a more permanent place. Thus two to three key players are targeted, such as an opening bowler, wicketkeeper or key batsman. Intriguingly, in a comprehensive review of the scorecards of suspect matches, the wicketkeeper is invariably the vice captain. While there are sound cricketing reasons for making the wickekeeper vice captain as he is in the best position to view the game, it bears pointing out that throughout the sorry saga of match-fixing accusations over the years, Pakistani whistle-blowers Aamer Sohail and Rashid Latif and Indian Manoj Prabhakar were all wicketkeepers and all-rounders. Alec Stewart, England's wicketkeeper captain, was named as the subject of alleged match-fixers' attentions in 1999 and the ICC's investigating team looked into allegations that a wicketkeeper was paid by a bookmaker to drop catches.[98] After all, it is the wicketkeeper who, in a batting innings, makes contact with the ball most often.

SK Shyam, a senior Indian sports editor, observed on record that 'For fixing a match, one will have to get at a large bunch of players, which is extremely difficult to do'. In Andrews' opinion, manipulation of the odds on total runs made would be 'an enormously difficult thing to control ... unless you had the co-operation of all concerned'. Because cricket is a team game, the majority of the team would have to be in on the fix.

It is not the first time that this view has been expressed. There is a significant degree of concurrence amongst the Indian journalists interviewed by Justice Chandrachud that fixing the ultimate outcome of a match is the most difficult way to manipulate the odds and presumably also the most lucrative.

Pakistan's star batsman Salim Malik, however, explained to undercover *News of the World* reporters:

> When you've got the main players in your hand you'll have to be really unlucky to lose. Really, there's no chance of losing money. We know which players are up for it. You pay and they will be out. He'll run himself out, whatever, but he will be out. You can throw your wicket … You'll have four or five players in hand and they will be playing just for you. No matter what the rest of the team do, they will do what they've agreed to do.[99]

In South Africa, Andrews agreed with Judge King's interjection that having four or five of the team's leading batsmen onside would be useful.

> It would certainly be an advantage and, of course, based on the fact that you are doing betting in running, that if your first 5 batsmen in, happened to put up particularly poor performances, getting back to the fact that we are betting in running, if it is 40 for 5 and you phoned your bookmaker, the spread would have come down to such an extent that you would be able to sell out with a handsome profit and, regardless of whether the tail wags or it doesn't, you would have made your profit, yes.

Exactly who is wagging that tail is cause for close observation. More than one journalist and former player pointed out the contribution of tail-enders in winning a game. Former Indian batsman Ajay Jadeja explained to Justice Chandrachud: 'A match can be fixed by getting at the star players in the team. But even tail-enders have turned the fortunes of a game as happened in the match which was played on 10 October 1997 between Pakistan and South Africa.' The first Test in Rawalpindi was notable for a number of record-breaking batting performances by the Pakistani lower order. From 231/8, Pakistan went on to close its first innings on 456 thanks to the efforts of debutante Azhar Mahmood, batting eighth, veteran number 9 Waqar Younis and last man in, Mushtaq Ahmed. The 45-run knock by paceman Younis and the 59 scored by Ahmed were their highest figures in Test cricket up to that point. Newcomer Mahmood outshone them both with his unbeaten 128, becoming the sixth Pakistani batsman to make a century on debut. The tenth-wicket partnership of 151 between Azhar Mahmood and Mushtaq Ahmed equalled the Test record first set by New Zealand against Pakistan in 1972/3. Ajay Jadeja's insights are valuable in that he was subsequently slapped with a five-year cricketing ban for corruption in 2000.

Back at the King Commission, in addition to external factors that help quantify the likely result of a game, such as the past history of a ground and the pitch and weather conditions on the day, Andrews stated that every batsman that comes to the wicket, be he opener or tail-ender, has a spread to his name that takes into account that individual's past performances and the bowling attack he is likely to face. An obvious advantage for an inside trader would be that, if the cricketer on the pay-roll had scored high in a previous innings but had arranged to score low in the following, the bookie could set a low spread while punters would be inclined to bet high based on past performance.

Cronjé's lawyer, Dickerson, put it to Andrews that the best way to secure a winning bet on an individual's performance would be to '... buy a particular player who would then be able to determine his own performance, going out for a duck, for example.' While Andrews concurred he added that, 'Whereas to effect a poor performance would naturally be easier ... in principle there's no reason to suggest that a cricketer couldn't back himself to do well, particularly if he's coming off a very bad piece of form and hoping to get runs ... he could back himself to do well or he could back himself to do badly'. Aniruddha Bahal, principal correspondent of *Outlook* magazine in 1997, elaborated on this point to the Chandrachud Inquiry:

> Corruption is a matter of individual susceptibility ... A player who has scored a half century has performed well for outward purposes but he may have scored those runs in twice the number of balls when his potential is that he can score 50 runs in 60 balls ... a bowler can bowl a few overs very well and then slide off, similarly a batsman or a wicketkeeper ... The fact that Indian players earn a high amount legally through the Board, does not mean that they would not be interested in making more money.

While it may be true that, to ensure the desired outcome of a match, a fair few players would be required, one man can influence the final result if that man is the captain. As Pakistani whistle-blower Rashid Latif told Aniruddha Bahal in an interview published in *Outlook* on 30 July 2000: 'When Salim Malik was captain, he would bowl himself at crucial stages of the match ... He would set an offside field and bowl on the legside. While batting, he would also run out his colleagues. I escaped being run out by him in England last year.'[100] Sunil Dev, former manager of the Indian team, made a similar observation at the Chandrachud Inquiry: 'It is easy to get run out or hit a lofted shot. Coaches can detect a deliberate under-performance and so can students of the game.' Yet, the cricketing public remains, for the most part, unenlightened. Ali Irani, disgraced team physiotherapist, identified the reason back in 1997 at the Chandrachud Inquiry: 'People are generally prone for [sic] forming opinions after hearing the TV commentary. That is why they talk the same way. If TV were made mute, very few people will be able to say or write anything original.'

Manoj Prabhakar, former Indian all-rounder whose allegations of dirty tricks in the Indian magazine *Outlook* prompted the Indian Cricket Board to appoint Justice Chandrachud to head the one-man inquiry in 1997, offered further insights to that body. According to Prabhakar: 'You approach players only when you want to influence the game, and it's best influenced when you're chasing.'[101] This dictum is startlingly illustrated in an online column written by Hansie Cronjé the day after losing the final game and the tainted ODI series to the Indians in March 2000. Cronjé wrote: 'What surprised me a little was the fact that the team batting second won four out of four. Considering that the pitches are reasonably dry and do turn as the game goes on, this has surprised me a bit.'[102]

But asked Prabhakar, 'Why approach a player on the team when you can get an ex-player?'[103] *Outlook's* underworld sources point out that 'Retired players who have a close rapport with the team have come in handy as a link between members of the team and the syndicate ... We cannot go into the dressing room or even to the hotel where the team is staying. But a former cricketer has access and has friends in the team.'[104] Clearly illustrating this triangular relationship, the well-heeled Indian bookie and gambler MK Gupta revealed to the CBI how retired players Manoj Prabhakar and Ajay Sharma had operated as his agents, organising introductions to the stars of world cricket.

But it is not only players and former players who are under suspicion. The members of the media interviewed by Justice Chandrachud in 1997 admitted that some of their number were on the bookies' payroll. The cricket commentators and journalists are acknowledged experts on the game, often having played international cricket themselves or coached the national team. They travel with the team and stay in the same hotels. To the bookies, such insider information is invaluable. And, one must assume, vice-versa. One South African journalist recalled being informed by Rameez Raja, former Pakistani player-turned-commentator, that Pakistan would lose to Bangladesh in their 1999 World Cup encounter, three days before the improbable event occurred. This is one of the matches Ali Bacher claimed was fixed in his testimony to the King Commission.

Umpires are also a target for their specialist knowledge and ultimate power over the game in play. Journalists interviewed by Chandrachud in 1997 acknowledged this fact. X Pradeep Vijaykar, then assistant sports editor for the *Times of India* said, 'Places like Sharjah where money power plays a large part, there can be pressure on umpires to fix matches'. ZH Natarajan, the sports editor for the *Indian Express* told of an Indian international umpire that had admitted to him that he was offered money to give certain decisions. Three years later, in the wake of Cronjé's midnight confession, the South African chief of the Cricket Board, Ali Bacher, indicated to an Australian newspaper that Pakistani umpire Javed Akhtar was under suspicion for the way he handled South Africa's 1998 tour of England when he gave nine lbw decisions in the last Test at Leeds. On 20 April 2000, South African umpire Cyril Mitchley made public an offer he had received during an Australian tour of Pakistan. $US50 000 was the proffered reward for ensuring that Pakistan did not lose the final Test. It would appear that the match referred to was the third Test in Lahore from 1–5 November 1994. Pakistan won the three-Test series 1–0. Mitchley claimed that he had immediately reported the exchange to ICC match referee John Reid. No more was heard of it. Similarly, a South African colleague, Rudi Koertzen, revealed a telephonic approach made to him in September 1999 during an ODI between India and the West Indies in Singapore where the two teams were playing in the Coca-Cola Singapore Challenge, a triangular tournament that included Zimbabwe.[105] Behind the scenes, groundsmen come in handy, preparing pitches for the home team or for a result, or perhaps are induced to tamper with the pitch overnight.[106]

A veteran South African sports writer, who has followed the national team since its return to the world stage, threw some light on what goes on in the wings.

> There's always money going around. There's always envelopes going around with money in them, exchanging hands. Look, Hansie would get paid R10 000 (US$1 400) in cash to go to someone's hospitality box after a day's play at a Test match. It's not declarable, is it? You go to someone's sports shop to sign bats and you get paid. Envelopes with money in them abound in the world of sport, not just cricket. I was always aware of that. Just to put the whole match-fixing thing and the taking of money into the perspective that I see it. If you're on tour in India on the subcontinent and a brown envelope with US$1 000 in used notes gets shoved under your hotel room door, it's great to think that we would all run downstairs to reception, find the manager and ask him to find its rightful owner. You're more likely to think, 'Mmm, someone's got the wrong room here' and you might keep hold of it until you move to the next city. Then somebody called Vijay, say, invites you to dinner, you get entertained. That's the environment. Often it was about pitches, how the team's doing, who's likely to open the bowling.

In his opinion, the current South African team has been 'squeaky clean' since Hansiegate, stressing the word 'since'. He admitted with a rueful laugh that he didn't think that they were 'squeaky clean' before but thought there was a kind of innocence about it. 'I think a lot of players took money and favours for information and team selection, things which they genuinely believed were innocent if maybe a bit naughty. There are ways of compromising sportsmen on tour. There are other favours apart from cash. You can't say, someone gave me US$2 000 in Sri Lanka and it was delivered by that woman …'

Lending credibility to such lurid claims, the British newspaper *The Observer* reported on 11 February 2001 that new allegations had come to light and were awaiting the attention of Condon's investigators. These included:

- four West Indian batsmen who threw their wickets away during a one-day match in Australia
- a New Zealand bookmaker who delivered prostitutes and porn to a Wellington hotel to show his appreciation for a job well done
- a top spin bowler who was given a video camera by a bookmaker in Singapore
- a batsman who fed a bookmaker insider information on his team and its tactics in exchange for money and gifts
- a batsman who committed to scoring less than 50 in his first innings in an Auckland Test for $1 000 and a gold bracelet
- a batsman who under-performed on tour in Australia, earning himself $8 000 and gifts worth $12 000 in the process
- a New South Wales doctor who made a fortune through her liaison with a famous bowler by paying players for 'information'.[107]

Nothing further was heard of these allegations.

The problem is endemic. The International Cricket Council released its Report on Corruption in International Cricket in April 2001. The report confirmed that there have been 'At least twenty years of corruption linked to betting on international cricket matches. Corrupt practices and deliberate under-performance have permeated all aspects of the game'. A man by the name of Imran Khan unwittingly introduced undercover *News of the World* reporters to Salim Malik in April 2000. Lending weight to the ICC's assessment, Khan was quoted in the article that stemmed from this media sting operation: 'Basically all the tournaments in the Middle East and Asia are fixed.'[108]

Ultimately, the responsibility must be laid at the door of the administrators of the game. The ICC was expecting to rake in some US$239 million dollars in profit from the 2007 World Cup in Jamaica.[109] The ICC and national cricket boards control vast amounts of money yet '... current corporate governance arrangements within cricket are inadequate for the task' according to the ICC's corruption report. As Inderjit Singh Bindra, the former President of the Board of Control for Cricket in India, stated in an online chat session on 15 April 2000: 'Whenever and wherever there is match-fixing, it is not possible without direct or indirect involvement or indifference on the part of administrators of the game.'[110] It can only be hoped that the optimism of at least one South African journalist is not ultimately misplaced. 'Perhaps the greatest thing about the game of cricket is that even the players, officials and spectators have been unable to kill it.'[111]

7

All for one and one for all

South Africa in India: October–December 1996

To fix a match, pre-decide a result, you need to bribe the whole team or at least seven to eight of them. The Pakistan, Australian and South African teams have that sort of unity ...[112]

'Crookes! Crookes! Crookes!' the word barrelled out of thousands of bellowing lungs, accompanied by the metallic thunder of drumming cans and pounding feet. Years later, that innocuous taunt would become invested with a blackly ironic significance. However, at the time it heralded nothing more sinister than Derek Crookes fielding at the boundary of Mumbai's Wankhede stadium during the final match of the South African tour to India in 1996. The frenzied atmosphere was a far cry from the oak-shaded langour of Newlands but, as a South African travelling in India, I couldn't pass up the opportunity to personally proffer my allegiance. Especially after watching South Africa lose to India in the Titan Cup final some weeks before.

I'd been in the northern hill station of Darjeeling, sipping gin and tonics at the Planters' Club and gamely hanging on to a confident smile as my countrymen were ground into submission on the small colour TV set at the foot of the room. Surrounded by lithographed black and white prints of a British Darjeeling in the 1920s, my fellow cricket enthusiasts were Indian professionals and academics for whom English was the lingua franca and who replicated in faithful detail the tweed jackets and pipes of their former colonial masters. An old-world chivalry prevailed, with the men relinquishing their seats to their womenfolk, eager for a better view of the 'gentleman's game'. All had high praise for the South Africans, despite their lacklustre performance, and didn't hesitate to proclaim, 'Oh, jolly good shot!' whenever the opposition got bat to ball – to no avail. After winning six out of six up to the last game of the series, the South Africans lost to the home side and I, salvaging what national pride I could, retreated with them from the field.

The Titan Cup (IND, AUS, SA) October/November 1996

Only later would an unsuspecting public learn that the triangular one-day series in India between India, South Africa and Australia had not been the clash of the Titans but rather the target of Machiavellian manipulations by bookie/punter MK Gupta and Mohammad Azharuddin and friends. All did not turn out as planned, however, and Gupta and partner Anil Steel lost a significant amount of money on a particular game in the tournament, thought to be the final. Word has it that counter-fixing was to blame.

Seventh ODI – IND v SA, Rajkot, 29 October 1996

Mohammad Azharuddin later confessed to fixing three matches to the Central Bureau of Investigation, the first of which was the seventh match at Rajkot, South Africa's third encounter with the Indians. Thus far, the visitors led 2–0. Azharuddin's candour may well have had something to do with the fact that Mumbai police allegedly had taped discussions between bookies and Azharuddin, Nayan Mongia and Ajay Jadeja during this series.

At the time, the outcome of this match filled *Rediff* commentator Prem Panicker with '... a sense of tragedy of almost Grecian proportions' befitting the name of the contest, the Titan Cup.[113] India, batting first, were all out in the first ball of the forty-eighth over for a less-than-intimidating total of 185. At the end of 25 overs they had been 104/2. Azhar was caught behind by wicketkeeper Richardson, bowled Boje for 9. Mongia was caught and bowled Boje for 2 and Jadeja was bowled Donald for 26 off 46 balls.

South Africa had made three changes to their squad, with Gibbs taking over from Hudson in the opening batting line-up, Boje replacing an out-of-form Crookes and Klusener standing in for McMillan, who had flu. Panicker, once again with uncanny prescience, remarked that '... unlike India, the Proteas' change of personnel was dictated by illness and indisposition, and not carried out with the casual, uncaring indifference of a bad gambler shuffling his cards'. [114] One such shuffle of the deck, according to Panicker, was the inclusion of right-hand batsman NS Sidhu, whose cricketing talents are described in his profile on cricketing website *cricinfo.com* as 'schizophrenic'. Sidhu took the place in the opening order of Ganguly, who'd injured himself fielding in the nets. Sidhu hadn't played international cricket in five months, yet he was brought into the squad at a crucial stage of the tournament. He survived 16 balls and added 2 runs to the board before pushing the ball straight to Cronjé at mid-on, who promptly ran him out. With Sidhu's departure, opening bowler Srinath was sent in as a pinch-hitter at number 3. This heady promotion up from the lower order worked like clockwork. With captain Tendulkar at the wicket with the pinch-hitting bowler, Panicker proclaimed that 'Srinath was the best Indian batsman on view'. [115] Srinath's 53 off 69 balls was his highest ODI score thus far in his career.

Panicker had little regard too for the umpires. The Board of Control of Cricket in India (BCCI) had fielded twenty umpires for the ten-match series, effectively meaning that each match would see a different pair. At Rajkot, V Chopra and BS Rao did the honours and in Panicker's opinion appeared '... to be the worst of a very bad bunch.'[116]

South Africa comfortably overshot the 186 target set by the Indians to win by 5 wickets with more than an over to spare.

Final ODI – IND v SA, Mumbai, 6 November 1996

With six for six under their belts, South Africa was the firm favourite going in to the Titan Cup final. India was the long shot but fate, or promised fortune, was on their side from the beginning. India won the toss and opted to bat. NS Sidhu had been dropped after two disappointing performances and had been replaced by Sanjay Manjrekar, who opened the innings with captain Tendulkar. Manjrekar failed to improve on his predecessor's performance and, after eking out 7 runs off 31 balls, was caught behind by wicketkeeper Richardson off the bowling of De Villiers. The South Africans had opted to use the swing bowler De Villiers rather than the medium-paced McMillan and, in a surprise move, Lance Klusener opened the bowling attack with '*Vinninge* (Fast) Fanie', rather than Allan Donald. Tendulkar took advantage of the young all-rounder and contributed to Klusener's disappointing figures of 26 for his first 4 overs. Following Manjrekar's speedy dismissal, bowler and lower-order batsman Srinath was back batting at number 3 but failed to emulate his previous success and was caught De Villiers bowled Donald for 5 off a mere 7 balls. Azharuddin stepped into the breach, belting off two 4s off successive deliveries, but thereafter the pace slowed and he too fell to the wicketkeeper's gloves off Boje's bowling on 26.

At the half-way mark, India found themselves on 99 for 3. Captain Tendulkar's 67 from 88 balls, which included six 4s, helped take India to 137/4. Specialist batsman Rahul Dravid also capitulated soon after, bowled by De Villiers for 31 off 41 balls. Robin Singh was unexpectedly sent in after Tendulkar, but he soon followed his captain back to the pavilion after being run out by Rhodes for 5. At 159/6 with 10 overs to go, a final tally of 200 was looking unlikely. However, it was Jadeja who helped get India to 220 runs in 50 overs, with a little help from the South African bowlers, who delivered 13 extras.

Prem Panicker, looking back at the unblemished South African record for the tournament, remarked that the key to their success had been their opening batsmen. Hudson and Kirsten had put together half a dozen over-50 partnerships in as many games. However, this time they failed to fire. With frontline bowlers Prasad and Srinath keeping them contained, Hudson lofted an easy catch to

Azharuddin at mid-wicket for 7 off 14 balls and Kirsten, who had, according to Panicker, looked like 'a fish out of water' since the start of play, succumbed to Kumble's spin and Dravid's dexterity at cover for 26 off 42 balls. Rhodes and Cullinan then took it upon themselves to push the pace, running between the wickets and managing to evade a number of close calls. Then, Rhodes bowed to Kumble, caught Joshi at cover, leaving South Africa at 60/4. Captain Cronjé, '… more impetuous than the ones who had gone before', managed only 6 off 28 balls before being dispatched, once again, by Joshi at cover, off Singh's bowling. Cullinan too hit out needlessly at Singh and was caught by Azhar at mid-wicket for 31. South Africa was at 92 for 6. Four runs later, Boje also went for the sweep that had already claimed victims and Azharuddin picked up the top edged ball at wide leg gully, 'cleverly placed there for just that shot'. With South Africa in desperate need of regrouping, Boje had managed only 3 and the scoreboard told the sorry tale – 100/8. Then tail-enders Symcox and Richardson put together a partnership that made it look like the favourite was still the team to put money on. However, Symcox was stumped by wicketkeeper Mongia, and Donald followed suit with Kumble's very next ball. South Africa folded in the forty-seventh over on 185 and India had 'defied the odds', defeated the hitherto undefeated and taken the Titan Cup.

According to MK's testimony to India's Central Bureau of Investigation (CBI), the gambler looked to Azharuddin to make up for his losses in the Titan Cup during the upcoming Test series against the South Africans. It was during the third and final Test at Kanpur, with the tally standing at one-all, that Azharuddin introduced MK Gupta to his old friend Hansie Cronjé.

Third Test, Kanpur, 8–12 December 1996

At the outset of the decisive third Test in Kanpur on South African's first full tour to India in 1996, South Africa occupied pole position on the Wisden cricket rankings as top Test nation in the world.

India won the toss and the *Daily Telegraph* online declared in its match report of the first day of play that 'India's batsmen displayed an inexplicable obsession with caution' in their first innings.[117] Thirty-three maiden overs on Day 1 would seem to back up this observation. After India's top 3 in the order had put together a respectable, if not decisive, 160/3, a pair of India's finest batsmen found themselves at the crease – the captain, Tendulkar, and Dravid – the 'most technically correct player in the side'. Despite his obvious abilities, Dravid had spent the two preceding Tests sliding up and down the batting line-up, appearing at number three, then four, then one. Here he came in at number five. Between Tendulkar and Dravid they managed to put on 14 runs in 16 overs. Dravid was out on an lbw decision to Adams for 7 off 55 balls and Azhar was caught and bowled Adams for 5 off 9 deliveries. Joshi went for a duck and India were at 193/5. Tendulkar, with his 43 off 151 balls, and Kumble assumed night-watchman responsibilities and Day 1 ended with India on 204/6. An online match report by Prem Panicker for *Rediff* observed that 'India, for its part, has patented its own speciality – namely, an ability to throw away advantages with effortless ease.'[118]

According to Peter Robinson of the Johannesburg newspaper *The Star*, Ali Bacher arrived in Kanpur on the second day of the match to watch the South Africans '… produce their worst day's cricket of the '96 tour.'[119] 15 wickets fell for 217 runs. Despite his snail's-pace in the previous day's innings, Tendulkar managed to hit 18 runs off 22 balls before being caught and bowled by Adams. Srinath too fell to the same fate, caught and bowled by Adams, who ended the day with bowling figures of 6/55. R Mohan, in his match report, observed that '… each of his six victims was guilty, in some measure, of complicity in his own dismissal.'[120]

With India all out for 237, Tendulkar set a defensive rather than an attacking field for the South Africans' first-innings reply. Two slips and a wide gully greeted the opening stand of Hudson and Kirsten, who had recently notched up a 200+ partnership in the previous Test in Calcutta. Kirsten survived a missed catch by Prasad to go on to 43 – the highest score of the South African's second innings. Hudson retired to yet another lbw decision on 15. Gibbs, who had earlier hit 371 runs off an Indian A side was bowled by Kapoor for 17 in '… another dismissal that is hard to credit to the wicket', according to the second day's match report on *Rediff*.[121] Cullinan, after his second innings century at Calcutta, soon followed suit and was out to Kumble on 29; Captain Cronjé joined him back in the box on 15. McMillan put a single on the board and Richardson went 3 better before being dismissed for 4. South Africa had lost 6 wickets for 42 runs and were all out for 177 in less than 2 sessions of play. 'It must be admitted that the tourists contributed, to a considerable extent, to their own downfall,' said the *Rediff* commentator.[122]

The Indian second innings began with just 4 overs to go before the end of the day's play. However, they managed to lose another wicket and packed up on 7/1 with a 67-run lead on the South Africans.

It was Mohammad Azharuddin that anchored the Indian lead on the third day, which ended with India on 270/5. Azhar had been joined at the crease by Dravid, this time coming in at number 6, and together they began to build a partnership upon which Robin Jackman commented on ESPN: '… if Azhar was the don, then Dravid was the ideal consigliere, executing the imperial will to perfection.'[123] As night-watchmen, they retired with Dravid on 33 and Azhar on 88. Three years later, in testimony to the King Commission, Cronjé affirmed that, at the time, South Africa's prospects of catching up with the

Indians' overnight lead of 250/270 were 'not good'. The lead was, in fact, over 330. Azharuddin introduced Cronjé to 'diamond dealer' Mukesh Gupta and left the two men alone in his room in the teams' hotel in Kanpur. MK revealed that he had money on the game and asked Cronjé to ensure that the South Africans did not snatch a surprise victory from the imminent defeat facing them. Cronjé said that Gupta had given him US$30 000 to seal the deal. Gupta said US$40 000. Whatever the amount, Cronjé regarded it as 'money for jam'.

On Day 4, the Azhar/Dravid partnership has proceeded to 165 when the declaration came at lunch with India on 400/7. Azhar retired unbeaten on 163 and South Africa were looking at a second innings run chase of 461. During the King Commission proceedings, Advocate Batohi read from a match report for the day, asking Cronjé to comment on the observation that '... the match was effectively over as a contest barely an hour after lunch on the fourth day. Both Kirsten and Gibbs played down the wrong line against the new ball bowlers of Srinath and Prasad. Cullinan was needlessly run out by Tendulkar'. Cronjé conceded that, 'As far as I can remember that was the state of the game and I was batting with Andrew Hudson at the time'. The South African fall of wickets proceeded as follows: Kirsten 1/21; Gibbs 2/26; Cullinan 3/29; Cronjé 4/97; Hudson 5/109. Cronjé's 50 was his highest second-innings score of the tour. At the end of Day 4, South Africa was at 127/5 and faced the prospect of chasing 334 on the final day.

Night-watchmen McMillan and Richardson both fell within the first 20 minutes of the final day's play without adding to their overnight totals of 18 and 5 respectively. Klusener and Symcox managed to put on another 45 runs before lunch. Seven balls after lunch it was all over, with Srinath and Prasad picking up the last 2 wickets of De Villiers for 2 and Adams for 1. When Brendon Manca, the UCB junior counsel, asked Cronjé if he agreed that the probabilities were overwhelming that Azharuddin was involved with MK, Cronjé disagreed, 'If you look at his average against South Africa, it certainly wouldn't suggest that'. Azharuddin, in fact, was named Man of the Match for his unbeaten 163 in the second innings and was also awarded Man of the Series as the home side took the series 2-1.

Mohinder Amarnath Benefit Match/ODI, Mumbai, 14 December 1996

The last match of the 1996 tour was to have been an unofficial limited-overs contest for the benefit of Mohinder Amarnath, the legendary Indian batsman who ranks in the top ten of the country's highest scorers. Ali Bacher's Indian counterpart at the time was Jagmohan Dalmiya and it was at his behest that the benefit match was upgraded to an official ODI. Bacher, in his deposition before the King Commission, explained:

> It was a late addition to the itinerary; the players were unhappy and quite rightly so. It is unheard of, in my opinion, to have a benefit match between two countries regarded as an official one-day international match. It was a Saturday morning, I phoned Mr Dalmiya and I expressed to him very strongly our unhappiness about this match. He implored me to speak to the players, to go through with the match, the match had been advertised, it had been promised to Mr Amarnath, there were television sponsorships, and reluctantly I spoke to the team and asked them to proceed with the match. I think that background is important. It was a very unhappy team that proceeded to Bombay for that particular match.

The game marked Cronjé's hundredth ODI and fiftieth as captain. Apparently, he was upset about the change of plans, as this landmark should have been the first game of the following season, to be played at his home ground, Bloemfontein. Instead, it came at the end of a long tour and two lost series and the team was plagued by injury. Rhodes and Donald had already gone home and Dave Richardson, Fanie de Villiers, Lance Klusener and the coach, Bob Woolmer, were ill. At the King Commission, senior player Patrick Symcox recalled the players' low morale by the end of the 1996 tour:

> So the tour was a really, really tough tour. It was, for me, one of the first times that we'd experienced playing at places like Eden Gardens, with 100 000 people, and the Bombays of the world. And the conditions were very foreign. Obviously under the food problems that one experiences, and the water problems, and people getting sick. So it was a really tough, tough tour. And we got to the point in the tour where, like all tough tours, at the end of the tour the resistance of people is down. People are feeling sick; people want to go home; you've lost the series, there's really nothing in it; and it just – everybody seems to spiral down to a slow grind of going home ... There were seven guys who – if I'm not mistaken, there were about seven guys that felt not fit to play. For instance, Fanie de Villiers had been sick. He had to get out of bed to come to the meeting and actually play the next day. We didn't have Jonty, we didn't have Allan. Dave Richardson was sick, so – Derek Crookes had been sick on and off [throughout] the tour. So it was going to be tough to win anyway.

The South African cricketers weren't the only ones to have succumbed to the inevitable dose of 'Delhi Belly'. My American partner too was recovering from a bad bout and I had organised tickets to the Amarnath game, confident that his first encounter with the game of cricket would go a long way to cheering him up. We arrived at the team's hotel in Mumbai on the morning of the match to pick up our tickets when who should step out of the elevator but Hansie Cronjé. Infused with patriotic fervour, I sidled up to wish him luck and was caught in a delightful dither when I realised that if I stepped into the elevator, I would be alone with the South African captain. My nerve failed at the last minute and I never approached him. Later, I would discover that just eight hours previously, at three o'clock that morning, he had been meeting with MK Gupta, ostensibly to tell him that all deals were off. Apparently, it was not only Gupta but the shadowy figure of Sunil that was also interested in manipulating the outcome of this match, but it was MK's offer of US$200 000 that was put to the team. There are numerous inconsistencies in the players' testimonies, including just how much money was on offer, how many meetings were held, who spoke out against the offer and whether team management, namely Bob Woolmer, was aware of the offer or not.

Of the contracted members of the SA cricket team in 2000, six were on the Indian tour of 1996: Daryll Cullinan and Jonty Rhodes were the most senior, followed by Gary Kirsten and Herschelle Gibbs and newcomers Nicky Boje and Lance Klusener. Klusener, aged 23, made his Test debut for South Africa in the second Test at Calcutta, and his best bowling figures to that point stem from that match – 8/64. Despite being party to Cronjé's illicit offer in 1996, when he was sounded out again in India during the 2000 tour he claimed that he thought Cronjé's approach was a joke. In his opinion, having only ever played for South Africa under Cronjé's captaincy, he was '... a wonderful captain and probably the best South Africa has ever seen'.

Rookie Nicky Boje was first selected for the national squad for the short 1995 tour of Zimbabwe. He was also a mere 23 years old on his first main tour to India in 1996. According to Boje, he wasn't approached by Cronjé beforehand and recollects only one team meeting. He maintained that Hudson, Crookes, Cullinan and Richardson were against the offer. Acknowledging the important role played by Cronjé in his career, he told the King Commission: 'Hansie's been my captain when we played together for Grey. He's been my captain in the same side as for Free State for probably the last ten years now, and he also was captain of the South African side, where I was a part. So he had a very big part in my career so far'.

Similarly, it was Herschelle Gibbs' second tour and he, like Klusener, made his Test debut in the second Test at Calcutta. He recalled a single meeting of the full touring squad but was hazy about the details.

> The meeting definitely took place before the game, one or two days, it could have been a day or even the morning of the game I am not sure, I can't

remember … I didn't know what to think. You know, being only my second tour I thought I'd leave it up to the senior players to have a discussion and if we were individually asked our opinions, I can't remember what my opinion was or if I did give an opinion, but I was happy to go along with whatever the general consensus of the meeting was.

The consensus must have been generally favourable as he remembers only Crookes and Hudson speaking out against the plan.

Senior player Daryll Cullinan added himself to the protesting voices of Crookes and Hudson in his testimony to the King Commission, but he too is sketchy on the details:

I do recall Hansie Cronjé, in passing, remarking that there was money on the game and we were going to have a team meeting about it … I think it was, we had like an informal practice before that game. It could have been then … I cannot recall if he mentioned figures then, he just fleetingly made the remark and we were going to have a team meeting … I recall the team meeting the night before, it could have been the morning of the game, I am not too sure … I laughed about it. I dismissed it as typical of his sense of humour.

However, Cullinan left the meeting in a '… very strong, very positive frame of mind, certainly more motivated and very clear … where we stood in regard to this matter'. He no longer regarded Cronjé's proposition as a joke but as a

… stroke of genius … I believe it was his way of testing his team. What we must understand at that stage that there was, this wasn't a new subject, it is not the first time we have heard of match-fixing, it was inevitable, it would be inevitable when we would be approached and I do believe it was the motive behind his putting it to the side. And we left that team meeting the better for that meeting, a much better side and very clear in our own minds that in no ways in the future would any player, or the South African side, entertain those sort of ideas.

Neither Rhodes nor Kirsten was interviewed at the Commission despite the fact that it was Rhodes who, although he wasn't present at that meeting, had allegedly informed Bacher of the offer put to the team by Cronjé, following his captain's confession. Several players testified that it had become something of a standing joke over the years and at least one South African journalist travelling with the team was aware of the offer at the time.

Derek Crookes, although not a regular member of the squad, was Man of the Series in the Hong Kong Sixes tournament of that year and travelled to India with the South African team in 1996. Despite the fact that Cronjé had initially proclaimed that the proceeds of the Hong Kong Man of the Series award, should it be won by a South African, would not have to be shared amongst the team, he changed his position and forced a divvying up when Crookes took the prize. Crookes would have been rightly put out by such a volte-face. Four years later, after being caught up in Cronjé's machinations during the one-day series against India in 2000, Crookes nonetheless continued to vouch for his captain's leadership abilities, as did his other team-mates. 'As far as I am concerned, I think he is probably one of the best captains South Africa has ever produced.'

Crookes recalled the events preceding the final match of the 1996 visit. He was approached by Cronjé on the plane to Mumbai. 'He said that he had spoken to the other team members and had only to speak to Andrew Hudson' about throwing the upgraded ODI. Later that evening, according to Crookes, there was another meeting held on the topic but he couldn't remember who was present. Versions disagree on who exactly was and was not in the room at the time, but Crookes indicated his presence and Hudson's. As roommates, they adjourned to their room to discuss the offer. Crookes declared that they '... thought that it was not the right thing, it was immoral and how it could jeopardise our future'. This phrase was repeated parrot fashion throughout his testimony at the King Commission. The following morning, Cronjé put the proposition to the whole team at a team meeting. Management, it seems, was not present. According to Crookes, the offer on the table was US$250 000. The Johannesburg newspaper *The Star* reported on 18 April 2000 that Hudson said, 'We were each offered $20 000 – so the amount of $250 000 seems to be correct.'[124] As Richardson himself said of the original figure mentioned, 'I do remember thinking though, immediately, that if you divide it by 15, it's not going to be that much money.'

Evocative of that stirring musketeer refrain, 'All for one and one for all', Crookes insisted that 'Hansie said that we were either all in or all out, whatever the decision was and if one of us was out, then we would not take the money'. Belying such rousing sentiments of solidarity, it seems that, despite the dissenting voices, another gathering took place of certain senior players and a phone call was made to MK to see if the amount on offer could be increased to US$300 000. Cronjé speculated that the bookie would have settled at US$250 000. Whatever the final figure, the offer was supposedly rejected, although Cronjé conceded that 'I probably would have gone for it if the team had gone for it'. Subsequently, a report appeared in the *Cape Times* of 10 August 2000 that confirmed that chief investigator Shamila Batohi was '... to call former players Brian McMillan, Pat Symcox and Dave Richardson to the stand when the hearing resumes in October because of concerns about an offer to the team to throw a one-day international in India in 1996'. The hearings, of course, never did resume.[125]

Dave Richardson, right-hand batsman and wicketkeeper, was part of the South African team from its return to international cricket in the 1991/92 season until his retirement in February 1998 at the end of the Australian tour. He was subsequently employed by ESPN Legends, the sports marketing company, and was also the commercial representative of the South African cricket team, fondly known to the team as 'Uncle'. Of that epithet Richardson commented, 'I mean, the fact that they called me 'Uncle' was not something which I enjoyed, but it was that type of relationship which I had with the team, including Hansie'. He represented the private interests of the new generation, Herschelle Gibbs, Mark Boucher, Roger Telemachus and Makhaya Ntini as well as up-and-coming wickie Thami Tsolekile. In January 2002 he was appointed as the International Cricket Council's first General Manager.

Dave Richardson is a man who wears many hats, including that of Attorney of the High Court of South Africa. This hat was the first to be remarked upon by Judge King at the outset of his testimony to the King Commission on 13 April 2000.

COMMISSIONER: I take it you don't need a good attorney to assist you.
MR RICHARDSON: It's debatable.
COMMISSIONER: I beg your pardon?

In the course of his testimony on the offer to throw the final game of the Indian tour, Richardson explained, like others before and after him, that team morale was at a low ebb. He himself did not play in the match as he was down with a virus and wasn't fit enough to play.

COMMISSIONER: We'll inquire into that in due course, Mr Richardson. I think what you're saying is that the players, for all the reasons you've given, were vulnerable.
MR RICHARDSON: Exactly. That's why I do need a good lawyer.

Richardson, like his team-mates, also suffered from imperfect recollections and imprecise details.

> Yes. As I said in my statement, it's quite difficult to remember exactly what I recall, and obviously since this whole news broke we've discussed it amongst ourselves, whether it's been in the commentary box, or wherever, so it's sometimes difficult to differentiate between what I remember and what people

have subsequently told me. But I think if I can best describe it – I think the way it arose was prior to the match, and certainly after the previous final, Hansie mentioned to a few of the senior players that he'd received an offer for us to influence the result of the game. I can't remember whether it was meant to be we were meant to lose, or whether we were meant to lose by a certain number of runs, or whether they were meant to get to a certain number of runs, and I also can't remember the actual figure that was mentioned ... The reaction of the players that he spoke to first was, 'We've got to have a team meeting'. Now I can't say that I – it was a meeting convened of senior players for that purpose. All I know is that it eventuated in a team meeting, and we all sat in, I think it was Hansie Cronjé's room, and again, Hansie just put the offer to the team. I don't recall it ever going to any kind of vote. I presume that a couple of the guys just spoke about it, and gave their views. There might have been some guys who said, 'Ja, we must go for it, we're going to lose anyway' but I do recall Andrew Hudson saying that he wouldn't want any part in it. I can also recall saying something about that, 'I would probably love to take the money more than all of you, but it's just not something that we can do' and that was said really after I had heard everyone talking about it and giving their penny's worth, and it was really almost summing up the meeting, and almost taking the responsibility of giving advice to what I thought the team should do. And that I was an attorney and if I, for instance, got caught or it came out, it would jeopardise my practice, and it was summarised as something that we just mustn't get involved in, no matter how much or how tempting the offer might be.

MR FITZGERALD: After the team meeting, was that the end of your involvement, or ...?

MR RICHARDSON: To be honest, only until recently when it has been put to me by various things, and I read about Pat Symcox's testimony, I do vaguely kind of recall one or two of us sitting behind and discussing the offer. The testimony that I have heard, that a phone call was then made to increase the offer, I honestly can't recall that, but I can say with safety that the result was the same. That we just can't get involved.

MR FITZGERALD: With the benefit of hindsight, do you think it was a good approach to have the team discuss the offer?

MR RICHARDSON: Well, I think in hindsight, knowing what we knew then, it was kind of the only way that it could have happened. But certainly with hindsight, and knowing what we do today and the seriousness of the matter worldwide, and the implications that arise from something like this and the seriousness, really, of the matter, there's no doubt that it shouldn't really have even got, I don't think, as a senior player you should have suggested to the captain that he take it to a team meeting. Definitely not.

The King Report noted of the offer: 'It is not at this stage clear whether or when it also came to the knowledge of the team management or the United Cricket Board.' Cronjé claimed that coach Bob Woolmer knew about the proposition on the same day of the game and Dave Richardson seemed to confirm this when he stated that Woolmer knew immediately after the meeting when he came in to talk about the game.

CRONJÉ: The next morning, before the match, there was a brief meeting at which it was confirmed that the offer was rejected. When Mr Woolmer, the coach, heard about the offer, he was very angry about it … He was angry in the way that he heard that there was a meeting and he wasn't part of it, I think he made a sort of joking remark to me at the end, 'Heh, you were going to cut me in' because I was like joking with him about it.

In an article in *The Hindu* on 16 October 2001, Bob Woolmer talked about one meeting: 'There was a meeting before the match in Mumbai in 1996. I attended only one meeting. What was said in that meeting appeared trivial, all fun and not as anything serious. As Dave Richardson said, "I think we have come of age because we have been approached." It was like a schoolboy prank. That's what it seemed at that point of time; down the line though, it took a more serious effect.'[126]

Despite the former South African coach's impassioned defence of Cronjé when the scandal first hit the headlines – 'If you told me the earth was going to stop rotating tomorrow I would not believe it. I have the same reaction to people saying Hansie is guilty'[127] – Woolmer didn't waste much time after Cronjé's confession on 11 April 2000. Two days later, he threw the 1996 offer into the bubbling brew in a report in the *Daily Sport* newspaper in London. Two months later, on the day before the King Commission was due to begin, Woolmer was quoted on the cricket website *The Pavilion*: 'We received this phone call out of the blue asking us to throw the game.' While this was the same modus operandi that distinguished Marlon Aronstam's approach to Cronjé before the Centurion Test match, clearly it was not a call out of the blue as Cronjé had met MK Gupta in person, days before this final match. Woolmer continued, 'I know that was the closest the team came to match-fixing and I did mention it in dispatches and in meetings of the board. Ali Bacher denies that I did, but I know that I did.'[128]

Ali Bacher, the Managing Director of the UCB, who has been described by many who know him as a man with his hands firmly on the reins of South

African cricket, claimed ignorance of that un-kosher team meeting. He claimed that it had not appeared in either team manager Robbie Muzzell's or Bob Woolmer's end-of-tour report and even when the story appeared in the *Sunday Times* in December 1998, Bacher still denied any knowledge of it to the King Commission.

DR BACHER: Sir, I have no recollection of Mr Woolmer ever saying to me or mentioning to me about that approach.
COMMISSIONER: And if he had, you'd have taken it further?
DR BACHER: Absolutely.

Ray White, former President of the UCB, was a member of the United Cricket Board in 1996. In a report in the *Cape Argus* of 29 June 2000, White revealed that he had known of the infamous gathering: 'I seem to recall discussing it with Dr Bacher in New Zealand in 1999 before an ICC meeting. I seem to recall that, but my memory is not faultless.' Bacher's response, relayed through UCB attorney Clifford Green, was that '... White was the President at the time; if he knew about it why did he not do anything about it?'

White had relinquished the presidency of the UCB abruptly in January 2000 to his deputy, Percy Sonn, and according to the *Argus* was 'forced out' as the UCB representative to the International Cricket Council, his place again occupied by Percy Sonn.[129] By the end of 2000, Bacher had also departed. His successor, Khaya Majola, had been an executive board member at the time of the 1996 team offer and he did not recall the matter being discussed at any meetings. Ray White's departure, rumoured to have been precipitated by a falling-out with new UCB Managing Director Khaya Majola over racial selection policy, went some way to ameliorating the views of former South African vice captain Craig Matthews on some of the errors of judgement made by cricket's ruling body. In Matthews' opinion, the UCB was stupid for having an all-white hierarchy, with Peter Kirsten as Convenor of Selectors, Ray White as President and Ali Bacher as Managing Director. Matthews insisted that 'Bacher was a good man for war. Not for peace'.

To summarise then, the South African team was in low spirits and a number of meetings were held to discuss MK's offer. Although Cronjé maintained that all had to be in on the deal, an attempt was made, despite some dissent, to raise the stakes. All concerned vowed that the money was ultimately rejected but South Africa did indeed lose the match in question.

South Africa went into the game with 4 spin bowlers and a sickly Fanie de Villiers, who managed only 5 overs. Gary Kirsten covered for an ill Richardson behind the stumps. South Africa utilised 7 bowlers during the Indian innings, but only Symcox and Boje bowled a full 10-over complement, with Symcox conceding more than 5 runs an over on completion. Indian captain Tendulkar won the toss and took up the opening stand with new partner Raman. Symcox, Crookes and Boje picked up the Indians' first 3 wickets but not before 90 runs had been notched up by their openers. Symcox drew first blood with the dismissal of Raman and Azhar then joined Tendulkar at the crease as they began to score runs off Symcox and Crookes. Boje collected Tendulkar, the other opener, but only after the Indian captain was dropped at 3 and 32 by Gibbs and McMillan respectively, going on to reach 114 and winning Man of the Match with his first century at his home ground.

Crookes ended his 6 overs with an average of just under 6, bowling 4 wides but running out the Indian third man, Azharuddin, with the help of Kirsten, who did the stumping. Azhar was unhappy with the decision and showed it. The crowd picked up on the ugly tenor of the game with India on 155/2 after 30 overs and started lobbing plastic water bags onto the pitch close to where Adams was fielding. In reaction, Cronjé led the South Africans off the field where they remained, until Azhar was persuaded by officials of the Mumbai Cricket Association and the Indian police to come out and placate the crowd. Play resumed twenty minutes later.

Now, it was Jadeja's turn to take Symcox and fellow-spinner Adams to the cleaners. He opened his middle-order fight-back with a mid-wicket flyer off Symcox and showed the same disregard for Adams, brought into the attack in the thirty-eighth over. There was 249 on the board as India went into the final over and Jadeja added 18 runs to the score, punishing Adams with 3 lofty 6s and ending with a swashbuckler off the last ball, on 54 not out. South Africa was chasing 268.

Azhar soon tasted revenge. It was Kirsten who bowed out first in the South African innings, notching up only 1 run before being dispatched by Prasad and caught by Azhar who repaid the favour with the score at 1/2. Captain Cronjé joined Andrew Hudson at the wicket but soon followed suit, scoring just 10 to put SA at 2/35. Hudson was next to go but had the consolation of the top score of the innings with 45. Cullinan on 44 was close behind but his fourth-wicket stand with Gibbs was cut short, leaving SA on 122/4. But it was when Crookes joined Gibbs on the field that Azharuddin found his vengeance complete. He ran out Crookes with a direct hit for 18 and the collapse picked up pace. From 161/5, Gibbs made it 166/6, Boje managed 3 and SA was at 174/7. Symcox added little impetus with his 3 not out, while McMillan steadied the ship somewhat but relinquished the helm on 16 with the visitors at 188/8. De Villiers was out for a duck, leaving the score unchanged, and Adams, as last man in, failed to add a run. Indian won by 74 runs.

Two years after that dismal performance, Colin Bryden's report, entitled 'Proud South Africans hit match-fixers for six,' was published in the South African *Sunday Times* on 20 December 1998.

> The record of the South African team in one-day cricket makes it obvious that they are not open to bribery or offers from bookmakers … It happened in Mumbai at the end of the 1996/97 tour of India. The South African captain received a telephone call in his hotel room on the eve of a benefit match for Mohinder Amarnath. Cronjé told the caller he was not interested. 'To be honest, I'm not sure whether he was a bookmaker or just a member of the public. We didn't get to the point of discussing any details.' Cronjé raised the issue at a team meeting. 'We basically laughed it off,' he said, 'but we did agree as a team that we would never be open to any such offers. One of the things that makes me proud to play for South Africa is the team spirit and the knowledge that every member of the side will always try his best to win for his country.'

8

A fix for the history books

Fifth Test, SA v ENG, Centurion, 14–18 January 2000

I am absolutely confident that England is absolutely clean in all this.

– Nasser Hussain[130]

In the opinion of South African sports writer Trevor Chesterfield, 'Hansie Cronjé stepped into Test history' after the final Test of the Millennium series between England and South Africa at Supersport's Centurion Park in January 2000.[131] Little did the journalist know just how right he was, but for all the wrong reasons. In 1 483 matches, spanning 123 years of cricket, the forfeiting of an innings by both teams had never happened. Until now. With the series already won 2–0 by their hosts, England went into the fifth and final encounter at Centurion from 14–18 January with nothing at stake but pride and prize money. The rain-delayed start of the Test was a harbinger of things to come. Poor English bowling and some disappointing South African batting saw both sides make heavy weather of the first day's abbreviated play.

England won the toss and sent the South Africans in to bat. Opener Kirsten was out for a duck on Gough's last ball of the first over with the score on 1/1. His partner Gibbs lasted another 6 overs, adding a total of just 3 runs before being caught by Adams off the bowling of Caddick with the South African tally at 15/2. Kallis brought his bulldog tenacity to the wicket and survived until the eighteenth over when Caddick struck once again, dismissing the South African batsman for 25. Captain Cronjé mimicked Gary Kirsten and was also out for a duck to Gough on the last ball of the nineteenth over. However, Gough's 2 wickets were marred by 10 no-balls and a wide. Thirty-year-old Pieter Strydom, in his debut Test appearance, joined veteran Daryll Cullinan at the wicket to steady the South African innings and the debutante put on a respectable 30 before being caught behind by wicketkeeper Stewart off Silverwood. Klusener and Cullinan were left to stitch the innings together. A modest crowd of 6 750 were on hand to watch Cullinan pass 3 500 career Test runs and then succumb 4 runs shy of his 50, caught and bowled by Alan

Mullally for 46. At the close of play, Klusener on 22 and Pollock on 9 assumed night-watchman responsibilities with the score on 155/6.

In the first of many surprises that this Test had in store, that same night Daryll Cullinan held a press conference and announced his retirement from one-day internationals, apparently without discussing this decision with his captain. Cronjé later speculated that Cullinan was feeling like a 'has-been' because he was not going on tour to Kenya and his participation in the 2003 World Cup was doubtful. The second highest run-scorer in South African cricket history proved that his shelf life had not yet expired when, at the end of this Test, he was named Man of the Millenium Series.

Summer showers and a sodden pitch put paid to the second, third and fourth day's contest and the Northerns Cricket Board and the UCB faced the prospect of empty coffers. Already on the second day of no-play, Richard Harrison, the Northerns President, announced that, far from reaping the R1,6 million (US$ 228 000) profit expected from this game, Northerns were facing losses of around R2,4 million.(US$ 340 000) [132] UCB Managing Director Ali Bacher presided over a press conference on the fourth day of the non-event and intimated that England had offered to turn the match into a one-day game. This was subsequently denied by the English captain, Nasser Hussain, who said he'd been thinking along the lines of an exhibition match.[133] Hansie Cronjé, in his statement to the King Commission, recollected that, sometime during the fourth day of the rain-soaked Centurion Test, there was a discussion about how to salvage the loss of three days of play. In attendance were the English captain, Hussain, the umpires, DB Hair, Rudi Koertzen and Cyril Mitchley, Barry Jarman, the Match Referee from Australia, Richard Harrison and Ali Bacher. Cronjé claimed that it was Bacher who had first mooted the idea of turning the Test into an ODI, but apparently there were sponsorship clashes and this proved impossible. Cronjé conceded that the double forfeit option may have been mentioned.

That same evening, following the meeting, Cronjé received a fortuitous phone call from a complete stranger who had somehow managed to obtain the South African captain's cellphone number. The man described himself as a cricket lover who was interested in seeing Cronjé make a match of the washed-out Test. He offered Cronjé a sizeable 'donation' to Hansie's preferred charity for entertaining his plan. 'My idea was to raise money for the United Cricket Board Development Fund,' he later told the King Commission. Marlon Aronstam, a career gambler with a background in horse racing and sports betting, was an unusual answer to a prayer.

Or was he?

A meeting was arranged between Cronjé and Aronstam for later that night. A number of calls passed between the two men before Marlon arrived at Cronjé's room in the Sandton Sun at 10 pm that evening. However, the R200 000 'donation' was no longer on the cards. (Cronjé claimed that the amount on offer had in fact been R500 000.) Aronstam contended that in the hours that had elapsed between the initial phone call and their meeting in Hansie's hotel room he had made a few calls and was unable to place any money on the game as betting had closed around the world as the Test was inevitably going to be a draw. Nonetheless, there was still talk about the Centurion game and Aronstam convinced Cronjé that providing some entertainment would go some way to improving his negative image in the eyes of the public. The skipper had had two consecutive ducks in his previous innings. Aronstam encouraged Cronjé to contact Nasser Hussain, but in his statement Cronjé said that, at that time, he didn't want to involve Nasser. 'He wanted to call Nasser Hussain, who was in the same hotel, up to my room. I refused because I did not want him to be involved.' Shamila Batohi, the King Commission's Leader of Evidence, did not allow this comment to pass unnoticed and asked Hansie what he meant by 'involve'. 'Surely it's up to both captains to make such an historic decision?' she inquired disingenuously. Cronjé brushed off the question.

While both men insisted that the 'donation' never materialised, they agreed that an amount of R50 000, in two instalments, did change hands. 'I paid Hansie Cronjé R50 000 for pitch reports,' Aronstam claimed, emphasising that '... in view of my position in cricket, for me, pitch reports are more important then anything, especially if they come from, who I regard as one of the best players in the world and best judges of world cricket, Hansie Cronjé.' Aronstam elaborated:

> ... I went to the hotel and I gave him an amount of R30 000 in cash and told him I would bring him another R20 000, and that this money was for the one-day Test [sic] series in which I requested him to provide me with pitch reports. I also requested him for his cricket jersey to be signed by all the players, which he arranged for me. The next day, I met him again at the hotel, where I gave him the balance of the R20 000 in cash and he handed me the jersey signed by all the South African players.

Judge King commented wryly, 'The most expensive cricket shirt in Christendom, I should think.' Aronstam continued:

> I further phoned Mr Cronjé and asked him, when he was in Johannesburg again for the last one-day game at the Wanderers, whether it would be possible for me to bring my son to have breakfast with him at the hotel. I met him together with my young son for breakfast and I gave him a further amount of R3 000 in cash, together with a lady's black leather jacket for his wife, which

was mainly due to the fact that he had given me some very good and well-judged pitch reports in the one-day series.

Despite the fact that no 'donation' was forthcoming and no international bets were being taken on the Centurion Test, the morning after his first meeting with Aronstam, on his way down to the nets, Cronjé put the bookie's proposition, not to his fellow captain, Hussain, but to Alec Stewart. Interestingly, this name is one that had come up in match-tampering allegations by English cricketer Chris Lewis in 1999. Stewart's name also appeared in the Indian CBI Report into cricket corruption. Stewart and Cronjé discussed a mutual forfeiture of innings and a target for the English of around 270 in 65/70 overs. Alec Stewart was 'very, very keen' according to Cronjé and went to speak to management. But the English had rejected the offer by the time the final day's play got underway and Cronjé sent an SMS message to Aronstam to tell him so.

The South African night-watchmen picked up where they had left off three days earlier. The unprecedented events that followed were negotiated 10 overs into the fifth day's play. Word came to Cronjé from Alex Tudor, the English twelfth man, that they were ready to negotiate and both captains left the field. From the initial offer of 270 in 73 overs to 255 in 73, agreement was finally reached on 249 in 76 overs, just over 3 runs an over. As Judge King pointed out in his interim report: 'Cronjé was obviously determined to see the plan carried out.' South Africa's first innings continued with Klusener going on to 61 and Pollock to 30 before the South African declaration came at 248/8 after 72 overs. England declared their first innings reply on 0/0, South Africa forfeited their second innings and England were set a contrived target, effectively turning a Test into a limited-overs game.

The game was on. South African wicketkeeper and vice captain Mark Boucher was involved in five of the eight English dismissals. He held on to former captains Atherton and Stewart and bowlers Adams and Caddick and helped Kirsten run out Maddy. Four of his victims succumbed on single-digit scores. England were at 102/4 by the thirty-eighth over when Alec Stewart, the English wickie and vice captain, bumped up the order to number 4, and Test rookie Michael Vaughn stopped the rot with a mid-wicket partnership of 126. Then, in the space of 27 balls, 4 wickets tumbled for 12 runs with Stewart on 73 leading the lemmings in the middle of the sixty-ninth over. Maddy took the leap 11 balls later with Caddick close behind 2 balls after that. Vaughn succumbed in the next over, the seventy-fourth, his 69 earning him Man of the Match. With 3 overs to go, England were on 240/8. Darren Gough hit the winning boundary off Hayward with 5 balls in hand, closing up shop for the English on 251/8 in 75.1 overs.

In an article in *The Guardian* on 10 April 2007, Darren Gough reminisced about the Centurion game:

> The night before the last day everyone was in the bar with Woosie (Ian Woosnam) and Lee Westwood. It had rained for three days solid and we thought there was no chance of play. So we got stuck in with Woosie and drank until half-past three. By the time we got to the ground they were using two bleeding helicopters to dry a sodden outfield. I'd been sick twice but Nasser made me bowl 10 overs on the bounce, just to teach me a lesson. And then we got this message that Hansie Cronjé wanted to offer us a run-chase – that was the game they said he fixed. Nasser made me sit in my pads all afternoon but I eventually went in at 10 and hit the winning runs in the last over. We thought it was odd at the time but I was so hungover I didn't know what was going on.[134]

South Africa's unbeaten run of 14 wins was at an end. However, Cronjé's popularity was restored and he was made Man of the Match. After the game Cronjé was congratulated by '… the Northern Titans President, one of the South African selectors, the former President of the UCB, Ray White and Ali Bacher'. There was obviously good reason for such jubilation. As IS Bindra, the outspoken Chairman of the Punjab Cricket Association, pointed out, 'One-dayers bring in as much money in a day as three Test matches do in fifteen days!'[135]

South African correspondent Trevor Chesterfield was of the opinion that the target set for the English was 'far from generous' although that may have been based on his mistaken assumption that the target was 249 in 72 rather than 76 overs. Chesterfield lauded the move as the '… most dramatic decision in the game for more than two decades'.[136] Chesterfield wasn't alone in his admiration. Sports writer Neil Manthorp recollected that he had written '… a thousand word eulogy to Cronjé and I still think it is brilliant. I think it's fantastic. I think it's exactly what Test cricket needs. I think it was superb. If it hadn't been for the leather jacket and the 50 grand, it would have been even better. I was totally and utterly deceived'.

Manthorp later disclosed at a Western Province cricketing dinner that Daryll Cullinan had seen his captain receive money in suspicious circumstances at the Sandton Sun after the Centurion Test. Acknowledging that his relationship with Cullinan had long been strained and he had thus received the story somewhat third-hand, Manthorp related how he had been told by a 'concerned Transvaal team member' that Cullinan had said in the dressing room during the Supersport final that he believed that Cronjé had received R30 000 in cash for the Centurion Test.

Now when I gave a talk at the Oaks, I just relayed that fact and I said, 'Who knows how he knew, maybe Daryll saw Hansie receiving an envelope, there's a lot of envelopes around in this game.' Cullinan has never actually dealt with it. He's always avoided that question but he did know and Cronjé did receive R30 000 and then another R20 000 so it was a hell of a coincidence if I made that story up and it turned out to be true.

The *AFP* report of the match remarked that 'South Africa's challenge seemed generous and became even more so when Adams had to leave the field.'[137] Off-spinner Paul Adams crashed into an advertising board with England one wicket down, broke his left middle finger and retired. Interestingly, Marlon Aronstam told the King Commission that he had phoned Hansie the evening of the game's conclusion and they had discussed the game. 'He was of the opinion that if Paul Adams had not broken his finger, South Africa would have won.'

In a press conference at the Supersport grounds after the game, Cronjé referred to having heard rumours of the ICC's concern about his decision. With unconscious prescience the South African captain announced that if that was the attitude then he would rather not be in the game. Ignoring coach Graham Ford's desire not to lose and his team-mates' initial reluctance, Cronjé maintained that 'When I arrived at the ground I found there were twenty-two players who wanted to get involved in a game and the mood was a positive one.' Apparently, this was not the case in the South African dressing room where a number of players were unhappy about Cronjé's decision. 'Of course I am disappointed we lost and our record of not losing in fourteen matches has gone but the choice was there and had to be taken,' the South African skipper told the media.[138]

Daily Telegraph reporter Michael Henderson, in an article entitled 'England win with perfect timing' on the day after the controversial Test, seemed sceptical. Henderson remarked that 'Cronjé, whose enterprise had enabled the day to take shape, certainly felt it hard, though he could understand why certain bookmakers had refused to take money yesterday'. Henderson quoted Cronjé's views on dissenting voices: 'If some people are unhappy about the way it went then I want to get out of the game. This was Test cricket at its best, in my opinion.' The writer disagreed: 'It wasn't that, but it was a strange day and, so far as England were concerned, one that ended with a most unusual victory.'[139]

English captain Nasser Hussain, despite his initial reluctance, had no such doubts after England's win. 'Hansie deserves every support for what he did. He gave us a chance, he gave his side a chance and we gave the public a great day.'[140] Three months later, after the Delhi police had publicised their allegations and Cronjé had confessed to his complicity, Hussain stuck to his guns on the Centurion Test. 'Let me say straight away that I am still totally satisfied that there was nothing improper about the circumstances that led to our dramatic win.'[141]

Michael Atherton, captain of England in 52 Tests and Hussain's team-mate in the Centurion Test, in an interview with the *New Statesman*, voiced his suspicions about Cronjé's decision, eight months after the fact:

> The declaration was out of character. I justified it initially by the thought that he had had a poor run with the bat, and his captaincy had been criticised throughout the series. Offering a generous declaration would look like creative captaincy, and he would come out smelling of roses. Then we lost a few wickets: at one stage, we virtually shut up shop when Stewie (Alec Stewart) and Vaughnie (Michael Vaughan) were in. At that point, he (Cronjé) brought on Pieter Strydom, an inexperienced bowler, and a couple of boundaries off him kept the game open. That was when I thought something was going on. South Africa were trying to win the game but it was clear that Cronjé was after a result.[142]

After the parade of South African cricketers had replayed the Centurion Test before the King Commission, Justice King agreed. In his interim report he confirmed that Cronjé had contrived to turn an inevitable draw into a positive result for the sake of financial reward.

> ... What occurred was that Cronjé engineered a formula whereby what would otherwise have produced an inevitable draw in the Centurion Test was transformed into a match which would in all probability (and did) produce a positive result – a win for England. Thus the decision was taken and the action pursuant thereto was influenced by the promise (and receipt) of a reward. Such other motive as there might have been is in this context secondary.

Verdict: Centurion fixed.

9

Long live cricket?

The end of the King Commission

If sin is as old as humankind, so too is corruption as old as government itself.

– President Thabo Mbeki at an anti-corruption summit, Cape Town, November 1998

Along with a colonial history of cricket, South Africa also shared India's greatest freedom fighter, Mohandas Ghandi, who had once lived and fought for human rights in South Africa. It was India that had led the drive to bring South Africa back into world cricket and India had been the first international country to host the prodigal's return. Almost ten years after that historic three-match encounter in 1991, Hansiegate precipitated a souring of relations between the two countries. The hostile South African reaction to the Delhi police charges did not go down well in India. Vindicated by Cronjé's confession and subsequent suspension on 11 April 2000, a *rediff.com* report quoted an Indian External Affairs Ministry official: 'It was Indians who were accusing white South Africans, and there is no doubt that South African whites think themselves superior. Had a European country accused the South Africans, they would not have created such a noise, but because it is us Indians making the charges, they get upset, doubting our ability.'[143] This same observation would ring true about the Jamaican police after the tragic events of the 2007 World Cup in the Caribbean. But that was still seven years in the future.

Despite the initial outcry at the accusations of the Indian police, the South Africans' prompt response to the unpalatable business earned them international kudos. In a paean of praise to Cronjé for coming clean, fellow cricketers for publicly admitting their wrongs and the King Commission, Tim Mitchell wrote in the *Weekend Argus* of 24/25 June 2000, that '... taking nothing away from Pakistan's Qayyum Report, ours is the first public inquiry that is entirely transparent.'[144] However, by the King Commission's untimely end, after postponements, legal wrangling and other delays, that first impression was to be severely tarnished.

In the wake of Hansie's confession, President Thabo Mbeki issued a government press release on 12 April 2000 designed to reassure the South African public that Hansiegate, unlike Watergate, '... is not a national political crisis at all'. However, the government's response to the non-crisis was an urgent one; Deputy Foreign Minister Aziz Pahad announced that 'It is the government's intention that we don't delay this matter longer than is necessary. It is impacting on very many aspects of South Africa's image abroad'.[145] The UCBSA President Dr Ali Bacher was in agreement with his long-standing friend Pahad. Expressing the Cricket Board's position on the inquiry in a magazine interview on 24 April 2000, Bacher said, 'We want it to be done quickly. We have to move fast. This thing must not linger on. There must be a finality to it'.[146] The International Cricket Council too was after a speedy conclusion to the inquiry. ICC President, and another old friend of Dr Bacher's, Jagmohan Dalmiya, said in Calcutta, 'We have advised them [UCB] to conduct the inquiry as soon as possible. His (Cronjé's) admission and other allegations made by the police in India require an immediate and thorough investigation and the ICC awaits an early outcome.'[147] By now, Ngconde Balfour, the Sports Minister at the time, had announced that an independent commission of inquiry headed by a judge would investigate the charges against the South African players. Balfour expected the judge's appointment to be made by the following Friday of the Easter weekend, 21 April, and the Commission's work to be finished by the end of May. On Wednesday 19 April, the South African team manager, Goolam Rajah, received an anonymous phone call claiming that Gibbs, Strydom and Boje had indeed been approached by Cronjé and, on Good Friday, inappropriately enough, Strydom and Gibbs admitted as much to Ali Bacher. Boje continued to deny the charge. With this fuel added to the Indians' fire, the South African authorities were trying unsuccessfully to obtain copies of the alleged taped conversations between Cronjé and Indian bookie Sanjay Chawla, but a police spokesperson admitted on 22 April that they had not yet received them.[148]

With the Easter weekend intervening, the announcement of the head of the inquiry was delayed until 4 May 2000. Newly retired Judge President of the Cape, Judge Edwin King, who had served fifteen years on the bench, was named head of the commission that would come to bear his name. The Judge was reportedly a keen cricket fan, but during the inquiry 'Sharkey' King would live up to the menace implicit in his nickname, prompting one journalist to describe him as an 'iron fist in a velvet glove'. Giving early indications of this tempered-steel approach, King told the media that he wished to pursue the inquiry in a 'congenial' atmosphere. 'I'm hoping people will come forward and open up to the Commission and make this almost a cleansing and healing process – but make no mistake: if I have to use firmer methods, I will.' King's was perhaps the only voice appealing for less haste in getting proceedings underway. 'But if we kick off without proper preparation, we will achieve the exact opposite of what we want to achieve,' he said.[149] His report was initially to have been prepared within a month but was now due by June 30.

Meanwhile, Ajay Raj Sharma, Chief of the Delhi police and related by marriage to disgraced cricketer Ajay Sharma, was reported by SAPA on 28 May 2000 to have denied the Indian foreign ministry copies of the tapes as they had a direct bearing on the case and would be submitted as evidence in court. He made it clear that South Africa would have to go through the relevant legal channels to obtain copies of the transcripts. Thus the King Commission went in to bat, without the tapes, on 12 June, three months after Hansie's confession. This first innings took ten days spread over three weeks, with holidays, constitutional challenges and legal manoeuvrings curbing the run rate. The witness list included an all-star XI of past and present South African cricketers, the communications manager, security head and managing director of the United Cricket Board of South Africa, a Reserve Bank official, a psychiatrist, a betting expert, a bookie and Banjo, the biltong man. The King Commission was into its third week of hearings before it was televised on 21 June 2000. An incredulous nation tuned in to Hansie's second day at the wicket at the Cape Town venue, the Centre for the Book, newly dubbed the Centre for the Bookie, where he outlined his meeting with bookie MK Gupta, introduced to him by Indian cricket icon Mohammad Azharuddin.

State Advocate Shamila Batohi was Leader of Evidence. With a law career spanning fifteen years, she was the first person of colour to become a Deputy Director of Public Prosecutions in her home province of KwaZulu-Natal before going on to become Director. The day before Cronjé's first televised sitting, Batohi said that the Commission was using 'every available avenue' to gain access to the tapes but co-operation seemed to be lacking. The Delhi police complained of the same tardiness from Interpol in responding to their request for a voice sample of Cronjé and information on the existence of English bank accounts in the names of Cronjé, Boje, William, Strydom and Gibbs.[150]

As a result, the preliminary hearing of the case against the South Africans scheduled for 9 June in Delhi High Court had to be postponed.[151] In a diplomatic stand-off, the Indian police had not received any sample of Cronjé's voice from the South Africans to help verify the tapes and the King Commission didn't have authentication of the transcripts. The South Africans continued to deny that an extradition request for Cronjé had come through from India although at least one report suggested that the application had been received but was not going to be considered if the tapes were not handed over by the Indians. Pursuing them through diplomatic channels, the Department of Justice and then President Thabo Mbeki himself, the Commission had no success.

With the state's team hampered by the absence of authenticated transcripts of the Indians' aural evidence, the first round of the public inquiry ended on Monday 26 June 2000. Unsurprisingly, given the extensive revelations made, the report, due to be completed by 30 June, was delayed until 11 August. Batohi continued to pursue the elusive Hansiegate tapes through 'diplomatic channels' and King Commission spokesperson John Bacon gave the assurance that further investigations would follow. However, there would be no second sitting. Despite talk of the hearings resuming in August, then September, an official date set for 2 October, then rumours of December and official proclamations of 25 January, the Commission's resumption was postponed five times in seven months and finally cancelled altogether in February 2001.

The King Interim Report was duly completed on 11 August 2000. On 24 August, Sports Minister Balfour handed over the document to Ali Bacher and then CEO of the International Cricket Council, Dave Richards. Balfour remained upbeat, convinced that South African '... cricket is in a very healthy state, it is not corrupt at all ... I am still of the opinion that there are only one or two people involved in this type of thing and we can easily clean up the game.'[152] While the King Report reserved final judgement on Cronjé's complete disclosure, it cast doubt on Cronjé's insistence that in mentioning his team-mates to Sanjay he was merely 'stringing them along'. Responsibility was laid squarely at the captain's door. 'Cronjé testified that in order to be able to contrive a result, i.e. fix a match, it was necessary to have the co-operation of other players, perhaps four or five of them. That is undoubtedly so. One must not, however, lose sight of the fact that one such player must necessarily be the captain ... It is no exaggeration to say that the participation of the captain is indispensable.' The report noted that 'It is interesting that the first time Cronjé was approached to fix a match, he was prepared to and did entertain the suggestion'. In its most explicit finding, the report confirmed that the Centurion Test-turned-ODI between England and South Africa had been influenced by Cronjé for a promised reward. Ending on a sobering note, the Judge cautioned, 'It will be appreciated that until all the evidence has been heard, no aspect of the inquiry can be, or can be regarded as finalised.' At the handing over of the first report in Cape Town, it was revealed that Batohi would travel to India to interview her counterparts and reach an agreement about the tapes. There was also a surprise announcement of a second interim report detailing measures to help clean up the game.

On 20 September, Batohi met Indian investigators in Delhi. On the same day, Delhi Police Commissioner Ajay Sharma predicted that the South African investigators would probably have to return for the tapes because of complex legal hurdles. Apparently, the South Africans would have to appeal to the Indian judiciary to release the evidence, sealed as court property, pending prosecution, perhaps the following month.[153] Batohi returned empty-handed after her week-long visit, without the tapes and without interviewing Mukesh Gupta, as the Indian authorities refused access because of the sensitive nature of the ongoing Indian investigations. The hearings scheduled for 2 October failed to materialise and John Bacon told the website *TotalCricket* that while no new date for the resumption had been set, the Commission was now looking at November. 'We're trying to procure some documents from the Indian authorities and didn't deem it fit to resume the proceedings. A formal request in that regard will be made this week through diplomatic channels,' Bacon said.[154]

This lack of international co-operation was one of the factors that led to the demise of the Commission. Graham Dawes, a member of the elite Scorpions unit working on the King Commission, when interviewed a year later, spelled out the bottom line. 'I think it's safe to say that we are still waiting for presentable evidence from India. In the end it was never forthcoming. We don't have the tapes.' Speculating on why such evidence was not forthcoming, Dawes explained, 'I think they have a similar procedure to what we have here, where basically those tapes are sealed as evidence and if you had then taken them out and given them to someone else to listen to, you'd then break that chain of evidence, which would lead to major problems later if you wanted to use them in prosecution.' Dawes, as an investigator, had not been privy to the reasons but he cautioned that '… that kind of exchange of information between countries is a lengthy process. So it's not necessarily that people weren't willing to give it but sometimes that kind of thing takes a lot longer to obtain in any procedure where you're dealing with evidence between two countries. You can wait years sometimes to get it.'

Vincent Botto, the Assistant Leader of Evidence to Shamila Batohi at the King Commission added, 'You must also understand that the obtaining of that kind of evidence is regulated by certain legislation, which obviously lays down for what use the required information should be. Like in terms of the Mutual Assistance Act it must be for criminal purposes. And clearly a commission is not a criminal trial. So there were those types of issues involved.' Colleague Dawes agreed, 'It's those political and legal issues that people tend to debate for a long time, especially when something is of exceptionally high profile; in a lot of matters, it gets tied up in bureaucracy. So I think it was a combination of all those factors that led to the fact that we never got those tapes.'

That was merely one of the frustrations that hampered the King Commission in its work. Vincent Botto described the pressure the investigating team were under.

What the people seem to conveniently forget is that you can hardly start a commission without being prepared. And the one problem that I've experienced … Given the opportunity to do it all over again is to say we will start with public hearings once all and every investigation and lead has been followed up. That is what I would have done. But what was expected and I suppose because of the hype, they wanted something to happen now. And you can't do that. It's like running a trial. And I only use that by way of analogy because I don't want it to seem as if I'm saying that this is a trial. But you can hardly start a trial if you haven't investigated the matter, haven't collated the evidence in a form that can be presented and that was one of the major problems that I experienced. You were under pressure.

INTERVIEWER: You were obviously acting at a disadvantage.

BOTTO: Exactly. And that to a large extent contributed to the stop-start, or the impression that was created that it was a stop-start type of thing.

INTERVIEWER: What were the reasons for those delays?

BOTTO: Now, again, you must also understand that this whole thing broke in India and that is where most of the evidence was. I think the Commission would have been failing in their duty if they did not explore the Indian connection, if I can call it that. The reason that was given for the first delay was precisely to follow up the Indian leads. Once that was followed up it was a question of weighing up whether it was feasible to proceed with whatever 'evidence' was uncovered in India.

INTERVIEWER: So then it was decided that it wasn't feasible to proceed?

DAWES: I think the basics were that we waited for evidence from India. That was the bottom line. And I think it's safe to say that we are still waiting for presentable evidence from India. In the end it was never forthcoming. We don't have the tapes.

The beginning of November saw the release of the Indian CBI Report into cricket corruption in which eight former international Test captains were named along with Australia's Mark Waugh and former Indian physiotherapist Ali Irani. The Indian evidence extended the list of suspect South African matches and the day following the report's publication, the South African cricket board banned Hansie Cronjé for life.

On 12 November 2000, some two weeks after the release of the Indian report, South African sports correspondent Neil Manthorp confirmed that, after a number of delays spanning nearly seven months, the King Commission would reconvene on 25 January 2001. Graham Abrahams, spokesperson for the South African Sports Ministry, told Manthorp that Minister Ngconde Balfour would be meeting with an Indian cabinet minister in Oslo later in the week to '... discuss issues around match-fixing both in South Africa and in India'.[155] Here, at a World Anti-Doping Agency conference, the Minister was interviewed by respected *Daily Telegraph* journalist Mihir Bose. In an article that appeared in that newspaper four days after the new date of the Commission was announced, Bose claimed that King had been told to cut short the inquiry with no further evidence being heard. According to the journalist, Balfour said, 'The King Commission will not have any more hearings and, depending on what his final report says, we will decide whether we should take any criminal action'.[156]

This was subsequently vehemently denied, the same day, by Ministry spokesperson Graham Abrahams on the Cape Town radio station *Cape Talk*. In a heated interview with broadcaster Martin Gillingham, Abrahams pounced on Gillingham's interpretation of the week's contradictions as 'bizarre'.

> I just find it strange that you term it quite bizarre. You're obviously taking what you saw in the *Daily Telegraph* as God's truth. Yes, the Minister was in Oslo and so was the reporter. Minister Balfour was supposed to see the Indian Minister of Sport but he couldn't make it. His secretary was present in the discussions in which an agreement was reached on the basis of Leader of Evidence Shamila Batohi's request for the Minister to expedite the authentication of the Hansie tapes. South Africa has made an official request to the High Commissioner in India. The Indian authorities have given us their assurance that they will expedite the evidence. The hearings have been postponed on that basis. Unless new evidence is forthcoming, there will not be a need for new hearings.

So far, so good. But then Gillingham questioned the fact that Abrahams' statement was a direct contradiction of the article in the *Daily Telegraph*. The Sports Minister's spokesman was at a loss for words and wanted to terminate the discussion. Gillingham didn't let him off the hook. 'Is the Minister's quote in the newspaper then a fabrication?'

'You have this way of playing with words,' the government mouthpiece spluttered, '... playing with listeners. If you are happy with what an English newspaper is telling you, you can swallow that.' Suddenly eloquent with rage, Abrahams did not stop there. 'You are an absolute liar!' he accused Gillingham, more than once. 'I've never used the word fabrication at all. It is a fabrication by you. We can terminate this discussion. Thank you.'

Callers' responses to the official's unseemly temper tantrum revealed that the public know spin doctoring when they see it. 'It just shows that politicians are unanswerable. They're not something special. They're answerable to us. We deserve the truth,' said one caller. 'Abrahams sounded like a National Party politician going back fifteen years,' said another.

Two days later, *AFP* reported on 14 November 2000 that Cronjé's lawyers had appealed to the High Court for yet another delay, pleading their unavailability on 25 January. Obligingly, King agreed not to hear any further evidence on Cronjé until 19 February 2001. However, the High Court application went ahead and on 23 December 2000, Cape High Court Judge Thembali Jali ruled in favour of Cronjé's lawyers, finding that the Commission had failed to honour its commitment to consult with them about a new date for the second session of hearings.[157]

The end of that *annus horribilis* of South African cricket marked the departure, too, of the longest-serving managing director of the South African Cricket Board, Dr Ali Bacher. Relinquishing the chair he had held since the inception of the UCBSA ten years previously, Bacher turned his attentions to securing the R130 million (US$ 18,5 million) profit projected for South Africa's hosting of the 2003 World Cup.[158] Bacher's successor, the first black man to head the non-racial body, was Gerald Majola. Reflecting on the past year, he quoted Shakespeare's Macbeth: 'What is done is done and cannot be undone … I still think the UCB should sit down with Cronjé after the Commission wraps up, and reach some arrangement.'[159]

By the New Year, it was clear that something was afoot. An article written by Paul Martin for *rediff.com* on 20 February 2001 bore the sinister title, 'King a pawn in a wider plot' and cast doubts on the South African government's commitment to cleaning up cricket. With both King and Minister Balfour protesting the Judge's independence, Cronjé's lawyer, Leslie Sackstein, brought that issue to the fore. In an interview with the Afrikaans Sunday newspaper *Rapport* on 4 February 2001, Sackstein revealed that he intended challenging the King Commission in court yet again, on behalf of his client. However, this latest tactic cast doubt on the legality of the Commission itself following a prior constitutional court ruling on the invalidity of a judge heading the Heath Special Investigative Unit (SIU).

Successful corruption-buster Willem Heath was compelled to step down from his government-appointed post as head of the SIU following a challenge by the South African Association of Personal Injury Lawyers (SAAPI). Heath had been probing allegations that attorneys were defrauding their clients and the Road Accident Fund. Heath was no favourite of the government despite his unit's successes and in the wake of a new scandal involving alleged government corruption in procuring arms, Justice Minister Penuell Maduna had already announced government's intention to dissolve the SIU when the Constitutional Court ruled for the separation of the powers of the Judiciary and the Executive.

Thus, Heath, as a judge, could not head a body appointed by the government. That meant that Heath and his unit would have no part in the investigation into irregularities in a billion-dollar government arms deal, which is the subject of ongoing international investigations.

I asked Vincent Botto, Assistant Leader of Evidence, if this constitutional challenge was the final straw that broke the back of the King Commission.

> You must understand that soon after, or during, the existence of the public hearings there was the judgement by the Constitutional Court on Justice Heath. Basically what the judgement said, I'm not saying that it was directly applicable on the Commission, I'm just saying that was one of the concerns of the Judge and that is what he said in his press statement; that there is this perception amongst certain people that what he is doing is illegal. And he then made a press release to the effect that those people who questioned his authority to sit as head of the Commission and viewed it as being illegal should take the appropriate step, which was to go to court and test it. And he said, in view of that fact, this question hanging, it wouldn't be right to continue with that question hanging over his head.

INTERVIEWER: What were the similarities between Heath and King?

BOTTO: They were both judges reporting to the Executive.

INTERVIEWER: But surely, both of them were appointed by the Executive?

BOTTO: That's precisely what the problem is. That there must be complete separation of powers and here the Judge was reporting on his findings to the Executive. You must understand that a judge, in his normal functions, does not report to the Executive. He's not answerable to the Executive."

INTERVIEWER: So who would be a better person to head up such a commission?

BOTTO: There is this generally accepted misunderstanding about a commission. They refer to it as a judicial commission only because there's a judge heading it. But there's nothing judicial about the commission. A commission is basically an appointment by the Executive. It's an executive function and therein lies the problem. That you have the Judiciary [which] is an independent leg of government doing the work for the Executive and there should, strictly speaking, be a separation of powers. But in the same breath, I'm not saying that the Commission had this problem. I'm saying that there was this perception from various quarters, and that made it untenable for the Judge to continue.

While the similarities between the two cases are clear, so too are the differences. King was, after all, a retired judge. Heath, now also retired and free to speak out against his former employers, told a South Africa/Israel Chamber of Commerce gathering on 4 April 2001 that South Africa was governed by corruption. 'I doubt that they are serious about corruption ... If government does not allow investigations or support investigations into corruption properly, then it allows corruption to increase. Until and unless we become enthusiastic and dedicated in the fight against corruption, we will not make progress in this country.'[160] In South Africa, at the time Heath was speaking, only 8,3% of white-collar crime was successfully prosecuted.[161]

Given that the weight of the Constitutional Court ruling was sufficient to help force out Justice Heath and end the King Commission, subsequent events are inexplicable. A year to the day that Cronjé had thrown South African cricket into its worst crises ever, it was the turn of the national game. On 11 April 2001, 43 soccer fans were crushed to death at an overcrowded Ellis Park Stadium in Johannesburg. In the aftermath, amid allegations of mismanagement and corruption, another commission was quickly assembled, this time headed by the Judge President of the Transvaal, all constitutional implications ignored.

A lack of political will to get to the bottom of the Cronjé affair was remarked upon by more than one commentator and investigator. With a presentiment perhaps of things to come, the cricket administrator, writer and sociologist Dr Ashwin Desai was quoted in an *Outlook* cover story in the month that 'Hansiegate' flooded the headlines:

> The unwillingness of Sports and Recreation Minister Ngconde Balfour to condemn Cronjé's actions is a reflection of the reality that the ANC government uses sport in its quest to bring white South Africans aboard the new nation it is trying to build ... The government's hands are tied. In its quest to build a notion of reconciliation they've always tried to reach the white constituency via sport. Mandela would pitch up at the Rugby World Cup; Bacher is touted as a person who has always stood for freedom of the masses and so on ... The government has been forced to mollycoddle the sports fraternity – particularly around white-dominated sports like rugby and cricket – because of the notion of nation-building.[162]

Another journalist who may have had an inkling of things to come was Kevin Mitchell, chief sports writer for *The Observer*, who referred to the 'uncommitted' reaction of the government and reported a cabinet minister as acknowledging that cricket was not the pinnacle of the government's sporting agenda. The hosting of the Football World Cup of 2006 was of more national interest.[163]

By the end of the Cronjé affair a year later, radio presenter Martin Gillingham was of the opinion that the Commission was:

> … quite clearly a witch-hunt to bury Cronjé on the part of the United Cricket Board. I think both the United Cricket Board and the government have let us down by grinding the thing into submission … I think on some parts there are sinister reasons because I think there are people involved who know that there's far more to come out and that we have really only scratched the surface. As far as South Africa is concerned, they grasped the nettle, didn't they? They actually did something here in South Africa. They said, 'Let's have a commission. Let's get this out in the open,' and there they led the world. The UCB, I think, can be praised for that; the South African government can be praised for that. We see what's happened subsequently, the Australians have covered up, the English are fudging, the Pakistanis, the Indians have led the world in many respects so take our hats off to them. But having got that far and having got through the first stage well, I'm afraid that things have been going on involving the role-players that in the end we ended up with Judge King being the only one who really wanted to see it carry on. The government had their own reasons. The UCB had their own reasons and obviously the players …

The inevitable announcement, long-denied, was made on 5 February 2001. The King Commission's second sitting was postponed indefinitely. Again, events in Jamaica in 2007 would follow a similar pattern. The following day, in an interview with Martin Gillingham on *Cape Talk*, Judge King revealed some of the events behind the scenes. Apparently, the question of the legitimacy of King heading the inquiry was first raised by Leslie Sackstein in December and in subsequent correspondence in January. When Sackstein made public this contention to the Afrikaans newspaper *Rapport* on 4 February 2001, King found himself in an untenable position. He made the unavoidable decision to postpone the inquiry indefinitely as he felt that his inquiry had been tarnished in the public's perception and 'I can't be a judge in my own cause,' the Judge explained to Gillingham. He would have to take stock of the future of the Commission and perhaps explore other avenues. A forensic report undertaken at the behest of the inquiry was underway and this evidence could be taken up perhaps by another agency, King postulated.

A South African journalist who had a source working on the forensic audit claimed that the auditors were '… desperately frustrated at how little assistance and help they've been getting'. Apparently, despite the fact that the auditors had the right to demand what financial documentation they required, they had not been getting it. The frustrated auditors came to the conclusion that the entire process was a waste of time and money as it was never going to happen. They were not alone in that conviction. In an *Electronic Telegraph* article entitled

'South Africa go soft on Cronjé' on 18 February 2001, Owen Slot quoted Shamila Batohi: 'There was a stage when I thought the Commission would definitely go on but as it stands now, I really don't know ... I wonder about our commitment to get to the bottom of it. There's got to be total co-operation and that seems to be lacking.' Lending credence to the Commission's determination to see the thing through, Slot reported that the investigators were processing subpoenas for a number of former international cricketers.

But by 22 February it was all over. King announced the closure of the Commission with immediate effect. Interviewed by John Maytham on *Cape Talk* on the same day, and continuing to assert his independence, King explained that the Constitutional Court threat and the further utilisation of taxpayers' money had precipitated his request to the President to terminate the Commission. This seemed to contradict the previous day's statement by his spokesperson, Marina Valentine: 'According to legislation it is up to Mbeki to decide whether the Commission of Inquiry should continue its work under the chairmanship of Judge King.'[164]

Continuing to explain his position, King pointed out:

> You can't keep the thing open indefinitely. Very strong and strenuous efforts have been made to obtain the tapes from India and that door remains closed. I won't go into the details of whether that is commendable or otherwise, I think certainly it's understandable, but that avenue's closed ... A fair number of people have been left on a string: players, administrators, managers and there is no evidence as far as they're concerned to justify them either being called to the witness box or if they've been there before, called back. They, we regard as cleared and I think it's right and proper that not only they, but the public should know that.

As regarded the progress report delivered by the forensic auditors commissioned by the investigators, King admitted that the evidence '... may well warrant further investigation and could be taken up by an appropriate agency.' As for Cronjé's indemnity issue, King hedged, '[This] must still be taken up with the National Director of Public Prosecutions. I still have to come to some sort of decision about whether I am still able to make an assessment. That's an open question at the moment.' That question remained unanswered with the release of King's final report on 29 June 2001. Despite his overt reservations about Cronjé's candour in his first interim report, in the final reckoning King declined to commit himself on this issue. 'The Commission was required to express to the National Director an opinion as to Cronjé's credibility. Due to subsequent developments the Commissioner is not in a position to express such an opinion and has advised the National Director accordingly. The National Director is in agreement with the Commissioner's decision.'

The loose ends that had dangled from the first interim report, such as the issue of whether cricket management had known about the 1996 team meeting to throw a game in India; the doubts that were cast on Cronjé's credibility in insisting that all the names he had mentioned to Sanjay were an elaborate smokescreen; none of these fraying threads were sewn up. The only indication that all was not cut-and-dried was the cautionary note that '... vast sums of money have changed hands in the course of betting on cricket matches; the industry is said to be controlled by a sort of mafia. One cannot readily assume that this will all disappear overnight. There's too much at stake and there are too many unscrupulous people involved.'

Six years later, on 16 March 2007, ICC watchdog Lord Condon's contribution to the British House of Lords' debate on the Corruption Bill would bear out Judge King's words:

> In cricket in the 1990s, match-fixing brought the international game to its knees and disgrace to cricket legends such as Hansie Cronjé and other international captains. The problem threatened the integrity and financial structure of the game. Some of that match-fixing was linked to organised crime and even terrorism ... In some countries, it is now more lucrative to engage in sports corruption than drug dealing or robbery.[165]

Despite the decades of match-fixing rumours, inquiries and life-bans, there has never been a successful criminal prosecution of any player or official involved in match-fixing. Corruption laws differ from country to country and even within countries. The law has yet to catch up with the crime.

Nonetheless, in the end, Judge King was satisfied that '... the Commission has achieved its main purpose, which was to uncover and investigate and cause the creation of international investigatory units and concentrate the minds of the cricketing authorities throughout the cricket world. I think all that's been achieved.' In closing his interview with John Maytham, 'Hercules' King was determinedly sanguine. 'May I say this, that I believe that the Commission has contributed to the cleaning up of the Augean stables. It would be naïve to think that it will disappear overnight but I would say that if I watch South Africa playing ... any one of the top ten sides, I feel comfortable and I hope that the cricket-loving public will share that view.'

10

Match-fixing on the Orient Express

The Indian connection

If I could ever reveal all that I have gone through and seen, you would see that in this human [bathroom] of Indian cricket almost everyone is naked.

– Manoj Prabhakar[166]

When the Hansie Cronjé match-fixing allegations hit the newsstands on 7 April 2000, India was agog, the country reeling with 'shock mingled with anger and disgust' as one local commentator put it.[167] This outpouring of reaction came despite the fact that New Delhi police had accused only South Africans of cheating, fraud and criminal conspiracy. Yet the Indian team too had long been the target of rumours and vague allegations; of payment proffered for under-performing, of leading players being approached by bookies to influence games and even murmurs of matches being thrown. Sunil Dev, former Vice President of the BCCI and one-time manager of the Indian team, was quoted in an online article in *India Today*: 'I have rubbed my eyes a few times in the past to figure out what's been going on in the field. Things have happened which can only be described as ridiculous. The public has been fooled.'[168] Atul Wassan, former Indian XI cricketer-turned-commentator, unwittingly echoed this sentiment two months later in an online chat session. 'It is the mystery of our time that we have got the top five players in the world in our own team and still we lose so much ...'[169] However, now names had been mentioned and the stakes had just gone up.

Initially, the New Delhi police claimed that only Hansie Cronjé, Nicky Boje, Herschelle Gibbs and Pieter Strydom were under suspicion and that they were not investigating any Indian cricketer. However, three months later, on 8 July 2000, in a web exclusive interview with *India Today*, India's Union Minister for Sports, Sukhdev Singh Dhindsa, stated that he had information that five to six Indian players were involved in match-fixing and added that it could be more. In his assessment of the prevailing mood of the Indian cricketing public, he declared, '... the nation trusts the cricketers very little.'[170] Subsequent revelations of cricketers' princely incomes did little to allay the public's suspicions. Dhindsa addressed the Chandigarh Press Club on the same day, 8 July 2000, and revealed that he had information that some of the country's senior cricketers were worth some Rs2 billion (US$49 million) and a number of the younger players, Rs100 million (US$2,5 million).[171]

In India, as in South Africa, cricketers get paid a salary from the national cricket board in addition to the prize money, incentive bonuses, Man of the Match and Series awards that are up for grabs.

In 2007, the top contracted Indian players earned an annual retainer of US$115 000. They collected US$5 800 in match fees for every Test they played and US$3 700 for each one-day game.[172] In the run-up to the 2007 World Cup the South African team pocketed US$175 000 in prize money for winning the annual ICC's One-day Championship. Australia earned the same amount for winning the ICC Test Championship.[173] The World Cup is the most lucrative of all cricket tournaments with US$2,24 million up for grabs for the winning team in 2007, US$1 million for the runners-up and US$450 000 each for the semi-final losers.[174] However, it is not retainers, match fees or prize money that make cricketers fabulously wealthy. Sachin Tendulkar is the highest-earning Indian sportsman with an annual income estimated at US$14 million.[175] Over the years he has been the face of Colgate, Pepsi, Visa, Philips and Adidas and also had a lucrative sponsorship contract with TV company WorldTel. Its chief, Mark Mascarenhas, was also his marketing agent. This contract, worth US$20 million, was renewed in May 2001 for a further five years, making Sachin Tendulkar the world's highest paid cricketer. When the WorldTel contract expired in 2006, Tendulkar signed a three-year sponsorship deal with Iconix, the marketing branch of Saatchi and Saatchi for US$40 million.[176]

However, long before Tendulkar, it was Kapil Dev, the face of Palmolive, who led the field in Indian cricket's money stakes. One of India's greatest legends in his own lifetime, Kapil Dev captained the Indian team that won the 1983 World Cup. The first Indian cricketer to own his own Mercedes, in the mid-1980s, Kapil Dev's high-flying, fast-living lifestyle was described in an article in the Indian magazine *Outlook* on 22 May 2000. It relates Dev's impromptu cellphone calls to far-away friends just to tell them the latest dirty joke. It speaks of his 'active bias towards a designer wardrobe' and his connections with the wealthy and the influential in Indian society – the 'fat cats' of the Delhi Golf Club, industrialists, high-ranking bureaucrats and media moghuls.[177]

Former Indian cricketer Atul Wassan again, in the same online chat session of 15 June 2000, defended the Olympian lifestyles enjoyed by cricket's elite: 'I think cricketers deserve every penny they make officially ... Also the game is so popular and makes a lot of money for the organisers so why should the players not get a piece of the action when they are the people because of whom the game is popular. What better way to be a role model than to be famous, young and rich.'[178]

Cricketers have other, non-taxable sources of income, it would appear. A report in *The Telegraph* claimed that Indian tax investigators had discovered that, during the mid to late 1990s, several leading international cricketers were receiving monthly retainers of US$80 000 from Indian bookmakers. The money was apparently deposited into offshore bank accounts in the Cayman Islands.[179]

At a press conference in Chennai on 9 April 2000, AC Muthia, the incumbent President of the BCCI, insisted that the Delhi police first prove the charges against the South Africans before the Board took a stand.[180] By November, Muthia was under investigation himself over a lucrative fertiliser scam.[181] Chandu Borde, former Indian captain, team manager and then Chairman of the Selection Committee, echoed his President's view: 'We have to wait for the full reports to come in before deciding anything.'[182] Showing somewhat more commitment to his own opinion, JY Lele, the Indian Board's Secretary at the time, defended the South Africans in a TV interview and proclaimed the charges '... all rubbish. Such charges are baseless and cannot be proved.'[183]

Indian cricket administrator Jagmohan Dalmiya was the outgoing President of the ICC at the time Hansiegate exploded. He assured the public on 9 April 2000, 'If there is any grey side, the ICC will handle it. We have our own way of working. We will cross the bridge when we come to it.'[184] By 28 April that bridge had been reached. After dusting off the unpublished 1997 Chandrachud Report into Indian match-fixing and reassessing the national team's dismal form, the Indian government directed the Central Bureau of Investigations (CBI) to determine whether any Indian cricketer or administrator was involved in malpractice. Speaking on behalf of the ICC, Dalmiya vigorously backed another inquiry, his second in three years, and insisted that players, administrators, managers and coaches should all be investigated, with more stringent punishments befalling complicit administrators. Sports Minister Dhindsa conceded that there was reason to believe that the people at the top were as responsible as the players for the rot. According to the Minister, 'The Board of Control of Cricket in India has failed the people ... It has failed to carry out its duty and take immediate action. An explanation is owed to the nation.'[185]

In the interminable jostling for personal power within cricket's boardrooms, personal rivalries and smear campaigns blur the bigger picture. The CBI's probe was not India's (or Dalmiya's) first foray into the murky waters of match-fixing. In February 1997, the Indian team returned from their tour of South Africa. Indian team manager Sunil Dev reportedly included his misgivings about betting among the Indian players in his tour report. Four months later, on 11 June 1997, Aniruddha Bahal and Krishna Prasad, writing for the Indian magazine *Outlook*, revealed 'Indian cricket's worst-kept secret'. Their match-fixing exposé included a signed article by former Indian cricketer Manoj Prabhakar. Prabhakar hinted at suspicious games going back to the 1987 World Cup, including vaguely dated one-day internationals played at Sharjah and a Test played at Kanpur against the West Indies. There was one match, however, that Prabhakar specifically identified, making his allegations public three years after the event. He claimed that an unidentified team-mate had offered him Rs25 lakh (US$61 500) to help influence a match against Pakistan during the Singer Cup in Sri Lanka in 1994.

The BCCI appointed the one-man Chandrachud Committee to investigate these claims. The outgoing BCCI Secretary at the time of the Chandrachud Inquiry was none other than Jagmohan Dalmiya. 'The Board will not spare anyone found guilty of betting and match-fixing and accepting bribes,' he told the media. 'If, however, the allegations are not proved, the Board will take appropriate action against those responsible for spreading such malicious and motivated rumours with a view to tarnishing the image of Indian cricket.'[186] The Board, in fact, threatened to sue Prabhakar, but in the end did not.

Unlike its South African cousin, the King Commission, the Chandrachud Committee was not conducted in the glare of TV cameras and the former Indian Chief Justice had no investigative powers. Even after declaring all Indian players innocent of wrongdoing, the Chandrachud Report was not made public until, in the fallout from Hansiegate, the Indian government demanded it from the BCCI, some two-and-a-half years after the inquiry's completion. In his newly released findings, Justice Chandrachud admitted that he was '... inclined to believe that a large amount of betting takes place on cricket in India' primarily because he had been apprised of this fact by senior police officials. According to contemporary estimates quoted in an editorial in the *Asia Times Online* on 15 March 2007, enthusiastic Indian punters bet more than US$250 million on any important one-day international, particularly between the home side and Pakistan.[187] Chandrachud, in his report, philosophised that 'Betting, like drinking, is a common human weakness since the beginning of the world'.

After interviewing a glittering galaxy of India's cricket stars of the past and present, many of whom had reincarnated themselves as cricket coaches, administrators and media commentators, the Judge found that 'The data before me does not show any Indian player, official or journalist has ever taken part in fixing a match or that any of them lays bets on cricket for the purpose of match-fixing so as to lose a match.' He accused Prabhakar of trying to '... dilute if not destroy the glorious uncertainty, the fun, the charm and the camaraderie of a great game.' Yet, he remained upbeat about the 'gentleman's game'. 'Cricket, I believe, will take care of itself. It is too deeply rooted in our lives and too widely liked and loved to be damaged by unexamined outbursts of misguided individuals.' When his report was finally made public on 20 April 2000, one Indian print commentator summed up the document as a 'tattered figleaf'. In response, Chandrachud was far less eloquent than he had been in his report. 'In the best traditions of judicial functioning, I have decided not to comment.'[188]

At the time, Manoj Prabhakar called the report '... factually incorrect ... with little regard for the truth' and claimed that he was not even asked to name the player who offered him money to throw a match.[189] He had described his reaction to this team-mate's approach to Chandrachud: 'At the time in question when the incident occurred, I had informed the concerned persons and had been told to play my game and they would do the needful.' Justice Chandrachud, in his report, told a different story: 'It defies understanding as to why Manoj is afraid of disclosing the names even of those 'concerned persons' by which is evidently meant the officials of the Board or the manager, the captain and so on. There was surely no danger to his life in disclosing those names.' Prabhakar would disagree. In an interview with Indian Zee TV, four days after his initial revelations to *Outlook*, Prabhakar said, 'I have come to know this now, that the very people I had told would probably have finished me.'[190]

These words are reminiscent of Cronjé's testimony to the King Commission in South Africa three years later. 'I think it will be very dangerous for me at this stage, Mr Commissioner. I don't want to get into a situation where I disclose my relationship with the UCB.' Lending some credence to such fears, *India Today* reported on 14 July 2000 that the Indian prosecutor investigating the Cronjé case had received death threats and had been provided with heavy security.[191]

In 1997, however, Justice Chandrachud did not probe underworld links and did not interview any bookies, in spite of Prabhakar's assertion in the *Outlook* article that gave rise to the inquiry that 'The commercialisation of cricket has changed its face – it's no longer just a game; it's a game where money is the main motivator. Sponsors and bookies have started exerting pressure and games are now being increasingly fixed'. Prophetically, as it proved, Prabhakar declared, 'I feel that the day is not far when, if the Board is not vigilant enough, a major scandal might erupt.'[192] Three years later, it was the South Africans that precipitated the match-fixing crisis that threatened to bring down international cricket and India was caught up in the maelstrom.

Unsurprisingly perhaps, Manoj Prabhakar featured once again. This time, he purportedly had hidden-camera footage, handed in to the CBI in May 2000, of a number of administrators and former players talking of match-fixing within the Indian team. These were said to include BCCI Secretary Lele himself and the former Indian physiotherapist, Dr Ali Irani. This Ali Irani is the man who, in 1992/3, introduced Kapil Dev to that jolly purveyor of biltong to the South African team, Hamid 'Banjo' Cassim. The two have since become very good friends, according to suspected 'bagman' Cassim's testimony to the King Commission. Kapil Dev, in his statement to the CBI, confirmed the relationship, saying that he knew Cassim very well.

The Hansiegate tapes and Prabhakar's candid camera footage was not the only technological evidence thrown up by the gathering tide of the CBI's investigation. Earlier tapes in the possession of the Mumbai police and the Directorate of Revenue Intelligence (DRI) dating back to 1993 and, subsequently, 1996 came to light.

One of the mounting number of international cricket matches that have been tainted over the years includes the Titan Cup final between South Africa and India played in Mumbai on 6 November 1996. The Mumbai police were said to have taped conversations between bookies and several Indian players about this game, which India won. Three of the players were reputed to be the Indian captain at the time, Mohammad Azharuddin, as well as the wicketkeeper Nayan Mongia and specialist batsman Ajay Jadeja. Manoj Prabhakar's name also cropped up. Apparently, the same three names, as well as Prabhakar's, had come up before (and more than once) in Revenue Department tapes of telephone conversations between bookies in Mumbai and Sharjah in Dubai in the early 1990s. The Directorate of Revenue Intelligence forwarded this information to MR Sivaraman, the Revenue Secretary. He, in turn, handed on the names to the BCCI's Madhavrao Scindia sometime in 1995. 'I did what I thought was best and gave this important body of information along with the four names to Madhavrao Scindia, whom I have known for long,' he told the Indian magazine *Outlook* in June 2000.[193] In his turn, in a deposition to the CBI, Scindia denied receiving any tapes as he was not the BCCI President at the time and thus was not the man to approach with such material. The BCCI President in 1995 was, in fact, IS Bindra. In their statements to the Chandrachud Committee in 1997, the three cricketers linked to the Mumbai tapes denied all knowledge of match-fixing.

MOHAMMAD AZHARUDDIN: I do not think that any match can be fixed … I do not know if there is betting on cricket. But I know this for certain, that none of my team-mates bets.

NAYAN MONGIA: Matches are not fixed at all. I have been playing Test cricket since November/December 1993. I came to know about the expression 'fixing of matches' from newspapers only. As a member of the Indian team, I have never experienced it … I have never heard even a whisper of it from any team-mate … The team meets very often, we are together for long hours, we discuss our strategy but never, never, is there even a whisper of fixing a match or of batting [sic].

AJAY JADEJA: I believe that people bet on cricket … Our style of living has changed significantly which leads to various guesses and allegations. People think that we must be making money by illegal ways since we live so well … I do not think that in today's Indian team there is any player who bets on the game. It is true that, at one time, friends used to have access to the players' enclosure and sometimes they used to speak on mobile phones. Now mobiles are not allowed after we leave our hotel. No friends are now allowed in the players' enclosure, much less in the dressing room.

And there, it would seem, the matter came to rest until the CBI released their report into match-fixing in November 2000. This time the underworld connection was not neglected and an impressive array of India's most influential bookies and punters were interrogated. One of the mobsters involved listed gun-running, supplying terrorists and cricket match-fixing as his principal sources of income.[194]

The report implicated five Indian players: Nayan Mongia, Ajay Sharma, Mohammad Azharuddin, Ajay Jadeja and Manoj Prabhakar who, ironically, had been the first to blow the whistle on Indian cricket. But the report didn't stop there. It also named nine international stars, eight of them former captains, from every Test-playing nation of the world with the exception of Zimbabwe and newcomer Bangladesh. The foreign players named included: Hansie Cronjé (South Africa), Alec Stewart (England), Martin Crowe (New Zealand), Mark Waugh (Australia), Brian Lara (West Indies), Arjuna Ranatunga and Aravinda de Silva (Sri Lanka), and Asif Iqbal and Salim Malik (Pakistan).

The CBI's star witness was New Delhi bookie Mukesh Gupta and much of the report is devoted to his revelations. MK Gupta identified Prabhakar as the man who, for a fee, introduced him to some of the world's leading cricketers. However, it was not Prabhakar but Mohammad Azharuddin who put Mukesh Gupta in touch with physiotherapist Ali Irani during the first Test against South Africa at Ahmedabad in 1996. The CBI Report claimed that Irani became Azhar's middleman in his illicit financial dealings with MK. 'Evidence has disclosed that Dr Ali Irani was collecting money on behalf of Azhar from MK and his associates and that he used to get a "commission" from Azhar for his service.'

Ali Irani was the Indian team's physiotherapist almost uninterruptedly between 1987 and 1997. As Indian journalist Pradeep Magazine remarked in his book *Not Quite Cricket*, 'Dr Irani, it was obvious to everyone, had a godfather on the Board. To have remained with the Indian team for so long as its trainer, when the Board is often used to changing coaches and managers every so often, with or without reason, was an extraordinary feat'.[195]

In the wake of the Indian Cricket Board's sentencing of the match-fixers named in the CBI Report, South Africans expressed astonishment at the five-year ban imposed upon Dr Irani. Mike Wills of *Cape Talk Radio* was bemused by the involvement of a physiotherapist in cricket's increasingly dirty dealings while Shaun Pollock, the new South African captain, joked with a radio presenter about South Africa's physiotherapist Craig Smith cooking up an injury to pocket some extra cash. Coincidentally Smith, like Irani, was one of the longest-serving members of the South African team, having been involved since the Proteas' readmission to world cricket in 1991. However, his contract with the UCB was not renewed in 2002. Given the surprise expressed at a team's physiotherapist being in on the fix, it would seem that the South African media had not been doing their homework. Irani's name had come up repeatedly in various international cricket inquiries, including South Africa's King Commission, where Hamid Cassim, suspected middleman in Cronjé's extra-curricular finances, testified to his association with the Indian physiotherapist.

Just after the sports boycott had been lifted, the Indians visited South Africa on the so-called 'Goodwill Tour' of 1992/93. Before arriving in South Africa, the Indians had first played in Zimbabwe and it was here that Hamid Cassim's sister-in-law met Dr Ali Irani. Brother-in-law Banjo was introduced to Irani at a warm-up game in Springs and that night, in Irani's room at the Sandton Sun, he met Kapil Dev, dined with him and showed him the bright lights of Jo'burg. Thus began Cassim's association with the cricket teams of South Africa and the subcontinent. The Pakistani and Indian teams enjoyed vegetarian dinners at Banjo's brother's place in Jo'burg, were wined and dined by Cassim's nieces in Cape Town and Ajay Jadeja, Javagal Srinath and Ajit Agarkar had medical treatment and surgery arranged in South Africa by Cassim himself. A busy Banjo met Hansie Cronjé later this same year while Cronjé was playing in the five-nation (India, South Africa, West Indies, Sri Lanka and Zimbabwe) Hero Cup in India in November 1993 and became 'friendly' with him during a 1996 tournament in Sharjah where they exchanged cellphone numbers. The final link in the chain that connects a Johannesburg sweet-shop owner, an Indian physiotherapist and two former disgraced international cricket captains is provided by Hansie Cronjé's deposition to the King Commission. It was Azharuddin who introduced him to MK at Kanpur during the third Test of that fateful tour of India in 1996. Former South African coach Bob Woolmer recalled that meeting in an article on *cricinfo.com* in October 2006. 'It was in Kanpur that Hansie Cronjé was invited by Mohammad Azharuddin to meet a keen cricket fan. I was present when they were introduced in the lobby and then they went off to a room. What happened then has been recorded at the King Commission held in 2000 in Cape Town.'[196]

In South Africa, the King Commission was following its own yellow brick road, beginning its public hearings into corruption in South African cricket on 7 June 2000. Ali Bacher, Managing Director of the South African Cricket Board and Jagmohan Dalmiya's former ICC colleague, phoned a number of people the day before his appearance before the King Commission to let them know the contents of his statement. He explained to the King Commission that:

> One was Mr Jagmohan Dalmiya, who is the President of the ICC, he's based in Calcutta. I have known him for more than a decade. He, in fact, was the driving force in 1991 to get South Africa back into international cricket. So we have a long, long association. He's under siege at the moment, which is sad. There are question marks about his integrity and I made it very clear to him yesterday on the phone that he has my support, I would not question his integrity.

Others, however, would.

Described as a 'shadowy character' by Greg Baum in an article on an Australian cricket website,[197] Jagmohan Dalmiya comes from a well-to-do Calcutta family and inherited the family's prosperous construction business at an early age. An opening batsman and wicketkeeper for one of Calcutta's foremost cricket clubs, he joined the Board of Control for Cricket in India in 1979. The revenue potential of televised one-day internationals became apparent after Kapil Dev captained the Indians to their 1983 World Cup victory, the same year that Dalmiya became Secretary of the BCCI. Ironically, the CBI Report traced the beginnings of the endemic scourge of cricket corruption to this cricketing milestone, which marked the start of regular TV broadcasts of Indian matches both home and abroad and now, 'Any cricket match which is shown live on TV, whether an international, domestic, veteran or festival match, activates the betting syndicate' concluded the CBI. Modern technology brought cricket to the world. Computers, the Internet, satellite TV and cellphones made gambling on the game an international, 24 hour-a-day pastime.

Inderjit Singh Bindra was President of the BCCI from 1993 to 1996 at the same time as Jagmohan Dalmiya was Secretary. It was the businessman Dalmiya, and the bureaucrat Bindra, that oversaw the commercialisation of cricket in India and the proliferation of one-day cricket, or so-called 'masala matches' (pyjama tournaments) in satellite venues like Sharjah, Toronto, Kenya and Dhaka. Together they waged and won a legal battle against the government TV channel Doordarshan's monopoly on TV rights. The Board then sold the Indian rights to TransWorld International and ESPN from 1994 to 1998 in a deal that garnered an estimated US$35 million and saw the Board's finances improve immeasurably.[198] Today, the BCCI is the world's richest cricket association with profits of some US$7,64 million in 2005/6.[199] Some nifty political machinations amongst cricket's minnows saw Dalmiya out-manoeuvre England for the right to host the 1996 World Cup, which took place in India, Pakistan and Sri Lanka. In a lucrative deal, the BCCI awarded the worldwide TV rights to the World Cup to Mark Mascarenhas of WorldTel. The estimated US$80 million success of the subcontinent's World Cup and the same minor cricketing nations helped Dalmiya to beat the Australian challenger to the title and become the first non-white President of the ICC in June 1997. This milestone year also marked the fiftieth anniversary of Indian independence from the British. Yet old attitudes die hard. Regarded as a safari-suited interloper in the hallowed halls of Lords, Dalmiya's celebration party in London was marred by the absence of the then England and Wales Board Chairman, Lord MacLaurin, as well as representatives from the West Indies, Australia, New Zealand and South Africa.[200]

The BCCI is a non-profit organisation whose task is to administer Indian cricket. It is exempt from tax on the condition that its income is spent '... wholly and exclusively to the objects for which it is established,'[201] namely the administration and upliftment of Indian cricket. In May 1996, the BCCI sanctioned £30 000 sterling '... to meet the expenses towards legal expenses, fees of solicitors, meetings with different member countries as well as dinner for the ICC members in connection with India's candidature of the ICC chairman elect.'[202] Thus at the exchange rates of April 2001, some US$60 000 was spent on getting Dalmiya elected to the ICC. Coaching expenditure for the same year was around US$20 000.[203]

The relationship between Bindra and Dalmiya deteriorated in direct proportion, it seems, to Dalmiya's elevation in the cricketing world. Faction fighting postponed the BCCI elections in November 1997. Bindra objected to Dalmiya continuing to involve himself in the Indian Cricket Board, despite the ICC's own prohibition on its President holding other cricketing posts. The following year, the issue had yet to be resolved and the *Indian Express* reported Bindra's comments to a colleague during a BCCI committee meeting on 10 August 1998. 'The Board is acting like a mafia,' the newspaper quoted Bindra as saying.[204] Bindra explained this falling out with the Board he once led as due to '... differences regarding the administration of the game in the country as well as globally. The main reason was the privatisation of Indian cricket in the garb of globalisation.'[205]

In the aftermath of Hansie's confession, Bindra took the opportunity to take another swipe at his old adversary. 'Virtually every match in international cricket is fixed in one form or another. Match-fixing is as old as the game itself,' Bindra told a press conference he had called in New Delhi on 19 April 2000: 'Cricketers from all countries are involved. Dalmiya is in the grip of mafia and sharks. Hansie has become a hero by confessing. If Dalmiya confesses, he will be a bigger hero.'[206]

Three days later, at another press conference, this time in Mohali, Bindra disclosed that he and his wife had received death threats aimed at his children just before the New Delhi media briefing. Undeterred, Bindra challenged Dalmiya to a public debate and repeated his previous allegations that '... the people behind match-fixing are a handful of cricket administrators and others with vested commercial interests.'[207] In the wake of the latest scandal to rock the 'gentleman's game', he affirmed that despite '... living with threats to my personal being, I will be first to help in any way possible ... If it is names they want, they will get names,' Bindra promised on 28 April 2000.[208] Dave Richards, the then Chief Executive of the ICC, confirmed receiving correspondence from Bindra: 'He has written to us indicating that he has a certain amount of information so we advised him to contact our solicitors.'[209] The ICC did not invite Bindra to their emergency session of 2 May 2000 at which incumbent President Jagmohan Dalmiya was cleared of allegations of malpractice by the ICC governing body shortly before stepping down from his position the following month. According to the accusations, the extra-India TV rights to the 1998 ICC Trophy in Bangladesh were sold, in a cut-price deal, to WorldTel, a company in which Dalmiya had an interest. Bindra was forced instead to submit his 360 pages of evidence to the CBI.

Undaunted by the ICC's response, and proving true to his word, two days later, in an interview with CNN on 4 May 2000, Bindra named names, saying that Prabhakar had identified former Indian captain and incumbent coach Kapil Dev as the team-mate who had paid him to under-perform in the Singer Cup against Pakistan in Sri Lanka in 1994. Kapil Dev had told the Chandrachud Inquiry in 1997 that 'In my entire career as a player, I was never approached by anyone for match-fixing. I guess that there is large betting on cricket but the evil of betting can be dealt with only by the police. Today, there is so much cricket that there is so much betting also. Those who lose their bets are the first to blame the players for playing bad deliberately.'

Interestingly, Bindra had been involved in a joint business venture with Kapil Dev for the floodlighting of his pet project, the Punjab Cricket Association stadium in Mohali.[210] Bindra was subsequently charged by the ubiquitous CBI with the misuse of his position in getting the stadium built. Arch-nemesis Jagmohan Dalmiya was fingered as being behind the CBI's probe.[211] Whatever Bindra's motives for the allegations against his business partner, Kapil Dev,

Prabhakar's were more open to speculation. His well-publicised fall-out with Kapil Dev went back to the Indian tour of Australia in the 1991/92 season. At the time, Azharuddin's captaincy was under threat and there was talk of bringing back Dev as captain. Prabhakar made some injudicious comments to a sports magazine about Azharuddin's leadership and, in the uproar that followed, Prabhakar subsequently blamed Dev for using him.

As the CBI's investigation gathered momentum in India, the weekend of the 20 July 2000 saw over three hundred revenue officials and CBI investigators swoop on eighty-four premises in seven Indian cities. The homes and offices of those raided included bookies, eight cricketers, two administrators, one of whom was Jagmohan Dalmiya, and a TV executive, one Mark Mascarenhas, the CEO of WorldTel, the company that was implicated along with Dalmiya in the 1998 TV rights malpractice charges.

In the tax raids of July 2000, code-named Operation Gentleman, Mohammad Azharuddin's flat was among those searched, as was the family home of his Bollywood actress wife Sangita and their own home. After this inspection, an income tax official in Mumbai was reported by the *Cape Argus* as saying that they had evidence of the '... stockpiling of massive undisclosed property and income'.[212]

While naming no names, Vishwa Gupta, a high-ranking Indian tax commissioner, told Australian reporter Liz Jackson that a 'leading cricket player' had some US$50 million in unexplained income.[213] Kapil Dev and batsman Ajay Jadeja were also on the visiting list, as was Nayan Mongia, Manoj Prabhakar and former Indian cricket player Ajay Sharma. Ajay Sharma's credentials come self-proclaimed: 'I am one of five cricketers headed by Sir Don Bradman to have scored over 10 000 runs', he pointed out in an online interview with *India Today's* principal correspondent, Sayantan Chakravarty, on 20 June 2000.[214] He was also on quite another select list, according to India's Central Bureau of Investigation. His phone records revealed hundreds of calls to bookies and a steady stream of calls to Azharuddin's mobile phone before every match of the past Indian season and the preceding four. The tax men also paid bookie Mukesh Gupta a visit.

Following a second raid on Dalmiya, Mascarenhas and Doordarshan officials on 13 November 2000, this time by CBI investigators, a case of criminal conspiracy was laid against Dalmiya, WorldTel's Mascarenhas and six TV executives from the government TV channel Doordarshan. Subsequently, Dhananjaya Kumar, the Indian Minister of State for Finance, publicly stated that Mascarenhas was involved in match-fixing and a CBI official revealed that they were investigating his links with Mumbai bookie Shobhan Mehta. Mascarenhas declared: 'Such an allegation is baseless and defamatory. Neither

WorldTel nor I have any connection with bookies.'[215] Mascarenhas died in a car crash in a game park in India in January 2002, the same year that a plane crash killed Hansie Cronjé.[216]

The First Information Report filed on 13 November 2000 charged Dalmiya with having a vested interest in WorldTel's bid for the TV rights to the 1998 ICC Tournament knockout championships, which WorldTel were awarded despite a higher bid from Doordarshan. Sunil Dev, the former Indian coach whose 1997 tour report had helped precipitate the Chandrachud Commission, had claimed that same year that Dalmiya had been doing business with WorldTel and Doordarshan regarding TV rights for the 1997 Independence Cup. The CBI was investigating these two tournaments as well as Wimbledon, the French Open and the 1999 World Cup, all deals concluded while Dalmiya was President of the ICC. Dalmiya was cleared by his ICC fellows on 2 May 2000, shortly before stepping down from his position, only to be elected President of the BCCI the following year.

By the end of 2000, the Indian newspaper *The Statesman* reported in December that Kapil Dev and Mohammad Azharuddin were likely to feature high on the list of cricket's tax defaulters.[217] Dev was cleared of all match-fixing charges but resigned his position as the Indian coach. Azharuddin was not so fortunate. He found himself under a life ban along with his good friend, Ajay Sharma. The CBI's Report on Cricket Match-fixing, released at the end of 2000, found that '… the facts disclosed during the inquiry, clearly establish that Ajay Sharma acted as a conduit between the players and the betting syndicates in fixing matches.' While Nayan Mongia escaped the axe, Prabhakar was banned for five years and with him, fellow cricketer Ajay Jadeja and physiotherapist Ali Irani.

Azharuddin should have seen it coming. With the Chandrachud Report safely shelved, he had imparted a little folk wisdom to Indian journalist Pradeep Magazine, during a Test against Sri Lanka in Nagpur in December 1997. 'Crabs from various countries are exported in sealed tins. Only from India are they exported with the lid of the tin open. Do you know why? Simple. These crabs are Indian. The moment one gets to the top, the one below him will pull him down.'[218]

But not for long.

Ajay Jadeja's ban was overturned by the Delhi High Court in January 2003 and by June he was back playing domestic cricket. Jadeja was appointed as captain and caretaker coach of the Rajasthan Cricket Association in 2005. Prabhakar sat out his five-year ban, running unsuccessfully for Parliament and promoting his company's aromatherapy beauty products. But by 2006, he was back on the cricket pitch, appearing in veterans' tournaments against Pakistan in 2006 and in February 2007, along with Nayan Mongia and captain Mohammad

Azharuddin. While Azhar's life ban from Test and first-class cricket remains in force, Azharuddin was honoured with a lifetime achievement award by the BCCI in November 2006. Today, Ali Irani is the President of the Indian Association of Physiotherapists.

Jagmohan Dalmiya lost the BCCI presidential election in November 2005 and his successor, Sharad Pawar, wasted no time in instigating an internal enquiry into alleged financial irregularities during Dalmiya's tenure as BCCI president. The charges related to the mishandling of funds from the so-called PILCOM account created when Pakistan, India and Sri Lanka hosted the 1996 World Cup. The BCCI filed criminal charges against Dalmiya and expelled him from the organisation for life on 16 December 2006. In July 2007, the Calcutta High Court issued a stay on his suspension from the BCCI and Dalmiya was once more on the come-back trail. To date, nobody implicated in cricket corruption has ever been found guilty of a criminal offence.

11

The bookies and the dons

The underworld connection

Cricket cannot be compared to horse racing where mafias rule the roost.

– X. Pradeep Vijaykar: Assistant Sports Editor, *Times of India*, to the Chandrachud Commission

The tortuous course of international match-fixing never did run smooth. According to the official version of events, a routine extortion investigation would lead to the phone tapping that precipitated cricket's biggest scandal. On 26 June 1999, a new case landed on the desk of Inspector Ishwar Singh of the Delhi Crime Branch. The Chairman and senior executives of Apollo Tyre Groups in New Delhi had complained of receiving extortion threats.[219] Inspector Ishwar Singh was tapping the phone of a certain Salim Hathela, allegedly a member of underworld don Dawood Ibrahim's D-Company.[220] Inspector Singh found a link between the cell numbers of the extortionists and threatening calls made to Bollywood film actor Kishen Kumar, younger brother of murdered music baron Gulshan Kumar. Big brother Gulshan was murdered in 1997 by suspected Mumbai underworld operatives who ran an extortion ring. The mob and the movies are inextricably linked in India. The populous country makes over 700 films a year, leading the world in film production. India's mafia fashions itself on the movies while India's filmmakers draw on the gangsters' experiences to make their films. The mob rubs shoulders with the glitterati, the cricketers and Bollywood stars, and movies are used to wash dirty money.

Attention turned to Kishen Kumar's phone records. By late February 2000, Detective Singh had identified two numbers that were regularly dialled – one belonged to Sanjeev Chawla, a native of Delhi who moved in the early 1990s to Britain, where he ran a clothes shop called Toro on Oxford Street in London. The second number belonged to a certain printing-press owner and illegal bookie, Rajesh Kalra. Further scrutiny of phone records showed Chawla and Kalra to have been in close contact with each other. Singh applied for permission to tap these phones and was given the go-ahead in early March, when the South African cricket team was on tour in India. It was during one of these recorded conversations that Sanjeev Chawla is said to have told Kishen Kumar, 'Matters have been settled with Hansie Cronjé.'[221] Kumar was interrogated on 6 April but was released for lack of evidence. Kalra, however, was arrested that same night, while Kumar checked into hospital the next day with angina pains, which prevented him from speaking to the police. Rajesh Kalra was more forthcoming. Apparently, he told the Delhi police that Kumar was '… an agent who collected money from different people and put them into betting in one-day matches.'[222] The *Cape Times* reported on 17 April 2000 that Chawla had booked into the Taj Hotel in Mumbai, where the South African cricketers were staying, three days before the start of the first Test. He reportedly paid his hotel bill by credit card – in the name of Kishen Kumar.[223]

However, Scyld Berry in *The Telegraph* tells a different story.[224] Apparently, some members of the Delhi police force had placed (and lost) substantial bets on the five-match ODI series being played between India and South Africa from 9 to 19 March 2000. The police then discovered that the Asian mafia had influenced these matches. In order to get their money back, the police tapped Hansie Cronjé's phone and the rest, as they say, is history. However Hansiegate came about, the tapping of Cronjé's phone snowballed into an avalanche of international investigations that would carry away a number of the world's cricketing icons.

Conspiracies and ironies jostled for pole position with the much-awaited release of the Indian Central Bureau of Investigation Report at the beginning of November 2000. The report confirmed that while betting on cricket is nothing new, never before has it been so widespread. TV, cable and now cellphones and STD booths all aid the bookies in their business and business, it seems, is brisk.

Despite the fact that betting on cricket is illegal in India, the billion-dollar cash industry is a finely-tuned machine. Chennai-based journalist Syed Ali Mujtaba explained how the machine works in an article published on the *indolink.com* website on 27 May 2007.[225] According to Mujtaba, the illegal betting operation is controlled by a foreign syndicate, believed to be Dawood Ibrahim's D-Company run out of either Dubai or Karachi. The syndicate defines its territories and selects people to control its operations in these territories. Mumbai is the Indian head office and most of the bookies involved are in Mumbai and New Delhi. The bookies operate according to a financial hierarchy with those on the bottom rung dealing in small stakes. The next tier interacts with the Mumbai head office while those bookies who deal in the most cash communicate directly with the overseas syndicate. It is the syndicate that sets the betting odds and these change as the cricket match progresses. A punter will watch the game on TV and check in regularly with the bookies to find out the changing rate and place his bets accordingly. Often these interactions are done by SMS. Punters use a prearranged codename to identify themselves and even the amount of money they bet is in code. The wager is recorded so there can be no debate. It is only at the end of the game that the punter will know how much he has won or lost. If fortune has smiled on the gambler, he will be given an address from where to collect his money. If not, bet collectors will arrive at his door and strong-arm tactics may be used to keep everyone honest. The bookies themselves also bet and thus work to influence the games so as to protect their interests.

Bookies are hand-picked based on their financial capacity and their relationships with the authorities, who allegedly receive regular pay-offs to ensure the bookies stay in business. Lending credence to this claim is the incident of the twenty-three bookies who were picked up by the Mumbai police in January 2003. The bookies had apparently got together to arrange a payment of Rs50 lakh (US$123 000) to the police so that they could operate unhindered during the World Cup in South Africa. Betting kingpin Shobhan Mehta and Jagdish Sodha of Stephen Fleming, Chris Lewis and Maurice Odumbe fame, were among those arrested. However, the bookies were released from custody soon after, allegedly on the instructions of Joint Commissioner of Police (Intelligence) Sridhar Wagal. Nine months later, on 7 November, Wagal himself was taken into custody on the charge of accepting bribes from Abdul Karim Telgi, a stamp counterfeiter.[226]

The CBI Report asserted that 'Betting on cricket is today ... perhaps the biggest organised racket in the country'. Although sports betting is illegal in India, the Public Gaming Act is not much of a deterrent. According to the lengthy report: 'The maximum punishment under this Act, for example in Delhi, for a first offence is imprisonment for 6 months and a fine of Rs1 000 (US$20) and for subsequent offences, a maximum punishment of imprisonment for 1 year and a fine of Rs2 000 (US$40).' Given the vast sums of money generated by crooked cricket, the rewards far outweigh the risks. The underworld seems to have come to the same conclusion and the CBI Report warned that '... it is only a matter of time before major organised gangs take direct control of this racket, a phenomenon that would have implications not only for cricket but for national security as a whole'. There is an array of evidence to suggest that this is, in fact, already the case.

In an early stage of their investigation into Cronjé and his cronies, the Delhi police revealed that they wished to question Indian cricketer Mohammad Azharuddin about the murder of a Mumbai diamond dealer named Ashraf Patel. The dead man was suspected of being the target of 'a ... powerful bookie network that stretches from Mumbai to Dubai' and the police confirmed that match-fixing as a motive in his murder could not be ruled out.[227]

One of the first links between the underworld and cricket fixing was unearthed in New Delhi when police raided so-called mafia boss Yudhishtar Kumar in

1996 and arrested his son Deepak Kumar for cricket-booking. Deepak's partner Poley and Hans Kumar Jain are other bookies who are said to operate for the alleged Delhi drug-lord. Many bookies who got into the cricket betting racket apparently started out in horse racing, as did Dubai-based businessman Sharad Shetty. After turning his attentions from the track to the cricket pitch, Shetty is widely credited with blazing the trail which others followed – such as Dawood Ibrahim, brother Anees Ibrahim and Chhota Shakeel of D-Company, [228] and D-Company's rivals, Mumbai-based Shobhan Mehta and Chhota Rajan, who started out as Dawood's lieutenant. Sharad Shetty, suspected of being Dawood Ibrahim's financier in his illegal betting industry, was gunned down at the India Club in Dubai on 19 January 2003, in the run-up to the World Cup in South Africa. Chhota Rajan's gang was thought to be behind the hit.[229]

Diverse sources claim that it is Dawood Ibrahim's D-Company that is the main player in cricket gambling. The son of an Indian police constable, Ibrahim failed to follow in his father's footsteps. For the past twenty years, Ibrahim has been one of the leading criminals in the Asian underworld. As head of D-Company he presides over an empire of prostitution, drugs and gambling. In 2003, the US Treasury Department labelled Dawood a Specially Designated Global Terrorist. According to the fact sheet attached to the press release: 'Ibrahim's syndicate is involved in large-scale shipment of narcotics in the UK and Western Europe.' Al Qaeda has a 'financial arrangement' with Dawood for the use of his drug-smuggling routes through South Asia, the Middle East and Africa. The US also contends that Dawood's syndicate financially supports Islamic militant groups working against India.[230] Along with his younger brother Anees, Dawood is wanted by the Indian government for the 1993 Bombay Exchange and Air India bombings in which 257 people died and more than 2 000 were wounded.[231] Sources quoted by *The Tribune* newspaper in India said that Anees was questioned by the Americans in connection with attacks on Israeli tourists in Mombasa, Kenya in 2002.[232] Anees Ibrahim has been linked with fallen Indian cricket icon Mohammad Azharuddin. Big brother Dawood has even closer ties with Pakistan's former cricket coach and captain Javed Miandad. Ibrahim's son is married to one of the don's daughters.[233] But it is not only cricketers with whom Dawood likes to consort. He has been connected to the Indian film industry, having allegedly financed a number of films and 'persuaded' Bollywood stars to act in them. Dawood's predilections are no secret. The don was spotted on Indian TV watching international cricket matches in Sharjah with some of Bollywood's finest.[234] After fleeing Mumbai to escape criminal prosecution in 1986, Ibrahim was based for a long period in the United Arab Emirates state of Dubai. It is said that he now directs his operations from Pakistan.

In the aftermath of the Cronjé affair, Indian police and bookies alike asserted that the cricket trade was controlled by Dubai. A top Mumbai bookie confirmed this in the Indian magazine *Outlook* on 24 April 2000. According to the source, the Mumbai mob stand aside for Dawood's people whenever there is an India/Pakistan match in Sharjah.[235] All roads, it seems, lead to Sharjah, the United Arab Emirates venue that has, since 1984, staged the most one-day internationals in the world.[236] The former Secretary of the BCCI Jaywant Lele admitted, 'The truth is that when India was going to Sharjah in 1987, a person approached us and said that he was a fan of the Indian team and that India should win. If it wins, he would give each of us a Toyota car. Then people said he was Dawood Ibrahim and that he was a big industrialist.'[237] Dave Richardson, former South African wicketkeeper, described the Sharjah competitions in testimony to the King Commission in June 2000: 'The United Cricket Board treats it as a place where they often allow wives and girlfriends to go, so it's a pleasant tournament to play in.' The International Cricket Council (ICC) moved its headquarters to Dubai in 2005.

Asif Iqbal is a former Pakistani captain who played 58 Tests for his country and earned the Wisden Cricketer of the Year award in 1968. His long association with cricket includes a stint as ICC Match Referee and ICC Cricket Ambassador 2000; he has been a '... commentator, columnist, tournament director and event manager'[238] as well as chief co-ordinator of the Cricketers' Benefit Fund Series (CBFS) in Sharjah until his resignation in April 2001. Such is his public face. Behind the scenes, the name of Asif Iqbal is one that comes up again and again in connection with cricket corruption. Former players, officials and bookies alike credit him with the entrenching of crooked cricket in the United Arab Emirates betting hub of Sharjah.

In his testimony to the Qayyum Commission, Sarfraz Nawaz, former Pakistani captain and special advisor to one-time Pakistani Prime Minister Benazir Bhutto, accused Asif Iqbal of paying to fix the 1987 World Cup semi-final between Pakistan and Australia in Lahore. The long-serving Pakistani team manager Intikhab Alam asserted on record to a Pakistani match-fixing inquiry that Asif Iqbal was linked to bookies. Indian bookie Anil Steel, who was in partnership with well-connected bookie/punter MK Gupta, admitted to the Indian investigators that he was 'very friendly' with Iqbal and often exchanged 'gifts' for 'information' provided by Iqbal on international matches. It was Anil Steel that introduced Iqbal to MK, according to MK's revelations to the CBI investigators. MK claimed that Asif Iqbal, in turn, introduced him to Sri Lankan all-rounder Sanath Jayasuriya, who, insisted MK, refused to do any matches for him.

South African journalist Neil Manthorp confirmed the general consensus that institutionalised match-fixing goes back '... probably to the beginning of Sharjah. That was what Sharjah was all about. Once again, there are so many clever fronts and ruses. Now Asif Iqbal had every reason to want to put on a good cricket tournament, he's got such a brilliant track record, so he was a very clever choice as front man. He knew exactly what he was doing. Of course, you get people in every sport who say, look, as long as it's a good show, who cares!'

In South Africa, the Northerns Cricket Academy nurtures the talent of up-and-coming young cricket stars. For a number of years they used an imported video called *Cover Point* to alert the young players to the dangers of bribery and corruption in cricket. The video was presented by Asif Iqbal.[239]

The CBI's investigations, however, centred on India and the report lists a choice selection of the country's most influential bookies and punters. Prominent Mumbai bookie and Dawood's arch-rival, Shobhan Mehta, is featured in the CBI Report. Apparently, in April 1999, during the Coca-Cola Cup in Sharjah, Dawood lost almost US$4 million on a Pakistan/England match. He discovered that a Mumbai syndicate had paid the Pakistanis to lose. The order was passed down to the bookies that all bets were off. However, Shobhan Mehta refused and so began a bitter rivalry that encompassed a failed assassination attempt on Mehta and culminated in Dawood shopping Mehta to the police in 2005. When Shobhan Mehta was arrested in Mumbai in May 2005, police sources claimed that he had confessed to receiving match-influencing 'tips' from prominent cricketers including: Nayan Mongia, Ajay Jadeja, Mohammad Azharuddin, Mark Waugh and Hansie Cronjé.[240]

MK Gupta is perhaps the best-known name on the CBI's roll of infamy. MK's erstwhile partner, Mumbai-based Anil Steel, is also named as a bookie. Punters on the list include the well-connected New Delhi restaurateur and high-roller Ratan Mehta and Rajesh Kalra, who bears the dubious distinction of being the first to be picked up in the cheating, fraud and criminal conspiracy charge laid by the New Delhi police on 7 April 2000.

The elusive Hansiegate transcripts reportedly reveal that Kalra was in touch with both Cronjé and Sanjeev Chawla during the contentious Pepsi ODI series in India in March 2000. Rajesh Kalra's association with Hansie Cronjé, although he claimed never to have met the ex-South African captain, is not Kalra's only cricketing liaison, it seems. As phone records would show, the Indian bookie/punter was also personally acquainted with Manoj Prabhakar, Ajay Jadeja and bowler Nikhil Chopra, who was cleared by the Board of Control of Cricket in India (BCCI) of all complicity with bookmakers in January 2001, despite the fact that his name appears to have come up more than once in the police recordings of that five-match, one-day series. Coincidentally, one must assume, Chopra also happened to live next to MK Gupta in Delhi's Defence Colony.

When asked by the CBI whether Chopra had provided Kalra with information about cricket matches, Kalra stated that once, probably in the India/South Africa one-day match at Nagpur, he had rung up to find out whether Nikhil Chopra was in the team or not. He further stated that he wanted this information since Sanjeev Chawla had asked him to 'get the same'. Chopra was in the team for the fifth ODI at Nagpur but failed to impress with his 10 overs going for 57 runs with only 1 wicket to show for the effort – that of Hansie Cronjé. Kalra also confessed to knowing Ajay Jadeja '... very well and has contacted him on the telephone on a couple of occasions'.

The CBI would learn much from this subcaste of Indian society, especially since co-operation from the cricket community was not forthcoming. According to the Bureau's report, investigators were confronted with a '... conspiracy of silence ... Not a single player/ex-player/official etc, other than those who had made vague and general allegations in the media, volunteered any information to the CBI.' Thus, much as in South Africa where the Jo'burg bookie Marlon Aronstam stole the show at the King Commission, so the CBI's star witness is a bank-clerk-turned-bookie and high-flying punter named Mukesh Kumar Gupta. The nexus between bookies and their agents, punters, players and former players is graphically illustrated in his lengthy depositions to the CBI.

MK's 'chequered' career follows closely the development of cricket gambling in India. A bank clerk in New Delhi from 1982 to 1989, he supplemented his official pay cheques with money won on cricket betting, both as a punter and as a bookie. He started off small, indulging in sidewalk bets on the street near his home in Delhi, but through reading and research his informed wagers steadily brought their own rewards. By 1986, MK had accrued a tidy sum and decided it was time to move on up to the big boys in Mumbai at that time, Mama and Kamate. It was through a bank client that he was introduced to Anand Saxena, a sports punter who was to become his first partner in this lucrative sideline. By all accounts the World Cup of 1987 brought both men excellent dividends. Saxena himself, when interviewed by the CBI, denied any personal involvement with cricket players and maintained that he was just the bookie who did the books. MK, however, admitted to a string of cricketing acquaintances over the years that included most of the captains of the Test-playing world. It was Indian cricketer Ajay Sharma who, in 1988, helped MK get a foot in the dressing-room door.

In 1990, at MK's request, Sharma introduced him to Indian team-mate, Manoj Prabhakar, who also, MK claimed, became a member of his regular payroll. When Ajay Sharma was dropped from the Indian team that same year, Prabhakar took over as a jack of all trades, providing MK with 'information', under-performing in Test matches and introducing the bookie to other players, both Indian and international. Gupta's list of cricketers introduced by Prabhakar reads like an inventory of international cricket icons: Sri Lanka's Aravinda de Silva and Arjuna Ranatunga, Australia's Dean Jones and Mark Waugh, Pakistan's Salim Malik, the West Indies' Brian Lara and Alec Stewart of England. Prabhakar denied the introductions to De Silva, Ranatunga and Dean Jones but confirmed the rest. For these services, his remuneration was both prodigious and varied, earning him, among other things, a Maruti Gypsy '... with wide tyres'.

However, by the end of 1994, Prabhakar's 'information' was turning out to be wrong more often than not, yet his financial demands were unceasing. MK also had a falling out with his partner Anand Saxena and, while Saxena and Prabhakar stayed in touch, MK embarked upon a new chapter in his cricket career, turning punter and becoming involved with Anil Steel. It was through Steel that MK met the head of Sharjah cricket, Asif Iqbal, at the inaugural ceremony of the 1996 World Cup in Calcutta. Ajay Sharma, in need of new wheels, resumed contact with MK and with an eye on a Zen car, offered to arrange a meeting with Mohammad Azharuddin. Azhar confirmed this encounter at the Hotel Taj Palace in Delhi, '... sometime in 1995'.

Over a year later, it was Azharuddin who, according to Cronjé, introduced him to MK in December 1996, on the third day of the final Test against India at Kanpur. Azhar corroborated this evidence. However, this wasn't the former South African captain's first encounter with a bookie. That was two years previously, in Cape Town. The South Africans were playing Pakistan in the first leg of the Mandela Cup Final at Newlands on 10 January 1995. Before the match, a man named 'John', posing as a journalist, came up to Cronjé's room and offered him US$10 000 to influence the game to his advantage. Cronjé asserted in evidence that this person was the same 'John' who paid Shane Warne and Mark Waugh for 'information' in 1994/95. In 1998, the Chair of the Australian Inquiry into Player Conduct, Rob O'Regan, made unsuccessful attempts to identify this bookie 'John'. 'According to a journalist familiar with cricket matters on the subcontinent, he is also known as Pinky.' This name also appears on the Pakistan Ehtesaab Bureau's list of bookies. Two years later, the Indians went one step further and the CBI Report released in November 2000 clearly identifies John as Mukesh Gupta. If John is MK, then Cronjé met the Delhi bookie and punter two years before he said he did, in January 1995 rather than December 1996, at home rather than on the subcontinent and possibly without the intervention of Azharuddin, who claimed to have himself only met MK 'sometime in 1995'.

Be that as it may, Azhar and MK embarked upon a business relationship. In interviews with the CBI, Azharuddin '…accepted that he had taken money on some occasions from MK but did not under-perform in most of the matches in which he had taken money'. This is reminiscent of Hansie Cronjé's testimony to the King Commission where significant sums of money changed hands merely for innocuous 'information'. The Indian investigators were under no illusions about the meaning of the word 'information' – the CBI Report asserts that the word is '… a euphemism for under-performing or fixing'.

While Azhar denied following through on the many gambling deals brokered over the years, he did confess to fixing three matches; the first of which was the seventh match of the Titan Cup series against South Africa at Rajkot in 1996. It was during this series too that Azhar, MK and partner Anil Steel had a falling out over a game plan that hadn't turned out as scripted. MK bankrolled the Rajkot endeavour, which, according to Azhar, included Ajay Jadeja and Nayan Mongia. These players are also mentioned in connection with match-fixing by Ajay Sharma in his submissions to the CBI. The names would not have come as a surprise to Mumbai police detectives who tapped bookies' phones in the city in November 1996 while investigating an underworld murder. At the time, India were playing South Africa in the final of the Titan Cup on 6 November. According to a report in the April 2000 edition of *Outlook*, the crime branch picked up calls between the bookies and several players on the Indian team including Azharuddin, Jadeja and Mongia. 'What are you doing for us?' one of the bookies was recorded as asking Azharuddin, who replied that everything had been done. The Indian captain signed off by saying, 'Put my money on the other side.'[241] However, India won the final by 35 runs. Anil Steel explained that some of Azharuddin's 'information' proved unreliable, instructions weren't followed and all concerned were practically wiped out financially. MK corroborated this account in the CBI Report, explaining that India did not lose the final to South Africa as planned. By his own admission to the CBI, Anil Steel had '… lost a heavy amount of money as a result of his association with Mukesh Gupta and stopped contacts with him some time in 1997'. *Outlook*'s underworld sources suggested counter-fixing. Apparently, the turnover of bookies in Mumbai was well over Rs43 crore (US$10,6 million) for the Titan Cup final. The same *Outlook* article maintains that Steel lost some Rs17 crore (US$ 4 million) in a single match.[242] Steel's statement to the CBI investigators seems to suggest that it was this Titan Cup series that bankrupted him. Unable to pay his clients, Steel fled to Goa.

Ajay Sharma confirmed to the CBI that the relationship between Azhar and MK became 'complicated' during the Titan Cup when the result of a particular match did not turn out as planned. MK held Sharma responsible for introducing him to Azharuddin and he prevailed upon Sharma to accompany him to Azhar's home in Hyderabad to help him recoup some of his losses. Azhar agreed to make up for the incident in the ensuing Test series at home against the South Africans.

During the first Test, in Ahmedabad, Azharuddin reportedly introduced MK Gupta to the Indian team's physiotherapist, Dr Ali Irani, who accompanied the team for the better part of ten years. Irani confirmed this meeting, but only after seeing a picture of MK Gupta, whom he identified as 'John.' According to MK, Irani reassured him that Azharuddin would make good MK's Titan Cup losses. The bookie claimed that he made future payments to Azhar through Ali Irani. India won the first Test against South Africa at Ahmedabad in November 1996 and MK recouped 30% of his Titan Cup losses. This would seem to suggest that matches don't need to be lost to be fixed. In the second Test in Calcutta, India lost and MK made up 60% of his losses. The third Test was played in Kanpur, where MK paid Hansie Cronjé 'money for jam' for ensuring a South African defeat.

By the Sahara Cup in 1997, the quality of Azharuddin's 'information' was suspect and MK deduced that either Azhar didn't have enough players on board with him or he was working with someone else. Shedding some light perhaps on these shadowy events, physiotherapist Ali Irani claimed that Azharuddin had told him that he was doing matches with Anees Ibrahim that he couldn't do with anyone else. Once again, a case of being double-bookied, perhaps? This would not be the first, or presumably the last, instance of such double dealings. Hansie Cronjé, in testimony to South Africa's King Commission, revealed that he had been in contact with a South African-based bookie, Marlon Aronstam, as well as Sanjeev Chawla from London in connection with the five-match ODI series in India in March 2000 and the controversial Test that turned into an ODI against England at Centurion in January 2000.

It would appear that many gambling cricketers associate with more than a single bookie or punter. Manoj Prabhakar's telephone records show a number of calls to bookies/punters such as Sanjeev Chawla, Rajesh Kalra, Sunil Dara and Ratan Mehta. While strenuously denying any association with Anees Ibrahim in Dubai, Mohammad Azharuddin was also on a number of payrolls, it seems. In addition to big-time bookie and punter MK Gupta, Azhar was a personal friend of Ajay Sharma. Sharma, who now shares a life ban with his former roommate, was MK Gupta's conduit to cricket's stars and Azhar's introduction to wealthy Delhi punters Ajay Gupta and family in 1998. Azhar admitted to the CBI that it was through them that he and his accomplices Ajay Jadeja and Nayan Mongia fixed the third match in the Pepsi series against Pakistan on 24 March 1999. A year later, phone records showed Azhar's calls to Ajay Gupta on the last day of the second Test at Bangalore against South Africa and another on the day of that infamous fifth ODI at Nagpur in March 2000. Hotel bills and Harrods bills were also paid for by the Guptas.

Indian batsman Ajay Jadeja's cellphone records reveal calls to and from an array of bookies and punters, including Rajesh Kalra, Ratan Mehta, Ajay Gupta and Uttam Chand. Interestingly, a cross-check of Chand's phone records show that, after speaking to Jadeja, calls were made to Hans Kumar Jain in Delhi and Shobhan Mehta in Mumbai. Jadeja was a close friend of the big-time Delhi punter Ratan Mehta and was a regular frequenter of his restaurant. Mehta has connections in both the Indian and Pakistani team. Questioned by the CBI, Ratan Mehta confirmed his association with former Pakistani captain Javed Miandad as well as Pakistani players, '...Wasim Akram, Waqar Younis, Inzamam-ul-Haq and Saeed Anwar'. Wining and dining members of the Pakistani team in his wife's Mini Mahal restaurant in Delhi's Vasant Vihar, on their last tour of India in 1999, Mehta admitted to also giving them 'small gifts'. An interesting anecdote related by *India Today* on 24 April 2000 described an unidentified businessman, in India on business, sitting with a well-known Indian bookie in his restaurant in Delhi's Vasant Vihar suburb. The man overheard his host's cell-phone conversations with the respective captains of the Pakistani and Indian cricket teams, Wasim Akram and Mohammad Azharuddin. The calls over, his friend reportedly told him, 'It's fixed. India will win. Put your money on India'. And sure enough India won their Super Six match against Pakistan in the 1999 World Cup.[243]

Mohammad Azharuddin was not excluded from the income tax swoop of July 2000, in which 750 officials descended on cricket players past and present, administrators, bookies and punters throughout 10 Indian cities. According to a report in *Outlook* magazine on 31 July 2000, links were found between the former skipper and MK Gupta as well as prominent Mumbai bookie Shobhan Mehta.[244] One of a handful of men who appear to control the pivotal Mumbai trade, Shobhan Mehta started out as a small punter in 1985 before moving into booking. Well-travelled and well-connected, the bookie also allegedly handles illegal financial transactions to and from Dubai. In interviews with the CBI, Mehta denied having any cricketing ties. However, two former Indian captains and a TV magnate have been linked to the money-man from Mumbai. Mohammad Azharuddin, in his statement to the CBI, fervently disavowed any ties with the Mumbai bookie: 'On being asked whether I received any gifts from Shobhan Mehta, I state that I have never received any money or a flat from him and I do not even know him'. When questioned by the Indian magazine *Outlook* on the reports that a Directorate of Revenue Intelligence tape showed four of Mumbai's top bookies in attendance at his wedding, former Indian captain Sachin Tendulkar insisted, 'As far as I am concerned, there was not a single person of that description at the wedding. I don't know why people are dragging my name into this'.[245] For his part, Shobhan Mehta 'categorically denied' being at Sachin Tendulkar's wedding. Mehta's father, Subodh, in an interview published in *India Today*, asserted that 'Knowing Sachin or his in-laws is not a crime.'[246]

That may be so but they say you can tell a man by the company he keeps. In its April 2007 edition, the South African investigative magazine *Noseweek* reported that, during the World Cup held in South Africa in 2003, a 'heavily-disguised' Dawood Ibrahim attended the cricket match between India and Pakistan at Centurion on 1 March in the company of South African Police Commissioner and head of Interpol, Jackie Selebi.[247] Cricket's match-fixing syndicates are well-connected and well-protected, it would seem.

12

Dirty laundry

The Pakistani connection

Match-fixing has been the scourge of the game. As the latest crisis in South Africa has shown, it is a global problem. No one country can point the finger at anyone else.

– Ali Bacher to the Australian media, 20 April 2000[248]

Before Hansie Cronjé was hoist by his own charade, a common perception, often expressed by the Australian, South African and English cricketing community, was that match-fixing was a pastime unique to the subcontinent. Even when Cronjé 'fessed up and took his medicine at the King Commission, both the former South African captain and the then Managing Directior of the South African Cricket Board tried to deflect attention towards Pakistan. Cronjé dated his first match-fixing encounter to Cape Town in January 1995 and implicated another former captain, Salim Malik of Pakistan. Despite Dr Bacher's initial assertion in the immediate aftermath of Cronjé's downfall that '… no one country can point the finger at anyone else', he then promptly proceeded to do so at the King Commission, naming Pakistan in two dubious World Cup matches in 1999, including the Super Six match between Pakistan and India at Old Trafford and a qualifying game between Pakistan and Bangladesh that was rumoured to have been fixed for US$1 million. Bacher claimed his sources were Majid Khan, former Chief Executive of the Pakistan Cricket Board (PCB), and an Indian bookie called Mr R who had been introduced to Bacher by his good friend Jack Bannister. Bacher, in his testimony to the King Commission, described Mr R as '… an acquaintance I have, whom I've met on five or six occasions during the past five to six years. He's an Indian bookmaker …'

IS Bindra, former President of the Indian Cricket Board and one-time head of Punjab Cricket, told CBI investigators that 'the way Mr Ali Bacher conducts matches in South Africa creates a lot of suspicion'. So did Bacher's submission to the King Commission on 12 June 2000. Unfortunately, it was not televised nor was it widely publicised, on the directions of the South African Cricket

Board's Managing Director. After a sweeping tale of unnamed bookies and strange confidantes, crooked umpires and contract killings, Bacher's lawyer, Jeremy Gauntlett, communicated his client's last word on the matter: 'He intends to say nothing about what he has testified here today again in any media disclosures. He has spoken to the Commission. And that is also, I think, to assist the task of the media representatives present here, who otherwise may be inclined to follow up with him. He cannot and will not say anything further.' He'd said enough, perhaps.

The shadowy figure at the centre of Bacher's bizarre story was known only as Mr R, as the UCB Chief feared for his safety should he name him. Bacher related how they had first met on a flight to Port Elizabeth for the Boxing Day Test match during the 1995/96 tour by England of South Africa. This game was noteworthy for the national debut of South African development star Paul Adams. Jack Bannister, former Warwickshire county player, BBC commentator and bookie, also met Mr R during this Test. Ali Bacher described Bannister as a '... long-standing friend ... and I would say probably, in the international cricket scene, he would probably be the best friend I've ever had over many decades ... nobody in international cricket, I can vouch, would ever question Jack Bannister's integrity'. According to Ali Bacher, Bannister appealed to Mr R's extensive experience for help in reviewing a book he had been working on, entitled *Tampering with Cricket*, which was published in 1996. Bannister, in a letter to Bacher on 23 April 2000 setting out relevant background to the recent developments, described how 'The Indian bookmaker confirmed my text and revealed why a betting row broke out in India and bets were called off. My manuscript was thus vetted during the third Test against England in Port Elizabeth by a man whose knowledge and integrity I trusted so much that we had several minor business dealings in England during the next three years'.

Bacher too maintained infrequent contact with Mr R over the next three years, usually meeting up for dinner in various international cricket venues where Mr R would divulge the inner workings of crooked cricket. On one such occasion, following South Africa's victory in the first Test of that tainted tour at Mumbai in February 2000, Bacher joined Mr R for dinner. The bookie told him that Javed Akhtar, the Pakistani umpire, was 'on the payroll' during the final Test between South Africa and England at Headingly in August 1998.

Confirming both Mr R's credentials and his impeccable cricketing contacts, Johannesburg bookie Marlon Aronstam, whose well-timed proposal to turn the Centurion Test into a one-day game helped salvage a washed-out draw, was also a friend of Mr R's, as he revealed to the King Commission: 'The person referred to by Mr Bacher as Mr R is definitely the same man. I know him personally.'

Explaining that his 'very good friend' was not a bookmaker but a globe-trotting, professional gambler with superb credentials, Aronstam described Mr R, '... dressed beautifully in his suit, tie and jacket' off to the cricket having been '... invited by Dr Bacher to the box at the Wanderers'. Aronstam related Mr R's tale that '... Dr Bacher allowed him to see the pitch at Newlands and he told me he'd become very friendly with Dr Bacher and one of his best friends was Jack Bannister'. According to Aronstam: 'Mr R is not a bookmaker, Mr R is a commission agent ... he's a professional gambler. Mr R, what he tries to do is place money for people. If a person would like to get a big bet on or something, they'll try and use Mr R to move the money. So he doesn't make a book.'

South African sports writer Neil Manthorp explained the seemingly cosy relationship between cricket administrators and bookies:

> Now, we say 'bookie' like it's a dirty word but they've been intrinsic to cricket. Ali Bacher's best friend is a bookmaker. There have always been bookmakers around. It's like the stock market, which goes through major purges of periodically cleaning up insider trading and then it dies down, but it doesn't stop it from going on. It happens all the time. Basically, that's what it's about. That's why bookmakers are friends with cricketers, because they need to be ... In 1996, if a cricket administrator was introduced to a bookmaker in a corporate hospitality box, they would regard each other as legitimate businessmen.

Influential Indian magazines *India Today* and *Outlook* identify Mr R as the well-connected Delhi restaurateur Ratan Mehta, whose restaurant, Mini Mahal, in the up-market suburb of Vasant Vihar, was frequented by the Pakistani cricket team. According to the CBI Report released later in 2000, Ratan Mehta is a professional gambler. Mohammad Azharuddin is said to have told CBI investigators that Mehta is a '... very big bookie who is also involved in ... narcotics and drugs.'[249]

The ICC's Anti-Corruption Unit (ACU), led by Lord Condon, investigated allegations that Ratan Mehta was 'actively seeking to match-fix' and was behind the two 'dubious' World Cup matches referred to by Ali Bacher in his testimony to the King Commission. An Indian businessman gave a statement to the ICC's Anti-Corruption Unit in which he claimed to have met Ratan Mehta by chance in London a few days prior to the Pakistan/India clash in the 1999 World Cup. The businessman's statement is outlined in an article in *Outlook* magazine on 16 February 2004.[250] According to him he spent the evening with Mehta at Monty's Cigar and Wine Bar in Sloane Street and watched as Mehta conducted business with the aid of two cellphones. Apparently, Ratan was using the one phone to place bets and move money around while on the other phone he had several conversations with cricketers whom Mehta identified as India's Mohammad Azharuddin and Pakistan's Salim Malik and Wasim Akram. Left-arm fast bowler Wasim Akram plied his trade for Pakistan between 1984 and 2003, periodically captaining both the Test and the one-day side. He faced a number of match-fixing accusations throughout his career from which he always managed to emerge unscathed. According to the Indian businessman's statement to the ICC, Ratan Mehta claimed to have 'sorted out' ten Pakistani players so that an Indian win was a sure bet. As it happened, India beat their arch-rivals by 47 runs. The same businessman claimed that Mehta had a hand in fixing the Pakistan/Bangladesh match, which Bangladesh won by 62 runs. Apparently, the ACU had similar information from another reliable source.[251] Ratan Mehta is well connected in the cricketing world, it would seem. The same Indian businessman, in his statement to the ICC's Anti-Corruption Unit, claimed to have seen Ratan Mehta leaving the Pizza Pomodoro Restaurant in Knightsbridge with Shane Warne and Brian Lara during the 1999 World Cup.

Despite these losses Pakistan went on to contest the final of World Cup 1999 against Australia. In what was described by one commentator as a 'parody of a World Cup final', Pakistan were all out for 132 runs in 39 overs.[252] Pakistani newspapers claimed that the players had sold the final for 400 million rupees, worth around US$8 million at the time.[253] The Pakistani government instigated an investigation into this match but Wasim Akram, batsman Ijaz Ahmed and Salim Malik were subsequently cleared of match-fixing in September of the same year.[254]

Back at the King Commission, Ali Bacher also singled out Salim Malik. Apparently, Mr R had told Bacher that the only player who came through repeatedly was Salim Malik and that in the second-half of the 1990s, the Pakistani captain had made US$1,5 million on the practice. During that same period, Pakistan had three inquiries into match-fixing – all featured Salim Malik.

The first was chaired by former Pakistani Supreme Court Judge Fakruddin G Ibrahim, appointed by the Pakistan Cricket Board in 1995, following a controversial tour by Pakistan to Southern Africa and public allegations by Australian cricketers against Salim Malik. Shane Warne, Mark Waugh and Tim May were not prepared to travel to Pakistan to testify and thus Ibrahim returned a verdict of 'Not Guilty'. A second probe headed by retired Justice Ejaz Yousuf and commissioned by the Pakistan Cricket Board was abandoned as a toothless tiger because it lacked the necessary judicial powers. It released its interim findings in August 1998, branding Wasim Akram, Salim Malik and his brother-in-law Ijaz Ahmed suspect and recommending that they should not be considered for selection until a formal commission cleared them of doubt. Almost immediately, a third commission was set up at the instigation of former team manager of Pakistan and erstwhile CEO of the Pakistan Cricket Board, Majid Khan. His request to the Pakistani President for a judicial inquiry resulted in the appointment of Justice Malik Muhammad Qayyum, a serving High Court Judge whose work commenced on 13 August 1998 and would end over a year later on 30 September 1999. However, the Qayyum Report was only publicly released some eight months after completion, at the end of May 2000, in the flurry of official inquiries made public in the wake of Hansiegate. Qayyum interviewed thirty-three Pakistani cricketers, former cricketers and cricket administrators along with four sports journalists and the three Australian accusers.

The initial investigation focused once again on Salim Malik and fast bowler and also one-time captain Wasim Akram, but as more names floated to the surface the inquiry cast its net wider. Six extensions were required before finally a cut-off date of 30 September 1999 was imposed and the final report was submitted more than a year after the Commission started work. As far-ranging as Qayyum's deliberations were, however, they did not extend to the World Cup of 1999, where minnows Bangladesh beat mighty Pakistan against odds of 33–1 or to Pakistan's slump to India and later Australia in the final. According to an exclusive in London's *Sunday Telegraph*, at the outset of its work, the Qayyum Commission had been instructed by none other than the Pakistani President, Rafiq Tarar, not to investigate any World Cup matches. Tarar also happened to be the patron of the Pakistan Cricket Board. Quoted in the exclusive report, Justice Qayyum said:

> After three days though, I was told not to investigate any World Cup matches. The President issued the order in writing, it came from the Ministry of Sport. The President of Pakistan is also the patron of the Pakistan Cricket Board and once he takes the mandate back, I have no jurisdiction. Initially, I was told I should look at match-fixing without restrictions. So I was going to look at that World Cup final and the game against Bangladesh. Then I was asked to withdraw. This was very unusual. Of course I was surprised. Anybody would be surprised if you are asked to do something and then told not to three days later. [255]

Then, in May 2001, the blackout was lifted and the go-ahead was given to pursue these allegations by yet another judicial inquiry.[256] However, Ali Bacher, whose allegations at the King Commission had precipitated this commission, reportedly declined to appear before it.[257] In June 2002, Justice Karamat Bhandari exonerated all the Pakistani players of match-fixing

Made captain during the 1993/94 season, Salim Malik's first tour as Pakistan's skipper was to New Zealand in February and March of 1994. A Test match and a one-day international from this New Zealand tour came under the scrutiny of the Qayyum Commission, although no firm findings were made. Much like Hansie Cronjé, who gained his captaincy in October 1994 only to reveal approaches by bookies as early as three months into his office, Malik too, it would appear, wasted no time. If Manoj Prabhakar's testimony to the Indian inquiry is to be believed, he introduced MK Gupta to Salim Malik in October 1991, well before he became captain and thus this tour is perhaps not the first that should have been scrutinised.

In the third and final Test in Christchurch, at the end of February 1994, New Zealand managed to pull off the impossible. Chasing 324 in their second innings, they won, with 5 wickets to spare. Qayyum found that there was insufficient evidence to call this match fixed. 'However', he wrote, 'in the matter of the fifth one-day match, also at Christchurch, there is stronger evidence.'

Vice captain Rashid Latif's allegations of misconduct during the 1994 New Zealand tour are corroborated by the evidence of team-mate Ata-ur-Rehman. In his first appearance before the Qayyum Commission, Ata-ur-Rehman initially denied his sworn affidavit before a previous board of inquiry, the Probe Committee, regarding this match. When presented with his signed statement in the Qayyum Commission hearings, he conceded that it was his. In it he told how he was asked by Akram to bowl badly in the final ODI between Pakistan and New Zealand at Christchurch and was given PKRs100 000 (US$1 700) for his trouble. The full price agreed upon had been PKRs200 000 (US$3 300), but he was paid half up front and promised the other half later if he continued to co-operate. He also stated that Akram told him that Ijaz Ahmed had fixed the game with the Pakistani bookie Zafar Ali, aka Jojo. According to Rashid Latif, it was Malik that probably fixed the Christchurch match with Ijaz Ahmed and Zafar Ali (Jojo). This person is identified in the Ehtesaab Bureau's list of bookies as Haneef Caddie, the same Cadbury who was allegedly seen in the rooms of certain Pakistani players during the 1994/95 tour of South Africa and who was subsequently gunned down in Johannesburg in 1999.

Pakistan went into the final game of the ODI series leading by 3–0 with the fourth match tied. With nothing to play for, Pakistan set the New Zealanders a target of 146 in 50 overs, which the home side reached within 34.1 overs with the help of 17 extras conceded by Pakistan's bowlers. Of the Pakistani batting innings, 8 of the 11 team members scored in single figures, each putting on less than the extras tally. These players included opening batsmen Saeed Anwar and Aamer Sohail, Inzamam-ul-Haq, Asif Mujtaba, Rashid Latif, Wasim Akram, Waqar Younis and Ata-ur-Rehman. Ata-ur-Rehman was Pakistan's next generation pace bowler, in the running to succeed Wasim Akram and reverse swing specialist Waqar Younis. Wicketkeeper Latif, Aamer Sohail, Salim Malik,

Akram, Younis and ul-Haq all captained Pakistan at one time or another. Long-time stalwart of the Pakistani team Inzamam ul-Haq batted first for his country in 1991. The portly ul-Haq was famed not for speed but for his ability to play against pace bowling and to get himself and others run out. He went on to become Pakistan's captain until his sudden resignation following the death of Bob Woolmer at the 2007 World Cup. Justice Qayyum acknowledged that '... the performance of the team was sub-par. There were misfields and there were wides. The batting collapsed'. He philosophised, 'But then again, that is the Pakistan team'. Thus, while Qayyum affirmed that there was 'stronger evidence', it failed to measure up to the 'requisite standard of proof'.

Recalled to the Commission, Ata-ur-Rehman elaborated. On tour in England, Wasim Akram had approached him to change his story, contradicting the first sworn statement. Rehman did so under threat of dire consequences from Akram's friends back in Pakistan. Akram then sweetened the deal by paying his airfare from Newcastle to London. Ata ur-Rehman claimed that Khalid Mahmood, Chairman of the Pakistan Cricket Board, had also wanted him to retract his statement. Apparently, the Chairman was in possession of his original statement. However, Ata-ur-Rehman's team-mate Aamer Sohail produced Rehman's sworn affidavit and Qayyum took this as proof of collusion by both to malign Wasim Akram.

Rehman made another guest appearance at the Qayyum hearings on 3 September 1999, this time brought back by popular demand of Akram, whose lawyers cross-examined him. This time he performed another volte-face and claimed that the accusations against Akram in his initial affidavit were fabricated. Qayyum reacted to these shenanigans by accusing him of perjury. Headlining again before Qayyum, Rehman stuck to his last sea-change and alleged that he was coerced by team-mate Aamer Sohail to make a statement against Wasim Akram because, he explained, Sohail had designs on the captaincy. He continued to insist, however, that Akram had paid for his flight to London by personal credit card. Some seven years later, after Bob Woolmer took the job of Pakistan's cricket coach, he would reportedly comment, 'Pakistan generally resembles a snake pit with the snakes continually crawling on top of each other and slithering about trying to get on top of each other'.[258]

Pakistan came up against New Zealand once more the following month in Sharjah, where they were joined by India, Sri Lanka, Australia and their hosts, the United Arab Emirates, in the Australasia Cup. Here, according to the CBI Report, Indian gambler MK Gupta approached Australia's Mark Waugh and Pakistan's new captain, Salim Malik. However, Gupta claimed that the two men declined to co-operate. Neither Waugh nor Malik acknowledge this alleged encounter.

After Sharjah, Sri Lanka was on the touring card for the Pakistani team in July and August of 1994. Malik remained captain and led his visiting side to victory in both the Test and one-day series. A fifteen-day break followed before the start of the Singer quadrangular one-day series between Pakistan, India, Australia and hosts Sri Lanka in September. Every team involved in this series would subsequently be tainted with suspicions of fixing. The second match of the Singer Cup between Australia and Pakistan has thrown up a tidal wave of rumour and allegation in inquiries and media reports the world over. The sixth game, involving India and Pakistan, was the now infamous match in which Manoj Prabhakar alleged that team-mate and Indian captain Kapil Dev offered him Rs25 lakh (US$61 500) to under-perform.

Prior to the start of the Singer championships, skipper Malik flew home to Pakistan. To Islamabad, he claimed. His arch-nemesis, Pakistani batsman/wicket-keeper Rashid Latif, insisted Lahore. Giving reasons for his trip home, Malik said because his son was ill, the management maintained it was because he wanted to attend a wedding and Latif alleged it was to make a deal with bookies.

Like Marlon Aronstam in South Africa and Mukesh Gupta in India, the well-connected Pakistani bookie Saleem Pervez would prove to be a most valuable informant for the Qayyum Commission. Reminiscent of Ajay Sharma in India, Pervez was a former opening batsman for the National Bank of Pakistan team. According to Rashid Latif, Pervez '...was a bookie...seen freely mixing with the players in their hotel rooms'. His name also appears on the Pakistan Ehtesaab Bureau's list of cricket bookies. Qayyum acknowledged Saleem's dubious credentials: 'It is, no doubt, true and admitted by Saleem Pervez that he has some criminal record and that he had even been involved in a murder case but that does not mean that the man is lying.' Qayyum accepted his version of events and concluded that the '... statement of Saleem Pervez holds a lot of weight'.

Saleem Pervez admitted being in Sri Lanka during the Singer Cup. Travelling with a bookie friend, a Mr Aftab Butt, he confirmed staying at the Taj and the Oberoi in Sri Lanka, the same hotels that housed the Pakistani team. Mr Butt had had a brief cricketing career himself as a first-class player between 1977 and 1979. Pervez went even further and 'categorically stated' that he had paid Salim Malik and Mushtaq Ahmed US$100 000 to throw the second game of the Singer Cup against Australia on 7 September 1994. According to Pervez, the deal was done in Lahore. Legspinner Mushtaq Ahmed played for Pakistan between 1989 and 2003 in both Test and ODI squads. He would become Pakistan's assistant coach to Bob Woolmer in September 2006.

In England, late April 2000 saw undercover *News of the World* reporters meet with an unwitting and garrulous Salim Malik at the Kensington Hilton Hotel in London. The reporters posed as businessmen seeking to invest in fixing matches. Malik referred to a match that was rigged by both Pakistan and Australia, unbeknown to each other.[259] Salim Malik was quoted in the *News of the World* exposé: 'Both sides were wondering what the hell was happening. We were trying to get them to score runs against us and they wouldn't. We were tying to get ourselves out and they wouldn't get us out. I was the captain in that game. What a lot of aggro that was! It was like we had to kick the ball just to get their runs up.'[260]

This double-fix fiasco is given additional credence by Pakistan's former team manager Intikhab Alam, who told the Qayyum Inquiry that after the match he had received an anonymous phone call complaining about the loss of Rs40 lakh (US$98 000) on the game. Why any gambler or bookie would phone the team manager to complain about his losses is not explained. The names of seven Pakistani players came up in connection with the fixing of this game.

In India, MK Gupta told the CBI that, despite Salim Malik's alleged resistance to his overtures back in April 1994 in Sharjah, he had rung up the Pakistani captain before an ODI during the Singer series in Sri Lanka. Malik apparently informed MK that Pakistan would lose the game against Australia, a 'prediction' which proved accurate and made MK some good money. This is also the match in which Shane Warne and Mark Waugh confessed to accepting money for information on pitch and weather conditions from 'John' later to be revealed as MK, friend and confidante to most of the world's Test-playing cricket captains. Warne claimed he received US$5 000 while Waugh got US$4 000. In addition to his match fees and extracurricular income garnered from this game, Shane Warne enjoyed another windfall as Man of the Match.

In summary then, we have two sets of bookies and two teams. One bookie has members of both teams on his payroll – MK confirmed paying Malik and both Warne and Waugh for their 'information'. At least one team member is being paid by two bookies – captain Malik was in contact with both 'John', aka MK, the Indian bookie, and Saleem Pervez, his Pakistani counterpart. And both teams, it would appear, did their damnedest to lose. Aniruddha Bahal, *Outlook* magazine's intrepid match-fixing reporter, told the Indian Chandrachud Commission of Inquiry in 1997 that there was a Singapore company behind the scenes that had organised the Singer Cup. According to Bahal's source, an Indian Board official was a beneficiary of the proceeds along with three other persons closely linked with cricket – one of whom was from Pakistan.

The events of that contentious second ODI of the Singer Cup unfolded in the following fashion: Australia lost the toss and was sent in to bat by Pakistan. Right-hand batsman Michael Slater and captain Mark Taylor opened the batting. Slater was dismissed first with the score on 11, comprising a personal contribution of 4. Mark Taylor doubled the ante to 8 before folding with Australia on 34/2.

By the time Boon and Steve Waugh had come and gone, Waugh lasting just 5 minutes for his single run scored, Australia had slumped to 49/4. Wasim Akram and Mushtaq Ahmed took 3 of those 4 wickets with Akram toppling the top order and Ahmed picking up Steve Waugh in the middle. Ahmed also felled Mark Waugh, batting number 4. Tail-enders Ian Healy and Shane Warne, batting number 8, injected some heart into the proceedings, with each reaching 30. Healy was not out but Warne bowed out to Akram. With Bevan top-scoring with 37 the Australian total of 179/7 in 50 overs was less than intimidating. Or so the punters would have thought.

Like the Australians, Pakistan's top-order failed to fire on all cylinders. Saeed Anwar and Aamer Sohail opened the innings for Pakistan but Sohail didn't tarry as he departed on a duck with the score on 1 for 2. Top-scoring partner Anwar's 46 helped stabilise the innings somewhat, but Basit Ali's duck at number 4 didn't help and when Anwar departed after seeing out the number 6 and 7 batsmen, Latif and Akram respectively, with the score on 129/6, the rot really set in. Steve Waugh collected the wickets of opener Anwar, as well as the captain and vice captain of the Pakistani team, middle-order batsmen Malik on 22 and Rashid Latif on 7. Captain Malik failed to add to the total before surrendering his wicket for 22. The wickets of Wasim Akram, Saeed Anwar and Malik were conceded for a mere 5 runs. Less than 20 runs later, Waqar Younis gave up the ghost, scoring 2 off 9 balls in a desperate situation, and just 3 runs later Raza sank Pakistan to defeat, ending the 50 overs on 151/9.

Shane Warne garnered the Man of the Match award for his 30 runs and the wickets of number 3 batsman Inzamam-ul-Haq (29), number 4, Basit Ali (0) and tail-ender Waqar Younis (2).

On the face of it, Saeed Anwar's performance was the only highlight in an otherwise dismal Pakistani innings but this achievement is marred by strange circumstances. Rashid Latif said he was told by Anwar that Malik had asked him to play badly in this game. Anwar denied this to Qayyum and the scorecard would seem to bear him out – 46 off 78 balls, five 4s and a 6. But he retired unexpectedly on 43 when Pakistan had consolidated on 80/2. The twelfth man came on and delivered a message from the dressing room to Anwar, who promptly left the field, according to the scorecard, with 'cramp' and sat out a number of overs in which the Pakistani team crumbled and crept from 80/2 to 124/5. Anwar then returned to the field, accompanied by a runner, and added 3 runs to his total before being taken out by Steve Waugh, still 4 runs shy of his 50. Aamer Sohail recalled this message from the twelfth man and Anwar retiring hurt for no apparent reason. In the following series in South Africa, Sohail claimed that Anwar had told him that his loss of form was because he had been cursed because of his match-fixing dabblings.

The Qayyum Report upheld the allegations of match-fixing on this game. However, the Australian Cricket Board, which launched their own inquiry into Malik's claims publicised by the *News of the World*, announced on 9 August 2000 that the allegations were unfounded.

After the Singer Cup, Pakistan went home to await the arrival of the Australians for three Tests and an ODI series spanning September and October 1994. It was this tour that would bring matters to a head and would see three Australian cricketers testifying under oath in the Qayyum Inquiry of 1998 that Salim Malik was a match-fixer. That was some way down the line, however. After entertaining the Australians at home, Pakistan left for a tour to Southern Africa at the end of that scandal-plagued year of 1994, but the scandals were far from over.

In Hansie Cronjé's initial testimony to the King Commission in June 2000, he dated the first of his match-fixing encounters to the one-day Mandela Trophy series in January 1995 where he was approached by 'John', and Pakistani captain Salim Malik to influence the Cape Town final. Pakistani bookie Saleem Pervez maintained that Pakistan deliberately lost the Mandela Trophy to South Africa. Lending credence to this claim, Pakistani batsman Basit Ali told the Qayyum Commission that he had seen Hanif Cadbury, a well-known Pakistani bookie who had since settled in South Africa, enter the hotel rooms of several of his team-mates on this tour, including Salim Malik.

South Africa, it appears, is a favoured destination for cricket bookies and agents. 'It is believed that all major Indian bookies have their Pakistani counterparts, many of whom have since settled in South Africa.'[261] Mohammad Hanif Kodvavi, aka Cadbury, was one such Karachi immigrant. He apparently helped arrange the 1994/95 Pakistani tour of South Africa as well as other cricket tournaments.[262] Cadbury's name appears on the Pakistan Ehtesaab Bureau's list of cricket bookies of the subcontinent. His crooked stable allegedly contained Wasim Akram and Salim Malik, as well as another player unnamed by former Pakistani captain/coach Javed Miandad. The Indian bookie/agent named Anil, described by Pradeep Magazine in his book, had visited South Africa as many as six times and explained that 'It is a great place for people like me to be in.'[263] Cadbury would ultimately have disagreed. According to a *Sunday Times* report by Simon Wilde on 23 April 2000, Cadbury was gunned down by 67 bullets on a Johannesburg street on 14 May 1999 and his bullet-riddled body was then cut into pieces.[264] In an interview with *India Today* in May 2000, Subodh Mehta, father of big-time Mumbai bookie Shobhan Mehta, insisted, 'We're bookies, not fixers. But bookies get involved directly or indirectly when the match is fixed. And nothing is possible without the underworld. They want to share your profit. Pakistani bookie Hanif Cadbury refused to part with his profit and he was killed last year in South Africa.'[265] According to Ali Bacher's testimony to the King Commission, Jack Bannister alleged that 'by January '96, Salim Malik had received US$2 million for betting and bribery favours paid in Johannesburg by an expatriate bookmaker then living in Johannesburg.'

In January 1995, going into the double-legged final having won five of their six qualifying games, Pakistan would have been favoured to take the Mandela Cup from the home side. The two matches were day/night games and Malik sent South Africa in first on both occasions, leaving Pakistan to bat in the shadows of the floodlights. Indian cricketer Manoj Prabhakar's axiom that a game is '... best influenced when you're chasing' echoes here. Pakistan lost the chase, by 37 runs in Cape Town and by 157 runs in Johannesburg.

According to a number of reports, there was much acrimony between vice captain Rashid Latif and his captain over these unorthodox decisions. Like Manoj Prabhakar in India who was also a wicketkeeper; who also took early retirement because of fixing allegations and who also taped conversations to back up his accusations, Latif acknowledged that there was a lot of talk of betting in the Pakistani dressing room and the players were required to take an oath of honour on the Quran. But their captain apparently did not as he was outside for the toss. Wisden, when reporting on the second final, understated the case: 'Again, Salim Malik asked South Africa to bat, creating divisions in Pakistan's dressing room.' Intikhab Alam, the team manager on the Southern African tour, admitted hearing rumours that his team was going to lose the final. His anonymous informant alleged that eight players had been bought: Salim Malik, Ijaz Ahmad, Inzamam-ul-Haq, Mushtaq Ahmed, Wasim Akram, Waqar Younis, right-hand batsman Basit Ali and Moin Khan. Like his fellow wicketkeeper/batsman Rashid Latif, Moin Khan also captained the Pakistan side. The Pakistani Ad Hoc Committee sent Saleem Altaf, a member of the Selection Committee, to examine the reports coming back from Southern Africa, but Altaf returned to Pakistan with nothing to tell.

The next leg of Pakistan's tour was to Zimbabwe and in the first Test in Harare, played from 31 January 1995, the visitors were beaten inside four days by a home team who had never won a Test since their ascension to the Test-playing ranks. Wisden points out that, before the match, Asian bookmakers had quoted the odds on a Zimbabwean win at 40-1. Talk from Mumbai was that the bookies had balked at paying out on Zimbabwe's victory, obviously suspecting tampering.[266]

Hard on the heels of the controversial visit to South Africa, a rash of fixing allegations hit the media while the Pakistani team were in Zimbabwe. On 16 February 1995, *The Sun*, a London newspaper, published Pakistani wicketkeeper/batsman Aamer Sohail's accusations that several of his team-mates were involved in match-fixing. Before the end of this Southern African tour, team-mates Basit Ali and wicketkeeper/batsman Rashid Latif would announce their retirement from international cricket.

It was on the eve of the third Test against Zimbabwe, which Pakistan went on to win, and with it salvage the series, that Malik first heard of the broadside fired across his bows by Australian bowlers Shane Warne and Tim May. Articles in the Australian press carried the two cricketers' claims that they had been offered US$70 000 apiece by Salim Malik to under-perform in the first Test against Pakistan in October 1994. Mark Waugh claimed his wicket was worth US$100 000 in the same Test. The Australian cricketers had waited five months before pointing fingers. Khalid Mahmood, PCB Chairman, described the Australian accusations as an extreme form of sledging: 'Australian cricket is known for indulging in tactics like terrorising the opposition in and off the field, which they call "sledging".'[267]

Malik explained Warne's accusations against him as a grudge because he was the only batsman that Warne couldn't get out. The Australian cricketers went further than making claims in the media. They signed affidavits, which were handed to the head of Pakistan cricket, Javed Burki, by the ICC's Chief Executive, David Richards, on 20 February 1995 in a meeting at Lord's cricket ground.

By March, Malik had been sacked as captain and with him manager Intikhab Alam, pending the outcome of the resulting Ibrahim Inquiry. However, in a startling reversal of fortune, that same month Malik's ban from first-class cricket was lifted. By May of 1995, Latif and Basit Ali had returned to the cricketing arena and Intikhab Alam had been reinstated for Pakistan's return tour to Australia. Despite their affidavits, the Australians were not prepared to travel to Pakistan to testify and Ibrahim's report submitted on 21 October 1995 exonerated Malik of all charges because of insufficient evidence. He went so far as to conclude that the Australian accusations '... appear to have been concocted for reasons best known to the accusers'.

Those reasons were only to become clear some three years later. As it turned out, eight days after the Australian cricketers' affidavits were handed to Pakistan by the ICC on 20 February 1995, the Australian Cricket Board (ACB) informed the International Cricket Council that Shane Warne and Mark Waugh had themselves admitted to accepting money from a bookmaker during the Singer tournament in Sri Lanka prior to the Australian tour of Pakistan. This information was kept from the Ibrahim Inquiry, by then already underway, and from the rest of the world until the Australian media broke the story in December 1998.

In March 1997, Sohail gave vent again in an article in a Lahore newspaper, claiming that several of his former team-mates were on the take and referring specifically to the final ODI match on the Pakistani tour of England in 1996. The third ODI, played at Trent Bridge, Nottingham on 1 September 1996, looked set to hand England a series victory of 3–0 until Rashid Latif's 31 not out helped Pakistan win the game with 2 balls to spare. The Man of the Match award went to the entire Pakistani team. Aamer Sohail claimed that Latif failed to follow instructions to throw away his wicket as big bets had been placed on an English series whitewash. England won the series, 2–1. A month after Sohail's media revelations, in April 1997, a PCB disciplinary committee slapped the cricketer with a two-year ban from international cricket for making allegations against the Pakistani team. A month later, after Sohail apologised to the Board, the ban was rescinded in favour of a fine of PKRs50 000 (US$800) and Aamer was back in the squad, destined a year later to lead the team he had once denounced.

Aamer Sohail's first appearance before the Qayyum Commission was when he was captain of the Pakistani team during their 1998 tour to Australia and Zimbabwe's visit to Pakistan. He claimed to know nothing about match-fixing. In his report, Qayyum does not try to hide his irritation at the fact that Sohail said little to him but was far more chatty to the press. Sohail explained that as the PCB was not doing anything about the match-fixing rumblings, he went to the media.

In January 1998, with media speculation rife, Wasim Akram stepped down as Pakistan's captain. He would be replaced for the tour of Zimbabwe and South Africa early in that year by Rashid Latif, the man that had resigned from the team during the 1995 Pakistani tour to Southern Africa because of his match-fixing denunciations. However, the final ODI against South Africa in Cape Town on 22 April 1998 was to be Latif's last appearance for Pakistan, until his career was resurrected in 2001.

After the appointment of the Qayyum Commission in August 1998, Wasim Akram resigned again – this time from international cricket on 15 September, getting out of the kitchen because of the heat, which had been steadily climbing all this while. Six days later, Akram was back, announcing his availability for the upcoming series against Australia and Zimbabwe at the end of that year. Sure enough, Akram's inclusion in the squad was announced on the 21 September, but he would not be rejoining the team as captain. Aamer Sohail would have that honour. Later, on 19 December 1998, Sohail was relieved of the captaincy and came to the Commission of his own accord, making allegations about the Pakistani tour of Southern Africa in 1995.

By that time, the third inquiry into Pakistani cricket was underway and the Qayyum Commission was three months into its investigation. In depositions to the Commission, Shane Warne claimed that Malik had offered him US$200 000 to bowl badly on the last day of the first Test match in Karachi and to solicit the help of Tim May. Both refused the deal according to their account. In addition, May was allegedly approached by Malik in his hotel room and offered a bribe for a one-day international on that tour in Rawalpindi. Warne apparently also overheard a conversation between Salim Malik and Mark Waugh at a Presidential function for the two teams at the end of October. Malik allegedly approached Waugh to throw the Rawalpindi ODI on 22 October with the help of four or five other players at the going rate of US$200 000. Both Warne and Waugh apparently reported the incident to captain Mark Taylor who informed the Australian officials on tour with them – Bob Simpson, the coach, and Colin Egar, the manager, although there is no record of this in the post-tour report.

Then, on 8 December 1998, *The Australian* newspaper and former Australian cricketer-turned-radio-talk-show-host David Hookes revealed Shane Warne and Mark Waugh's financial dealings with a bookie named John during the same tour of Pakistan by Australia in the fall of 1994. Neither Warne nor Waugh had made any mention of this in their appearance before the Qayyum Inquiry and now their testimony was suspect. The Judge makes it clear that 'They had not revealed these material facts as to why they precisely were approached by Malik … Malik had possibly heard these two had some connections with bookies and so were approachable'. Both Mark Waugh and Shane Warne are well-known gamblers.

Pakistan demanded that Warne and Waugh return to Pakistan to elaborate on their testimonies. This, they were reluctant to do. In the end, Muhammad came to the mountain, courtesy of the Australian Cricket Board, and a special session of the Pakistani judicial inquiry was convened in Melbourne to accommodate the Australian cricketers. On 8 January 1999, Justice Abdul Salaam Khawar, the Registrar of the Lahore High Court, stood in for Justice Muhammad Qayyum in the first public questioning of any cricketer on charges of match-tampering. Despite their previous omissions, Qayyum considered the testimonies of the Australian cricketers credible and found Malik guilty of fixing both the Rawalpindi ODI and the Karachi Test match. Qayyum confirmed too the Singer Cup fix.

While Qayyum poured cold water on '… the allegation that the Pakistani team is, as a whole, involved in match-fixing' he passed judgment on more than half the Pakistani team. He found 'clear evidence of match-fixing' against Salim Malik and recommended that both he and Ata-ur-Rehman, who perjured himself, be banned for life. He fined Malik PKRs10 lakh (US$16 500) and Ata-ur-Rehman a total of PKRs5 lakh (US$8 000). In addition to these two, Qayyum fined the following players for bringing the game into disrepute and failing to co-operate with the inquiry: Wasim Akram, Mushtaq Ahmed, Waqar Younis, Inzamam-ul-Haq, Saeed Anwar and Akram Raza.

Wasim Akram, in particular, was heavily censured by Qayyum, who, in addition to a PKRs3 lakh fine (US$5 000), recommended that he be removed from the captaincy and his assets investigated. 'The captain of the national team should have a spotless character and be above suspicion. Wasim Akram seems to be too sullied to hold that office.' Qayyum recommended a similar penalty and fine for Mushtaq Ahmed, advising that '... he be censured, kept under close watch and be not given any office of responsibility (selection or captaincy) in the team or on the Board'. Regarding the allegations against Waqar Younis, Qayyum found there to be sufficient substance to the allegations to warrant censure, observation and investigation. Qayyum also found Younis to be unforthcoming and fined him PKRs1 lakh (US$1 650). Saeed Anwar was also suspected of withholding evidence, as was Inzamam-ul-Haq and Akram Raza and they were similarly fined.

While the Pakistan Cricket Board followed Qayyum's suggestions, they did so only in May 2000, following the public release of Qayyum's Report in the fallout from Hansiegate. Salim Malik and Ata-ur-Rehman were banned for life, joining that pantheon of fallen heroes that include Mohammad Azharuddin of India and Hansie Cronjé of South Africa.

Malik tried to overturn his life ban and, at the time of writing, was awaiting a ruling from the Pakistan Supreme Court on his appeal. On 4 November 2006 the ICC lifted Ata-ur-Rehman's life ban so that he could play league cricket in England and, by May 2007, he was officially back in the international swing of things. Wasim Akram continued to play for Pakistan until he announced his international retirement in May 2003. Inzamam-ul-Haq was appointed the new Pakistani captain and Mushtaq Ahmed was named as Pakistan's assistant coach in the same year. Despite being mysteriously sacked in 2006 and then reinstated within three months, Ahmed travelled with the Pakistan World Cup squad to the Caribbean in 2007, as assistant to Pakistan's coach Bob Woolmer. As for Shane Warne, he was selected one of the top five cricketers of the twentieth century before retiring at the end of the 2006/2007 Ashes series.[268] As Salim Malik reportedly pointed out to the intrepid *News of the World* reporters, '... the thing about white players is you just can't trust them'.[269]

13

Kangaroo court

The Australian connection

Whether you're an honest man or whether you're a thief,
Depends on whose solicitor has given me my brief.

– W S Gilbert, British dramatist and comic writer (1836–1911)

The Australians' answer to the Qayyum Report in Pakistan and the Chandrachud Report in India was the O'Regan Report, commissioned by the Australian Cricket Board in the wake of the public outcry over the Shane Warne and Mark Waugh saga, which had its beginnings on the Australian tour of Sri Lanka in 1994. However, the ACB Player Conduct Inquiry was only set in motion four years after the events of that Sri Lankan tour. On 15 December 1998, the Australian Cricket Board appointed Rob O'Regan AM QC of the Queensland Bar to head the investigation.

The Commission was handicapped from the beginning by its limited investigative powers (it had no powers to subpoena witnesses or documents or take evidence under oath), as well as its restricted time frame, (the report was to be finalised by 28 February 1999). This left a scant two months in which to investigate '... whether any of its contracted players had engaged in certain conduct relating to betting, bribery, match-fixing, the unauthorised receipt of moneys or other benefits and related matters' during a seven-year period dating from 1 January 1992 to 31 December 1998. Showing a special talent for fashioning a silk purse out of a sow's ear, O'Regan was of the opinion that '... a private, low-key and relatively informal inquiry was much more likely to get to the truth'.[270]

Unlike his counterparts in India and Pakistan, who bore the brunt of the questioning themselves, O'Regan's Counsel, Mr Jordan of the Victoria Bar, interviewed sixty-four people during this time while O'Regan himself interrogated a further ten. With no powers to enforce attendance at the inquiry, dozens of people were unavailable. Nonetheless, O'Regan enthused, 'I am pleased to report, however, that, as anticipated, I received substantial co-operation from past and present players, officials, directors and others'. Such apparent eagerness to assist the Inquiry was in stark contrast to other international probes, such as the later investigation by the Indian CBI, who described the response of the cricketing community to their inquiries as a 'conspiracy of silence'. The head of the ICC's Anti-Corruption Unit, Sir Paul Condon, seconded that sentiment in his 2001 report on corruption in international cricket.

The evidence heard by O'Regan stretched back to 1992. However, it was the 1994 tour of Sri Lanka and Pakistan that gave rise to the O'Regan Report of 1999. In early September of that year, in the team's hotel in Colombo, key Australian batsman Mark Waugh was approached by an Indian man named 'John'.

> One evening during that period I was with some team-mates at the Taj Hotel, where the team was staying, when a man who introduced himself to me as John, said that he had met me in Hong Kong at a six-a-side tournament, and that he loved the way that Australia played cricket. During cricket tours I meet many people, and I had no recollection of having met him. We had a brief conversation during which he said he was from Delhi. He told me that he had a business proposition to put to me and invited me to have a discussion with him. He invited me to have a drink and a chat with him after dinner.[271]

This 'John' is thought to be the same man who introduced himself to Hansie Cronjé in Johannesburg, some five months later, in early 1995. He has subsequently been identified as Mukesh Gupta. Despite Waugh's protestations under oath that he had no recollection of meeting 'John' prior to this encounter in 1994, Gupta's deposition to the Indian CBI investigators indicated that former Indian cricketer, Manoj Prabhakar, his agent at the time, had effected an introduction to Waugh during the Hong Kong Sixes Tournament in September 1992. Prabhakar confirmed this meeting. Apparently, Waugh was paid US$20 000 for 'information' whenever Australia played. Some two years later, in 1994, 'John', was in search of 'information' about team selection, pitch and weather conditions for the current tour as well as the upcoming summer season in Australia.

At the time, O'Regan had no luck in identifying 'John' but observed, 'Whatever his full name, he appears to have had no difficulty at all getting through to the players at various hotels around the world when he phoned … I should add that other material indicates that it was common at that time for bookmakers to stay in hotels on the subcontinent where international teams were also staying and where apparently they had ready access to the players'. Revelations from South Africa's King Commission the year after the O'Regan Report was finalised would seem to suggest that little had changed. Hotel records showed reputed match-fixer Sanjeev Chawla frequenting the same hotel as the South African players during the controversial Indian tour at the beginning of 2000.

Back in 1994, Waugh acceded to John's request for pitch and weather information but apparently drew a principled line at team selection or tactics. The deal was done for $US4 000, according to Waugh, although this would reflect a substantial reduction in the going rate for 'information' since 1992. There were at least ten phone calls made between the two men over a five-month period while Waugh was in Pakistan, in Australia during the England tour of 1994/95, in New Zealand in February 1995 and finally in the West Indies the same year. O'Regan pointed out that the phone calls were in fact more numerous than the Board had at first thought when the relationship was discovered in early 1995. John, seemingly not content merely to have one of Australia's leading batsmen on his books, asked Waugh for an introduction to Shane Warne, Australia's star spin bowler. The meeting took place the next evening, fittingly enough, in a Colombo casino, where Waugh introduced John to Warne as a man who 'bets on the cricket'.[272] The following evening Warne received a phone call from John who was staying in the team hotel and he went up to see him in his room. John gave him an envelope 'with no strings attached' containing US$5 000 as a 'token of his appreciation for meeting him'. Apparently, Warne received three phone calls from John during the Ashes series in Australia at the end of that year in which he provided general information on team composition and pitch reports. As Mark Waugh was also providing information during this period it would seem an unnecessarily expensive duplication of 'information'. According to Warne, contact with John ceased after February 1995.

O'Regan pointed out that, even if the information passed on was innocuous, the '... acceptance of the money creates a basis for blackmail ... It is naïve to think that a gift of a large sum of cash would ever be made by an unknown benefactor with no strings attached'. Throwing further doubts on the two men's wide-eyed innocence, O'Regan surmised that Warne and Waugh may have seemed likely players to John as both men were well-known gamblers. However, O'Regan seemed to contradict his own logic when he distinguished between the players' individual roles in the transaction. Accepting that Shane Warne was naïve enough to believe that he was under no obligation for the US$5 000, O'Regan concluded that Warne hadn't entered into a business relationship with John. According to O'Regan, there was, however, a business agreement reached between John and Mark Waugh to the tune of US$4 000. If there was no reciprocal agreement between Warne and the bookie, why then did Warne receive the lion's share of the cash when it was Waugh who was actively conveying 'information' for at least five months?

In February 1995, five months after the eventful tour of the subcontinent,

Pakistan were visiting Zimbabwe and Australia were playing in the quadrangular Centenary tournament along with India and South Africa in New Zealand. Some time during this competition, Australian team manager Ian McDonald received a call from a journalist who had been tipped off that an Australian player had been on the payroll of a bookie in Sri Lanka. McDonald called the head of the ACB, Graham Halbish, who gave McDonald the go-ahead to investigate the allegation. Warne and Waugh admitted their involvement and two handwritten yet unsigned statements to that effect were faxed to Halbish. The players' statements, a cover note from McDonald to Graham Halbish and a media release written by McDonald but never issued, is the sum total of the documentation of the incident. There is no record of the cricketers' interview with the ACB upon their return to Australia; no signed statements, no transcript or summary of evidence and no record of the decision to fine them.

At the same time that Shane Warne and Mark Waugh were being outed, the accusations made by Tim May and Shane Warne against Salim Malik were publicised. The New Zealand Centenary tournament took place between 15 and 26 February 1995. Salim Malik was informed by *The Telegraph* on 14 February in Harare that Australian newspapers, the following day, would be naming him as the man who had attempted to bribe Tim May and Shane Warne during the Australian tour of Pakistan the previous October. The Australian cricketers had waited five months before pointing fingers. On 27 February, with the Australian team back in Sydney, the players were questioned by Mr Alan Crompton OAM, the ACB Chairman, and Halbish at the Park Royal Hotel prior to their departure for the West Indies the next day. Warne and Waugh admitted their complicity and were fined A$8 000 and A$10 000 respectively.

The following day, the ACB held a meeting at the Sheraton Airport Hotel; present were Sir Clyde Walcott, Chairman of the ICC, and David Richards, CEO of the ICC since 1993. Prior to his elevation, Richards had formerly led the Australian Cricket Board. The two men were there to discuss the allegations levelled by Warne and Waugh against Salim Malik on the same contentious Sri Lankan tour. The Australian players' involvement with bookies was brought up at the end of the meeting after several members had already left and there was little time for discussion. However, the minutes report that '... the actions of the Chairman and the CEO were approved by the Directors present'. The ICC was informed confidentially of the contretemps and there the matter was buried, only to be exhumed in December 1998, thanks once again to the media.

On the afternoon of 8 December 1998, the Australian Cricket Board was informed by *The Australian* newspaper that they had concluded a lengthy investigation into the goings-on during that fateful Sri Lankan tour and would be publishing the full story on the front page of the next day's edition. That evening, the ACB issued a brief press release indicating that two unnamed Australian players were fined in 1994 for taking money from a bookmaker. Later that same evening, in his nightly Melbourne radio show, former Australian player David Hookes named Warne and Waugh as the culprits and the cat was out of the bag with a vengeance. A press conference was held the following day in Adelaide, where the Australian team were preparing for the third Test against England. Warne, Waugh and Malcolm Speed, the Australian Cricket Board's CEO, were present. Warne and Waugh read prepared statements while Speed read a statement from Alan Crompton, the ACB Chairman at the time of the disciplinary hearing in 1994. No questions were permitted.

Following Warne and Waugh's confessions, further revelations tumbled out of the antipodean locker. On 11 December 1998, *The Australian* newspaper reported that another Australian player at the time, all-rounder Greg Matthews, had also turned down a similar offer during the 1992 tour of Sri Lanka. Matthews did not report the dubious approach to team management. The same day, the Wellington-based newspaper *The Dominion* described former New Zealand fast bowler Danny Morrison's account of a phone call and an offer of US$1 000 to provide information during the Hamilton Test on India's tour of New Zealand in 1994. Some reports suggest that the offer came from an Indian player. A week later, on 15 December 1998, the Australian Cricket Board's Player Conduct Inquiry was instituted. Two days thereafter, on 17 December, Australian batsman and keen punter Ricky Ponting went public with an offer made to him by a Sydney bookmaker at a greyhound meeting in 1997. Apparently a four-figure sum was mentioned in exchange for information about the Australian cricket team. O'Regan was going to be busy.

During the Commission's inquiries, Australian captain Allan Border related how a former Pakistani cricketer had visited the Australian dressing room during the Ashes tour of England in 1993. The cricketer was hoping to elicit Border's help in ensuring that England won the sixth and final Test in order to win a £500 000 bet. Border refused, he said. Apparently, this encounter was common knowledge among several Australian players, but Border did not remember telling the team manager Des Rundle about it and once again the team manager's report does not include this incident.

O'Regan's verdict on all the evidence heard was that 'There is, in my opinion, no basis for recommending any disciplinary action against any player or official'. Warne and Waugh he considered to have been dealt with already, although '... in my opinion, this punishment was inadequate ... I do not think it is possible to explain their conduct away as the result merely of naivety or stupidity ... A more appropriate penalty would, I think, have been suspension for a significant period of time'. Once more displaying an ability to be equivocally even-handed, he then came to the defence of the penalty, explaining that the financial punishment was not insubstantial for the time. Furthermore, the players had suffered public humiliation since disclosure in December 1998 and one player had suffered significant loss of income. 'Finally, it must be emphasised that their conduct, although reprehensible, was at the lower end of the scale of misconduct. It was not bribery or match-fixing or anything like those grave offences ... compared with the very serious allegations of bribery made against Salim Malik.'

Finally, O'Regan advised the publicising of penalties imposed for serious offences to act as a deterrent and ensure public confidence in the process. This spur to transparency proved less than persuasive. While the ACB, breaking with normal procedure, did publish O'Regan's findings, they held back a confidential chapter which contained '... additional facts relevant to the Terms of Reference which may affect the right of identified third parties'. In other words, this is the chapter in which names are named and '... matters of suspicion and impressions mentioned by one or more witnesses interviewed ...' are aired. Apart from international cricketers named in this chapter, two other senior Australian players also make an appearance despite an ostensible lack of conclusive evidence.

The Indian investigation released its first report at the beginning of November 2000. The CBI had relied extensively on evidence given by bookie/punter Mukesh Gupta, identified in the report as the oft-mentioned 'John'. Following the release of the report in which his name came up once again, Mark Waugh put on a suitably stoical face: 'I've been through two inquiries, the Pakistan inquiry and the O'Regan Inquiry, and all my evidence is there. But of course I'm willing to co-operate with any further investigations with the ACB or the ICC.' With the mask slipping somewhat, he wistfully admitted, 'It'd be nice to bury it and get on with cricket.'[273]

Waugh found support in expected quarters. The CEO of the Australian Cricketers' Association was none other than fellow whistle-blower Tim May. May focused the minds of the ACB on the fact that providing 'information' was not deemed illicit prior to the signing of a revised players' declaration in 2000. Thus Waugh could not be punished retroactively, much like the salutary position in which Herschelle Gibbs and Henry Williams found themselves in South Africa.[274] Taking Waugh at face value, however, the ACB announced that its investigator, Greg Melick, and members of the ICC's Anti-Corruption Unit would interview Mark Waugh early in February 2001. Malcolm Speed, CEO of the Australian Cricket Board, wrote a letter to Waugh informing him that his co-operation would be required.[275] In a press release issued by the Board on 22 January, disappointment was expressed at Waugh's unaccommodating response. The cricketer had declined Speed's invitation as a 'fishing expedition'. While the ICC's Anti-Corruption Unit lacked the necessary powers to enforce compliance, Malcolm Speed, on 24 January, cordially threatened Waugh with omission from the Australian team if he did not address the following issues with the investigators:

- the number of times he had met bookies and received money for information
- the total amount of money received for such information
- the identity of the bookie/s
- details of any meeting with MK Gupta in 1992/3.[276]

Living up to his name, Speed set a deadline for written consent from Waugh's lawyers for 4 pm the following day, 25 January. Less than two weeks later, Waugh was at the meeting with investigators at Melbourne's Hilton Hotel. His story remained unchanged. His only bookie contact was the elusive 'John' and he did not know Mukesh Gupta. Waugh played on.

In an online chat session, a week after the Delhi police had filed their charges against the four South Africa cricketers, Inderjit Singh Bindra, the then President of the Punjab Cricket Board and former President of the BCCI, stated that the '... Australian reaction in the case of Shane Warne was as lopsided as the initial reaction of the Indian and South African Boards when the Hansie episode was disclosed by the Delhi police. It is such like actions or indifference to public sentiments which has resulted in this problem becoming a major malaise and a cancerous growth in international cricket'.[277] Once the carefully staunched wounds had been reopened by the Cronjé affair, O'Regan's remarks upon the release of his report were resurrected: 'Australian cricket is clean, and it's important that it's kept that way.'[278]

14

The green fields of home

England's contribution to cricket and corruption

I contend that we are the finest race in the world and that the more of the world we inhabit, the better it is for the human race.

– Cecil John Rhodes, Businessman, politician and imperialist (1853–1902)

Cricket arose from folk games long disappeared into the murky reaches of England's medieval past. The modern name of the game was derived from the French, *criquet*, testimony to the Norman conquest of England in 1066, but was not played by the French-speaking nobility who preferred the chivalric diversions of hunting and jousting. Indeed, the word 'chivalry' comes from the French *cheval* for horse. Later, however, it was the aristocracy and their love of gambling that would appropriate the game and eclipse cricket's rustic origins. School cricket too would reinvent and popularise the game, endowing it with the status of a 'virility cult' that achieved a world following.

In the earliest existing record, the game was being played by schoolboys in Surrey around the 1550s. When Elizabeth ascended the throne in 1558, cricket was still a leisure pursuit of the lower classes and there is no evidence of its having attracted any commercial interest yet. A century later, with civil war sweeping the land, Charles I put to death in 1649 and Oliver Cromwell at the head of a newly established Republic, cricket escaped the Puritan purges of the interregnum. Sporting events attracted crowds and the Protestant regicides were wary of 'unlawful' gatherings. However, school and university cricket flourished. Public schools such as Eton and Harrow and the great medieval universities of Oxford and Cambridge would become the elite nurseries of 'the gentleman's game'.

Once the monarchy was restored to Britain in the person of Charles II in 1660, sport made a spectacular come-back and gambling soon became a national pastime. By 1668, cricket had become a commercial event. The brewing industry was one of the earliest sponsors of cricket, canny tavern-keepers recognising the ale-selling potential of spectator sports. The famous Lord's Pavilion was funded in 1889 by a loan of £21 000 supplied by gin-maker William Nicholson.[279] This association has continued to the present day. In South Africa, the brewing giant SAB has been involved with cricket for over twenty years.[280] Reinforcing cricket's manly image, the first sponsors of the modern one-day game were the razor-blade company Gillette in 1963.

With horse racing firmly established as the 'Sport of Kings' and the aristocracy enthusiastic punters, by the 1700s the nobility were involved in cricket, heading teams of household retainers expected to win their masters' wagers. As Derek Birley points out in *A Social History of English Cricket*: '... the involvement of the gentry in the cricket games of their inferiors was a by-product of their penchant for gambling'.[281] Echoes of cricket's contemporary malaise reverberate throughout this period. As with modern-day spread betting, bets were taken on individual performances and players backed themselves with the bookies or 'blacklegs,' so-called from their leggings muddied by the racetrack. Then, as now, '... money was the oil that greased the wheels of cricket'[282] and matches were being bought and sold, as one cricketer's recorded fate reveals.

The Reverend James Pycroft, who published the first history of cricket in 1851, and bequeathed the phrase 'not cricket' to posterity, related the tale of an 18-year-old Buckinghamshire farm labourer with cricketing talent who was spotted by George Finch, Earl of Winchelsea and President of Hambledon club from 1787. Young William Fennex was swept off to London to play for Hampshire against England. Witness to the extravagant lifestyles led by the professional players, which were often funded by illicit arrangements, the farm boy soon followed suit. In his dotage, he confessed to selling a match and revealed that this match had been sold by both teams, a tradition that continues to this day. Then, as now, the punters were involved in fixing matches. The Reverend Pycroft illuminated the temptations laid before such rustics: '... the 'blacklegs' skulking in the Green Man were quick to tell the lads, "Your backers, my Lord this, and the Duke of that, sell matches and over-rule all your good play so why shouldn't you have a share of the plunder?"'[283] Presumably, Fennex got his share, but died penniless in the workhouse. His belated confession, however, has a prophetic ring, '... matches were bought and matches were sold and gentlemen who meant honestly lost large sums of money, till the rogues beat themselves at last. They over-did it; they spoilt their own trade'[284] scaring off potential backers and attracting the ire of the establishment.

Such matches were high-society events that were further elevated by the patronage and participation of Frederick Louis, Prince of Wales, heir-apparent to King George II. As enthusiastic a player as he was a punter, Frederick's passions were embraced by the aristocracy. A second Prince of Wales, son of George III, continued the royal association with cricket begun by his predecessor. The royal gentlemen conducted their betting and batting contests at White Conduit

Fields in Islington, London until they objected to the increasing attendance of the lower classes at their matches and sought a private ground. Thus were born the elite private clubs such as the White Conduit, the Star and Garter, patronised by Frederick, Prince of Wales, and the Marylebone Cricket Club. The MCC was founded in 1787 and its rules of play were codified the following year. To this day, the MCC continues to be the custodian of the Laws of Cricket as well as cricket's best-known landmark. The gentleman's club eventually made its home at St John's Wood and a duck pond became the most famous ground in cricketing history, commemorating that young London bowler, Thomas Lord, who had arranged the lease of that first ground in Dorset Fields in the Marylebone district.

Derek Birley quotes the *Morning Chronicle* of 1774, which editorialised: 'The game of Cricket ... has too long been perverted from diversion and innocent pastime to excessive gaming and public dissipation.'[285] By 1817, matters had come to a head and William Lambert, the disgraced Sussex cricket star, was banished from Lords for deliberately under-performing, along with the bookies, who were only allowed back some 160 years later. However, in the aftermath, little changed. Mary Russel Mitford, writer and cricket enthusiast, wrote an impassioned letter to a friend about a game between Hampshire and All-England on 24 August 1823 where bets were taken, not only on the final outcome of the Test, but also on individual performances. An indignant Mitford declared, 'To think of playing cricket for hard cash! Money and gentility would ruin any pastime under the sun ... So be it always when men make the noble game of cricket an affair of bettings and hedgings and maybe of cheatings.'[286] School cricket too was not exempt from the influence of gambling. The long-standing cricketing rivalry between the aristocratic sons of Eton and Harrow began in 1805, with their first encounter played at Lords. Pycroft, in an aside on the match of 1825, reflected that 'there was much betting in those days'[287] as there had been for many years preceding. £20 000 was bet on a series between Old Etonians and England in 1751.[288]

By the Victorian era, which encompassed the greater part of the nineteenth century, cricket had become a repository of imperial values and a means of propagating them. The national conviction, expressed by an earlier clerical sports writer, Reverend John Mitford, editor of the *Gentleman's Magazine* in 1833, was that cricket was an Englishman's game. 'Cricket is the pride and privilege of the Englishman alone. Into this, his noble and favourite amusement, no other people ever pretended to penetrate: A Frenchman or a German would not know which end of a bat they were to hold.'[289] Despite, or perhaps because of, such nationalistic fervour, cricket expanded with the Empire into its colonies, carried by soldiers and administrators, missionaries and teachers. The myth of the noble game was thus perpetuated, as was the superiority complex that underpinned it.

The interwoven strands of cricket and colonialism were embodied in the person of Lord George Harris, the Eton-educated fourth Baron in a family of colonial administrators. Captain of Kent in 1875, Harris led an English side to Australia in 1878/79, to help spread the game. His idealised view of the sport has been much quoted from the following passage:

> You would do well to love cricket for it is more free from anything sordid, anything dishonourable than any game in the world. To play it keenly, generously, self-sufficiently is a moral lesson in itself. And the classroom is God's air and sunshine. Foster it, my brothers, so it may attract all who find the time to play it. And protect it from anything that may try and sully it ...[290]

At a farewell dinner before departing to take up his post as Governor of Bombay in 1890, the cricket-playing imperialist declared, 'I have done my best to promote the noble game in this country and I intend to extend my patronage to the promotion of cricket in India.'[291]

The Victorian Pycroft summed up the implicit virtues embodied by cricket in *The Cricket Field*: sobriety and self-denial, patience and fortitude, obedience, good humour and an 'unruffled temper'.[292] *Tom Brown's Schooldays*, written by Thomas Hughes and published in 1857, six years after Pycroft's tome, added the essential element of 'all for one and one for all'. In a passage from the book, a schoolmaster muses on the meaning of cricket, during a match. 'The discipline and reliance on one another which it teaches is so valuable, I think it ought to be such an unselfish game.'[293] However, as Birley points out, 'A ball game, no matter how elaborate, is ethically neutral: any moral qualities it exhibits are those brought to it by the players.'[294]

Or not.

Cricket's greatest heroes have long had feet of clay. WG Grace, whose imposing figure adorns the famous Long Room at Lords, is acknowledged as the father of the modern game and one of cricket's earliest superstars. He was also, by all accounts, a selfish player with a shrewd and acquisitive approach to the game. Fiercely competitive, he was willing to do whatever it took to win. Born in Gloucestershire in 1848, into a family of cricketers, Gilbert's elder brother EM led the way, touring Australia with England in 1863/64. 1864 proved to be a seminal year for cricket's greatest traditions. That year saw the younger Grace playing for the South Wales Club against England and the MCC. Cricket's bible, the *Wisden Almanac*, was first published that year and contained '... the Laws of Cricket as revised by the Marylebone Club'. In 1866, the 18-year-old WG made 224 not out for England against Surrey and a star was born.

The Grace family, while doctors, made cricket a second family business, becoming administrators of the county club founded on the Bristol Cricket Club nurtured by Dr Henry Grace, the family patriarch. First-born EM was Secretary and in charge of finances and WG, aged 21, was captain. (He captained Gloucestershire from 1871 to 1898.) Young though he was, by all accounts Gilbert was already adept at cashing in on his growing renown. Sought after by both the United South of England team and the MCC, WG managed to milk both cash-cows, sporting MCC colours and reaping expenses while arranging matches for United and playing in them. He became so popular that extra admission was charged to see him play and umpires were under pressure to ensure the crowd's expectations were satisfied before giving him out. A famous remark attributed to him was occasioned when he refused to leave the crease after being bowled first ball in front of a large crowd. 'They came to see me bat, not to see you bowl.'[295] Grace wasn't shy to intimidate umpires directly if the need arose and controversy dogged the family over inflated expense claims, gate-taking scams and even kidnapping.

1868 marked Australia's first tour to England – with an aboriginal team. Ten years later, a white team arrived on a speculative venture led by Captain DW Gregory. The eleven-man squad planned to pick up the twelfth man in the person of William Midwinter, an Englishman who had adopted Australia as his home. He had returned to England to pursue his cricketing career but was to play for the Australians on their English tour. Padded up and waiting to open the batting for Australia at the Oval, Midwinter was kidnapped by EM Grace, WG and some rugby-playing muscle who hustled him off to play for them as they were a man light. Notwithstanding such contretemps, a benefit fund raised £1 458 – the equivalent of £75 000 today – for Grace in 1879. Sixteen years later, when he was 47, another testimonial fund earned him £9 703 – around £385 000 today. The following year, 1896, Grace became captain of England at the ripe old age of 48. His long cricketing career finally ended in 1908 and cricket's first modern icon died in 1915.

While determinedly unacknowledged, cricket's history is as much about the baser side of human nature as it is about its heroes, as more recent events attest. Two days after the Delhi police held their momentous press conference to announce corruption charges against Hansie Cronjé and friends, a report by Scyld Berry appeared on the web version of England's *Telegraph* newspaper, dated 9 April 2000: 'England's cricketers are above suspicion, or perhaps away from suspicion, in that apart from a brief visit for the World Cup of 1996, they have not toured Pakistan since 1987. They have not toured India since 1992/93, shortly before the start of match-fixing allegations.'[296] Ironically, English captain Nasser Hussain, himself of Asian descent, echoed these self-righteous sentiments a week later, in a report on the *Electronic Telegraph* on 16 April.

'… I am absolutely confident that England are absolutely clean in all this. I have never received an approach from any bookmaker and I am sure that any players who have been, have immediately reported them, like Chris Lewis last year and Adam Hollioake before that in Sharjah. We have been lucky, in some respects, that we haven't toured the subcontinent for some time so we haven't been targeted by these people …'[297]

In December 1997, England played in the Akai-Singer Champions Trophy in Sharjah. The ODI competition was a quadrangular tournament between England, India, Pakistan and the West Indies.

Right-hand batsman Adam Hollioake had taken over the captaincy of England's one-day side from Mike Atherton earlier that year. Alec Stewart was vice captain. Stewart's background is noteworthy; his father was also an England cricketer and his grandfather was a bookie.[298] A year later, in December 1998, as media revelations compelled the Australian cricketers Shane Warne and Mark Waugh to come clean about their dealings with bookmakers, Adam Hollioake also joined the fray. He told the *Mail on Sunday* on 13 December that he had been contacted twice by two different men during the Sharjah tournament the previous year. The first man phoned him in his hotel room wanting to know about the team, the pitch and what would happen should England win the toss. Hollioake initially thought that the man was a reporter but when he asked him what newspaper he was with the man explained that he was 'making a book'. Hollioake said, 'I told him where to get off'. He was subsequently contacted by another man, who promised to make him a millionaire if he co-operated. Instead, Hollioake claimed, he reported the matter to David Graveney, England's Chairman of Selectors.[299]

On 21 May 2000, the *News of the World* reported on a meeting its undercover reporters had had with Pakistani cricketer Salim Malik. The reporters, pretending to be businessmen interested in getting involved in match-fixing, were introduced to Salim Malik by a man identified only as Iqbal Khan. In the article that outlines this meeting, Khan referred to this tournament: 'The England v Pakistan match in Sharjah, when Adam Hollioake led his side to victory, was fixed by my people. England would never have won otherwise.' On 15 December 1997, in the fifth match of the series, England beat Pakistan by 8 runs. England went on to defeat the West Indies by 3 wickets in the final.[300] By 1999, Scotland Yard was investigating allegations of corruption within the English team. England hosted the World Cup that year in May and June but failed to reach the Super Six stage of the competition, for the first time ever, because of their poor run rate. The match against India that sealed their fate would return to haunt the English team.

After the 1999 World Cup, New Zealand toured England in July and August.

On 12 September 1999, the *News of the World* published match-fixing allegations by former English all-rounder and Leicestershire cap, Chris Lewis. Lewis, who is a black man born in Guyana, played 32 Tests and 53 one-day internationals for England between 1990 and 1998. By many accounts, a talented bowler, batsman and fielder, he was never fully accepted by the national cricketing establishment. The victim of erratic selection, he wasn't named, even in the preliminary list, for the World Cup squad of 1999, despite being on form. So Lewis was not part of the English team when he claimed he was offered £300 000 a head to approach team-mates Alec Stewart and Alan Mullally in order to fix a Test match against New Zealand the previous month.[301] In the same article, the *News of the World* relates how Stephen Fleming, the New Zealand captain, received a similar offer before the third Test against New Zealand began on 5 August. Strangely, Lewis insisted that he had not given an exclusive to the *News of the World* but that the story was leaked by someone inside the English Cricket Board. He maintained that he had not received any money for the story[302] and this was corroborated by James Millbank, the reporter.[303] Be that as it may, the cat was out of the bag.

The *News of the World* article recounts how Lewis had met an 'old sporting acquaintance' named Mr Patel in a newsagent's in north London, '... just days before last month's vital game'. While the newspaper does not spell out which game, the article implies that it is the third Test against New Zealand at Old Trafford from 5–9 August 1999. England had won the first Test in the series, with New Zealand taking the second encounter. There were, however, still two Tests to go. Lewis told the *News of the World:* 'I was introduced to some people who had what they called a business proposal. But it was a bribe wrapped up as a business proposition.' Controversial Indian sports promoter Ashim Kheterpal was reportedly present at this meeting, although his name was not mentioned in this initial article. The men required Stewart to fumble his wicket-keeping duties and Mullally to bowl wides and drop catches. Lewis commented, 'You can lose a match like that. For instance, in a one-day game, if a keeper goes out and makes no attempt or drops catches off one end, he has a major effect on the actual runs scored.'[304]

As it happened, Stewart didn't keep wicket for the third Test, Mullally didn't play and rain forced a draw – luckily for England, who were on a hiding to nothing. However, the fourth and final Test of the series was lost by the home side and with it the series. Commentators remarked that England's batting had 'failed them miserably'.[305] Alec Stewart made a scant 11 in his first innings and went one better in the second for 12. England had failed to reach 200 in their first innings of any of the 4 Tests. The series loss earned England the unofficial Wisden ranking of worst Test team in the world. In the aftermath of defeat, the

English Chairman of Selectors, David Graveney, commented, 'The past couple of years have been littered with collapses that sometimes are beyond belief.'[306]

According to Chris Lewis, he refused the syndicate's offer and immediately informed the England Cricket Board (ECB). A police spokesperson confirmed that 'An allegation of attempted corruption was reported by a player to the England and Wales Cricket Board on 3 August.'[307] In the aftermath of Hansiegate, Lewis would later maintain that, although he had provided the ECB with all the details, including the hotel in which the fixers were staying, they sat on the matter for a week.[308] Lewis told the *News of the World* on 16 April 2000: 'When I did report the details about the plot to fix the New Zealand game, the ECB effectively didn't tell the police about it until Kheterpal fled the country.'[309]

In the media maelstrom that followed Hansie Cronjé's confession in April 2000, the magazine *India Today* harked back to the Lewis incident and described the encounter in more detail.[310] The magazine claimed that Chris Lewis received a call from a Kamlesh Patel on 2 August 1999. Mr Patel, it would seem, was acting as the representative of a betting syndicate. Apparently, there was a meeting at Patel's London home at which sports promoter Ashim Kheterpal was present, among other Asian men, including Jagdish Narain Sodha, a Mumbai businessman with Bollywood connections.

The Indian cricket writer Pradeep Magazine describes Ashim Kheterpal as 'a self-styled sports promoter' who was also '... a man with a special knack for getting into trouble, especially when it came to money'. Kheterpal moved from organising tennis and billiard tournaments into cricket and was involved in the 1993 Hero Cup and the 1996 World Cup. He also specialised in organising veteran matches that featured past Test players from South Africa, Sri Lanka, Pakistan and India. Kheterpal claimed that he had launched Ajay Jadeja's sponsorship career with a contract with Liberty Shoes and boasted to the Indian journalist that 'I have also signed most of the Pakistani cricketers like Saqlain Mushtaq and Wasim Akram. There is very little money in Pakistan cricket. I will get these players good sponsorship deals from India.'[311]

Interestingly, a UK *Sunday Times* article on 21 May 2000 links then ICC President Jagmohan Dalmiya to Kheterpal.[312] The article reported that, after Lewis's allegations were made public and Kheterpal found himself under investigation by Scotland Yard, Kheterpal approached Jagmohan Dalmiya for help. The *Sunday Times* quoted Dalmiya's response in a letter dated 22 October 1999: 'I object to your comment that I have known you for years and that we shared a certain bond.' However, it would seem that over the years both men were involved in organising a number of international and domestic cricket tournaments in India, including the Asia Cup of 1990/91 and the Hero Cup of 1993.

Kheterpal and Sodha explained to Lewis that they organised veterans' cricket competitions in the subcontinent and also arranged tournament sponsors. They wanted Lewis to approach two or three English players who would be willing to under-perform and thus influence the third Test against New Zealand at Old Trafford and perhaps other matches. They were willing to pay between £300 000 and £500 000 for these services. Alec Stewart and Alan Mullally's names were mentioned but the article does not name any third player. According to the *India Today* article, Sodha and Kheterpal were found to have shared hotel rooms and aeroplane flights on this visit to England. Kheterpal is thought to have been fronting for an Asian betting syndicate, which included Sanjeev Chawla, whom various newspaper reports describe as a close friend and associate although Kheterpal maintained that he had never met Chawla.

Lending credence to Lewis's allegations, Stephen Fleming, the then New Zealand captain, had received a similar offer from Kheterpal around the same time, which he said he had turned down. Fleming described the encounter in his biography, *Balance of Power*. He claimed that Kheterpal invited him to join '… the syndicate that's going on around the world right now, speculating on the likelihood of certain results of occurrences … He'd pay me £200 000 straight up, then another £100 000 in a year's time.'[313] According to Fleming, Kheterpal told him that top athletes were involved in the syndicate and alluded to a soccer match in which Manchester United suffered an unexpected upset and a major tennis tournament from which Andre Agassi had been eliminated. 'He said that those things were not coincidences,' wrote Fleming.[314] Kheterpal's revelations were echoed by the ICC's corruption-buster Lord Condon, in a 2007 debate in the House of Lords: 'But cricket is not alone now. Horse racing, soccer, tennis and other sports all have their problems. The sums of money involved are huge.'[315]

For his part, Kheterpal admitted meeting Lewis, as well as New Zealand captain Stephen Fleming and West Indies captain Brian Lara in England between 29 July and 2 August but claimed that the meetings were in connection with a benefit match that he was organising. A criminal case was opened and the Organised Crime branch of New Scotland Yard stepped in to investigate Fleming and Lewis's stories, the first police investigation of match-fixing allegations.[316] However, ultimately, the Scotland Yard investigation cleared the English team of any wrongdoing and little else was heard of the matter until Hansie Cronjé broke ranks on 11 April 2000.

On 16 April 2000, the *News of the World* carried a piece in which Chris Lewis claimed that Ashim Kheterpal had told him that three well-known English players were on the take. Lewis told the *News of the World*: 'They are all famous players hero-worshipped by millions of young fans in this country … The amounts the three received went into thousands. I was told everybody was at it, including players from South Africa, India and Pakistan … I was told one of the three – a batsman – had received a "substantial figure" to get himself out deliberately during a one-day international against Australia.'[317]

In reaction to the latest bombshell from Lewis, David Lloyd, who had coached England between 1996 and 1999, said, 'Allegations of England players being involved in match-rigging are complete nonsense unless I've been walking around with my head in the sand … I would note that these allegations don't come from Mike Atherton or Alec Stewart. You would take them seriously then but this is coming from Chris Lewis'. [318] ECB Chairman Lord Maclaurin, who also sat on the Board of the corporate giant Vodafone, sponsor of the national side, commented on Lewis's latest allegations: 'Chris Lewis had a lot of guts to come forward in the first place. He should get on with being a professional cricketer and I hope he isn't booed every time he goes to the wicket.' However, as in the case of whistle-blower Manoj Prabhakar in India, no action was taken by the English Board against Lewis.

On 27 April 2000, Gerard Elias QC, author of the elusive Elias Report and Chairman of the England and Wales Cricket Board's Discipline Standing Committee, cleared all English players of corruption, both past and present. In an official statement Elias declared:

> Having been given information by Chris Lewis at a meeting on April 18, following an article under his name in a Sunday newspaper, I have investigated the matter and met with police officers of New Scotland Yard. As a result, I conclude that there is no evidence whatsoever to justify the bringing of disciplinary charges in relation to betting and/or match-fixing against any member of the England international squad, past or present.[319]

To date, the players mentioned by Lewis have never been named by the Board and the ECB's Elias Report on its in-house investigation has never been released.

But this was not the end of the revelations of 16 April. In the same edition, the *News of the World* identified three cricket matches involving England that were being investigated by Scotland Yard.[320]

The three matches were:

1. South Africa in England, May to August 1998

Fifth Test, ENG v SA, Headingley, 6–10 August 1998

Alec Stewart was both captain and vice captain for the Leeds Test. This is the same Test referred to by South Africa's Ali Bacher in his testimony to the King

Commission where he claimed that Mr R had told him that Javed Akhtar, 'the umpire concerned, was on the payroll'. The match referee was none other than Zimbabwean Ahmed Ebrahim, the man who would ban Kenyan cricketer Maurice Odumbe from the game in 2004. England won by 23 runs, the team's first win in a 5-Test series since 28 December 1986.

2. 1999 World Cup

Twenty-fifth match, ENG v IND, Group A, Edgbaston, 29–30 May 1999

'England's worst performance in this competition' and Zimbabwe's 'extraordinary victory' over South Africa at Chelmsford helped India to qualify for the Super Sixes and eliminated hosts England from the World Cup in the early rounds.[321] The Group A match between England and India in Birmingham was marred by a dismal batting performance by the home side, bad weather, which turned the one-day international into two, and dubious umpiring decisions, particularly when to end play on the first day.[322] Darrell Hair of Australia and Javed Akhtar of Pakistan were the umpires. Mohammad Azharuddin captained the Indian side with Nayan Mongia, his vice captain. Ajay Jadeja also played in this match. Alec Stewart was wearing both the captain and vice captain caps yet again. The match reports consistently speak of the poor batting performance of Stewart in the tournament. Since notching up 88 in England's first outing – against Sri Lanka – he managed a total of only 37 runs in the next 4 innings. This match proved to be no exception and Stewart was caught by Azhar on 2. Once again, the English batting performance was described as 'miserable'. Graham Hick, Mark Ealham and Alan Mullally all went for ducks and Adam Hollioake succumbed to Kumble on 6. On Day 2, chasing 232, England was eliminated by India after a spectacular batting collapse saw the team slump to 169 all out after 45.2 overs. India won by 63 runs.

3. England in South Africa, November 1999–February 2000

Fifth Test, ENG v SA, Centurion, 14–18 January 2000

This Test, which effectively was turned into a one-day game, was found by the King Commission to be fixed. England won by 2 wickets.

England was touring Pakistan for the first time in thirteen years, in November 2000, when the Indian Central Bureau of Investigation released their report into match-fixing on 1 November 2000. Along with the four Indian nationals named, nine international players, with a preponderance of captains past and present, were implicated – by another of Cronjé's extra-curricular associates, MK Gupta. One of those cricketers was former English captain Alec Stewart, on tour in Pakistan. Indian bookie MK Gupta claimed to have paid Stewart £5 000 for 'information'. The ECB did not see the need to withdraw Stewart from the Pakistani tour following the release of the report. In fact, Alec Stewart was appointed English captain, for the second and final Test match of the return series against Pakistan at Old Trafford, two days before the ICC Corruption Report was made public on 23 May 2001.

By July 2001, Alec Stewart had been officially cleared of corruption charges by the ECB. The Board referred to a confidential report from Lord Condon, who could find no evidence to justify the allegations against Stewart.[323] Stewart's career continued to ascend to new heights. In 2002, he became England's most-capped Test cricketer, before finally retiring in 2003. Today, he is an Ambassador for the Professional Cricketers' Association (PCA), a role described on the Association's website: 'As representatives of the PCA, ambassadors uphold the values and integrity of the Association.'

The ICC, world cricket's governing body, reacted to the Cronjé crises with an emergency meeting on 2 May 2000 at which the Code of Conduct Committee proposed the drafting of a declaration detailing any knowledge of corruption within the game to be signed by the ten Test-playing nations, along with associate members Scotland and Kenya. The Imperial Cricket Conference, described as the MCC's 'colonial branch' by Derek Birley[324] and comprising England, Australia and South Africa, was formed in 1909 to champion commonwealth cricket and standardise the rules governing international matches played between these three sides. In 1926, New Zealand, the West Indies and India were welcomed into the ICC's fold of Test-playing nations. Pakistan followed in 1952. In 1965, the organisation was renamed the International Cricket Conference and the inner circle expanded to encompass associate members who, unlike founder members, were only entitled to a single vote each. Sri Lanka joined the ranks of full membership in 1982 followed by Zimbabwe in 1992 and Bangladesh in 2000. The last metamorphosis of the erstwhile International Cricket Conference took place in 1989 when the organisation was christened the International Cricket Council. Its mission statement promises to '... lead by promoting the game as a global sport, protecting the spirit of cricket and optimising the commercial opportunities for the benefit of the game.'[325]

The ICC officials involved in the Code of Conduct Committee read like a Who's Who of Commonwealth peerage. Lord Hugh Griffiths, a past chairman of the Marylebone Cricket Club, was the Chairman.[326] Alongside the Right Honourable Lord sat Sir Oliver Popplewell of England and Sir Denys Williams of the West Indies. The head of England's Cricket Board at the time was Lord MacLaurin. Three hundred years after cricket was taken up by the aristocracy and formalised by the MCC, the social hierarchy remained intact.

The first draft of the declaration was reviewed by the ICC's Board in June 2000. Showing more alacrity in the inception than the implementation of the idea, the final version appeared only five months later, in October. Submissions from all cricket's participants were due the following month, November. As of 31 March 2001 only two of the twelve countries canvassed had fully completed the exercise. Of the nine hundred and eleven declarations received, only twenty-one admitted any knowledge of corrupt practices and of these only five were found to warrant further investigation. Thus, with the benefit of hindsight, the Director of the ICC's Anti-Corruption Unit pointed out what should have been obvious from the first. The self-declaration idea was '... intrinsically flawed because corrupt people were unlikely to respond honestly'. So much for the ICC's initial salvo in the match-fixing skirmish. The Anti-Corruption Unit (ACU) was another weapon in the ICC's war on wagering.

Sir Paul Condon was appointed Director of the new unit on 26 June 2000, the same day that South Africa's King Commission had its final public sitting. Condon, an Oxford man, was the youngest Commissioner of London's Metropolitan Police in 150 years, reaching the position in February 1993 aged 45. He was knighted in 1994. On 22 April 1993, less than three months after Condon became Commissioner, 18-year-old A-level student Stephen Lawrence was stabbed to death at an Eltham bus stop in south-east London. He was black. His alleged attackers were white. The Lawrence case almost led to the premature end of Condon's career in 1999. After a string of start-stop inquests, several trials ending in dismissed charges and acquittals, internal reviews of the investigation, and finally a public inquiry in 1998, the Macpherson Report found that the Lawrence investigation had been '... marred by a combination of professional incompetence, institutional racism and a failure of leadership by senior officers'.[327] On the eve of the Macpherson Report's release on 24 February 1999, Condon was grimly hanging on to his job with ten months to go before his retirement. After the *Sunday Telegraph* leaked news of the contents of the report on 21 February 1999, calls were raised for Condon's dismissal as he had neglected to act on the Lawrence family's accusations of a bungled investigation until the Police Complaints Authority found cause for concern in its 1997 inquiry. He also continued to deny charges of institutional racism in his department. With the support of Home Secretary Jack Straw, Condon held on to his position. In fact, he went one better and was made a life peer by the Queen on 27 June 2001. After his retirement from the police force, Condon was seconded to the directorship of the ICC's new Anti-Corruption Unit (ACU), which was renamed the ICC Anti-Corruption and Security Unit (AC&SU) in 2003.

In Condon's introduction to his cricket report, produced a month shy of a year since his appointment, he expressed his unit's '... humility and respect for religious and cultural differences ...' in their international investigations. Evidence of his even-handed approach is found in his assertion that 'In many ways the Indian betting industry has been the engine room which has powered and driven cricket corruption'. At the same time, Condon acknowledged that '... the blame for the spread of cricket corruption is a shared responsibility and must not be unfairly laid upon the Indian subcontinent'. The introduction to the report also professed a commitment to transparency. However, no names were named, no fresh allegations were published, no suspect matches were identified and no new investigations were detailed in the report. Instead, Condon and his crew compiled a Beginner's Guide to Match-fixing, which provided a general overview of world cricket corruption mostly summarised from various inquiries around the world. The report traced the genesis of corruption, the elements of and reasons for the fix as well as matches that are vulnerable to manipulation. There were no surprises in the fact that corruption in cricket has been rife for the past twenty years or that it continues to this day. Nor were there any new revelations in Condon's observation that the allegations so far made public are only 'the tip of the iceberg'. No indication was given of how much of the iceberg has been plumbed. Former England captain-turned-commentator Ian Botham used the same metaphor in an interview on the BBC TV show *Panorama* on 20 May 2001. 'I think we've just touched the tip of the iceberg ... It's not just the players that are involved, it's a much wider network. I've heard figures of as much as a billion US dollars changing hands on a Test match.'[328]

Echoing the Indian investigators complaints of a 'conspiracy of silence', Condon extrapolated on the reasons behind the general reluctance of the cricket community to co-operate. Players feared ostracism by the team as whistle-blowers have not been embraced in the past. They feared the end of their international careers and, in some cases, they feared for their personal safety. Players complained also of the absence of a credible body to whom to turn with such information. Condon acknowledged that his team, which is appointed and funded by the ICC, had been regarded with suspicion in certain quarters because of the perception that the ICC had been '... dragged reluctantly into public discussion of corruption'. Condon reassured the public that he reported not to the ICC's CEO, Malcolm Gray, but to his fellow peer, Lord Griffiths of the ICC's Code of Conduct Committee.

Careful not to bite the hand that feeds him, Condon sought to explain the ICC's '... ambivalence to face up to the challenge of corruption'. Cricket's governing body was portrayed as an under-funded, fragmented institution with limited powers and inadequate infrastructure for the task. As the contemporary game generates so much money that organised crime has climbed onto the bandwagon, this seems, at best, a disingenuous portrayal. In 2007, the ICC expected the World Cup to bring in some US$239 million, making it the most lucrative World Cup in the organisation's history.[329]

Lord Condon proclaimed his integrity in an interview on the BBC World Service's *Sportsworld* on 7 April 2001: 'For me the most important thing is to help restore the faith in the game for millions of followers around the world. What happens on the field should be about skill, courage, luck and endeavour, not about seedy deals with bookmakers, mobile phones and the fixing of matches for betting purposes.'[330] In his report, Condon promised that before the World Cup in South Africa in 2003, '... corruption in cricket will be under control and reduced to an absolute minimum'. However, subsequent events would prove his confidence misplaced.

The former British colony of Kenya inherited the game of cricket from its erstwhile imperial masters in the nineteenth century. In 1982, Kenya played its first Trophy match as an ICC associate member and in 1996 the African country took to the world stage to take on the best of the best in the Wills World Cup. Kenyan all-rounder Maurice Odumbe was one of the star performers and captained his country in its first World Cup. He would go on to play in sixty-one ODIs for Kenya. Eleven days after their ODI debut, in a cricketing version of the biblical tale of David and Goliath, the Kenyan team toppled the mighty West Indies in one of the biggest upsets in World Cup history. In a Group A match at Pune on 29 February 1996, Kenya beat the West Indies by 73 runs.

The West Indies won the toss and sent Kenya in to bat. The African team posted a modest total of 166 all out in 49.3 overs. The West Indies' bowlers added to the Kenyan total with 14 wides, 13 no-balls and a grand tally of 35 extras. Odumbe's batting performance was disappointing and he went out, hit wicket, for six. Interestingly, if perhaps incidentally, New Delhi restaurateur, professional gambler and allegedly 'active match-fixer' Ratan Mehta, in an interview with *Outlook* magazine on 12 July 2004, commented on the odds of a batsman dislodging the bails and being out hit-wicket: '... the odds on cricketers getting out hit-wicket is 80:1. Brian Lara has got out like this frequently. Recently, Graeme Smith got out stepping on his wickets.'[331] However, what seemed like an easy target proved out of the reach of the West Indies batting line-up, which crumbled to 93 all out in 35. 2 overs, notching up their second-worst score ever. The opening order managed a grand total of 17 runs with captain Richie Richardson contributing 5 and Brian Lara adding 8, having narrowly escaped being run out on 4. Odumbe took 3 wickets for 15 runs and earned himself the Man of the Match award.

Odumbe picked up another Man of the Match award, this time in a day/night game against India on 6 March in Gwalior, during the 1998 Coca-Cola Triangular series. In another stunning upset, Kenya racked up a total of 265/5 in the allotted 50 overs while India were all out within 47 overs on 196. Mohammad Azharuddin captained this match with Nayan Mongia as his deputy.

Although Kenya didn't manage any giant-beating in the 1999 World Cup in England, Odumbe earned himself another Man of the Match award for his 82 against Sri Lanka in a Group A match at Southampton on 30 May 1999. Then, in the 2003 World Cup, which Kenya co-hosted with South Africa, Odumbe covered himself in glory once again, as did the Kenyan team. The minnows of world cricket marched through to the semi-finals of the tournament by defeating Canada, New Zealand (by default as the New Zealanders forfeited the game because of security concerns about playing in Nairobi), Sri Lanka, Zimbabwe and Bangladesh. Odumbe's 52 not out against Bangladesh and 4 wickets for 38 runs in 10 overs earned him the Man of the Match award again.

However, a year later, Odumbe's achievements were overshadowed by match-fixing allegations. In contrast to the confidential inquiry and conclusion to the English match-fixing allegations, on 12 March 2004, the ICC announced that, as a result of the AC&SU's investigations, Odumbe would face a formal public hearing into claims that he had had '... inappropriate contact with a bookmaker and influenced the result of matches'.[332] The suspected bookie in question was none other than Jagdish Sodha, of Chris Lewis and Stephen Fleming infamy.

Former Zimbabwean Supreme Court Justice Ahmed Ebrahim led the official inquiry. The preliminary hearing on 19 May 2004 was followed by the judicial hearing in Nairobi, which began on 27 July. Witnesses included Odumbe's estranged wife Katherine Maloney, girlfriends Caitlin Patterson and Kajta Neilson, a serving member of the Metropolitan Police whose identity was not revealed because of his undercover work, and several investigators from the ICC's Anti-Corruption and Security Unit. Their evidence would prove to be damning.

Niranjan Virk, an ACU and former CBI investigator, cast some light on the identity of Jagdish Sodha. According to Virk, Sodha had confessed to him on 17 August 2000 that he had been a bookmaker since 1985. Apparently, Sodha had met Ashim Kheterpal at a party at the Sun-'n-Sand hotel in Mumbai in 1998. This was one of the hotels at which Odumbe enjoyed free accommodation during his four visits to India in 2002. Mr Virk said Sodha had come to the attention of the Indian police again in 2003 during the Cricket World Cup in South Africa. Virk told the Odumbe Inquiry that Sodha had been brought in by the Mumbai police along with twenty-three other bookmakers the night before the match between India and Australia. Based on newspaper accounts, this would be the match on the 15 February, rather than the March final. Virk added that Sodha was again brought before the Mumbai police on 1 March during the India/Pakistan game.

The unidentified Metropolitan Police officer also testified that Sodha had admitted to him that he bet on cricket matches. The policeman was part of the investigation into Stephen Fleming's and Chris Lewis's attempted bribery allegations. He testified that a telephone analysis had revealed numerous phone calls that had been made between Jagdish Sodha, Ashim Kheterpal and a certain Sanjeev Chawla.

Odumbe's wife Katherine Maloney explained how she had met her husband while he was still involved with Caitlin Patterson. Odumbe, it seems, was reluctant to end the relationship with Patterson because she knew too much about his illicit cricketing activities and had threatened to go public with the knowledge. Apparently, Odumbe had told Maloney that Patterson was aware that five or six members of the Kenyan cricket team had been involved in match-fixing, earning US$5 000 each for their efforts, or lack thereof. The going rate would appear to differ markedly from what other international cricketers claimed they had been offered for similar services. Unfavourable exchange rates, perhaps? Maloney told the inquiry that she had met Sodha in person and that Odumbe had told her he was a match-fixer. She had collected US$10 000 from Sodha for Odumbe upon one occasion and on another had found US$8 000 in the family home. She referred also to a phone call from Sodha on 3 March 2003, looking for Odumbe during the World Cup in South Africa.

According to the testimony of Caitlin Patterson, she had also been introduced to an Indian man called Jagdish by Odumbe at a cricket tournament in Nairobi in September 1999. She recounted her understanding that this Jagdish was involved in match-fixing and recalled the many telephone calls between Jagdish and Odumbe that followed that initial meeting. In December 1999, Patterson claimed, Odumbe went to Zimbabwe where he told her he would make US$5 000 for match-fixing.

Based on the evidence at hand, Justice Ebrahim found that Odumbe had:

- associated with a known Indian bookmaker
- accepted hotel accommodation in Mumbai from Jagdish Sodha and/or his associates on at least five occasions in 2002
- accepted a total of 16 317 rupees
- received cash from Sodha amounting to US$18 000
- admitted to receiving US$5 000 to fix an unidentified match
- admitted to receiving US$5 000 for fixing a match in Zimbabwe.

Intriguingly, Justice Ebrahim found that the allegation that Odumbe had received an unspecified amount of money from a Mr Kush Patel to perform 'a service' during the Cricket World Cup 2003 was not proved. Be that as it may, could this Mr Kush Patel be the same Kamlesh Patel that introduced Chris Lewis to Kheterpal and Sodha in London in 1999? Justice Ebrahim concluded: 'He has not been found guilty of match-fixing but, as I have indicated, his conduct was outrageously reprehensible. In my view, a five-year ban would meet the justice of the case and I so recommend.'

Accordingly, on 17 August 2004, Odumbe was banned by the Kenyan Cricket Association for five years. Maurice Odumbe, therefore, had the dubious distinction of being the first and last cricketer to be thus penalised since the fallout from Hansiegate – perhaps because, as the ICC's website proclaims, '... corruption has been suppressed to an "irreducible minimum" level ...' Or perhaps not?

15

Pulling the wool

The death of Bob Woolmer

Where there is gambling, there is money
and where there is money, there is murder.

– Sarfraz Nawaz [333]

Robert Andrew Woolmer was born in the Indian city of Kanpur, Uttar Pradesh, on 14 May 1948. His father, Clarence, was a manager with a textile company, British India Corporation, and a keen cricketer. Legend has it that when Bob was born Clarence placed a bat and ball in his cot. Whether the power of such suggestion took effect or whether cricket was simply in the family genes, Bob Woolmer developed into an all-rounder whose talent is described in the *Wisden Almanack* of 1976: '... the only argument about Woolmer's undoubted cricketing ability and future in the game was whether he might become a better bowler than batsman or vice versa.'[334] On debut for English county side Kent in 1968, Woolmer hit an unbeaten half-century against Essex. He went on to make his cricketing debut for England in the first ODI of the Prudential Trophy against Australia at Old Trafford in Manchester on 24 August 1972. Although he didn't get to bat, he bowled 10 overs at an economy rate of 3.3 runs an over.

In South Africa in the 1970s, apartheid meant international sporting isolation. However, English sports promoter Derrick Robins arranged four private tours of the country with international cricketers such as Robin Jackman, Peter Willey, Tony Greig, Trevor Chappel, Ian Chappell, Dennis Lillee and Bob Woolmer, who played in the 1973 end-of-year tour. Woolmer stayed on to coach at the Kingsmead Mynah Club in Durban under South African batsman Barry Richards, whose prodigious talents, like Bob's, would later be showcased in Kerry Packer's break-away cricketing spectacle. It was here in Durban that Bob met his wife, Gill. Barry Richards was best man at their wedding in 1972.

Bob kept his hand in, batting number five for Natal before returning to England in 1975 when he made his Test debut in the second Test of the Ashes series against Australia. This time he earned 33 and 31 with the bat and maintained his tidy bowling figures. This Test was noteworthy in other ways. It was the first English Test match where a 'streaker' took to the field, signalling a new era of cricketing spectacle. Bob went on to make 149 against Australia in the fourth Test of the same Ashes series in August/September 1975 and earned the accolade Wisden Cricketer of the Year in 1976. Nonetheless, Woolmer chose to risk his burgeoning cricket career in England to join Kerry Packer's opposition World Series Cricket in 1977.

Australian media tycoon Kerry Packer is the man responsible for the game of cricket as we know it today. In the 1970s, Packer headed a business empire built on magazines, TV networks and casinos. 'Packer's Circus', as it became known in certain circles, popularised the one-day game, introduced day/night cricket and was responsible for other innovations, including batsmens' helmets and the cameras placed at each end of the pitch, enabling viewers to see every stroke of the bat. Ironically, and yet perhaps fittingly, given Packer's business interests, in helping spread the game of cricket through TV, Packer's legacy has also led to the widespread gambling that threatens the integrity of the game today.

In 1974, after the death of his father, Kerry Packer took over the reins of Australia's Channel Nine TV. With the advent of colour TV in 1975, Packer realised the opportunities offered by sports programming. First, he secured the TV rights to the Australian Open golf tournament before approaching the Australian Cricket Board for the TV rights to Australia's Test matches, rights that were held by the Australian Broadcasting Corporation. However, his generous offer was turned down. Not a man to take 'No' for an answer, Packer orchestrated a breakaway professional cricket tournament, World Series Cricket, which was aired on Channel Nine between 1977 and 1979. With the lure of match fees far in excess of what cricketers could earn from their country's own cricket boards, Packer succeeded in signing up some of the world's greatest cricket players of the time including:

- Greg Chappell, Ian Chappell and Dennis Lillee (Australia)
- Clive Lloyd and Viv Richards (West Indies)
- Javed Miandad, Asif Iqbal, Imran Khan and Majid Khan (Pakistan)
- Barry Richards, Mike Procter, Garth le Roux, Clive Rice, Kepler Wessels and Eddie Barlow (South Africa)
- Tony Greig and Bob Woolmer (England)

Bob Woolmer played what was to be his last Test for England in July 1981 at Lords. Then in 1982, he went on the first major rebel tour of South Africa, in defiance of the world's policy of sporting isolation. The South African rebel tours were organised by the South African Cricket Union under the leadership of Ali

Bacher and cricketers from England, Sri Lanka, the West Indies and Australia risked life bans by participating in these lucrative tours.

Incidentally, a Johannesburg lawyer named Peter Soller alleged, in a statement to the King Commission of Inquiry, that it was during the West Indies rebel tour of 1983 that Dr Bacher had fixed a match. Soller said that, during a one-day international at the Wanderers in Johannesburg, the West Indies team refused to return to the field after a change of innings unless they received more money. According to Soller, Dr Bacher agreed to their demands in exchange for their promise to lose the match. Bacher emphatically denied this charge.[335]

By the time Woolmer's playing career came to an end in 1984, he had appeared in over 300 first-class matches for Kent and the South African provinces of Natal and Western Province, as well as 19 Tests for England with an average of 33 runs. The following year he immigrated to South Africa, where he coached hockey and cricket at high schools in disadvantaged areas of Cape Town.

It was for his coaching talent that Bob Woolmer would be remembered. He became coach of Kent for a brief spell in 1987 before going on to become Director of Coaching at Warwickshire, which, under his guidance, won the NatWest Trophy in 1993 and three out of four domestic trophies in 1994. This was the same year that Woolmer brought the West Indies' master batsman, Brian Lara, to play for Warwickshire. In the space of 2 months, Lara broke 2 world records, 375 in a Test and an unbeaten first-class 501 against Durham, at Edgbaston. It was in the wake of this successful year that Bob Woolmer became coach of the South African team.

Following South Africa's readmission to international cricket in 1991, the team that Bob Woolmer took over in 1994 was new to world cricket. Woolmer would go on to shape the careers of iconic South African cricketers Jonty Rhodes, Gary Kirsten, Allan Donald and, of course, Hansie Cronjé, who became captain of the national team on 7 November 1994. In an article in the Indian newspaper *The Hindu*, Woolmer is quoted as saying that '... he and Cronjé were "made for each other" as coach and captain.'[336]

Woolmer guided the South Africans through two Cricket World Cups: 1996 on the Asian subcontinent and 1999 in England. In 1996, in only their second World Cup, South Africa reached the quarter-finals, losing to the West Indies by 19 runs. Woolmer said, 'We had a good plan in 1996, but were undone by a great performance by (century-maker) Brian Lara in the quarter-final ... It was cruel to lose by a run rate of 0.01 which was the closest of margins. It was very depressing.'[337]

By 1999, the South African team was one of the star attractions of the tournament and made it as far as the semi-finals, only to lose in singular circumstances.[338] However, the semi-final tie against Australia was not the only South

Africa match in this World Cup to attract untoward attention. The Pakistan Cricket Board (PCB) called for an inquiry into this game as well as a Group A match in which giant-slayers Zimbabwe toppled the South African Goliath.[339] South Africa's very first game of the tournament against India has also been investigated on suspicion of match-fixing. And then there was that infamous dropped catch by Herschelle Gibbs in the Super Six game against Australia at Headingley, which has gone down in cricketing history. Nonetheless, the King Commission in South Africa, just over a year later, never explored the extraordinary events of this World Cup.

In 2006, some seven years after the 1999 World Cup, Indian police asked the British Home Office to aid their inquiries into whether gambling syndicates had fixed matches during the 1999 World Cup. The Indians wanted video footage of South Africa's first match, against India at Hove on 15 May 1999, which detectives referred to as a 'curious incident'.[340] Both Cronjé and Allan Donald were wearing earpieces in this match, ostensibly to communicate with the coach, but '... Indian detectives believe they could have been used in a betting scam'.[341] The police also requested specific details of Cronjé's English bank accounts and phone records, as they continued, some four years after his death, to explore Cronjé's dealings with London-based Indian national Sanjeev Chawla.[342]

Bob Woolmer defended the earpieces in an *Indian Express* article that was published days after the match in question: 'Instead of using the twelfth man and sending out gloves or whatever with him, I thought we could use this innovation to save time ... Some of the guys enjoyed using it, and only a player who wants to use one wears it.' The story went on to claim that physiotherapist Craig Smith was also seen wearing the device in the players' enclosure. Craig explained that the earpieces '... were used to keep us in touch with our satellites and that '... all of us have ear infection'.[343]

Following the resurgence of police interest in this game in 2006, Woolmer addressed the issue once more in a self-penned article on *cricinfo.com* in October 2006: 'Even more bizarre is that the detectives have asked to take a look at the earpieces (and microphones) that were used at Hove during the game against India. I say bizarre because, quite frankly, the earpieces were used for one hour and ten minutes before we were instructed to stop by the match referee.'[344] Incidentally, Pakistan's Talat Ali, who would feature again in the unprecedented events of the 2007 World Cup, was the match referee in question. 'The players then did not have any microphones or transmitters with them – it was only one-way communication, from the coach to the player. The practice has since been banned by the ICC. Allan Donald and Cronjé were wearing the two earpieces but any suggestion that we were using them for betting purposes is mere speculation and far removed from the truth.'[345]

Three other matches in the 1999 World Cup have subsequently come under the scrutiny of the New Delhi police: 'Of particular concern is Bangladesh's defeat of Pakistan in a group game, although claims have also surrounded South Africa's loss to Zimbabwe and a second phase match between India and Pakistan. Zimbabwe and Bangladesh won when their opponents had already assured qualification.'[346]

On 29 May, in a Group A match between South Africa and Zimbabwe at Chelmsford, Zimbabwe pulled off one of the upsets of the tournament, beating the South African favourites, for the first time ever in an ODI, by 48 runs in the forty-eighth over. A loose South African bowling attack conceded 28 extras followed by a batting collapse that saw 8 out of the 11 South African batsmen leave the crease on single figures with opening bat Kirsten, described as '... the most dependable opening batsman in the world' and stalwart Kallis both departing on ducks.[347]

Coach Bob Woolmer discussed this match in a column on *cricinfo.com* in October 2006:

> South Africa's game against Zimbabwe at Chelmsford is suspect because Zimbabwe beat us. The first games looked at were those slating minnows against the big boys, and now recent newspaper reports suggest that South Africa's game against Zimbabwe at Chelmsford is suspect because Zimbabwe beat us. On the day Zimbabwe played better cricket and we were extremely disappointed – in fact, Cronjé and I had an argument over the way we had prepared for the game, having gone to Holland for the match before, which he felt was disruptive. Our travel plans were poor and we stayed in a hotel miles out of town. The dressing-rooms at Chelmsford are too small for touring teams and the net bowlers were poor at practice. A lot of small things started to conspire against our preparation. By the time the Zimbabwe game arrived we were all pretty ratty. That, more than any other reason, was why we did not perform to our best. Also, in those days Zimbabwe were a good team and not the complete underdogs they are now. They were quite capable of beating anyone in the tournament. There was no question of any betting or bookie involvement that I knew about.[348]

By the Super Six stage of the competition, South Africa were '... well on course to win this World Cup' as one commentator put it.[349] South Africa had already earned themselves a place in the semi-finals but Australia had to win this match to avoid being sent home. South Africa won the toss and backed themselves to bat first, putting on a sizeable total of 271, thanks to a century by Herschelle Gibbs. Captain Cronjé, however, was bowled by Warne, leg before wicket for a duck.

When Cronjé's counterpart, Steve Waugh, came to the crease, Australia were struggling at 48 for 3. Waugh played a captain's innings to steer his team to victory with 2 balls and 5 wickets to spare – with some help from Herschelle Gibbs. Gibbs is described in match reports of the game as '… one of the safest catchers in the contemporary game' [350] and '… one of the two best fielders in a side that is not short of good ones.'[351]

The following exchange between Gibbs and Mr Fitzgerald, the lawyer representing 37 players and former players at the King Commission on 8 June 2000, reinforced Gibbs' cricketing credentials.

FITZGERALD: Just for the record, you are a right-handed batman and a specialist fielder.

GIBBS: Correct.

FITZGERALD: A specialist catcher too!

GIBBS: Well, it's the dropped catch as well.

With Waugh on 56 and Australia 120 short of the target, Gibbs caught Waugh comfortably off the bowling of Klusener. Gibbs threw the ball up in the air in celebration only for it to slip from his fingers and with it the game. Gibbs was not alone, however, in letting Waugh off the hook. Just after reaching his 100, Waugh survived a catching chance off the bowling of Cronjé. As one match commentator described the incident: 'Klusener, whose catch it should have been, stood back and watched Boucher running 30 metres only to get nowhere near the ball.'[352] Waugh went on to make 120 not out and Australia took the game by 5 wickets with 2 balls to spare. The outcome of this match meant that, instead of Zimbabwe, South Africa would have to face arch-rivals Australia once again, in the semi-final.

Gary Kirsten, in his autobiography, *Gazza*, recalls the Headingly game:

> Herschelle Gibbs had scored his best one-day century and we had a match-winning score of 271 on the board, at a ground where it was infamously difficult to post large scores, let alone chase them. Australia were in early trouble at 48/3 but Steve Waugh was fighting like crazy to keep them alive. He had just reached 50. Moments later we saw the ball flying to Herschelle at mid-wicket. He caught it. We were going to win. I started to feel the thrill of victory. He had dropped it. What the hell was going on? It was the strangest catch, or drop, I've ever seen. It was too bizarre for words. I still shudder when I think back to the moment. Hersch actually caught the ball but lost it in the act of throwing it up in the air to celebrate. Instead of coming to terms with it as the years have passed, I find it harder and harder to believe.[353]

Then came the 17 June and the semi-final, which Gary Kirsten describes as '... equally bizarre but far, far more painful'.[354] What South African cricket fan will ever forget Allan Donald mired at his end, bat flung beside him on the pitch and Lance Klusener flailing across the wicket, unable to prevent the incredible semi-final draw that saw arch-rivals Australia go through on points to the final to win the 1999 World Cup?

Bob Woolmer's good friend Professor Tim Noakes remembers that semi-final all too well:

> You see, I was at that World Cup semi-final and that was the most devastating day I've ever been through. What happened was, I watched the game in the company of Australians. I was at the game and, I mean, I'm not a Bob Woolmer but there were things on the field that happened that day which I couldn't explain. The first example is you don't bat second at Edgbaston, you bat first. I asked the captain of Warwickshire who was at the Institute, whom Bob was coaching – now, he's totally independent, he didn't even know when South Africa had batted. I said, "Tell me, when you play at Edgbaston in a one-day game what do you do?" He said, "You bat first". I said, "Why?" He said, "Because the pitch deteriorates and it's always difficult batting second". So then I said, "Fine, but it's raining and it's wet and it's overcast as it was on that day and the game was held up for half an hour to an hour". He said, "You still bat first". I said, "Why?" He said, "Because the white ball seams around a lot for the first 7 overs and then it goes straight. The red ball seams around and moves all day so then, if it's a five-day game or a three-day game, then you would consider batting second. But in a one-day game you bat first". Now, South Africa won the toss and they batted second.

According to Luke Alfred in an article in the South African *Sunday Times* on 25 March 2007, 'Woolmer's advice to Cronjé on winning the toss was that he should bat. Cronjé won the toss and bowled.'[355] Noakes continued:

> There are other things I know ... The final question is, why did Klusener come in at 45 overs? Why didn't he come in at 35 overs? Why did Cronjé only bowl one over in that game? One over for 2 runs. There may be very good cricketing reasons; that's always the problem in cricket. But I was phoned by one of the ex-players and he expressed his concerns about the game. I think a lot of cricketers have concerns about that game, as well. But they don't speak up about it because it's a closed shop and if you speak up you're in trouble.

Bob Woolmer's tenure as South African coach came to an end with South

Africa's harrowing departure from the 1999 World Cup. Notwithstanding the fact that Woolmer's period as coach coincided with Cronjé's crooked captaincy and despite the extraordinary circumstances surrounding the South African World Cup campaign and the investigations that would follow, Bob Woolmer was never called to testify at the King Commission. A cricketing contemporary of Woolmer's from way back in those heady days of Packer's World Series Cricket, South African batsman Clive Rice, has said: 'Bob knew a lot of what went on during the match-fixing scandal in which Hansie Cronjé was nailed. I found it odd that he was never called as a witness by the King Commission.'[356]

Prosecutor Shamila Batohi explained that she '... did not call Woolmer to give evidence because he had no knowledge of match-fixing prior to the inquiry.'[357]

However, as has been detailed in an earlier chapter, Bob Woolmer knew, at least, of the match-fixing offer put to the South African team at the end of their 1996 tour of India. And apparently a lot more, according to Rice, who, when the match-fixing story broke in 2000, was coaching Nottinghamshire at the same time as Woolmer was coaching Warwickshire. 'We were actually involved in a match in England at the time and Bob and I discussed it. He told me a lot that never came out. I'm not just talking about other players being involved but officials too.'[358] Bowler Fanie de Villiers, another South African player who had been coached by Woolmer, echoed Rice's sentiments. 'Bob knew too much. He knew everybody in the system ... Match-fixing is the biggest problem in world cricket. The guys who are the closest are the players and the coaches. They can see if anything odd is happening on the field.'[359] Nonetheless, Woolmer was quoted in an article in *The Hindu* on 16 October 2001: 'I did not know it [match-fixing] was happening. Unless you knew it was happening, how do you stop it?'[360]

Despite the disappointing climax to his time with South Africa, it was widely reported that Bob Woolmer was England's first choice for their national coach. However, Duncan Fletcher got the job and Bob went on to join the ICC as their High Performance Manager in 2001, helping the coaches of fledgling cricket sides Kenya, Holland, Canada and Namibia. Then, in June 2004, he took on the job of Pakistan's coach, a job that was to end in tragedy at yet another ill-starred World Cup.

Woolmer took over as coach from Javed Miandad, whose son, incidentally, is married to Dawood Ibrahim's daughter. He was hired by PCB Chairman Shahryar Khan, Pakistan's former foreign secretary,[361] who would hold the reins of cricketing power for more than six years before his sudden resignation in October 2006.

Why Woolmer took the job is not easily explicable. As Shahryar Khan said, 'When Bob took over as coach, Pakistan were languishing in the lower levels of both Test and ODI rankings of the ICC tables'.[362] Woolmer didn't speak the language and could have made more money coaching an English county side in familiar surroundings. Moreover, he knew of the taint of match-fixing that had clung to the Pakistani team over the years. During the mid- to late-1990s Pakistan had held three enquiries into allegations of match-fixing within the national team. Just two years before Woolmer's appointment as coach, another inquiry, this time into the 1999 World Cup, had cleared all Pakistan's cricket players of match-fixing. Woolmer's ghostwriter, Ivo Tennant, explained in Bob's own words:

> I had heard a lot about the intolerance of failure when I took on the job. There was much to put me off – many stories and rumours of match-fixing and ball-scratching – and yet the talent emerging from the country appeared to be endless. Indian and Pakistani cricket, turning pitches, wristy batsmen, reverse swing, held a sort of mystique for me. I felt I could see the game and coaching in a completely different light.[363]

Professor Tim Noakes couldn't explain his good friend's decision to live and work in Pakistan, but he said that Bob's wife Gill didn't want him to go.

Woolmer's time with the team was not easy. Just six months after taking over as coach from Javed Miandad, media reports were already describing Woolmer as 'Pakistan's embattled coach'.[364] During an end-of-year tour of Australia in 2004, Pakistan lost a warm-up match against a Western Australia second XI, prompting Woolmer to comment: 'I've been with Pakistan for five months now, and we've done this three or four times. We're unpredictable; you can take what you like out of this. I don't know what's going on either.'[365] Pakistan went on to lose the first Test against Australia in Perth by 491 runs and the Test series by 3–0.

International media reports would later assert that, during his tenure as Pakistan coach, Woolmer had submitted anti-match-fixing recommendations to Shahryar Khan, Chairman of the PCB. These recommendations reportedly included: [366]

- regular monitoring of the bank accounts of players
- bans on the use of mobile phones during Test matches
- bans on cricketers associating with bookies or anyone with known ties to match-fixers
- a zero-tolerance code of conduct backed up by life bans
- bigger win bonuses to prevent temptation
- rigorous appraisals of captains to prevent abuse of leadership.

However, Khan, PCB Chairman during most of Woolmer's tenure as Pakistan's coach, maintained that Bob had never shared 'any doubts about match-fixing' with him[367] and apparently no such recommendations had been implemented by the time of the 2007 World Cup.

Media reports abounded about differences between Woolmer and the top brass of the PCB as well the players, both past, like Javed Miandad and present, like pace bowler Shoaib Akhtar and captain Inzamam ul-Haq. Shahryar Khan, in an interview on BBC's Radio Five Live programme *Sportsweek*, claimed that Bob Woolmer '... never really had full control of the team, either spiritual or cricketing, because this lay with the captain most of the time ... Inzamam was the leader, the unquestioned leader of his team.'[368] Former Pakistani fast bowler Wasim Akram echoed Khan's sentiments in an interview with ESPN: 'Inzy definitely had become a dictator. He had obviously become very powerful ... I have seen senior PCB officials sitting at his residence and awaiting orders. These things are not good for cricket.'[369] This is markedly similar to descriptions of Hansie Cronjé's reign as South African skipper while Bob was coach.

As in Hansie's time too, a religious element had suffused the Pakistani dressing room, which sometimes made life challenging for Woolmer as he attempted to train players who were fasting or praying. The born-again Christianity of the South African cricket team during Hansie's time as captain is mirrored in the Pakistani team's Islamic revivalist beliefs under Inzamam ul-Haq.

A secretive, worldwide, apolitical religious organisation that encourages Muslims to return to a pure form of Islam, the Tablighi Jamaat (TJ) is a party of preachers. However, there are conflicting reports about whether the TJ is more than it says it is. In 2003, the *New York Times* quoted Michael J Heimbach, the deputy chief of the FBI's international terrorism unit: 'We have a significant presence of Tablighi Jamaat in the United States and we have found that Al-Qaeda has used them for recruiting now and in the past.'[370]

Despite high-level political assertions that there is evidence that the TJ recruits for and even funds terrorist organisations, Eva Borreguero, a Fulbright scholar who has researched the movement intensively, maintains that she has found little evidence to prove the TJ's links to Islamic militants. However, she concedes that the TJ may be a fruitful hunting ground for recruitment to militant Islamic organisations.[371] British 'shoe bomber' Richard Reid, for example, was reportedly a member of the Tablighi Jamaat.[372] Borreguero also admits that militant groups may use the TJ as a cover for their members to move freely across borders under the guise of peaceful proselytising.

In Pakistan, where religion and politics go hand in hand, TJ-affiliated members have, over the years, occupied positions of power in government and the intelligence services[373] – and in the Pakistani cricket team. Inzamam ul-Haq,

Mushtaq Ahmed, Shoaib Malik, Mohammed Yousuf, Saqlain Mushtaq, Shahid Afridi and Yasser Hamid are reportedly TJ members.[374] Religion is said to have divided the team with vice captain Younis Khan, Shoaib Akhtar, Mohammad Asif, Danish Kaneria, Imran Nazir and Abdul Razzaq on the other side of the religious divide. Captain ul-Haq has been accused of favouring TJ members over non-TJ members, charges which he has denied.[375] Amid displays of religious fervour on the cricket pitch, some cynical fans apparently feel that such overt piety is merely politics in disguise.[376]

By the time of the World Cup in March 2007, the Pakistani team were ranked fourth in the world in the one-day game and Bob's three-year contract was due to expire in June. After their loss to the home team, the West Indies, in the opening match of the tournament, the Pakistani team remained in Kingston, Jamaica, preparing for their second game, against Ireland on 17 March. In his web blog on *cricinfo.com*, two days before the Irish match, Bob Woolmer described how Mushtaq Ahmed, his assistant coach, broke his nose while fielding during a practice at the Kensington Oval. Ahmed explained the incident to *Reuters*: 'I was going to collect the ball and it bobbled and then hit me.' He was taken to hospital where he received two stitches.[377] This seemingly innocuous incident would assume greater significance in the days to come.

Mushtaq Ahmed was appointed Woolmer's assistant coach on 15 September 2006, despite the fact that he had been penalised for bringing the game into disrepute following Justice Qayyum's match-fixing report seven years previously. Judge Qayyum himself later spoke out against the appointment saying, 'Mushtaq Ahmed's appointment as assistant coach was in violation of my recommendations that he should not be given any position in the squad, as a member or official.'[378] Apparently, it was captain Inzamam ul-Haq, who had also been named, shamed and fined in the Qayyum Report, who wanted Ahmed in the team.

On Friday 16 March, in what turned out to be his last diary entry on the *cricinfo.com* website, Bob Woolmer described his team's preparations for the match against Ireland the following day. 'We netted at the Kensington Oval and then to Sabina Park for fielding practice, which formed our final preparations for tomorrow's game.' Hamid Mir, the CEO of Pakistani TV channel GEO TV, would later allege that ul-Haq and Ahmed, '... had some kind of an argument with Woolmer on Friday when the coach pushed them for net practice and they went outside the ground.'[379]

Pre-tournament, British bookmaker William Hill gave 1992 World Cup champs Pakistan 10–1 odds on winning the 2007 World Cup while debutantes Ireland were a long shot at 750–1.[380] Ireland, along with five other second-tier Associate members of the ICC – Kenya, Bermuda, Canada, Scotland and the

Netherlands – had played in a warm-up league tournament in Kenya prior to the World Cup. Ireland had won only one of its five games. On the day of the Pakistan/Ireland match at Sabina Park in Kingston, the odds on an Irish win were 500–1. In the run-up to the game, the odds shortened to 8–1.[381] The ICC's Anti-Corruption and Security Unit (AC&SU) would end up investigating unusual betting patterns in this match as well as in Pakistan's earlier defeat by the West Indies.

The legendary luck of the Irish conspired, on St Patrick's Day, to oust Pakistan from the tournament. Ireland won the toss and sent Pakistan in to bat. The first wicket fell in the first over, signalling the beginning of an early batting collapse that took the team to 72 for 6 by the twentieth over. By the forty-fifth over, it *was* all over. The entire Pakistani batting line-up had succumbed on 132 with 7 of the Pakistani batsmen managing only single-figure scores. The Pakistani bowlers gave away 14 extras and the team was fined for a slow over-rate as the Irish reached the required total with 3 wickets in hand. When asked by journalists at the post-match media conference what went wrong, Woolmer replied succinctly, 'Bad batting.'[382] With his team out of the World Cup in the opening round, Woolmer told reporters that, 'I'd like to sleep on my future as coach. I've had bad days before – the worst of them was at Edgbaston in 1999. Things like this happen in cricket.'[383]

After the press conference, the Pakistani team returned to their Kingston hotel, the five-star Jamaica Pegasus. According to later media reports, there was a heated argument between Woolmer and some of the Pakistani players, either in the dressing room or on the team bus on the way back to the hotel. The *Mail on Sunday* quoted a Jamaican police source: 'When Mr Woolmer boarded the coach to go back to the hotel, he was very, very angry. Our investigators are looking into a report that he confronted some members of the touring party on the bus. They did not perform up to standard and he vented his disgust verbally.'[384] However, other media sources claimed that the argument became physical. *Sky*'s Asia Correspondent Alex Crawford reported: 'There was a very heated row on the team coach on the way back from the match which developed into a physical row.'[385] *The Independent*, on the other hand, claimed that '... if there was a row, it was in the dressing room immediately after the match, some people heard it and the mood on the bus was subdued.'[386] Such reports, however, were later denied by PCB officials, Jamaican police as well as the bus driver, Bertram Carr. The two Jamaican policemen that had accompanied the Pakistani team on the bus were, however, never directly quoted.

Apparently, the rest of the Pakistani team went off to have dinner at the Kingston home of wealthy Pakistani car-dealer Tariq Malik, leaving Bob Woolmer behind in the hotel. Malik later said that the players had told him that they had left Bob behind with a bottle of Scotch.[387] However, blood tests would later reportedly show that although Woolmer had been drinking, he had not been drunk.[388]

Subsequent media reports differ on what time Bob went up to his room, number 374 on the twelfth floor, and stepped out of the public domain for good. Pervez (PJ) Mir, the Pakistani media manager, would later say that Bob went up to his room at 7 pm,[389] but the police would say 8:30 pm.[390] Sometime between 8:30 and 9 pm, according to the police, Woolmer ordered a lasagne from room service and wrote an e-mail to his wife. A member of the hotel staff was apparently the last person to see Bob alive, at 8:45 pm, although some media reports claimed that PJ Mir had that dubious honour – allegations that Mir denied.[391] Nasim Ashraf, the new Chairman of the Pakistan Cricket Board, who had succeeded Shahryar Khan in 2006, later claimed that Bob had sent him a resignation e-mail at six o'clock on the Sunday morning. However this e-mail was never verified and no copy was ever released by the PCB.

Woolmer was sharing the twelfth floor with players and managers from his own team as well as Zimbabwe, Ireland and the West Indies. Pakistani leg-spinner Danish Kaneria had the room next to Bob, team manager Talat Ali, captain Inzamam ul-Haq and the South African support staff, physiotherapist Darren Lifsun and fitness trainer Murray Stevenson, were all on the twelfth floor. Brian Lara's room was across the corridor, while West Indies manager Clive Lloyd and Irish captain Trent Johnson also had rooms on this floor.

What really happened in room 374 that Saturday night and early Sunday morning will probably never be known. Media reports disagree on when Bob was found, where and in what condition; what he was wearing and even whether he was alive or dead. Right from the outset there were two distinct theories on the coach's death – death by natural causes or by murder. All reports agreed, however, that it was a chambermaid that first discovered the stricken coach. However, no media source ever gave an eye-witness account of her version of events. As the most widely reported story went, Bob Woolmer was found by a chambermaid in his hotel room at 10:45 am. This is the official time given and the time that is most often quoted in the media. However, at least one local newspaper suggested that Woolmer was discovered earlier – at 8 am.[392] There were conflicting reports too about whether Pakistan's coach was alive or dead when he was found.

It was widely reported that he was 'unconscious' as asserted first by the Pakistani team's spokesperson Pervez Mir. The world first found out that something was amiss early on Sunday afternoon in Jamaica when Mir issued a statement:

> We have taken Bob Woolmer to the hospital and he is in the emergency ward. We don't know anything more at the moment. We saw him last night but having not seen him early today two of our officers went to his room and with the help of hotel staff entered. He was found unconscious there. It is too early to say whether he has suffered a heart attack. We are awaiting medical reports.[393]

The first statement had barely hit the wires when Mir made the shattering announcement that Woolmer was dead:

> Robert Andrew Woolmer has passed away today and the entire Pakistani team and management are shocked and saddened by his passing. His next of kin have been informed and we extend our deepest condolences to his family. The Chairman of the Pakistan Cricket Board has also been informed. There will be a coroner's inquest and, in keeping with Jamaican law, an autopsy will take place into his death. Further information will be released by the PCB at the earliest opportunity once it has been received from the hospital. Hotel staff found him about 10:45 am. He had blood on him and there was vomit on the walls.[394]

In Jamaica, coroner's inquests take place when there is '… reasonable cause to suspect that deaths are violent or unnatural.'[395] However, apparently inquests are standard practice in deaths that occur when the deceased is not under a doctor's treatment for any specific ailment.

According to the police's version of events: 'Mr. Woolmer was found in his hotel room by cleaning staff shortly before noon in an unconscious state. He was attended to by medical personnel at the hotel who also accompanied him to the hospital.'[396] Manager Talat Ali, assistant manager Asad Mustafa and Murray Stevenson also apparently travelled with Woolmer to the hospital.[397]

While some news stories stated that Woolmer had been taken to the hospital in an ambulance, as befitting someone in urgent need of medical attention, a 'confidante' told the *Jamaica Gleaner* that Woolmer had arrived in '… a diplomat van and he had police escorts.'[398] The *Jamaica Gleaner* questioned also why an hour had elapsed from when Woolmer was purportedly discovered to his arrival at the hospital at 11:45 am when the hospital was a ten-minute drive away.[399]

Six members of the Pakistani team were reportedly present in Woolmer's room soon after he was discovered: team manager Talat Ali, assistant manager Asad Mustafa, media manager Pervez Mir, assistant coach Mushtaq Ahmed, all-rounder Shahid Afridi and captain Inzamam ul-Haq. PJ Mir claimed that Talat

Ali was the first person to reach Woolmer's room.[400] Ali said that he was the first member of the management team to arrive and told the media: 'When I reached the spot, medical staff was giving Bob some medical treatment and according to the doctor, the coach was breathing. But sadly, he was later pronounced dead in the hospital.'[401] PJ Mir said that he was the third person from Pakistani team management to see Woolmer '... lying on the floor there. There was no sign of violence'.[402] Mir said that he had asked the medical staff to '... give him oxygen but they told me he was stable, he had a pulse'.[403] Pakistani captain Inzamam ul-Haq wrote in his online diary on *bigstarcricket.com* on the day that Woolmer died and he resigned from one-day international cricket: 'The first time I knew of Bob's illness was when our assistant manager rang me Sunday morning and said the coach is not feeling well and maybe he is upset. When I went to see him he was lying on the floor and it was shocking for me.'[404]

Jamaica's Major Investigation Team Task Force led by Deputy Superintendent Colin Pinnock was called in to investigate. But it would be Jamaica's Deputy Commissioner of Police (DCP) and former Scotland Yard detective Mark Shields who would become the public face of the investigation. Mark Shields was seconded to the Jamaican Constabulary Force (JCF) from Scotland Yard in March 2005 on a three-year contract to help combat violent crime and police corruption. After graduating from Essex University with a degree in government and politics, the 48-year-old Londoner began his career with the City of London police in 1976. He rose swiftly through the ranks to become Detective Chief Superintendent of the City of London's Special Branch before he turned 30, at a time when the IRA was targeting the British capital. By 2001, he was Detective Chief Superintendent of Scotland Yard and in 2004 he headed up Special Branch's counter-terrorism and covert operations unit. Shields is no stranger to high-profile cases. Over the years, he has pursued money-launderers and mobsters, drug-runners, contract killers and terrorists, was responsible for the security of Lady Thatcher and British cabinet ministers and worked on the alleged plot to kidnap Spice Girl Victoria Beckham. He is reported to have said: 'I've got this sixth sense that I can see when something is going on. So my arrest rate has been extremely high.'[405] Lending credibility to this claim, after his first year as Deputy Police Commissioner, murder figures in Jamaica were down by 20%.[406]

Shields lived up to his promise to run an open and transparent investigation by giving interviews and calling regular press conferences, sometimes as many as twice a day. He elaborated on the circumstances of Bob's death:

> It was about 10:45 am when a housekeeper let herself into the room and found Bob unconscious. A nurse was called and a doctor very soon after that,

> and he was rushed to the University of West Indies hospital, which is about 10 minutes away, where he was pronounced dead at around 12 noon.[407] He may even have been dead when he was found but that has yet to be confirmed. I do know they treated it as though he was still unconscious and did everything they could to get him to hospital for resuscitation. Unfortunately, he was pronounced dead at the hospital.[408]

The police averred that Bob had never regained consciousness. 'That'll be part of the postmortem, to discover exactly what time he died.'[409] If Woolmer was unconscious when he was found, his time of death should not have been difficult to pinpoint, given that there was medical help on hand from soon after he was allegedly found. On the other hand, finding someone alive who has been strangled is 'most unusual' say those who know.[410]

Where was Bob found – in the bathroom or in the bedroom of his hotel? Once again, reports disagreed. The *Jamaica Observer* reported that when the housekeeper tried to enter Bob's room, his prone body was blocking the door. 'She (the housekeeper) could not open the door fully as the body was lying in the way, just by the door to the bathroom … She had to call some of her co-workers to help her push open the door in order to get in.'[411] On the other hand, diverse media sources noted that the coach had been found on the bathroom floor, between the bath and the toilet. Other media accounts claimed that Woolmer was moved from the bathroom to the bedroom in the attempt to resuscitate him.[412] However, it is not clear who moved him. Mr Mir revealed that the coach had been moved from the toilet to the bedroom, but did not mention by whom, saying, 'That is a matter for the police.'[413]

But perhaps the most contradictory reports related to the cause of death and the physical condition in which the coach was found. PJ Mir said, 'When I reached the room, he was lying on the floor, with his mouth wide open and there was blood in the bathroom and there was vomit all over the wall, and there were signs of diarrhoea.'[414] These symptoms were confirmed by a Jamaican police source in the *Sunday Mirror* who said that Bob had vomited violently over the floor and mirror and had diarrhoea.[415] Media accounts listed a bewildering array of injuries: blood and faeces on the floor, vomit high up on the walls and blood on Bob's cheeks and eyes. The news of vomit high on the walls was pounced on by many media sources as signs of a struggle although projectile vomiting would have a similar effect. Woolmer also had facial injuries, including a scrape on the right cheek, an abrasion on the left-hand side of his forehead above the eye and a cut across the nose. These wounds were verified in a picture of his body taken in the morgue the day after his death. A number of UK media sources noted that Bob was found on his back, '… wedged between the toilet bowl and the basin'[416] in the 'cramped bathroom'.[417] How he got these facial injuries in a terminal fall in a 'cramped bathroom' and landed up on his back, wedged into a confined space, is hard to imagine.[418]

If, however, he had time to fall and pick himself up, would he not also have had time to call for help? An unnamed Pakistani team official said that apparently Woolmer didn't have enough time to call anyone for help. He described finding Bob: 'The condition in which his body was discovered was very tragic. His face had gone blue and his hands and feet were white.'[419] According to pre-eminent South African forensic scientist Dr David Klatzow, a blue face could indicate strangulation. Other media reports, however, spoke of 'blue hands and feet',[420] 'blue extremities'[421] and even 'a body turned blue'.[422] These symptoms, said Klatzow, could indicate heart failure.

While the world waited for word from the police, Nasim Ashraf, Chairman of the Pakistan Cricket Board, told Pakistani TV station Geo TV that, just before the Pakistani team left for the West Indies, Woolmer had told him that he was having breathing problems at night and was also diabetic. 'Woolmer told me it was nothing new for him as he wore a mask during sleeping.'[423] The refrain continued. Two days after Woolmer's death, an unnamed team official was quoted as saying that the Pakistani camp thought their coach '... might have died of a heart attack' although he also claimed that there was a blood sugar testing kit lying nearby. However, Gill Woolmer, in an interview on Indian TV affirmed that while her husband had Type 2 diabetes he was not on any medication for the condition.[424] She also told South African reporters that Bob had been '... on a diet, swimming regularly and trying hard to slim down. After the Ireland match he was absolutely fine. He e-mailed me on Sunday morning and there was no sign of illness. There was nothing wrong with him, he was perfectly fit'.[425] Bob's friend, Clive Rice, agreed: 'He wasn't so unfit that would have died from poor health.'[426] Frans Cronjé, Hansie's brother, had seen Bob a few weeks before he died. 'He looked healthy and leaner so I was shocked when they said he'd died because of poor health as he'd looked so good when I'd seen him. It just didn't ring true for me.'[427]

Members of the world's press showed that they were one step ahead of events, as they would continue to do throughout the three months of hype and hypothesis that would follow. That Thursday morning, the 22nd, before the police had officially cried foul, the headlines in two Jamaican newspapers announced categorically 'Woolmer strangled.' A report in the *Jamaica Gleaner* quoted an unnamed but 'high-ranking' police officer: 'A bone in the neck, near the glands, was broken, and this suggests that somebody might have put some pressure on it. We are now treating this as a homicide.'[428] The *Jamaica Observer* also quoted unnamed sources close to the investigation as saying that bones in the lower part of Woolmer's face were broken. The article also referred to 'marks on the throat'.[429]

The task of making sense of this bewildering array of physical injuries fell to Dr Ere Seshaiah, the Head of the Pathology Department in the Jamaican Ministry of National Security. Dr Seshaiah, who has reportedly performed over 1 000 autopsies, moved to Jamaica in 1995 from the state of Andhra Pradesh in India. He performed the autopsy on Woolmer's body on the Tuesday morning after Bob's death. That afternoon, Jamaican police and Pakistani team management held a press conference at which they announced that they still didn't know the exact cause of death. PJ Mir told the press that 'The pathologist's findings were inconclusive and he is awaiting results of toxicology and histology from the government national laboratory and the government forensic laboratory'.[430] Shields explained: 'In a case like this I would think the pathologist would want to be absolutely sure and so I see nothing unusual in that. He wants to make sure that whatever his findings are they are accurate. Therefore, conducting further tests is quite legitimate and sensible in these circumstances.'[431]

Blood and tissue tests may not have been all the Jamaican police were waiting for. The issue of a second postmortem would come up more than once in the weeks to come. Despite official denials, whether a second autopsy actually took place remains unknown. A press release issued by the JCF's Director of Communications Karl Angell, on Wednesday 21 March, confirmed that a second opinion was being sought. 'Following consultations today involving representatives from the Government of Jamaica and the police, a decision was taken to seek the opinion of a second pathologist.'[432] Shields reportedly told the media that an American pathologist had been called in.[433] The pathologist, said to be from Florida, would help to determine whether Woolmer's death was caused by strangulation or a heavy fall.[434]

Shields was adamant that police would not announce the cause of death until they had received the American pathologist's opinion.[435] At least one correspondent, the UK's Channel 4 News, claimed that the Florida pathologist had confirmed the original murder finding. The broadcaster predicted that a murder announcement was imminent.[436] However, *The Times* of London reported later that, on the same day that Seshaiah carried out his postmortem, the Tuesday, the body had been embalmed, making a second postmortem difficult but not impossible.[437] When the murder announcement came the very next day, there was no further mention of the second pathologist or his report. Why then was the murder announcement made so soon, despite Shields' earlier pronouncement? Or were the police, in fact, in receipt of the results of an independent postmortem? It is worth remembering that the Caribbean was in the midst of hosting a major international sporting event, which would be marred, perhaps irretrievably, by the high-profile murder of one of the best-known coaches in contemporary cricket. Bear in mind also that the world's media was in town, in full force. Presumably no one would have wanted to cry wolf without good reason.

The cause of death was announced on the Thursday evening at a press conference. Police spokesperson Karl Angell read a statement on behalf of the Jamaican Constabulary Force's Commissioner of Police, Lucius Thomas:

> Consistent with our approach from the time Pakistan's cricket coach, Mr Robert Woolmer, was found in his hotel room on Sunday 18 March, the Jamaica Constabulary Force (JCF) has updated the media on all developments concerning our investigations of this case. The Jamaican police are in a position to inform that it is now in possession of the official postmortem report from the government pathologist who conducted the autopsy on the late Mr Woolmer.The pathologist report is now available and states that Mr Woolmer's death was due to asphyxia as a result of manual strangulation. In these circumstances, the matter of Mr Robert Woolmer's death is now being treated by the Jamaica police as a case of murder … It is our belief that those associated with or having access to Mr Woolmer may have vital information that would assist this inquiry. We appeal to these individuals to come forward now to assist us with our investigation. Our condolences go out to Gill, Bob's widow, and their sons, friends and members of the Pakistani team.

Speaking of Gill Woolmer, Deputy Commissioner of Police Shields told reporters: 'She's very, very upset and she's grieving. She has just lost her husband in extraordinary and evil circumstances.' He described the murder as 'particularly horrific'.[438] At this point, Shields seemed to contradict earlier media accounts of Woolmer's scratched and bleeding face, bruised neck and broken facial bones. He told the assembled media: 'There were no real visible signs externally … If there had been any clear visible signs it would have been easier for us to determine cause of death.' The Deputy Commissioner confirmed that it was unusual to find no visible external signs of strangulation but, he said, '… there are circumstances surrounding this one which render it not so unusual.'[439] These circumstances were never revealed but later a blood-soaked pillow would assume ominous significance.

At the press conference, Shields maintained, 'There was very little evidence of a struggle' despite the fact that, as the Deputy Police Commissioner pointed out, 'Bob was a large man and it would have taken some significant force to subdue him and cause his strangulation'.[440] Pakistani leg-spinner Danish Kaneria was rooming next door and he said he '… did not hear any noises coming from Woolmer's room'.[441]

Therefore, Shields surmised that there could have been more than one attacker.

However, another explanation for the apparent absence of a struggle was that the coach was subdued chemically rather than physically and whispers of poison would snake their way through the ensuing investigation like mustard gas.

Theft was ruled out as nothing of value was missing from the room, as was a random Jamaican killer as they typically use guns and knives. 'I think there's plenty of evidence in the room to suggest that it is not an opportunist who actually went there to steal money, passport, credit cards, laptop, cellphone, because all of those things are intact,' Shields said. 'Therefore, unless it was a specific object we're not aware of, it would seem that the purpose was to murder Bob Woolmer as opposed to stealing his possessions.'[442]

There was also no sign of forced entry. Guests at the Pegasus are given an electronic key card that allows them to access both the lift and their rooms. Each key has its own identification code and thus guests' entries to their rooms are recorded. Police would reportedly discover that after Woolmer entered his room at 8:30 pm his key card was not used again, despite earlier unconfirmed reports that Bob's card had been stolen some hours before he died.[443] Shields revealed in a later interview with *BBC Radio*: 'It looks as if it may be someone who is linked to him because, clearly, he let somebody into his hotel room and it may be that he knew who that person was.'[444]

Pakistan's coach must have felt comfortable enough with the person at the door to let them in despite the fact that he was only partially clothed, wrapped in a towel or clad only in boxer shorts, depending on the news source.

The investigation therefore focused on the people closest to Woolmer, the Pakistani cricketing contingent and the other inhabitants of the twelfth floor. Thus the CCTV cameras positioned to cover the entries and exits to the floor – the lift doors and the stairway – became a crucial part of the investigation, particularly as there appeared to be some doubt about whether two security guards who were assigned to the twelfth floor were actually at their posts that Saturday night.[445] However, no cameras were directly trained on the door of Woolmer's room.[446] The Pakistani team was questioned and fingerprinted. They were also swabbed for DNA samples as were West Indies captain Brian Lara and team manager Clive Lloyd and the entire Irish team. All the inhabitants of the twelfth floor were questioned too.

After the murder announcement, the autopsy results were almost immediately criticised in the media and the initial finding of an 'inconclusive' cause of death would return to haunt all involved in the investigation. The *Jamaica Gleaner* quoted several expert pathologists who questioned Dr Seshaiah's findings. Dr Garfield Blake, head of the Jamaican Association of Clinical Pathologists, pronounced: 'The final conclusion of this being a manual strangulation, I would not expect the first word to be inconclusive.'[447] Another postmortem expert quoted by the *Gleaner* admitted that while, 'They may not be able to say what is the cause of death … you could say what is not the cause of death.'[448] Dr David Klatzow agreed: 'There are certainly postmortems that are inconclusive. However, generally you would expect to find a reason for death.'

If the stated cause of death was finally strangulation, what then was the motive for murder? Match-fixing was the leading contender.

On the Monday, the day after Woolmer died and three days before the police delivered their murder verdict, outspoken former Pakistani fast bowler Sarfraz Nawaz, who now works for Pakistan's Sports Ministry, told reporters in Pakistan: 'Certain top players in the (Pakistan) team are involved in fixing the matches against the West Indies and Ireland. The theory going around in West Indies police circles is that Woolmer might have been killed by those who wanted to silence him on the issue of match-fixing.'[449]

However, in a *Reuters* TV interview, Nawaz denied saying that he believed match-fixers had killed Woolmer. 'I never said such a thing. Someone made up the story. But I definitely did say that in the first match against the West Indies, the body language of the Pakistani players was suspicious. It showed they played under par and didn't try to win, as if they lost intentionally.'[450]

Sarfraz Nawaz has long denounced corruption in Pakistani cricket. He was the first witness to appear before the Qayyum Commission in 1998 and also testified to the Bhandari Commission in 2001 that two of Pakistan's World Cup games in 1999 had been fixed. In 2003, he publicly levelled corruption allegations against senior officials in the Pakistan Cricket Board. In the latest scandal to rock Pakistani cricket, Nawaz was to prove no less vocal.

Nawaz reportedly told Indian TV station *Sahara Samay* that:

> Bob must have seen how the Pakistani team went about its business against the West Indies. You could sense it from their body language that something was amiss. I believe he was writing a book and he would have come off with sensational disclosures … I surely feel that he has been bumped off. It was the betting mafia which eliminated Hansie Cronjé. It was the same betting mafia which killed 'Cadbury', the well-known bookie from Pakistan who later settled in South Africa. Cadbury's body was cut into pieces. Now that has been the fate of Woolmer.[451]

Sarfraz went on to claim that captain Inzamam ul-Haq, Rana Naved-ul-Hasan, Mushtaq Ahmed, Mohammad Yousuf and Shoaib Malik were involved in betting and that the ICC was 'actively promoting' match-fixing.[452] Nawaz alleged that the bookmakers were so influential that they had a hand in appointing coaches, managers, selectors and cricket board members in various countries.[453] Nawaz also claimed that informants from inside the Pakistan Cricket Board had told him that five top Pakistani bookies were in the West Indies for the World Cup and had contacted 'heavyweight' players in the Pakistani team.[454]

Indian media sources would also report that leading Indian bookies and betting mafia were in the West Indies for the World Cup. A report quoting sources 'close to India's Central Bureau of Investigations' named all the usual suspects: Anees Ibrahim, Mukesh Kumar Gupta of Hansie Cronjé fame and his erstwhile partner Anil Steel, and a certain Sanjeev Sachar of New Delhi. The article also identified three Pakistani bookies that the CBI had reportedly tracked to the West Indies around the time of the World Cup – Khwaja Arif Pappu, Raja Zagfar Ali Iqbal (Jojo) and Saleem (Koki) who had all been named in the Qayyum Report back in 1999.[455] The report named Khwaja Arif Pappu as the operations head of Dawood Ibrahim's betting syndicate in Pakistan.[456] Pappu started out as a government income tax collector before being sacked for corruption. Nevertheless, he is reportedly well connected within President Pervez Musharraf's administration,[457] despite being wanted by Pakistani police in connection with more than sixty charges relating to murder, attempt to murder and extortion.[458] Indian news sources claimed that Pappu had been in touch with Woolmer and went missing on the day of the murder.[459]

On the Thursday, the day that the police cried foul, imprisoned Indian criminal Babloo Srivastaya echoed Safraz Nawaz. Described as a 'notorious gangster',[460] Babloo is said to have worked as a hit-man for Dawood Ibrahim. In the reversal of fortune that goes with the business, he later found himself on Ibrahim's hit list.[461] On his way to a Lucknow court for a hearing into a murder case of his own, Babloo aired his insights into the reasons for Woolmer's death on Indian TV channels. 'The Pakistan/Ireland match must have been fixed … The D-Company may have lots of money at stake. Woolmer may have got an inkling of the fixing and hence he was killed.'[462]

On Friday, the day after the murder announcement, PJ Mir, the Pakistani media manager, fanned the flames, alleging that Woolmer had told him that the only hard-copy proofs of a book he had been writing had gone missing.[463] However, Bob's family said that his book was on coaching cricket and asserted that the publishing proofs only arrived the day after his death.[464] Speculation now swirled around this exposé Woolmer was allegedly assembling. An unnamed PCB official theorised that Bob's upcoming book, *Discovering Cricket,* may have been about to lift the lid on match-fixing. The South African publishers and Woolmer's co-writer, Professor Tim Noakes, denied that this was the case. Woolmer was updating his 2000 autobiography as well and his ghostwriter

Ivo Tennant also rejected any speculation that Woolmer was planning to expose corruption in cricket. The next day Sarfraz Nawaz in an exclusive interview with *dnaindia.com* alleged that the diary that Bob had used to 'jot down his observations' was also missing.[465]

The unidentified PCB official went on to claim that Woolmer had met with Delhi police officers in 2005 while researching his book.[466] This is corroborated in a contemporary article by veteran Indian sportswriter Pradeep Magazine in the *Hindustan Times*. Magazine related how he had arranged Woolmer's hour-long visit with Delhi Police Commissioner KK Paul on 18 April 2005. In the meeting, Pradeep claimed, Woolmer defended Cronjé and denied the Proteas were involved in anything underhand at the 1999 World Cup. The journalist also revealed that Woolmer had told him he was writing a book on '... corporate corruption in cricket, especially in the selling of TV rights, and about the way money is made from it by those connected with the game.'[467]

Adding to the groundswell of corroboration for this potentially explosive yet elusive book, Woolmer had approached Pakistani journalist Osman Samiuddin, for his help with a third book – on his time as Pakistan's coach. Woolmer had sent an e-mail to Samiuddin the previous year on 18 September:

> I am going to write a book on my tenure as Pakistan's coach and wanted (a Pakistani collaborator – hopefully yourself) also an SA and English one as well so that I can cover probably one of the more interesting periods of my cricket career. I shall only start after the World Cup but I need to show a lot of different perspectives and the culture correctly which is where I had hoped you would come in. I have not approached a publisher yet so not sure what is in it for anyone at the moment but I believe, regardless of the money, the story is worth telling and has to be told and in the correct way. I am not a name and shame guy – just the honest facts. Let the punter make up his mind etc. No hurry, but hoped you might be interested.[468]

Samiuddin confirmed the e-mail but he claimed that no details had as yet been discussed.

Former South African captain Clive Rice 'had absolutely no doubt' that his friend had been killed because of what he knew.[469] Speaking to *Cape Talk Radio* in Cape Town on 27 March, Rice was convinced that Woolmer's death had come about much like Hansie Cronjé's – as the result of information they both had on the mafia-style illegal betting industry that makes billions from international cricket matches. 'Bob got wind of what was going on,' he said '... and perhaps things got out of hand for the Pakistani team.'[470] Rice said that Hansie Cronjé too had been planning a book. 'I went to see him six months before he died.

He signed over the rights to me. Like Woolmer he knew a lot more of what was going on. His so-called accident was just a lot cleverer than the one that killed Bob.'[471] Another good friend of Woolmer's, Barry Richards, shared Rice's view. 'There is a strong feeling around that Bob was going to expose something … People are asking that question and I must admit it is one I am asking myself. Why else would this happen? It may have been a fight gone wrong.'[472]

Former Pakistani captain and match-fixing whistle-blower Rashid Latif added his voice to the chorus. 'Whoever murdered Woolmer was clearly desperate or else he would not have been killed in the middle of a World Cup.'[473]

Meanwhile, another erstwhile Pakistani captain, chief selector Aamer Sohail, denied the match-fixing rumours on the Pakistani TV Channel Geo TV: 'Neither are the allegations of gambling against the Pakistani cricket team true, nor are they (players) involved in the death of coach Bob Woolmer.' Sohail had been a TV commentator for both of Pakistan's contentious matches and was adamant that neither had been fixed.[474]

Deputy Commissioner Mark Shields admitted that one of the theories on motive '… that keeps coming to light … is around match-fixing and bookies, so therefore that's the clear line of inquiry, but it is not the only one.'[475] Shields confirmed that police would be looking into the betting patterns during Pakistan's World Cup matches and that Jeff Rees, head of the ICC's Anti-Corruption Unit, was in Jamaica to investigate possible match-fixing links to the murder.[476] Shields admitted, 'I know a lot more about match-fixing than I did a week ago.'[477]

Lord Condon's Anti-Corruption and Security Unit had not been idle in the months leading up to the World Cup. In early February, the AC&SU had been called in to investigate a young Jamaican batsman from Kingston who found himself in the same situation that Hansie Cronjé had been in seven years previously. Indian police in Nagpur claimed to have taped conversations between Marlon Samuels and an alleged Indian bookmaker, Mukesh Kochchar, in which Samuels provided information about the West Indian batting line-up and bowling order as well as other confidential team information during a one-day international between India and the West Indies in Nagpur at the beginning of the year. The Nagpur police sent a letter to the Board of Control of Cricket in India (BCCI) outlining their accusation: 'This is to inform you that during our watch at the time of the One-Day International match played between India and West Indies on 21/01/07, West Indian all-rounder Marlon Samuels, staying in room number 206 of Hotel Pride, Nagpur, was contacted by one Shri Mukesh Kochchar telephonically on a number of occasions.'[478]

New Delhi TV in India published the following excerpts from the several alleged conversations Samuels had had with Kochchar:

ROOM 206: Early in the morning batting moves around the pitch.
BOOKIE: In the evening you move down?
ROOM 206: Low down.
BOOKIE: What do you think, who will bat?
ROOM 206: Well.
BOOKIE: Who, who?
ROOM 206: Dwayne, he's making a debut tomorrow.
BOOKIE: New batsman or bowler?
ROOM 206: No, he is an all-rounder.
BOOKIE: He's good?
ROOM 206: Yes, he's making his debut.
BOOKIE: Ya, I can understand that. Chris is in form.
ROOM 206: Not clear.
BOOKIE: How is your batting going on?
ROOM 206: My batting is good.
BOOKIE: Big score tomorrow?
ROOM 206: Not clear.
BOOKIE: So how are the things with you and how are the preparations?
ROOM 206: Preparations good enough.
BOOKIE: Wish you all the best.
ROOM 206: Thanks.[479]

The Dubai-based Kochchar is said to have started out as an international bookie on the Mumbai racecourse circuit. Kochchar is now 'handling the betting accounts for the Dawood gang' according to Mumbai police.[480] However, Kochchar told an Indian news channel that he was not a bookie but a businessman who had been in Dubai for the past 22 years.[481] The Mumbai police also suspected the involvement of a certain Kamal Kishore Chadha, an alleged bookmaker[482] also based in Dubai.[483] 'We are looking for Kamal Kishore Chadha, who does land deals for Dawood Ibrahim,' Maharashtra Director-General of Police PS Pasricha told a press conference.[484] Kochchar and Chadha admitted knowing each other, and Chadha told a news channel that he also knew Dawood Ibrahim. 'I know him. There is no crime in knowing him. However, I do not have any relation or any transactions with him.'[485] The Nagpur police handed the Marlon Samuels case over to the ICC for investigating. Nonetheless, a month after the Nagpur police had fingered him, Samuels was selected for the West Indies team and played in the opening match of the World Cup – against Pakistan. Five days later Pakistan's coach was dead.

The Jamaican police's murder allegations threw a pall of suspicion and speculation over the 'gentleman's game'. Then, hot on the heels of the murder announcement, came unconfirmed reports that a suspect had been arrested. Hamid Mir, Geo TV's Chief Executive Officer, told New Delhi TV (NDTV) that the man had been a regular visitor to Bob Woolmer and was '... in contact with many members of the Pakistani team.'[486] Hamid Mir also revealed that Pakistani captain Inzamam ul-Haq and bowling coach Mushtaq Ahmed had had an argument with Woolmer the day before the Irish game.[487] More details followed. A Mumbai newspaper carried a report out of Karachi quoting a one-time Pakistani Test batsman who had been named in the match-fixing scandal of the 1990s. Speaking anonymously, '... because of the people who are involved in this fixing racket,' he said, 'From what my informers have told me, they have arrested one man and he had telephone numbers of some players which are now being looked into'. Optimistically, as it turned out, he remarked, 'Woolmer's death should now reveal a lot of truth if the investigations are carried out professionally and without any interference from the ICC'. The player alleged that the police had short-listed six suspects in the Woolmer case. [488]

Then, on Saturday, six days after Woolmer had been found 'unconscious' in his hotel room and several hours before the Pakistani team were due to leave Jamaica for London, detectives arrived unannounced to question Inzamam ul-Haq, assistant coach Mushtaq Ahmed and team manager Talat Ali once again, because of 'discrepancies' in earlier statements. According to Pakistani spokesperson PJ Mir, police asked Inzamam and Ali why they had changed hotel rooms and what time Inzamam had got to bed on that fateful Saturday night. Inzamam, it appears, changed rooms from the twelfth to the fifth floor shortly before Woolmer's death. When asked why, he apparently explained that it was because he wanted to be nearer the players. After the coach's death, Talat Ali moved from his hotel room on the twelfth floor up to the seventeenth, under the assumed name of Newman. When the police asked him why, he reportedly said, 'We were all scared.' An unnamed source quoted in an India newspaper insisted that Talat didn't make the move voluntarily but was moved by hotel management and the ICC as a security measure and to protect him from being pestered by the media. PCB sources were quoted in the same report as saying that Talat was not the only person to shift rooms after the murder. According to the source so too did Murray Stevenson, Darren Lifsun and Danish Kaneria, Brian Lara and Clive Lloyd.[489] The Jamaican police, PJ Mir said, questioned Mushtaq Ahmed about cuts on his face. Mir said that the assistant coach had received the cuts during a practice at Sabina Park on the morning of the Ireland game.[490] Ahmed confirmed this. If true, then these cuts were new and not related to the broken nose Ahmed suffered at fielding practice two days before the Irish game.[491] The Pakistani contingent then left the Caribbean for London and travelled on to Pakistan.

Mark Shields told a press conference that although the Pakistani team had been allowed to leave the island, this did not mean that they had been excluded as suspects.[492] He explained to *The Times* in London that he had to let the Pakistani team leave Jamaica because '... holding people against their will ... would have caused a significant diplomatic incident and would have had an extremely adverse effect on the World Cup'. There is no extradition treaty between Jamaica and Pakistan.

The fourth estate was being kept busy. Next, *The Guardian* broke the story that, hours before Bob Woolmer died, he had thrown a Mumbai-based bookie out of his room after a 'blazing argument'. *The Guardian* identified its source as a senior Pakistani government official who claimed that two Pakistani cricketers had mentioned this incident to the Jamaican police. The source went on to say that this was one of three bookies who had checked in to the Jamaica Pegasus Hotel prior to the World Cup.[493] Mark Shields and Indian cricket officials scorned such reports. Then, news coming out of India and the UK named the bookie thrown out of Bob's room as none other than Kamal Chadha, whose name had come up in connection with the Marlon Samuels episode. *The Sun's* sources, identified as 'intelligence officials who tour with the Indian cricket team' claimed that Chadha was in Jamaica for the World Cup with Anees Ibrahim, Dawood's brother. Chadha, the newspaper alleged, was linked to Dawood Ibrahim, an 'Al-Qaeda fundraiser'.[494]

Indicative of the worldwide interest in Woolmer's death, even baseball-playing America sent journalists to the Caribbean, such as ESPN correspondent Patrick Hruby. In a feature story entitled 'Murder by Cricket' Hruby tells a strange tale. He speaks of meeting an unnamed 'guy in the information acquisition business' who had no doubt that Woolmer's mysterious death was murder. Hruby's shadowy companion told him that he had it from well-placed international intelligence sources that, ever since 9/11, Al-Qaeda has suffered from an American financial squeeze. Thus the terrorist organisation has turned to illegal sports gambling in India and Pakistan for funding. He floated the theory that Al-Qaeda may have lost a lot of money on the Pakistani team during the World Cup. Al-Qaeda, he said, is linked to Dawood Ibrahim and to Pakistan's Inter-Services Intelligence (ISI) Agency, which has an operative on the Pakistani cricket team's touring party. Hruby's source claimed that Woolmer had found out that three international umpires had illicit bank accounts funded by Chinese money and opened by ISI operatives, who, he believed, were involved in Woolmer's murder. For all these reasons, he says, Pakistani 'diplomats' were sent to Jamaica to keep tabs on the Woolmer investigation.[495] As former Pakistan Test captain and match-fixing whistle-blower Rashid Latif pointed out, 'I don't think the Pakistani government would have sent its diplomats to Jamaica if players had been questioned routinely.'[496] Whatever truth there is in this theory, the *Jamaica Gleaner* reported on 1 April that Condon's Anti-Corruption Unit was probing three top ICC umpires and their offshore bank accounts, believed to be linked to match-fixers. That Dawood Ibrahim has connections within the Pakistani government and within Pakistani cricket is not a new allegation. The *Asia Times*, back in 2003, claimed that '... it is an open secret that Mumbai's underworld kingpin Dawood Ibrahim lives in housing provided by the Defence Housing Authority in Karachi.' The story goes on to allege that PCB Chairman at the time, Lieutenant-General Tauqir Zia, would visit Dawood, despite the fact that the Pakistani government denied Ibrahim's presence in the country.[497]

If match-fixing was the front-runner for the motive behind the murder, then poison was the leading contender to explain how Woolmer was strangled without putting up a fight.

It was spokesperson PJ Mir who first revealed the presence of vomit in Bob's room. The press then brought word of traces of poison found on the floor.[498] As early as 21 March, while Woolmer's death was still being described as 'suspicious', a news report from the *Deccan Chronicle*, India's fourth-largest newspaper, quoted sources at the National Forensics Laboratory where the vomit found in Woolmer's hotel room was being examined. The sources claimed that it was very likely that Woolmer was poisoned, possibly by a slow-acting substance.[499] Unsurprisingly, the police ordered further toxicology tests as they investigated whether Bob's room-service meal was contaminated. The ever-communicative Mark Shields told reporters that, 'He was 6ft 1in and a big man, and unless he was drugged or impaired it would perhaps have been difficult to restrain him. We are looking at whether his food was drugged. The meal was thrown away after he put the tray outside his room, but we are conducting toxicology and tissue tests.'[500]

According to South African forensic scientist Dr Klatzow, if following standard procedure, police would have done a 'proper screening test for drugs or toxins'. The normal profile of blood is known, so the test would pick up anything out of the ordinary. Then additional tests would have been done to identify the unusual elements. News of these toxicology reports remained elusive until 14 April. However, before then, the poison theory got a shot in the arm with the news that police were taking one poison tip-off among many very seriously:

According to the London *Sunday Mirror*, police in Kingston received an anonymous telephone call from a man, thought to be from Pakistan, alleging that Bob Woolmer had been poisoned with aconite.[501] Dr Klatzow described aconite as a 'poison of ancient pedigree'. Derived from *Delphinium* species such as larkspur, which thrive in the wet and mountainous regions of the northern hemisphere, aconite is an alkaloid-type substance and not difficult, Klatzow said, to detect in blood tests. Ingesting aconite gives rise to a slew of non-specific symptoms including: nausea, vomiting, numbness, tingling of the mouth, hands, blurred vision, weak pulse, drop in pulse, chest pains, shallow respiration, convulsions and death. Mark Shields said, 'The symptoms Bob suffered before he died are identical to aconite poisoning, which is why it is a major line of inquiry now. It would also explain how such a physically imposing man, at 6ft 1in tall, died without putting up a fight. You'd struggle to get two people into his bathroom let alone three, so it could be no one was there'.

In the wake of the aconite story, a Metropolitan Police team from London, led by Detective Inspector John Sweeney and two forensic experts from Interpol in France, arrived to 'review' the investigation – ostensibly at the request of the Jamaicans. You will recall that Jackie Selebi, South Africa's Commissioner of Police, heads Interpol. The Europeans were joined by two Pakistani investigators, Zubair Mahmood, who investigated the beheading of US reporter Daniel Pearl, in Karachi [502] and Mr Kaleem Imam, '... an additional director of the Federal Investigation Agency.' Mahmood told reporters: 'We are going there to basically assist them. That is our agenda. But that also depends entirely on their response. I think our primary task will be to keep our government and the Pakistan Cricket Board informed of any progress in the case.'[503] Jamaican Police Commissioner Lucius Thomas would later say that the Minister of National Security '... extended an invitation to Pakistan to deploy police officers to work alongside the JCF team.'[504] If any Pakistani players were still under investigation, then this would be akin to inviting the fox into the hen-house. On the other hand, if members of the Pakistani team were not suspects in the ongoing investigation, then why the presence of Pakistani investigators and Pakistani 'diplomats'? Then, like the eye of a hurricane, the media frenzy that had swept the globe since Woolmer's death fell quiet. Not much was heard from the talkative Mr Shields and the world drew its collective breath and turned its attention to other things. Then, at a press conference in Kingston on 14 April, the first in two weeks, official word came of the receipt of the results of the toxicology tests. Shields explained the two-week lull in media briefings by saying that, '... there has been simply nothing to report.'[505]

Uncharacteristically, the Deputy Commissioner remained uncommunicative, simply acknowledging, without elaborating, that police had received the preliminary toxicology results and would be carrying out further tests – in the UK. 'If he was manually strangled and asphyxiated, why didn't he put up a fight? I've always said there was a possibility that he was incapacitated by something else. If I tell you they (the results) have come back and we are conducting further tests, I suggest you draw your own conclusions.'[506] Presumably, if the tests had revealed nothing out of the ordinary, further tests would have been unnecessary.

The wires buzzed anew with the news, scant though it was. The *Jamaica Gleaner* threw into the brew the revelation by a government official that a foreign substance had been found in Woolmer's stomach, blood and urine.[507] The newspaper's sources did not name the poison, however, and Jamaican police discounted aconite. In the UK, on its 30 April broadcast, *Panorama*, the BBC's longest-running investigative programme, added its voice to the chorus of 'poison'. Without identifying its source or the poison, *Panorama* said that toxicology reports showed that Woolmer had been incapacitated by a drug.[508] In addition, the documentary claimed that CCTV footage did not show anyone getting out of the lift at the time that police believe Woolmer was attacked. The conclusion drawn is that the attacker or attackers were already on the twelfth floor. The British tabloid *The Sun* quoted its own police sources as confirming 'significant traces of aconite' revealed by the toxicology tests. *The Sun*'s 'senior police source' said, 'We are now entirely convinced that he was poisoned. The fact that aconite has also previously been used in Pakistan may also be highly relevant'. Aconite has been suspected in a number of high-profile political assassinations in Pakistan, according to the S*unday Mirror*.[509] *The Sun* quoted another unidentified source: 'This murder proves that truth can sometimes be stranger than fiction. It is now an international inquiry and could ultimately involve high-level diplomatic discussions.'[510]

Whether such discussions took place will probably never be known, but if they were, their results soon became apparent. On 19 April, five days after the Jamaican police acknowledged they had the blood test results, the news came that the Woolmer inquest, due to start on the 23rd, had been postponed indefinitely because of 'new and material developments'. These developments were never revealed and no inquest ever took place, despite the requirements of Jamaican law. If the blood tests had not revealed anything suspicious, why then did the inquest not go ahead, if only to confirm that it had now been established that Woolmer had died of natural causes? It would be another seven weeks before such an announcement came. Woolmer's body was released and finally returned to his adopted South Africa, where the coach was cremated in a private ceremony.

Nonetheless, the reports of poison continued to circulate, with stories of 'significant traces' of weedkiller found on a champagne glass that Bob had used. Such reports were followed up soon after by tales of champagne bottles given to Bob, some time before he died, by Mushtaq Ahmed – an act witnessed by Talat Ali, said PJ Mir.[511] Word also filtered down the wires that a suspect had been identified from the enhanced security camera images. *The Independent* quoted a source close to the investigation: 'The cleaned-up images from London show at least one individual of considerable interest to the inquiry. The time of the footage and its location mean that this individual must be considered a suspect. Further work is being done on statements given by individuals to look at any inconsistencies. It is good progress.'[512]

At the same time, the case for accidental death was also gathering momentum. Zubair Mahmood, one of the Pakistani detectives, stated publicly that the Jamaican police had no real evidence that Bob had been murdered.[513] As high-level meetings took place between Mark Shields, Colin Pinnock and John Sweeney in London, media reports announced that a pathology report commissioned by Scotland Yard had concluded that Woolmer had died of heart failure, not strangulation, and Dr Ere Seshaiah was now under pressure to resign. Seshaiah responded, 'I can't comment. I didn't get any report'.[514]

The swelling tide of media comment turned now to flawed autopsies performed by underpaid and overworked pathologists, bungling detectives and a 'desperately ill' coach despite several people's assertions, including his wife's, that Bob was not in poor health. Reports now claimed that only small amounts of weedkiller of a type commonly used on cricket pitches had been found, and that the coach had chipped his neck bone in a fall.[515]

Amid calls from PJ Mir for legal proceedings against the Jamaican police, Mark Shields himself, at the beginning of June, signalled what was to come: 'Usually we investigate a murder and we look for suspects, but on this occasion, because of the lack of evidence to support the pathologist, what we've done is gone out to prove it's not a murder.'[516]

With the findings of the original autopsy now officially called into question, let's consider the evidence at hand.

Dr Seshaiah said that he had based his determination of asphyxiation due to strangulation on three things:

- a fractured hyoid bone
- bleeding around the hyoid bone
- three bruises inside the neck tissues and a larger bruise at the base of the tongue. [517]

Dr David Klatzow explained the significance of these findings: 'All of these things are very important because the bruising should have immediately raised the suspicion of a possible strangulation.' The hyoid bone is an unusual little C-shaped bone in the neck by the Adam's apple. Damage to the hyoid bone is often an indicator of strangulation, though not always. As Dr Klatzow explained:

> There are two little horns on the posterior aspect of the hyoid bone called the greater horns of the hyoid bone. When you are young these bones are very

cartilaginous. As you get older they become more calcified and brittle. They become easier to fracture. However, when you fall over as in collapsing from a heart attack, generally your throat is well back from your face and it's very difficult to fall on your throat unless you fall onto a sharp object such as a windowsill or a ladder or a chair back.

Now, if the hyoid bone is fractured, either by strangulation or in a fall, … there will be a clear sign of that having happened. It's surprising to see no marking on the skin or bruising on the skin but it is also possible.

INTERVIEWER: In what circumstances would that be possible?

KLATZOW: One of those strange things when not enough pressure was applied to stretch or damage the skin.

INTERVIEWER: But enough pressure was applied to damage the hyoid bone?

KLATZOW: Depending on how fragile the hyoid bone is. It's very unusual … no one would say impossible but very unusual. When you fracture the bone, you get bleeding under the layer covering the bone. There would be bleeding associated with the fracture. You'd expect to see markings on the skin, especially if there was bruising underneath in the big strap muscles of your neck.

In addition to Scotland Yard's consultant forensic pathologist Dr Nat Carey, two other pathology experts were brought in to assess Dr Seshaiah's postmortem findings. They were:

- Dr Michael Pollanen, Chief Forensic Pathologist, Canada
- Professor Lorna Martin, Chief Specialist for Forensic Pathology Services for the Western Cape, South Africa, and Professor and Head of Forensic Medicine and Toxicology, University of Cape Town.

All the experts confirmed Seshaiah's assessment of the bruising and bleeding – apparently you can bleed for a substantial time after you are dead – although Nat Carey and Dr Pollanen reportedly concluded it was more likely that the bruising in Woolmer's neck was the result of the postmortem examination itself.[518]

However there were inconsistent reports of whether the hyoid bone was fractured or not. Dr Pollanen was quoted in two separate Jamaican newspapers on different days.

The *Jamaica Observer* first said that Pollanen had agreed that there was damage to the hyoid bone but surmised that the damage may have been caused by a '… terminal collapse or falling in the hotel room in the period before death'.[519] However, in a report in the *Jamaica Gleaner* three days later, Pollanen was quoted as saying, 'It is clear from the X-ray that there is no fracture of the hyoid bone. This is a straightforward and non-controversial finding'.[520] All the experts concluded that death wasn't by strangulation but was probably due to heart disease.

Bear in mind that Seshaiah had had a body to dissect while these pathologists reportedly based their findings on photographic, X-ray and video evidence of the postmortem and the 'crime' scene. From published excerpts of their reports, which have never been revealed in full, it does not seem that the consultant experts saw histology and toxicology reports, although the Jamaican police had preliminary toxicology results by the time Dr Nat Carey was called in to review the case.[521] According to Police Commissioner Thomas, the investigation team acted on the Metropolitan Police Service's recommendations and '… compiled a package of all the information, photographs and results of forensic tests that had been conducted at the Government of Jamaica Forensic Lab. This package was taken to Dr Carey …'[522]

Yet a published extract of Carey's report says, 'The question of any toxicological contribution to his status in the period prior to death, including any possibility of poisoning, should be investigated through toxicological analysis of any samples taken at postmortem examination'.[523]

Similarly, extracts from Professor Lorna Martin's report raise the same question – did the experts base their assessment on all the available evidence? Dr Klatzow, who knows the Cape Town professor Lorna Martin and holds her in high regard, commented, 'I would not go into a witness box on that sort of evidence. I would be very loath to get myself under oath to say what I thought. You can speculate. That's easy. Cross-examined on it you might find it a little less easy. I hate going anywhere near a witness box second-hand'.

As it turned out, no one had to go near a witness box.

The long-anticipated announcement from Jamaican police came on 12 June, almost three months after Bob Woolmer's death. For the first time in the 140-year history of the Jamaican Constabulary Force, a cause of death was overturned.[524] At a Kingston press conference, Jamaican Police Commissioner Lucius Thomas declared that Woolmer was not murdered after all and that no match-fixing had taken place. Mark Shields reiterated throughout the press conference that the JCF had conducted a 'thorough and professional investigation' and in defence of the police force he maintained that it was not the police's job to second-guess the pathologist. Presumably that was the job of the three pathology experts. Mark Shields presented 'The facts as they are today' to a packed room of avid reporters.

- Bob Woolmer died of heart failure, not strangulation.
- A lack of facilities made a second postmortem impossible.
- The broken bone in Woolmer's neck was actually intact.
- The toxicology reports showed no poison.
- The blood-stained pillow was not used to smother him.
- The CCTV records made it impossible to say whether anyone entered the room from the same floor.

As news of the impending turn-around had already been broached a month earlier, the case of the dead coach ended with a whimper. The world, it seemed, was all too willing to accept that the Jamaican police had erred. At least one Cape Town newspaper reader, however, had questions. 'Reports indicated blood and vomit on walls, bruising and a fractured neck bone that indicated strangulation, and later poison being allegedly detected. These were all factors emanating from the West Indies Keystone cops and forensic medical fraternity. One wonders what has caused this apparent gross incompetence.'[525] Dr Seshaiah and Clive Rice were the lone voices in the wilderness. 'I am sticking to my findings. He was murdered,' Seshaiah told the *Jamaica Observer*.[526] In an interview with *Times Now*, Rice said, 'I'm afraid this is a cover-up again and there needs to be a whole lot of explaining done to satisfy all the cricketing public ... Suddenly, all the players and coaches are feeling vulnerable that it could happen to anyone if such a thing can be covered up citing natural causes. That is why we need a whole lot of answers.'[527]

Such answers were not forthcoming. Mark Shields, who had been so 'open and transparent' that Talat Ali had reportedly confronted Shields about the way in which '... Jamaican police officials kept on leaking out news to the media,'[528] would no longer speak to the press, gagged by Commissioner Lucius Thomas's 'strategic communications policy'.[529] Similarly, the Pakistani players were now not allowed to speak to the media without permission from the PCB.[530] When I asked Dr Klatzow whether, in his extensive experience with murder cases in South Africa's courts, he had ever come across such a case, he admitted, 'I must say, this is, in terms of a florid display of incompetence, fairly unique'. Despite such assessments, Deputy Police Commissioner Shields announced that he had no intention of resigning and Dr Seshaiah remained in his post. The Pakistan Cricket Board would not be taking action against the Jamaican police; nor would the Woolmer family. As for the world's media, who had also got it so very wrong, since no complaints had been received about the *Panorama* programme that had unequivocally cried foul on 30 April, the BBC would not be having a formal inquiry.

And all was as it had been before. Except that Bob Woolmer was dead.

16

King Commission of Inquiry into Cricket Match-fixing and Related Matters

South African matches under suspicion: 1995–2000

December 1994/January 1995, Mandela Cup in SA (SA, PAK, SL, NZ)

First final, SA v PAK, Cape Town, 10 January 1995

Hansie Cronjé had been named South Africa's new captain in November 1994. He claimed that the first approach he received from a match-fixer was before the first leg of the ODI final between South Africa and Pakistan in January 1995. An offer of US$10 000 to 'throw the game' came from a man called 'John' in his room at the team's hotel, the Cape Sun. Cronjé thought that this may have been the same John who approached Shane Warne and Mark Waugh for 'information' during the Singer Cup in Sri Lanka in September 1994. Cronjé responded, 'Let me think about it' and approached senior player Patrick Symcox for advice. Symcox, according to Cronjé, said that the offer was too low and thus it was rejected. As South Africa walked onto the field for the game, Cronjé said that Salim Malik had asked if he had spoken to John. Cronjé nodded in response but denied accepting John's offer.

Ali Bacher related to the King Commission how, in January 1995:

> We had a quadrangular one-day international tournament here. We got permission, support from our most distinguished President Mandela at the time to allow his name to be associated with this tournament. We invited New Zealand, Sri Lanka and Pakistan to come to South Africa and participate in this quadrangular tournament, to pay tribute to President Mandela. We now have the final, and it was a two-legged final between South Africa and Pakistan. The first leg was in January of 1995, in Cape Town at our very historic Newlands Cricket Ground. Prior to this match, a week before, I'd received correspondence from the United Arab Emirates Cricket Board, and they are an associated member of the International Cricket Counsel, requesting that

the United Cricket Board provide VIP treatment to two of their cricket administrators. The Cricket Board and South Africans are warm, hospitable people, we like to entertain people from abroad and I responded only with pleasure. The match took place and the two alleged administrators came to the ground. I would normally place the VIPs at the various tables with the President and the Vice-President, and I invited both these administrators to be my guests at my particular table at the dinner break. After dinner, Qamar Ahmed, now Qamar Ahmed is a Pakistani living in London who has covered more than 250 Test matches. He is well known in world cricket, a great friend of South African cricket, and great personal friend of mine. He called me aside, because I'd also invited him to one of the tables for dinner. And he said to me, 'Ali, what's going on here?' And I said, 'Well, I've got this letter from the United Arab Emirates Cricket Board.' He said to me, 'Ali, nonsense. They're bookmakers, man!'

Cronjé speculated in his testimony to the King Commission that one of these men may have been Mukesh Gupta, later introduced to the South African skipper in 1996 by former Indian captain Mohammad Azharuddin. While acknowledging that this observation was 100% speculation, Cronjé retorted, 'Maybe if Dr Bacher was in his statement full and complete then there wouldn't have been room for that speculation'. The same might be said for Cronjé. According to the Indian CBI report into cricket match-fixing, 'John' and MK Gupta are one and the same person. South Africa won the match by 37 runs.

Second final, SA v PAK, Johannesburg, 12 January 1995

Cronjé was also approached by 'John' before the second leg of the final at the Wanderers. Once again, Cronjé rebuffed his overtures and claimed never to have spoken to him again. If 'John' was MK Gupta then this clearly was untrue. South Africa won this match by 157 runs.

April 1996, Pepsi Sharjah Cup, Dubai (SA, IND, PAK)

Final ODI – SA v IND, 19 April 1996

Hansie Cronjé, Herschelle Gibbs and exercise specialist Paddy Upton were befriended by an Indian man called Sunil who lived in Mumbai. They went out to dinner and an illicit approach was made to Cronjé probably before the final ODI. South Africa won by 38 runs.

October–December 1996, SA in IND

October 1996, Titan Cup (SA, IND, AUS)

While sketchy on details of this triangular ODI series, Cronjé related that Sunil asked him to contact him in the future or on the tour, if he wanted to make some money. Discussions took place during the ODI series or during one of the matches in Mumbai. Cronjé, however, said he turned down Sunil's approaches. The Indian CBI Report released in November 2000 identified this tournament as having been the subject of manipulation by Mohammad Azharuddin and MK Gupta. The final between India and South Africa reportedly did not go as planned and the match-fixers lost a fortune. It has been suggested that this was due to counter-fixing. MK insisted that Azharuddin help him make good his losses in the upcoming Test series against the South Africans.

Third Test, Kanpur, 8–12 December 1996

Three to four weeks after Sunil's approaches, Azharuddin, who, according to Cronjé, was friendly with a number of South African players, not only himself, introduced the South African captain to Mukesh Gupta and left the two men alone in his room in the teams' hotel in Kanpur on the evening of Day 3 of the Test. The Indians were already more than 300 runs to the good yet, despite South Africa's poor prospects, MK, who revealed that he had money on India to win the game, asked Cronjé to ensure that South Africa didn't perform any miracles in their upcoming second innings. According to MK, Cronjé accepted US$40 000 from him to seal the deal while Cronjé put the figure at US$30 000, regarding this as 'money for jam.' Whatever the amount, both parties agreed that the money was to ensure that South Africa would lose the Test. They did, and with it the series, thereby ending South Africa's unbeaten Test series run since readmission to the ICC in 1991, five years before.

Mohinder Amarnath Benefit Match/ODI, Mumbai, 14 December 1996

Cronjé was approached by Sunil before this game as well as MK but it was MK's offer of US$200 000 to under-perform that was put to a number of players in the aeroplane including Kirsten and Crookes, and Dave Richardson on the bus on the way to the team hotel in Mumbai. Then the offer was put to the entire team at a team meeting. Said Cronjé, 'I made it clear that … if we were going to do it, then the whole team must be in on it.' According to Cronjé, junior players such as Boje, Adams, Klusener, Gibbs and 'I think, Kirsten, didn't really say much.' Hudson, Cullinan and Crookes were strongly opposed but a number of senior players stayed behind to discuss the offer further. These included McMillan, Richardson and Symcox. A phone call was made to raise the original offer from US$200 000 to US$300 000. Whatever the final figure, the offer was allegedly rejected although Cronjé conceded: 'I probably would have gone for it if the team had gone for it.' India won by 74 runs.

Daryll Cullinan, despite his avowed resistance to the idea, defended Cronjé's actions to the King Commission. The veteran batsman remarked that it was a 'stroke of genius' on his skipper's behalf to pose this moral challenge to his team who emerged all the stronger for having resisted the temptation. Journalist Colin Bryden's report in the *Sunday Times* entitled 'Proud South Africans hit match-fixers for six' was published on 20 December 1998, two years after the event. While several South African players recalled this incident becoming a standing joke among the team, the question of whether management or the administrators knew of this democratic gathering has never been satisfactorily answered.

December 1996–February 1997, IND in SA

First Test, Durban, 26–30 December 1996

MK was in daily telephonic contact with Cronjé, who admitted feeding the gambler information on team selection and daily forecasts. He recalled MK asking him what would happen in the first Test against India in Durban. Cronjé responded, 'I think South Africa has a very good chance of beating India handsomely'. South Africa did indeed win – by 328 runs.

Second Test, Cape Town, 2–6 January 1997

MK was staying at the team hotel, the Cape Sun, and received information from Cronjé about South Africa's declaration. South Africa won this Test too – by 282 runs. On 10 January a deposit of US$50 000 was made into Cronjé's Bloemfontein bank account, followed five days later by a similar money transfer for US$30 000. This amount was previously undisclosed in Cronjé's initial statement to the Commission. Hansie conceded that both amounts may have been from MK. In total, then, from the alleged first meeting in Kanpur during the third Test in India on 10 December 1996 up until the deposit of 15 January 1997, MK had invested around US$110 000 in the South African captain in just over a month.

Third Test, Johannesburg, 16–20 January 1997

In his statement Cronjé claimed that he had refused to speak to his team-mates about losing this Test and turned down an offer of US$300 000 from MK. The match was drawn, leaving the home side victors in the series.

November 1997, Wills Quadrangular ODI Tournament, Pakistan (PAK, SA, SL, WI)

Cronjé acknowledged being contacted by MK on 'a few occasions' during this tournament. He claimed that he turned down any offers made and never saw MK again, emphasising that he had had '... no contact with or from bookmakers or punters until the fifth Test against England at Centurion this year'.

Judge King, in his first Interim Report, stated that 'The evidence does not disclose that anything untoward happened from about January 1997 to January

2000'. However, the Judge found it pertinent to include all the intervening series in this period played by South Africa and captained by Cronjé. These included:

February–April 1997, AUS in SA (3 Tests, 7 ODIs)
October/November 1997, SA in PAK (3 Tests, ODI series – SL, PAK, WI, SA)
November 1997–February 1998, SA in AUS (3 Tests, ODI series – AUS, NZ, SA)
January–March 1998, PAK in SA (3 Tests)
March/April 1998, SL in SA (2 Tests, ODI series – PAK, SL, SA)
May–August 1998, SA in ENG (5 Tests, 3 ODIs, ODI series – ENG, SL, SA)
October/November 1998, ICC Knockout in Bangladesh
November 1998–February 1999, WI in SA (5 Tests, 7 ODIs)
February/March 1999, SA in NZ (3 Tests, 7 ODIs)
May/June 1999, World Cup in ENG

May–August 1998, SA in ENG

Fifth Test, Leeds, 6–10 August 1998

Ali Bacher, in his testimony to the King Commission, claimed that Mr R had told him that the umpire of this match was 'on the payroll'. Pakistan's Javed Akhtar shared umpiring duties with England's Peter Willey. England won the Test by 23 runs and with it the series after umpire Akhtar dished out 9 lbw rulings, 8 of them going against South Africa. Bacher said Mr R had told him that one of Karachi's biggest bookmakers had travelled to Leeds before the Test to make sure his client complied.

November 1998–January 1999, WI in SA

Ivo Tennant, writing in *The Times* of London on 22 April 2000, reported the then West Indian team manager Clive Lloyd's disclosure that Ali Bacher had introduced him to a bookie at the Wanderers in Johannesburg on the 1998/99 tour. 'Ali introduced me to a bookmaker. I can't remember his name and I thought it was some kind of joke. We had a short conversation but neither he nor anybody else approached me to fix any matches.' Tennant implied that the bookie in question was none other than Sanjay Chawla, Hansie Cronjé's alleged paymaster. The article in *The Times* drew Dr Bacher's personal attention in the King Commission:

> I think it was the Saturday of the Easter weekend in *The Times* of London, written by Ivo Tennant, there are two or three paragraphs where Clive Lloyd had alleged that I'd introduced Sanjay to Clive Lloyd. Now I've never met Mr Sanjay, I don't know who he is. What did take place, at our invitation, that on two or three occasions, we would invite Jack Bannister, overseas guests and

also 'Mr R' to come and spend a day at the cricket, a good vantage position, enjoy some good company. But certainly I have never, ever met Mr Sanjay.

However, Tennant claimed in the same article that Bacher and Bob Woolmer knew Chawla frequented the South African dressing-room. According to Tennant, Woolmer thought Chawla was 'measuring the players for new suits'.[531]

November 1999–January 2000, ENG in SA

Fifth Test, Pretoria, 14–18 January 2000

With the Test series already won and nothing at stake, this Centurion Test qualified for what Sir Paul Condon of the ICC's investigative unit would term a 'vulnerable' match. With rain washing out the second, third and fourth day's play, a draw was inevitable. However, a result was contrived on the final day's play with both sides forfeiting an innings – the first time in 123 years of cricketing history that this was done in a Test match. According to Cronjé, the mastermind behind this epic ploy was Johannesburg bookie Marlon Aronstam.

On the late afternoon of the fourth day, Cronjé received a phone call from a man who described himself as a cricket lover who was interested in seeing Cronjé make a match of the waterlogged Test. According to Cronjé, Marlon Aronstam mentioned making a donation of some R500 000 to a charity of Cronjé's choice as well as an unspecified 'gift' for Cronjé himself. This 'gift' cropped up for the first time in Cronjé's affidavit, subsequent to his confession letter of 11 April. Marlon, meanwhile, did not remember the 'gift' but did recall mentioning a charitable donation of R200 000 for entertaining his idea. By the time that Aronstam arrived for his prearranged meeting with Cronjé at the Sandton Sun, it would appear that the 'donation', whatever the amount, was no longer on the cards as Aronstam had been unable to get any odds on the outcome of the Test. A result was engineered, however, during the final day's play and money did change hands. South Africa lost the Centurion Test to England by 2 wickets. Both Cronjé and opener Kirsten were out for ducks, Gibbs was out on 3 and Paul Adams retired injured. It was South Africa's first loss in fourteen matches.

As Justice King emphasised in his Interim Report, the unprecedented events of the Centurion Test were engendered by the promise of financial reward. Cronjé received R50 000 from Aronstam in two instalments, the first on the Wednesday night after the Test, as well as a previously undisclosed sum of R3 000 and a leather jacket for his wife. As Cronjé understood it, the R50 000 was for future information and the R3 000 was for helpful pitch reports. Some thirty phone calls and SMS messages passed between Aronstam and Cronjé from the Centurion Test, throughout the triangular ODI series involving England and

Zimbabwe, up until the second Test against India in Bangalore in the first week of March. Cronjé explained that 'There's a lot of people that ... used to talk to me as captain quite a lot and give me suggestions and Aronstam was one of them'.

January–February 2000, Standard Bank Triangular in South Africa (SA, ENG, ZIM)

While Cronjé could not remember the particular conversation he conceded that the throwing of at least one game in the ODI triangular series was discussed with Aronstam as long as South Africa was through to the final. It was acknowledged that to make money on a cricket game you had to have people on your side to co-operate. Aronstam went on to say that Cronjé had mentioned the names of Boje, Strydom and Gibbs in this regard. Hansie denied this. Pieter Strydom, aged 30, had made his Test debut in the controversial Centurion Test. Although South Africa eventually won the ODI series, suspicion was cast on the entire tournament because of Cronjé's extensive communications with Marlon Aronstam, Hamid Cassim and Sanjay Chawla.

First ODI – SA v ZIM, Johannesburg, 21 January 2000

On an unidentified occasion that did not appear in Cronjé's original statement to the Commission, Aronstam inquired what a good score would be in one of the matches and Cronjé gave an approximate figure. South Africa went on to bowl out Zimbabwe for this same approximate figure. The match in question is thought to be the first ODI in Johannesburg where Zimbabwe got 226 and South Africa won by 6 wickets. Cronjé was Man of the Match for his unbeaten 83.

Second ODI – SA v ENG, Bloemfontein, 23 January 2000

An SMS message was sent by Cronjé to Aronstam before this game. South Africa were bowled out for 184 without completing the 50 overs. England won by 9 wickets.

Sixth ODI – SA v ZIM, Durban, 2 February 2000

A day or two before this game, Cronjé met a man named Sanjay in the team's Beverly Hills Hotel. He was subsequently identified as London-based Indian businessman Sanjeev Chawla. Sanjay was introduced to Cronjé by Hamid Cassim, a Johannesburg sweet-shop owner with connections to the Indian and Pakistani cricket sides as well as the South African team. In his statement, Cronjé affirmed that the two men wanted information on the ODI games and that Sanjay was 'keen to get involved' in South Africa's second encounter with Zimbabwe, in Durban. Topics of discussion included losing a match and influencing other players. Sanjay handed Cronjé an unspecified sum of dollars in a cellphone case and this money, uncounted, was carried, undeclared, first in a briefcase and then in an Adidas bag, through a number of international customs before landing up in the filing cabinet in Cronjé's home. A subsequent revelation, not contained in Cronjé's initial statement, was that the money, which could have been ten or twenty or sixty or eighty thousand dollars, Cronjé was unsure, was intended as a deposit on the US$100 000 discussed for throwing a match. Zimbabwe won the Durban ODI by 2 wickets after the bowling attack of Pollock, Klusener, Williams, Kallis and Hayward conceded 18 extras and Jonty Rhodes missed a crucial run-out 8 balls before the end of the game. Hansie Cronjé managed a meagre 10 with the bat while Rhodes went 3 better and Pollock succumbed on 14.

Seventh ODI – SA v ENG, East London, 4 February 2000

Aronstam was receiving pitch and weather reports from Cronjé and Sanjay, it seems, was around too. South Africa beat England by 2 wickets.

Eighth ODI – SA v ZIM, Port Elizabeth, 6 February 2000

Aronstam was receiving pitch reports from Cronjé and there were twelve calls from Cassim logged the day before the game. The last was at 12:35 pm that night. South Africa won by 53 runs and went through to the final in which 149 all out in the allotted 45 overs was sufficient to beat England by 38 runs and win the competition.

February/March 2000, SA in IND

First Test, Mumbai, 24–28 February 2000

Aronstam phoned during the first and second Tests and Cronjé also spoke to Sunil during this tour. In the build-up to the two Tests in India, Cronjé received regular calls from Cassim and Sanjay. He told Sanjay he had spoken to Gibbs, Strydom and Boje, but maintained that he was merely stringing Sanjay along and had not propositioned the players mentioned. As the King Commission would reveal, Gibbs and Strydom were, in fact, approached by Cronjé on separate occasions, while Nicky Boje, who made his Test debut in this match, continues to plead ignorance to this day.

Pieter Strydom confirmed that Cronjé sounded him out in Mumbai before the first Test and offered him R70 000 to under-perform so that South Africa would score no more than 250. Both concurred that Strydom turned down the initial offer and Cronjé upped it the following day to R140 000. This was still rejected, apparently. Coincidentally, the South Africans scored well below 250 in both their innings, racking up 176 in the first and 164 in the second. Such modest totals were enough to overwhelm the Indians by 4 wickets. When asked why he chose Strydom for his overtures, Cronjé replied, 'It could have been anyone'.

Second Test, Bangalore, 2–6 March 2000

Wicketkeeper Mark Boucher, batsman Jacques Kallis and all-rounder Lance Klusener testified that Cronjé approached them before the second Test in Bangalore. All claimed that they regarded the offer as a joke. When the UCB and the team met on 10 April after Cronjé's dubious dealings had come to light, no reference was made by any of the players to any of Cronjé's solicitations. South Africa won the second Test too, by an innings and 71 runs, putting paid to India's 13-year record of being unbeaten on home soil.

After the second Test, Cronjé spoke to Aronstam on the phone for the last time before returning to South Africa. Aronstam was passing through India on his way to a horse race in Dubai, the South African team's next stop. The possibility of doing something in the first of the upcoming one-day internationals in Kochi was broached once more, yet Cronjé allegedly told Aronstam that that was no longer feasible.

March 2000, Pepsi ODI Series (SA, IND)

First ODI, Kochi, 9 March 2000

According to Aronstam's testimony, he and Cronjé discussed the fixing of the first ODI in Kochi and Gibbs, Strydom and Boje were mentioned at some stage. Cronjé denied this, saying that these were the names he misleadingly mentioned to Sanjay. Aronstam added that after Kochi, Cronjé's attitude towards him seemed to cool. Meanwhile, Sanjay and Cassim phoned on the morning of the match and urged Cronjé to go ahead. Sanjay was staying in the same hotel as the South African cricketers in Kochi and, on the morning of the match, Cronjé phoned Sanjay in his room and confirmed that South Africa would keep the score below 220 and 5 or 6 names were mentioned. These included Gibbs, Boje, Williams and Hayward. Under cross-examination at the King Commission, Cronjé conceded that an arrangement was made that Sanjay would pay the players if they played along in Kochi. As it happened, instead of the alleged 220 agreed upon between Cronjé and Sanjay, South Africa went on to score a seemingly unassailable 301/3 but this score reflected a drop in the run rate at the end of the innings when at one stage the projected target was looking like 335/340. Gibbs reached 111 after surviving 3 chances that the Indians missed. Cronjé hit 19 off 20 balls and failed to score a boundary with 7 wickets in hand. Of Boje, Williams and Hayward's bowling spells, Hayward was the only one to pick up a wicket – that of Tendulkar, caught Williams, but at the cost of 2 no balls and 5 wides. The 7 South African bowlers gave away 27 extras between them and

South Africa lost to India after Azharuddin and Jadeja put on the runs. Cronjé insisted that Sanjay was upset that the game had not gone according to the script. The question, however, must be asked: Whose script?

Second ODI, Jamshedpur, 12 March 2000

Sanjay phoned wanting to influence the outcome of the second ODI and Cronjé alleged that he used the other players as an excuse to refuse, saying, 'No, no. They were saying that they were already doing Kochi. The other guys are already angry with me because I have not received their money, you know'.[532] South Africa lost this match by 6 wickets.

Third ODI, Faridabad, 15 March 2000

The Indian police, when publicising their charges against Cronjé, Strydom, Gibbs and Boje, released a phone transcript that they identified as occurring the night before this game. The conversation prefigures in many ways the events of this match. Cronjé, in his statement to the King Commission, conceded as much; that if the transcript was accurate, then it probably concerned a conversation he had had with Sanjay prior to the third ODI in Faridabad. In the telephone transcripts the names of Strydom, Boje, Gibbs, Williams and Klusener are mentioned. Gibbs is meant to get less than 20 runs and the Indians, if batting first, are to be restricted to no more than 250 runs.

Cronjé won the toss and sent India in to bat their way to 248/8. Cronjé's 10 overs with the ball were the most costly, giving away 69 runs. Boje's 4 overs cost 22 runs while Strydom's 3 overs went for 15 runs with 4 wides dished up in the process. Klusener only bowled 2 overs after conceding 11 runs and Williams did not play in this match. Nonetheless, South Africa won by 2 wickets, no thanks to their second and third batsmen, Gibbs and Boje, who managed a modest 19 and 14 runs respectively. Klusener, batting seventh, was sent packing by Tendulkar for 6 and Strydom, batting last, was 1 not out. Cronjé earned himself the Man of the Match award for his 66 despite the fact that Gary Kirsten scored 93. That night Sanjay met Cronjé in his hotel room at the Taj Palace in Delhi to congratulate the South African skipper on his team's victory.

Fourth ODI, Baroda, (Vadodara) 17 March 2000

Sanjay, who was now back in London, was still in phone contact with Hansie. Once again, the undated phone transcripts record that Cronjé told Sanjay that he had looked at the pitch today and in his estimation, it could 'turn big'. This was the case in both the fourth and fifth high-scoring ODIs. With India 2–1 ahead in the series, the home team won with 1 ball to spare, chasing a sizeable South African target of 282. The hosts now led the limited-overs tournament 3–1.

Fifth ODI, Nagpur, 19 March 2000

Sanjay phoned about Nagpur. Once again, this could be classified a 'vulnerable' match as South Africa was out of the running in this series. It is this game that Herschelle Gibbs and Henry Williams admitted to agreeing to fix at the behest of their captain. However, they insisted that they never followed through on the deal as Williams retired injured in his second over and Gibbs forgot about the deal in the heat of the moment. Those concerned maintained that the script plotted for the Nagpur game was that outlined in the transcript released by the Delhi police. In other words, Gibbs would get less than 20, Williams had to give away more than 50 runs in his 10 overs and South Africa were to get less than 270 in their innings. However, as we have seen, these details follow the events of the third ODI at Faridabad more closely.

South Africa were sent into bat by Indian captain Saurav Ganguly, who won the toss. As things turned out, for the first time in this series, the team chasing lost. Gibbs survived two near dismissals and went on to score 74 off 53 balls before being run out. Cronjé hammered 38 off 31 balls only to be caught by Dravid. At the end of their innings, the South Africans had managed to set a record-breaking target of 320 runs for the Indians to chase. Henry Williams, surprisingly, opened the bowling with Derek Crookes but didn't manage to finish his second over. After conceding 11 runs, bowling 6 wides and collecting the wicket of captain Ganguly, Williams retired with a shoulder injury. Nonetheless, 320 proved to be enough and South Africa ended a disappointing series with a record-breaking win despite losing the series 3–2.

As the *AFP* match summary on 7 April pointed out, however, such are the vagaries of the gentleman's game that 'Two days after the final match, India and South Africa shifted the battle to the desert venue of Sharjah – with a remarkable transformation in the results. India lost three of their four matches and South Africa won three before losing the final to Pakistan.'[533]

March 2000, Coca-Cola Cup, Sharjah (SA, IND, PAK)

Sunil, first mentioned by Cronjé during the Sharjah Cup of 1996 and the subsequent South African tour to India, had a VIP pass to the players' restaurant, apparently because he knew one of the tournament's organisers and shared breakfast with the South African, Indian and Pakistani cricketers every morning. Sunil was in contact with Cronjé during this tournament, as was Hamid Cassim.

Sixth ODI – SA v PAK, 28 March 2000

This is yet another 'vulnerable' game on 'neutral territory', as South Africa was already through to the final and the outcome of this match was unimportant. Cronjé did not play in this penultimate game. Sunil was seeking information on the South African team selection for this game as he wanted to put some money on Pakistan. This emerged at breakfast that morning with Cronjé and Corrie van Zyl and their wives.

Having been set an unintimidating target of 169 by the Pakistanis, the South Africans made a good start and were 71/1 at the end of 15 overs. Then they lost 7 wickets for 20 runs, Boucher, Benkenstein and Klusener all departing without moving the score from 74, with Pollock, Strydom, Crookes and Hayward close behind. Pakistan won the game by a convincing 67 runs as the entire South African team bowed out for 101 in 26.5 overs.

Final ODI – SA v PAK, 31 March 2000

The night before the Coca-Cola Cup final, Cronjé and Klusener were approached by an unnamed man who wanted the players to promote his product. An offer was made in two instalments – US$100 000 now and US$100 000 later – for a poor performance from the South Africans in the final. Cronjé claimed that Klusener knew nothing of this offer. In this, Cronjé's last official match for South Africa, he top-scored 79. Klusener, however, went for a duck, as did Nicky Boje, while Gibbs managed 5 followed by Crookes (1), Elworthy (5) and Hayward (4). Neil McKenzie and Mark Boucher were the only other two batsmen to feature with half-centuries. In pursuit of 263, South Africa surrendered in the forty-ninth over on 247. Pakistan won the final and the series.

A senior South African sports correspondent was under no illusions that this game was fixed.

> I think it was one of the most obviously fixed games – as obvious as the Bangladesh/Pakistan fixture in the World Cup … Cronjé threw his wicket away in highly obvious circumstances, I felt. Earlier, Derek Crookes had bowled the best spell ever, by his own admission. He'd bowled 5 overs for 16 with Inzamam going like a steam-train but Cronjé took him off and he didn't bowl again. Why did Cronjé bring himself on, bowl 3 overs for 20, wide half-volleys with no man on the cover boundary, late in the innings? This game is one of the most graphic examples of one man, the captain, being able to totally manipulate the game.

17

CBI Report on Cricket Match-fixing and Related Malpractices

Indian matches under suspicion: 1979–1999

India's Central Bureau of Investigation's star witness was bookie/punter Mukesh Gupta (MK) whose detailed revelations form the substance of the CBI's Report on Cricket Match-fixing. It goes further than any other official inquiry in crafting a comprehensive definition of match-fixing:

> As regards the word 'information' used by MK, it is difficult to believe that in an age when television has brought cricket to our drawing rooms and expert commentators thoroughly analyse various aspects of a match like pitch, team strengths, probable result, etc, such information provided by a player is of any use to a bookie. So, in this respect, it has to be construed that the word 'information' is a euphemism for under-performing or 'fixing'.

Thus, match-fixing when used in the CBI Report encompasses the following:

- receiving money to under-perform
- placing bets in matches in which you play
- passing on of information regarding team composition, probable result or pitch conditions
- fixing of piches by groundsmen
- current and ex-players used to get access to other players.

November 1979–February 1980, PAK in IND

Sixth Test, Calcutta, 29 January–3 February 1980

The 1979/80 Pakistani tour of India is best remembered for the sixth and final Test at Calcutta in January 1980. Indian captain GR Vishwanath lost the toss but Asif Iqbal, the Pakistani captain on that tour, insisted that his Indian counterpart had made the right call. There was speculation that bets had been placed on the outcome of the toss. Later in the same Test, Iqbal declared with Pakistan 59 runs behind with 6 wickets still in hand.

October/November 1987, World Cup in IND and PAK

In the World Cup of 1987, both MK and his partner Anand Saxena earned good money through betting. Former Indian cricketer and match-fixing whistle-blower Manoj Prabhakar told *Outlook* magazine on 11 June 1997: 'During the 1987 World Cup, rumours were rife about the team's performance but sometimes it seemed so obvious that it had me wondering.'[534]

1988, Ramcharan Agarwal Tournament, New Delhi

In a club tournament in New Delhi in 1988, MK watched Ajay Sharma score a 'quick 50 or 100'. As a token of appreciation for this performance, he slipped Rs2 000 (US$50) into Sharma's pocket as the player was escorted from the grounds. Two weeks later, Sharma got in touch and thus began a long and lucrative association, or so it would appear.

January/February 1990, IND in NZ

MK was getting 'information' from Sharma on India's tour of New Zealand in early 1990. Gupta requested an introduction to the Indian all-rounder Manoj Prabhakar, who was also on tour, and spoke to him on the phone from India. A 'personal introduction' took place sometime after the New Zealand tour but before the Indian team's tour of England in 1990.

July/August 1990, IND in ENG

MK requested a meeting with Prabhakar in person after Sharma was dropped for the English tour. Prabhakar was paid Rs40 000 (US$1 000) for his help on this tour. He provided 'information' about all the matches played and underperformed in one of the Test matches, which was a draw. By a process of elimination and deduction this may well have been the drawn second Test at Old Trafford from 9–14 August 1990. Prabhakar, batting at number 7, lost his wicket for 4 runs. After the tour, MK came up with the promised cash to purchase Prabhakar a Maruti Gypsy with wide tyres. While having dinner together one night, Prabhakar agreed to introduce other players to MK at the asking price of Rs50 000 (US$1 200) a head. They phoned batsman Gus Logie of the West Indies that same night but, apparently, he wasn't interested.

November/December 1990, SL in IND

MK claimed Prabhakar introduced Sri Lanka's Aravinda de Silva to him at a price and in MK's words they 'established good rapport'. Later, MK arranged a meeting with New Zealand's Martin Crowe through Aravinda de Silva. MK met Martin Crowe in 1991 in New Zealand and had lunch at his house with his wife Simone. He offered to pay Rs20 000 (US$500) for '… information in any game in which New Zealand played'. MK also said that he had paid Crowe US$20 000 for 'information.' According to MK, Crowe refused to fix any matches. Crowe was exonerated of any wrongdoing by the New Zealand Cricket Board in July 2001.

November 1990–May 1991, Ranji Trophy

Third quarter-final, Delhi v Mumbai, New Delhi, 16–20 April 1991

During the 1990/91 Indian domestic season, Prabhakar told MK that the Delhi players were prepared to throw this game because if they won they would have to play in further Ranji matches, which clashed with their overseas English league commitments. Former Indian XI cricketer-turned-commentator Atul Wassan was one of the players in this match, as was Ajay Sharma, who corroborated MK's evidence. MK paid Prabhakar for the information and, although the match was drawn, this was sufficient to knock Delhi out of the tournament.

October 1991, Super Wills Cup

Wills XI (Domestic) v Habib Bank Limited, New Delhi, 13 October 1991

MK refers to a match between Wills Cup winners Pakistan and Wills Cup winners India. MK asked Prabhakar to arrange an introduction to Salim Malik, with whom he conspired to fix this 45-over match, allegedly without the knowledge of captain Javed Miandad. Pakistan lost after a close finish. Malik was paid Rs8 lakh (US$20 000) for his contribution, while MK made an equivalent amount. MK claimed not to know who else had helped Malik to ensure the desired result.

October 1991, Wills Trophy, Sharjah (IND, PAK, WI)

Following this tournament, India refused to play in Sharjah because of match-rigging suspicions. As one media account explained, 'The Indians, who lost regularly to their arch-rivals at Sharjah since … the 1986 Australasia Cup final, were convinced Dubai bookmakers were hand-in-hand with the organisers.'[535] The penultimate match between India and Pakistan came up in evidence to the CBI investigators, while the final between the same two teams was the subject of media attention after revelations by former Pakistani cricketers Imran Khan and Intikhab Alam. India returned to the United Arab Emirates venue only in April 1994 for the Australasia Cup, where once again they met arch-nemesis Pakistan in the final. Oaths on the Quran and suspicious phone calls to the Pakistani dressing room were once more the order of the day, according to evidence heard by the Qayyum Inquiry.

Sixth ODI–PAK v IND, 23 October 1991

This match, which Pakistan won by a scant 4 runs after India looked set for the win, came up in two Indian inquiries – Chandrachud in 1997 and the CBI in 2000 – as well as in media reports. The events described bear a marked resemblance to what transpired sixteen years later, during the final of the 2007 World Cup in the West Indies.

Manoj Prabhakar, in a sensational story published in *Outlook* on 11 June 1997, recalled this game: 'I also distinctly remember that match at Sharjah in 1991 when I was at the crease with Sanjay Manjrekar, when we decided to walk off because of failing light. To our surprise we received a signal from the team management to play on. This decision still baffles and angers me.'[536]

Prabhakar's team-mate, Sanjay Manjrekar, remembered the incident somewhat differently in his disclosures to Justice Chandrachud: 'Our match at Sharjah against Pakistan in October 1991 started late. We were on the right path when the umpire said that the light was bad. There was a brief stoppage. But it is untrue that Manoj Prabhakar and I went to the pavilion. Ashok Mankad was the manager of the team.' Ashok Mankad didn't seem to remember the game in question: 'The Sharjah match of which he speaks did not take place at all. Besides, it was an inconsequential match since India had reached the final.' However, Pakistan's narrow win in this match ensured that they too would reach the final.

Pakistan won the toss, batted first and made 257 in the allotted 50 overs. In reply, the Indians were on target right up until the forty-fifth over of the match, when the fading light finally vanished. Had play been stopped at this point, India would have won the match on run rate. However, after the umpires stopped the game briefly to discuss the situation with the organisers, they asked the Indians to play on. In light so bad that the street lights were on for the last 6 overs, the Indians lost Tendulkar and Kapil Dev on successive balls and with that the match. Sandeep Patil was cricket coach of the Indian team from 18 March 1986 to September 1996. While he did not refer specifically to this match, he told Chandrachud, '... my long experience shows that no Indian player has ever laid a bet to lose a match. It has never happened and I am sure that it'll never happen in the future.'

The match report for the game described the unusual circumstances. Apparently, there was great confusion about the outcome of the match in case it was abandoned due to bad light. The umpires were uncertain as to the procedure, as were the organisers, and in a welter of confusion, the Indians batted on. The umpires claimed that the Indians did not appeal; Manjrekar and Prabhakar insisted that they did appeal but that the umpires were confused about the procedure and, as a result, asked the Indians to bat on.

Two former Presidents of the BCCI referred to this match in their statements to the CBI in 2000. IS Bindra mentioned a match that '... was played under failing light between India and Pakistan.' He stated that there was a possibility that this match was continued because of some foul play, especially since '... matches in Sharjah were played for money'. Bindra's counterpart, Madhavrao Scindia, was at the game as he was the President of the BCCI at the time. When asked by the CBI why the match was allowed to go on in darkness, Scindia replied that '... as a matter of principle, office-bearers of BCCI do not interfere with decision making on the field. Such decisions are taken by the coach, captain and team management'. The captain was Mohammad Azharuddin who, incidentally, was out for a duck in this match, as was team-mate Kapil Dev who kept him company.

November 1991–February 1992, IND in AUS

December 1991/January 1992, Benson and Hedges World Series Cup (AUS, IND, WI)

India toured Australia just before the World Cup in Australia and New Zealand in February/March 1992. MK arranged to fix some matches in this series with Prabhakar, who claimed that team-mate Navrot S Sidhu was his willing accomplice. Apparently, with the help of Prabhakar's 'information' MK made some good money in two unspecified ODIs against Australia.

February/March 1992, World Cup in NZ and AUS

MK lost big when nothing went according to plan.

September/October 1992, World XI v IND XI, Sri Lanka

According to MK Gupta's testimony to the CBI, '... there were some festival matches in Sri Lanka and many international players were also taking part'. Manoj Prabhakar was one of the players.

MK phoned Prabhakar from India, wanting introductions to other international players. Prabhakar informed MK that the teams were staying at the Hotel Taj Samudra in Colombo and that he could arrange a meeting with the Australian Dean Jones.

MK flew to Colombo, met with Jones and offered him US$40 000 for 'information'. After MK returned to India, apparently on the same flight as Prabhakar, which Prabhakar claimed was purely accidental, Dean Jones phoned MK to decline the offer as he was afraid that Allan Border had seen him talking to the bookie in the hotel lobby. MK testified that Prabhakar had also introduced him to Sri Lanka's Arjuna Ranatunga and Brian Lara of the West Indies during this festival series, although no money changed hands. While Prabhakar conceded Brian Lara, he denied introducing either Ranatunga or Dean Jones. Thus Prabhakar received Rs2 lakh (US$5 000) for facilitating 'information' that had failed to pay off despite Prabhakar's assertion to the CBI that '... he was paid only when his information was of use to MK'.

Based on Dean Jones's submissions to the Australian Player Conduct Inquiry of 1999, the O'Regan Report described this same encounter. The Australian Cricket Board-appointed inquiry heard allegations that the second game of this series was fixed (and duly lost) by the World XI and that MK, aka 'John', was present during this tournament. The ACB Report went on to discuss this evidence and the two Australian players involved in the event in a confidential chapter that has never been made public.

September 1992, Hong Kong Sixes

Prabhakar was paid for introducing Mark Waugh to MK, who gave the Australian batsman US$20 000 in exchange for 'information' whenever Australia played. While Prabhakar corroborated MK's evidence on this point, Mark Waugh maintained that he first met MK or 'John' in Sri Lanka in 1994, some two years later.

November 1992–January 1993, IND in SA

Ajit Wadekar, former Indian captain and manager, recalled a game during this so-called 'Goodwill Tour' when he rebuked Kapil Dev for failing to run out Peter Kirsten even though the South African top order batsman repeatedly left his crease before the ball was bowled. 'This appeared odd now but he had thought that Kapil really wanted to have good relations with South Africa.'

January–March 1993, ENG in IND

During England's tour of India in 1993, MK claimed to have arranged a meeting through Prabhakar with English vice captain Alec Stewart, who refused to fix matches but accepted £5 000 for conveying 'information' whenever the English team played. Prabhakar was paid for the introduction. Stewart was subsequently publicly exonerated of this allegation by the English Cricket Board on 11 July 2001 with the approval of Sir Paul Condon of the ICC's Anti-Corruption Unit. It seems that as MK Gupta did not further substantiate the claims he had made and no further evidence was forthcoming, Stewart was in the clear.

First Test, Calcutta, 29 January–2 February 1993

MK's payroll funded umpires as well as cricketers and MK arranged with umpire Piloo Reporter for his assessment of matches during the tour. Reporter was paid 'a small amount of money' for correct 'information' in the first Test in Calcutta.

Third ODI, Bangalore, 26 Feb 1993

MK made money on the ODI in Bangalore thanks to Prabhakar's information. According to MK, Prabhakar claimed that in most of the matches he fixed he was aided by Indian batsman NS Sidhu.

Fifth ODI, Gwalior, 4 March 1993/Sixth ODI, Gwalior, 5 March 1993

MK lost money on the 'information' that Prabhakar provided during the final two ODIs at Gwalior.

January/February 1994, SL in IND

First Test, Lucknow, 18–22 January 1994

According to MK, during Sri Lanka's tour of India in early 1994, captain Arjuna Ranatunga and Aravinda De Silva offered to under-perform and claimed they didn't need any other players on-side because they could fix the match themselves. Ranatunga notched up 9 in his first innings and a duck in his second. De Silva got 13 and 11 in his 2 innings. India won the match by an innings and 119 runs. Sri Lanka's loss in the first Test proved very lucrative for MK and he claimed to have paid De Silva US$15 000 for his help. Ranatunga and De Silva were ready to fix others but, according to MK, the odds were unappealingly low.

The business relationship between MK and Prabhakar deteriorated around this time. MK suspected that Ranatunga and De Silva were dealing with someone else through Prabhakar, who was now involved with other bookies in Delhi and Mumbai and some big punters so he didn't 'take much interest'. Prabhakar admitted being friendly with a punter called Tipu Kohli and a Mumbai bookie by the name of Mashaal.

Following this Sri Lankan tour of India, in which the visitors lost all three Tests by an innings, the Board of Control for Cricket in Sri Lanka (BCCSL) instigated an internal inquiry into their team's poor results. The Skanda Kumar Report found that 'There is evidence that a bookmaker of Indian origin has attempted to make his presence felt in the national cricket scene.'[537] The Skanda Kumar Report was never made public.

When the CBI Report was released in November 2000, MK Gupta's allegations against Ranatunga and De Silva were made public and a second inquiry was ordered by the Sri Lankan Cricket Board. Lawyer Desmond Fernando subsequently cleared the two of any wrongdoing in July 2001. His report, however, like the Skanda Kumar Report, was never released. The head of Sri Lankan cricket at the time was the controversial Thilanga Sumathipala. Sumathipala was President of the BCCSL, on and off, from 1998 to 2005. Over the years Sumathipala has been the subject of a number of allegations, which included financial irregularities and irregularities in awarding contracts and TV rights as well as intimidation in the Cricket Board's presidential elections and involvement in the gambling industry – the family business is bookmaking. However, the charge that finally stuck was that of passport fraud. In 2004, he was accused of violating immigration controls and using the Cricket Board's money to get alleged gangster Dammika Amarasinghe into England to watch the 1999 Cricket World Cup. During the trial, Amarasinghe was shot dead outside a Colombo courtroom by a gunman posing as a lawyer. Despite this setback to the prosecution's case, on 4 April 2007, Sumathipala was eventually found guilty and sentenced to two years' hard labour.

April 1994, Australasia Cup, Sharjah (IND, AUS, SL, PAK, NZ, UAE)

Final ODI – IND v PAK, 22 April 1994

Prabhakar was not included in the Indian team for this tournament. MK travelled to Sharjah where he approached Australia's Mark Waugh and the new Pakistani captain, Salim Malik. According to MK, both players rejected his advances and he returned to India 'a dejected man without any gains'. According to evidence heard by the Qayyum Commission in Pakistan, several Pakistani cricketers were approached by bookies before the India/Pakistan final and the Pakistan team was asked by management to take an oath of honesty on the Quran.

September 1994, Singer World Series, Sri Lanka (IND, PAK, AUS, SL)

Second ODI – PAK v AUS, Colombo, 7 September 1994

MK referred to the controversial Singer Cup of 1994, which also features in the Qayyum Report and the O'Regan Report. Despite Salim Malik's alleged resistance to his overtures back in April, MK told the CBI that he had rung up Pakistan's captain before an ODI during the Singer series in Sri Lanka. Malik apparently informed MK that Pakistan would lose the game against Australia, a 'prediction' that proved accurate and made MK some good money. Shane Warne and Mark Waugh admitted taking money from 'John' aka MK Gupta for 'information' during this tour.

Sixth ODI – IND v PAK, Colombo, 15–16 September 1994

The 1997 Chandrachud Inquiry resulted from allegations made by Prabhakar in a cover story in *Outlook* magazine on 11 June 1997 entitled, 'I was offered Rs25 lakh by a team-mate to sabotage a match in Pakistan's favour'. In the CBI Report, Manoj Prabhakar finally came clean on the well-publicised approach made to him by Kapil Dev to under-perform in this game, which, as it happened, was washed out. The amount on offer was said to be Rs25 lakh (US$61 500). Prabhakar alleged that his roommate NS Sidhu was an eyewitness to the encounter, which took place in their hotel room. According to Prabhakar, a cricketer in an adjoining room, Prashant Vaidya, also happened upon the conversation. Both alleged witnesses denied that they were present, although Sidhu admitted that Prabhakar had told him of the approach. Prabhakar claimed further that he had informed the coach, Ajit Wadekar, and the captain, Mohammad Azharuddin, of the incident. In an interview with *Zee TV* on 15 June 1997, Prabhakar said cryptically, 'I have come to know this now, that the very people I had told would probably have finished me.'[538]

For his part, Wadekar maintained that, had Prabhakar indeed made such a revelation, it would have appeared in the tour report. Prabhakar claimed also to have told former Indian cricketers-turned-commentators Ravi Shastri and Sunil Gavaskar a few days later. Shastri confirmed this but also stated '... that it was a well-known fact in the Indian team that Manoj Prabhakar and Kapil Dev did not get along very well'. Dev admitted as much to the CBI while denying all allegations. He also offered to take an 'unconditional lie detector test'. The CBI concluded that '... the inquiry has so far not disclosed any evidence of Kapil Dev's role in match-fixing and related malpractices'. After the CBI Report was released in November 2000, the Board of Control for Cricket in India imposed penalties on some of those named in the report. Prabhakar earned himself a five-year ban while Kapil Dev, newly resigned as Indian coach, was exonerated.

October–December 1994, WI in IND

MK referred to this West Indian tour of India in his revelations to the CBI. He said that he again met Brian Lara, who offered to give of less than his best in two one-day matches. MK's bets paid off and he paid Brian Lara around US$40 000.

October/November 1994, Wills World Series, India (IND, NZ, WI)

Fourth ODI – IND v WI, Kanpur, 30 October 1994

Six weeks after the final of the Singer Cup, another game involving India created a furore within cricket circles and the newspapers rang with the scandal. As Dr Ali Irani, the now-disgraced physiotherapist of the Indian team, testified to the CBI: 'It was in 1994, in the India/West Indies one-day international at Kanpur, that everybody, for the first time, felt that something was wrong.' To go by the scorecard, Prabhakar's 102 not out looks like a heroic innings. However, match reports, media accounts and eye-witness testimony tell a different tale.

This match had come up previously in the 1997 Chandrachud Inquiry in which Prabhakar testified:

> There are times that things are so obvious, the entire nation has watched it happened. In Kanpur, when we were chasing the West Indies score, Mongia

came into bat and conveyed the management's instructions to try and get as close to the target. The resultant hullabaloo about my going slow should be directed at the team management and not me as I was doing so under their instructions. Of the 48 balls in that period, I played just 11. I scored 9 off those 11 balls. In fact, due to someone else's fault, I was dropped and humiliated.

With India chasing a West Indies opening stand of 257, Nayan Mongia, last man in before close of play, joined opening batsman Prabhakar with 5 wickets in hand. However, instead of chasing the target, the two men batted as though playing in a Test match. According to Irani, the incumbent coach at the time, Ajit Wadekar, was sitting oblivious in the dressing room until one of the selectors, GR Vishwanath of that infamous Iqbal toss, rushed in shouting whether Wadekar knew what was going on in the field. Prabhakar maintained that Mongia had joined him at the crease with instructions from the dressing room to bat out the remaining balls and not lose their wickets. According to Prabhakar and Irani, Mongia never revealed just who had issued those instructions. On the return journey from the ground, Irani heard Prabhakar fulminating against Wadekar and captain Azharuddin, presumably because he had learned that both he and Mongia were to be dropped for the following two games.

In his statement to the Chandrachud Inquiry, LH Sahi, sports editor for *The Telegraph* in India, described press reaction to this match. 'The way Manoj Prabhakar and Nayan Mongia batted shocked everyone. The reports which appeared in the newspapers the next day almost unanimously doubted the integrity of these two players ... The general feeling was that their omission from the next two matches had everything to do with their involvement with the bookies.'

April 1995, Asia Cup, Sharjah (BDESH, IND, PAK, SL)

Third ODI – IND v PAK, 7 April 1995

Six months later, more damning reports appeared in the Indian media; this time about the Asia Cup in Sharjah in 1995. In his testimony to the CBI, IS Bindra, former BCCI president, referred to an incident reported by Mr LP Sahi of *The Telegraph* newspaper, Calcutta, in which Ajay Jadeja brought a bookie into the Indian dressing room to see Azharuddin. The media got wind of this and tried to photograph the encounter but the bookie was swiftly hustled away. The Indian magazine *Outlook*, in April 2000, mentioned another incident during this series in which members of the gambling syndicate D-Company were seen entering the press enclosure during a Pakistan/Indian match. A former BCCI President reportedly revealed that 'They (the bookies) told media persons that an Indian reserve player had given them access. When they were finally evicted, they had a tête-à-tête with the Indian player concerned.'[539]

Eyewitness media accounts were not, however, the only evidence of illicit dealings during this match. *Outlook* again reported on 24 April 2000 that the Mumbai branch of the Indian revenue service in the course of investigations into illegal money transit (*hawala*) had stumbled upon telephone conversations before an Asia Cup match in 1995 in which bookies discussed the involvement of three to four Indian international players in cricket gambling. *Outlook* asserted that its investigations had turned up the names of Mohammad Azharuddin, Ajay Jadeja and a relative of a former Indian cricket captain. Apparently, the revenue service's taped library was quite extensive and the evidence was forwarded to the then President of the BCCI, Madhavrao Scindia. No action was forthcoming from the BCCI.[540] Explaining why, Scindia told the CBI that he had never received the tapes or transcripts and that, as he was not BCCI President at the time, there was no reason that he should have received the alleged tapes.

October/November 1996, AUS in IND

Only Test, New Delhi, 10–14 October 1996

MK said that he had paid Ajay Sharma Rs3 lakh (US$7 000) for his enterprise in this match in which he ensured a definite result (and lucrative winnings) by arranging a spinner-friendly pitch with the head groundsman of the Ferozeshah Kotla ground in Delhi. India won by 7 wickets in three-and-a-half days.

October–December 1996, SA in IND

October/November 1996, Titan Cup Series (IND, AUS, SA)

The Titan Cup series towards the end of 1996, involving hosts India and the visiting Australians and South Africans, proved to be a morass of match-fixing. The Mumbai police apparently had taped evidence of suspicious conversations between bookies and Mohammad Azharuddin, wicketkeeper Nayan Mongia and specialist batsman Ajay Jadeja during this one-day competition. Prem Panicker, cricket correspondent for *rediff.com*, described the Titan triangular tournament as a series in which India 'slid from defeat to disaster'. [541] The reverse was true for the South Africans. Their perfect record of wins throughout the competition was marred by their unexpected loss to India in the final. According to MK, Azharuddin agreed to 'do' matches for MK in this series.

Seventh ODI – IND v SA, Rajkot, 29 October 1996

Azharuddin confessed to fixing three matches to the CBI, the first of which was this game.

MK confirmed that Azhar was working for him and Anil Steel at this time. India went into the Rajkot game with the visiting South Africans ahead in both their previous encounters. India won the toss and went in to bat. Opening batsman NS Sidhu was run out by Cronjé for 2. Rahul Dravid, batting 4, followed suit – run out by Jonty Rhodes on 21. At 111/4 the appearance of Azharuddin signalled a middle-order collapse. Azhar put on just 9 runs before being caught behind by Richardson off the bowling of Boje. India's own wicketkeeper Nayan Mongia followed soon after with 3 and, with the loss of Jadeja on 26, India found themselves at 172/9. By the forty-ninth over they had succumbed entirely on 185. Despite losing their captain to a run out by Azharuddin when Cronjé was on 27, South Africa reached the required total, also in the forty-ninth over, to make it 3 for 3.

Final ODI – IND v SA, Mumbai, 6 November 1996

It was during the 1996 Titan triangular ODI series in India that Azhar, MK and partner Anil Steel apparently had a falling out over a game plan that hadn't turned out as scripted. Mumbai police are said to have taped telephone conversations between bookies and Indian players, Azharuddin, Jadeja and Mongia which apparently revealed that, in exchange for sums of Rs20 lakh each (US$49 000), the players conveyed information on which team would open the batting, the Indian batting order and the names of the first four players to go out.[542] In his statement to the CBI, Anil Steel referred to some matches in the Titan Cup that MK Gupta had fixed through Azharuddin but said that the information provided had proved incorrect. India failed to lose this final to South Africa and MK and Anil Steel lost heavily on this match. MK told Indian investigators that he had arranged that Azhar would make up his losses in the forthcoming Test series against the South Africans. Despite the alleged taped evidence and allegations by Steel and Gupta, this was not one of the matches that Azharuddin confessed to fixing.

First Test, Ahmedabad, 20–24 November 1996

While this is also not one of the matches that Azharuddin confessed to fixing, MK claimed that Azharuddin told him that the first Test against South Africa at Ahmedabad would not end in a draw. Sure enough, India won and MK recovered 30% of his Titan Cup losses.

Second Test, Calcutta, 27 November–1 December 1996

According to Gupta, Azharuddin told MK that India would lose the second Test, which they did, and MK made up 60% of his losses.

Third Test, Kanpur, 8–12 December 1996

MK was in Kanpur for the third Test and asked Azhar for an introduction to Hansie Cronjé. At the end of the third day's play, with India ahead by 330 runs,

MK, in the guise of a diamond merchant, extracted from Cronjé the assurance that South Africa would lose. MK said that he paid the former South African captain US$40 000 for this 'information' and as a future investment. India won the Test by 280 runs and took the series 2–1.

Mohinder Amarnath Benefit Match /ODI, Mumbai, 14 December 1996

According to MK, Cronjé asked the bookie to meet with him in Mumbai before the final game of the tour – the Mohinder Amarnath Benefit game on 14 December. This match, which was upgraded to an ODI, came with an offer of US$200 000 to throw the game. All involved claim they turned the offer down, although it reportedly took three team meetings to do so. South Africa lost this final match resoundingly.

December 1996/January 1997, IND in SA

First Test, Durban, 26–30 December 1996

Despite MK's generous payments to both Azhar and Irani prior to this tour, Azhar's 'predictions' were not panning out, so MK decided to concentrate on the South African team. MK admitted that he had arranged to 'fix' matches with Cronjé during this tour and accordingly was in South Africa for the first and second Tests in Durban and Cape Town respectively. However, MK claimed that most of the matches did not turn out as planned. Cronjé, in his testimony to the King Commission about this same match, seemed to remember things differently. He recalled telling MK that South Africa would achieve a decisive victory over the Indians in this first Test, an accurate prediction as the game turned out.

Second Test, Cape Town, 2–6 January 1997

While MK did not have much to say to the CBI about this Test, he was in Cape Town during this match and, according to Cronjé's testimony to the King Commission, stayed at the South African cricket team's hotel. The magazine *India Today* related a well-known anecdote about this Cape Town Test, which involves a century-scoring Indian batsman who, '... having hit a savage 100' nudged the ball to slip and strolled down the pitch for the run, continuing on to the pavilion without breaking his stride. The magazine quoted a touring Indian team official as saying, 'There was something fishy about the way he ran. It was a single even a schoolboy wouldn't attempt.'[543] While both Sachin Tendulkar and Mohammad Azharuddin scored centuries in this Test, Azhar's 115 came off 110 balls before he was run out by Hudson. The King Commission's Interim Report states that MK made two payments of US$50 000 and, five days later, US$30 000 into Hansie's bank account following this Test match, for '... team selections, daily information and in respect of the second Test at Newlands ...'

Third Test, Johannesburg, 16–20 January 1997

MK returned to India between the second and third Tests. From India he phoned Cronjé who told him that South Africa would lose the third Test. However, the Wanderers Test was drawn because of rain. MK admitted depositing US$50 000 into Cronjé's South African bank account 'sometime during that period'.

January/February 1997 – Standard Bank International ODI series, South Africa (IND, SA, ZIM)

MK returned to South Africa for this triangular ODI series. He insisted to the CBI that Cronjé had misled him in the third Test and had subsequently called to apologise. According to MK, Cronjé offered to provide 'exact information' and was willing to lose some of the upcoming one-day games. However, once again, all Cronjé's 'information' turned out wrong and MK suffered major losses. Cronjé blamed the Indians for playing so badly that they didn't take their chances. Why MK persevered with such an obviously poor investment was not explored in either the CBI or the King Reports.

March–May 1997, IND in WI

Third Test, Bridgetown, 27–31 March 1997

Indian physiotherapist Dr Ali Irani voiced his suspicions to the CBI that a match during the West Indies tour was 'deliberately lost' after the Indians, with wickets in hand, couldn't manage to put on the few runs needed for victory. Irani recollected that some of the players came up with the 'silly excuse' that the opposition had been practising voodoo. The ICC's Condon Report identifies this match as the third Test of India's 1997 tour to the West Indies. This Test had received some attention in the media – for all the wrong reasons. *Outlook* magazine, on 24 April 2000, reported that the Indian coach on that tour, Madan Lal, told BCCI officials that an inquiry was needed after the Indian team failed to put on the requisite 120 runs in their second innings.[544] Another member of the Indian press, Pradeep Magazine of *The Pioneer*, wrote an account of his dealings with a bookie/agent named Anil during this Indian tour of the West Indies.[545] Could this have been MK's old partner Anil Steel?

July 1997, Pepsi Asia Cup, Sri Lanka (BDESH, IND, SL, PAK)

This series marks the second match that Mohammad Azharuddin confessed to fixing, although he did not indicate which game. He alleged that the deal was done through Mukesh Gupta, although MK did not mention this series in his depositions to the CBI. A witness at the Qayyum Commission in Pakistan alleged that another of these matches was fixed – the first game of the tournament, between Pakistan and Sri Lanka.

September 1997, Sahara Cup, Toronto (IND, PAK)

Upon his return to India, Azhar promised MK he would 'do' matches in this tournament and he had his Bollywood wife Sangita phone MK with the requisite 'information'. MK got the feeling that the couple was misleading him, either because Azhar didn't have enough players to ensure the required outcome or because he was involved with rival bookies. India lost the final after winning four games on the trot. Up to this point, MK claimed, he had invested Rs90 lakh (US$220 000) in Azhar, but his 'information' had proved useless and MK wanted to recoup some of his investment. After the Sahara Cup, MK retrieved Rs30 lakh (US$73 000) in instalments from Azhar's locker in the Hotel Taj Palace in Delhi. Anil Saxena, Food and Beverages Manager at the hotel, was a good friend of the Indian batsman and the keeper of his locker. Ajay Sharma also deposited money in this same locker, according to Saxena.

April 1998, Coca-Cola Cup, Sharjah (AUS, IND, NZ)

Fourth ODI – IND v NZ, 20 April 1998

Former BCCI president IS Bindra related to the CBI how the Secretary of the Pakistan Cricket Board had overheard a conversation between Sharjah cricket administrator Asif Iqbal and TV mogul Mark Mascarhenas that the Indian team would be out for less than 185 runs and the top 4 Indian players would throw their wickets. Batting first, the Indians were all out for 181 in 49.3 overs. Three out of the four top-order batsmen – captain Azharuddin, Sachin Tendulkar and Ajay Jadeja – got the worst of wicketkeeper Parore and were run out, Azhar and Jadeja both bowing out on 11 while Tendulkar top-scored with 38. Tendulkar's opening partner Ganguly played second fiddle on the scoreboard with 31.

June/July 1998, Singer Akai Nidahas Trophy, Sri Lanka (SL, IND, NZ)

Mohammad Azharuddin apparently met Ajay Gupta through Ajay Sharma in 1998. The CBI Report described Ajay Gupta, cousin Nishit Goel, friend Gyan Gupta and his son Ameesh Gupta, as '... big-time punters of Delhi who operate in unison as a group. They seem to have got into match-fixing some time in 1998'. Nishit Goel told of a deal made by his cousin with Azharuddin to lose certain matches during this triangular tournament in Sri Lanka. However, India won the matches and Goel had heard that the Gupta contingent had lost a lot of money. While Goel did not specify the matches, a process of elimination leaves only two possibilities. Of the seven matches India played in this series, four were abandoned because of rain, one was won by Sri Lanka and two were won by India.

First ODI – IND v SL, Colombo, 19 June 1998
India took the first match against Sri Lanka in Colombo by 8 wickets.

Final ODI – IND v SL, Colombo, 7 July 1998
By a far less comfortable margin, India also beat the home team in the final – this time by a mere 6 runs.

September 1998, Sahara Cup, Toronto (PAK, IND)

Again, according to Nishit Goel, Ajay Gupta and Ameesh Gupta had 'perhaps' travelled to Toronto during the Sahara Cup hoping to fix some matches with Azharuddin. Apparently, things did not go as planned and the Guptas once again lost a sizeable portion of the family fortune.

May/June 1999, World Cup in ENG

Nishit Goel told the CBI that he had heard that the same Ajay and Ameesh Gupta had visited England in July 1999 during the World Cup. Under duress, Ajay Gupta confirmed that he had offered to shoulder the travel costs of Ajay Sharma and his family to the UK during this tournament. The Gupta family apparently knew Ajay Sharma through Delhi's Roshanara Club and contrived Mohammad Azharuddin's participation in their match-fixing escapades through Sharma.

Eighth match – IND v ZIM, Leicester, 19 May 1999
IS Bindra, the Indian cricket administrator, mentioned an India v Zimbabwe game during this World Cup that had attracted the ire of former Indian cricketer-turned-commentator, Sunil Gavaskar. Gavaskar had claimed on TV that word had arrived from the dressing room to hurry up the innings although there were plenty of overs remaining in which to finish the job. Zimbabwe won by 3 runs after India were all out in 45 overs.

March/April 1999, Pepsi Cup, India (IND, PAK, SL)
Third ODI – IND v PAK, Jaipur, 24 March 1999
Nishit Goel, relative of the high-rolling Gupta family, once again proved to be a fount of underworld rumour. He had heard, presumably on the best authority, that the 1999 India v Pakistan match in Jaipur had been fixed by Azhar and the Guptas and everyone involved had made good money. The Rajasthan Cricket Association is responsible for Jaipur's Sawai Mansingh Stadium, where this match was played. In addition to the evidence of the Guptas' chatty cousin, the CBI Report pointed out that a suspected denizen of the underworld, one Ayub Gauri of Jaipur, was head of security for this game.

September–November 1999, NZ in IND

The CBI investigations hit pay-dirt with the phone records of Indian batsman Ajay Jadeja. They had a list of more than 380 phone calls between Jadeja and one-time bookie-turned-punter Uttam Chand from Madras. Chand, when questioned by the CBI, admitted to meeting Kapil Dev once some years before and denied knowing any other Indian cricket player, past or present. However, he changed his tune when confronted with the telephonic evidence of his relationship with Jadeja. He admitted meeting Jadeja at a function at the Sheraton Hotel in Madras some two to three years before this interview with the CBI investigators in 2000. Chand revealed that he had paid Jadeja Rs1 lakh (US$2 500) at this initial meeting. Chand claimed never to have fixed any matches through Jadeja but only paid for 'information', which he used to place bets with bookies such as Shobhan Mehta.

For his part, Jadeja too, initially claimed that he didn't know any Uttam Chand until shown his phone records. He then recalled that the man in question was a particularly enthusiastic fan whom he regarded as a lucky charm and thus always returned his calls.

The tell-tale telephone records span both the Test and the ODI series played by the visiting New Zealanders in 1999. The calls accrete around various matches, including the first and third Tests and the fourth and fifth ODIs.

First Test, Mohali, 10–14 October 1999

Phone records show a total of eighty calls made by Chand to Jadeja, stretching from the first to the final day of the first Test match in Mohali which ended in a draw.

10/10/1999 – Two calls from Uttam Chand to Jadeja. They were made on the first day of the first Test match between India and New Zealand at Mohali.

11/10/1999 – Eight calls from Uttam Chand to Jadeja. These were made on the second day of the Mohali Test match.

12/10/1999 – Twenty-three calls from Uttam Chand on the third day of the Test match.

13/10/1999 – Forty-six calls from Uttam Chand on the fourth day of the Test match.

14/10/1999 – One call from Uttam Chand on the last day of Mohali Test match.

Third Test, Ahmedabad, 29 October–2 November 1999

Deepak Rajouri, a cricket bookie of some six years' standing, pointed the CBI investigators to big-time Delhi punter Ratan Mehta. Mehta, he claimed, had had advance information that the third Test would end in a draw. Corroborating this tale, New Delhi interior decorator and enthusiastic sports punter Pawan Puri recalled how he had picked up Mehta to go to a party on 31 October 1999. On the way, Ratan Mehta had asked him to place a bet for him with Shobhan Mehta in Mumbai to the effect that the Test underway in Ahmedabad would be a draw. Puri regarded this as an unlikely outcome as, at the end of the third day's play, New Zealand were in a precarious position and a result looked certain to be on the cards. However, this Test also ended in a draw, leaving India the winner of the series after the only result in the series, India's 8-wicket win in the second Test at Kanpur. Later, a well-oiled Mehta allegedly boasted of his insider information that India would not enforce the follow-on and placed more bets with other bookies. Kapil Dev, the Indian coach at the time, explained to the CBI that the decision not to enforce the follow-on was taken in consultation with the captain, vice captain and other senior players during lunch on the fourth day – 1 November. Captain Sachin Tendulkar corroborated his coach's evidence on both the timing and the collective nature of the decision and the CBI Report concluded: 'There is no evidence that Kapil Dev had passed on any information to the betting syndicate about this match.' However, at least one member of the Indian team was in close contact with a gambling man during the third Test. The CBI have a list of 193 phone calls between Jadeja and Chand, dating from the day before the start of the Test to the final day's play.

28/10/1999 – Twenty-four calls from Uttam Chand. This was one day prior to the third Test match between India – New Zealand at Ahmedabad.
29/10/1999 – Thirteen calls from Uttam Chand. This was the first day of the third Test.
30/10/1999 – Sixty-two calls from Uttam Chand on the second day of the Test.
31/10/1999 – Thirty calls from Uttam Chand. This was the third day of the Test.
01/11/1999 – Fifty calls from Uttam Chand on the fourth day of the Test.
02/11/1999 – Fourteen calls from Uttam Chand on the last day of the Test.

An Indian media report alleged that Dawood Ibrahim's right-hand man, Chhota Shakeel, lost a large bet on this Test because Shobhan Mehta had apparently fixed the match.[546]

November 1999, ODI series, NZ in IND

Sunil Dev, former Vice President of the BCCI, accurately predicted the progress of the five-match ODI series against New Zealand in a TV programme. According to Dev, the two teams would go into the final match at a two-all deadlock, which is exactly what happened. After losing the first match in Rajkot and the fourth game at Guwahati to the New Zealanders and winning the second and third matches, India broke the tie and took the series in the last game in Delhi, Dev's home association. The administrator later claimed that he had been given the information by an unnamed bookie.[547] He demanded a judicial inquiry.

Fourth ODI, Guwahati, 14 November 1999

The day before the fourth ODI at Guwahati, Uttam Chand made forty-eight calls to Jadeja, who returned the favour once. On the day of the match, Chand rang five times. New Zealand won this game by 48 runs to level the series 2–2.

Fifth ODI, New Delhi, 17 November 1999

Phone records for 16 November show that Jadeja received fifty-five calls from Chand and placed one in return on the day prior to the fifth and final ODI. The home side won the final by 7 wickets and took the series 3–2.

18

The Justice Qayyum Report

Pakistani matches under suspicion: 1980–1999

November 1979–February 1980, PAK in IND

Sixth Test, Calcutta, 29 January–3 February 1980

Of those early rumours of dodgy doings on the cricket pitch, the toss at Calcutta in the final Test of Pakistan's tour of India is one of the best remembered. At the time of the Qayyum Commission, the longest-serving official of the Pakistan Cricket Board (PCB) was the alliterative Arif Ali Abbasi, who had spent almost seventeen years under the auspices of Pakistan cricket. In his long experience he claimed to have had no acquaintance with match-fixing or gambling on cricket other than rumours he'd heard about the Iqbal toss.

Asif Iqbal captained Pakistan on the 1979/80 tour. His Indian counterpart, Gundappa Vishwanath, maintained that even before completing the toss, Iqbal affirmed that India had won. Later, in Pakistan's first innings, Iqbal declared with Pakistan lagging by 59 runs with 6 wickets still in hand.

Former Pakistani pace bowler Sarfraz Nawaz dates the genesis of Pakistani match-fixing to this tour. The practice then spread to Sharjah in Dubai, where it flourished, allegedly under the nurturing of the same Asif Iqbal. It would seem that Nawaz knows what he is talking about. Imran Khan, politician and former Pakistani captain, described Sarfraz as '... the biggest gambler there is. In England you always found him in Ladbrokes'. [548] Many years later, Iqbal referred to this tour in a report in the *Sunday Times*: 'The first time I heard rumours of that kind was in 1980 when I captained Pakistan in India and lost 2–0. After that, there were rumours that we had been paid money to lose. It was, of course, ridiculous. These rumours have regularly resurfaced, particularly when India and Pakistan play in Sharjah and whenever a team loses it is alleged to have taken bribes.'[549]

October/November 1987, World Cup in IND and PAK

First semi-final – PAK v AUS, Lahore, 4 November 1987

Pakistan, led by Imran Khan, lost unexpectedly to Australia in the semi-final. Sarfraz Nawaz told Qayyum that the semi-final was fixed – with the help of two other players – by Javed Miandad, who later captained and then coached Pakistan. Interestingly, it was Javed Miandad who stood in as wicketkeeper after vice captain Saleem Yousuf was injured. Nawaz later accused Asif Iqbal of proffering Rs30 000 000 (US$500 000) to lose the match.[550] The Indian CBI Report heard evidence that bookie Mukesh Gupta was active during this World Cup and apparently did very well out of betting on the cricket.

April–September 1991, English County Championship

Essex v Lancashire, Manchester, 23–26 August 1991

Justice Qayyum, in the introduction to his report, mentions the following incident although the match did not involve any Pakistani players. This allegation also appears in the ICC's Report on Cricket Corruption. Dan Topley, a former Essex player, writing for the *Sunday Mirror* in 1994, asserted that two domestic fixtures between Essex and Lancashire back in 1991 had been arranged by both teams so that Lancashire won the Sunday League contest and Essex won the County Championship. If true, then this match presents early evidence of corruption in domestic tournaments as well as international competitions. In addition, it reveals both teams colluding to manipulate results. No action was taken by any official cricketing body, either at the time or in 2000 when the allegations surfaced again.

October 1991, Wills Trophy, Sharjah (IND, PAK, WI)

Justice Qayyum pointed out in his report that India refused to play Pakistan in Sharjah, claiming matches were fixed, after losing the Wills tournament to Pakistan in what they perceived as suspicious circumstances. While Qayyum did not hear any evidence from Pakistani cricketers or officials about this series, the sixth match between Pakistan and India attracted attention in the CBI Report and the final between the same two teams also featured in media reports – and not because of the cricket.

Sixth ODI – PAK v IND, 23 October 1991

Manoj Prabhakar and Sanjay Manjrekar of India apparently accepted the offer to leave the field because of bad light. With India ahead on the run rate, the unfinished match would go to India. However, inexplicably, the batsmen return to the crease and India lost by 4 runs. This match is referred to in evidence detailed in the CBI Report of 2000.

Final ODI – PAK v IND, 25 October 1991

Imran Khan revealed at a press conference in Karachi in September 1994 that as captain of the Pakistan side in Sharjah in 1991, he and Pakistan's manager,

Intikhab Alam, himself a former Pakistani captain, had taken measures to stamp out the possibility that four unnamed Pakistani players were paid to lose. They bet the team's earnings on a Pakistani win. It turned out to be an effective ploy and Pakistan won the game by 72 runs. Pakistani bowler Aaqib Javed won Man of the Match for single-handedly removing seven Indian batsmen from the field. His hat trick dispatched Shastri, Azharuddin and Tendulkar in three successive balls, all leg before wicket, and effectively put an end to Indian hopes of winning this match.

June–August 1992, PAK in ENG

Third ODI, Nottingham, 20 August 1992

Four journalists deposed before the Qayyum Commission. Ms Fareshteh Gati-Aslam of *The News* maintained that match-fixing, as far as Pakistan was concerned, began on this English tour. In her opinion, 'Wasim Akram, Salim Malik and Ijaz Ahmed were primarily responsible for match-fixing'. Gati-Aslam's colleague Ms Kamala Hayat, editor of *The News*, told the Qayyum Commission of a conversation between Pakistani cricketers overheard by an Englishman named David Monroe. Ijaz Ahmed, Mushtaq Ahmed and Wasim Akram were discussing how the next match in England was to be fixed. Her tale is evocative but not conclusive, based as it is on hearsay evidence and hazy detail.

Writing in the press, Fareshteh Gati-Aslam had singled out an ODI game played at Nottingham in which, according to her, Akram and Waqar Younis deliberately bowled badly against England, allowing the home team to score more than 300 runs, even though Pakistan had won the preceding Test series convincingly.

Rashid Latif made his debut in this match, both as wicketkeeper and vice captain. Pakistan won the toss and sent England in to bat. They promptly racked up 363/7 in 55 overs. For Pakistan it was all over on the first ball of the forty-sixth over, as they retired on 165 all out. The scorecard fails to back up Ms Gati-Aslam's criticism of Younis and Akram's bowling. They were by no means the worst of the seven bowlers used on the day. Waqar Younis, in fact, picked up 4 wickets, including those of the opening pair of captain Graham Gooch and vice captain Alec Stewart, as well as those other captains of English cricket, Allan Lamb and Ian Botham. Khalid Mahmood, the incumbent PCB Chairman at the time, didn't know whether match-fixing occurred or not, but he was certain that the ODI in Nottingham in 1992 was not fixed.

February/March 1994, PAK in NZ

Third Test, Christchurch, 24–28 February 1994

Pakistan had taken the first two Tests convincingly and, in this third and final outing, had set New Zealand a second-innings target of 324. The home team pulled off the seemingly Herculean task with 5 wickets to spare. Pakistan's coach at the time, Intikhab Alam and journalist Fareshteh Gati-Aslam, sportswriter for *The News*, testified that this match was fixed. Qayyum was of the opinion that there was insufficient evidence about this match. Pakistan won the Test series 2–1 and Wasim Akram was Man of the Series.

Fifth ODI, Christchurch, 16 March 1994

Wicketkeeper and former Pakistani vice captain Rashid Latif testified to Qayyum that his captain, Salim Malik, had called him to his room the evening before this game and offered him PKRs10 lacs (US$16 500) to 'throw away the match' – an offer he refused. According to Latif, four players were in the room at the time: Waqar Younis, Inzamam-ul-Haq, Akram Raza and Basit Ali. Three of the four denied being in the room and suffered collective memory loss regarding the details of the match. Inzamam ul-Haq went a step further, affirming that 'He did not think the match was fixed as he gave 100% from his side'. Basit Ali did not comment. Latif maintained that Salim Malik and Wasim Akram were the chief culprits in ensuring that Pakistan did indeed lose this match, with Akram feigning injury and declaring himself unfit before the first ball was bowled. Chasing 145 in 50 overs, the New Zealanders got there comfortably after 34.1 overs with 7 wickets in hand. Qayyum hedged, 'The fact is that looking at the match one cannot reach any conclusion with certainty that the match was fixed although much can be said otherwise'.

April 1994, Australasia Cup, Sharjah (IND, AUS, SL, PAK, UAE, NZ)

Final ODI – IND v PAK, 22 April 1994

The Indian CBI Report alludes to this match, as does Qayyum. MK Gupta said he went to Sharjah and approached Mark Waugh and Salim Malik, but claimed to have returned disappointed. Pakistani players also touched on this game. Wicketkeeper/batsman Aamer Sohail had more information to impart. He claimed to have received a call from an Indian bookie who offered him PKRs25 lacs (US$41 000) to get himself out for less than 10 runs and to ensure that opening partner Saeed Anwar was run out. Instead, Sohail received the Man of the Match award for his top-scoring 69 off 87 balls. Sohail's evidence was bolstered by fellow cricketer Basit Ali who played for Pakistan between 1993 and 1995. He testified to receiving a phone call at 8 am on the day before the final. Someone named Raqeeb offered him PKRs10 lacs (US$16 500) to ensure that he went out for less than 10. Ali said he informed Intikhab Alam, the team's manager, who called the team together and insisted they take an oath of integrity on the Quran.

At the time of the Qayyum Commission, former team manager Intikhab

Alam had had a seventeen-year long association with Pakistan cricket and was himself once captain of the national side. In an incident reminiscent of that other ex-Pakistan captain, Asif Iqbal, and the Calcutta toss in 1980, Alam was involved in a controversial toss against his West Indian counterpart, Clive Lloyd, in the first Test in Lahore from 15–20 February 1975. According to West Indian star Viv Richards, Clive Lloyd claimed that Alam had awarded the opposition the toss although Lloyd had made the wrong call.[551] Alam told Qayyum that during this final he received phone calls claiming that the match was fixed. He confirmed that he had asked the Pakistani team to take an oath on the Quran. Pakistan won the game by 39 runs and with that the tournament.

July/August 1994, PAK in SL –

Despite the vagaries of his first tour as captain to New Zealand, Salim Malik retained his position for the tour of Sri Lanka in July and August 1994. Under Malik's leadership the visitors won both the Test and ODI series. Allegations surfaced that Malik had flown home to meet with alleged bookie Khalid Gitti and had arranged to fix one of the Singer Cup games. Sarfraz Nawaz corroborated this story, saying that Khalid Gitti had told him that Malik was called to Lahore during the Sri Lankan tour and the match in question was fixed for PKRs40 lacs (US$66 000). Javed Burki, past Chairman of Pakistan's Selection Committee and the Ad Hoc Committee controlling cricket in 1994, recalled giving permission to Malik to fly home for a wedding during this tour in the 15-day hiatus before the Singer quadrangular ODI tournament began in Sri Lanka in September.

September 1994, Singer World Series, Sri Lanka (PAK, IND, SL, AUS)

Second ODI – PAK v AUS, Colombo, 7 September 1994

This match has attracted a great deal of interest in the media and in international investigations.

According to MK Gupta's revelations to the CBI, Salim Malik informed MK that Pakistan would lose a certain match against Australia. This proved accurate and MK made good money. Not everybody made money on the game, however. In testimony before the Qayyum Commission, the Pakistani team manager, Intikhab Alam, said that he had heard that certain bookies had lost heavily on the match. Australian cricketers Shane Warne and Mark Waugh confessed before both the Australian Cricket Board and the Qayyum Commission that they had received money from MK Gupta during this tournament for providing 'information' to the Indian bookie. It is this match that is thought to have been double-fixed by both the Pakistani and the Australian team. The second match of the Singer World Series in Sri Lanka was the only encounter between Pakistan and Australia in that tournament. The Pakistani Judge was quick to make connections: 'The match on which the two Australians had admitted giving information for consideration from John was the same match for losing which Saleem Pervez said that he had paid Salim Malik and Mushtaq Ahmed.' Saleem Pervez was the former opening batsman of the National Bank of Pakistan team and had played a single ODI for Pakistan against the West Indies in Lahore on 19 December 1980. Pervez is named as a gambler in the Ehtesaab Bureau Report. In his statement to the Qayyum Commission, Pervez admitted paying Salim Malik and Mushtaq Ahmed US$100 000 to throw the Pakistan v Australia game. Pervez revealed that he and his bookie colleague, a Mr Aftab Butt, had struck the deal with Mushtaq Ahmed in Lahore, three days prior to their departure for Sri Lanka and the Singer Cup. Former Pakistani captain and coach Javed Miandad acknowledged knowing Saleem Pervez and his reputation. He was suspicious of the team's conduct during the Singer Cup of 1994 and claimed that Mushtaq Ahmed had confessed to him his involvement.

Mushtaq Ahmed acknowledged Pervez as an acquaintance and confirmed that Pervez was staying in the cricketers' hotel at the time of the Singer Cup. However, he denied taking any money from the bookie and pointed out that his performance in that match was good. When asked by counsel which match he was referring to, Mushtaq Ahmed had no answer. If, in fact, he was referring to this match, his bowling figures of 34 runs conceded in 10 overs with 1 maiden and the wickets of both Waugh brothers would seem to endorse his assessment. Team-mate Aamer Sohail confirmed that he was approached in his hotel room during the Singer Trophy in Sri Lanka by Pakistani bookie Saleem Pervez, who offered him PKRs10 lacs (US$16 500). Sohail also named Salim Malik, Mushtaq Ahmed, Waqar Younis and Inzamam-ul-Haq as players that were on the payroll of Salim Pervez, who had informed him of this. In reply to these allegations, Salim Malik insisted that as he had been exonerated by Justice Ibrahim's Inquiry '… the allegations against him … were false and baseless'. Waqar Younis, in turn, '… maintained that he had no knowledge of match-fixing and betting …' and Inzamam ul-Haq, for his part, asserted that the Singer Cup match was not fixed and that '… no match-fixing takes place in Pakistan'.

Nonetheless, Javed Burki asserted that Saeed Anwar had told him that he was asked not to perform in this game. However, Anwar never produced a written affidavit to this effect and Anwar denied having this conversation. Rashid Latif's statements back up Burki's story. Latif told Qayyum that Anwar had claimed that Malik had approached him in August 1994 with an offer to throw the Singer match. Like Prabhakar in India, who went to extreme lengths to bolster his allegations by surreptitiously recording conversations with interested parties, Latif also introduced into evidence audio cassettes containing dialogues with, among others, Ata-ur-Rehman and Saeed Anwar. Qayyum regarded the tapes with less enthusiasm than might have been expected, convinced that they had been doctored. Anwar denied both Latif's claims and Burki's allegations.

Intikhab Alam, the team manager for the tour, recalled that Saleem Pervez was staying in the same hotel as the cricketers in Sri Lanka in 1994. Pervez confirmed staying at the Taj and the Oberoi in Sri Lanka during the Singer Trophy. Alam also related how, after the match, he had received a phone call from an anonymous caller, who complained about losing PKRs40 lacs (US$66 000) on the game. According to Alam, Asif Iqbal had also mentioned that the bookies had lost Rs40 lacs and wanted to get it back. The caller claimed four to five players had been bought and Salim Malik, Waqar Younis and Basit Ali were interrogated by Alam. According to the manager, Malik and Younis denied everything, but Basit Ali broke down and confessed his part. There is no official record of this incident, however, and manager Alam received a show-cause notice for that oversight and subsequently lost his position, only to be reinstated soon after. When Basit Ali was called upon by Qayyum to explain this charge, he denied ever being implicated in match-fixing.

Not displaying much confidence in the integrity of the team that he managed for so long, Alam considered only Aamer Sohail, Rameez Raja and Aaqib Javed to be clean. Rameez Raja, former Pakistani captain, claimed that these allegations were the only incident he had come across of match-fixing in his whole career. Wasim Akram's lawyers pointed out that the accusing players, Rashid Latif, Aamer Sohail, Ata-ur-Rehman, Aaqib Javed and Rameez Raja, all came from the same team, the Allied Bank of Pakistan.

Pakistan won the toss and sent the Aussies in to bat first, lending credence to Manoj Prabhakar's truism that the game is '... best influenced when you're chasing'. The Australians managed a total of 179/7 in 50 overs. In reply, Pakistan lost their first wicket on 2/1 when Aamer Sohail went out for a duck, half the team failed to score in double digits and they all gave up the ghost on 151/9, 28 runs short. Qayyum judged the allegations against this game justified.

September–November 1994, AUS in PAK

Immediately after the Singer Cup Trophy, Australia travelled to Pakistan for a three-Test tour followed by a one-day triangular series. Arif Ali Abbasi, Pakistan's manager at the time, deposed that, four to five months after this tour, Phil Wilkins, a senior Australian journalist, had told Abbasi that three Australian players had signed affidavits accusing Malik of attempting to buy them off in the first Test match at Karachi and a one-day match during the same tour. These players were Shane Warne, Mark Waugh and Tim May. A Pakistani inquiry was instituted, chaired by former Pakistan Supreme Court Judge Fakruddin G Ibrahim, to explore the Australian allegations. Warne and Waugh refused to travel to Pakistan to give evidence under oath and Ibrahim concluded on 21 October 1995 that the allegations against Malik are '… not worthy of any credence and must be rejected as unfounded'.

However, this was not to be the end of the matter. Around the same time as the Australian allegations, Pakistani cricketers Rashid Latif and Basit Ali accused some of their team-mates of match-fixing. A one-man judicial commission was appointed on 13 August 1998 to probe the betting and match-fixing allegations against the Pakistani team.

Representatives of the Qayyum Inquiry flew to Australia in 1999 to cross-examine Mark Waugh and Shane Warne. Waugh admitted that he was a 'frequent bettor', placing bets on '… golf, rugby and horse races but never on cricket'. Warne too admitted that he was a 'frequent gambler'. In his report, Qayyum ventured the opinion that the reason Malik had approached Warne and Waugh was that he had '… possibly heard these two had some connections with bookies and so were approachable'.

First Test, Karachi, 28 September–2 October 1994

Shane Warne claimed that Salim Malik had approached him in September on that tour to offer US$200 000 to throw the first Test Match in Karachi and to solicit the help of Tim May. Both refused the deal, according to their testimony. Signed affidavits to this effect were handed to Javed Burki, the head of Pakistan cricket, by the ICC's Chief Executive, David Richards, on 20 February 1995 in a meeting at Lord's cricket ground.

Wills Triangular Series (AUS, PAK, SA)

Sixth ODI – PAK v AUS, Rawalpindi, 22 October 1994

Mark Waugh deposed how, at a Presidential function for the two teams at the end of October, Malik approached Waugh to throw the Rawalpindi ODI with the help of four or five other players at the going rate of US$200 000. Warne was nearby and heard the conversation. Both players apparently reported the incident to captain Mark Taylor, who informed the Australian officials on tour with them: Bob Simpson, the coach, and Colin Egar, the manager. This was confirmed by Mark Taylor before the Qayyum Commission and Taylor made a written statement to this effect.

October 1994, Pakistan domestic season, National Bank v Habib Bank

According to Sarfraz Nawaz, Salim Malik and Ijaz Ahmed were '… involved in gambling at the domestic level too'. Nawaz claimed that Salim Malik was paid PKRs10 lacs (US$16 500) in a match between National Bank and Habib Bank. Malik denied this charge.

December 1994/January 1995, PAK in SA

After the Australians' eventful visit, the Pakistanis travelled to South Africa for the Mandela Trophy, a quadrangular ODI series involving Pakistan, South Africa, New Zealand and Sri Lanka, which was followed by a single Test. Pakistani team manager Intikhab Alam admitted to hearing rumours that Pakistan was going to lose the Mandela Trophy finals. He claimed to have received a call in which an anonymous informant alleged that eight players had been bought: Salim Malik, Wasim Akram, Inzamam ul-Haq, Basit Ali, Ijaz Ahmed, Mushtaq Ahmed, Moin Khan and Waqar Younis. Mushtaq Ahmed did not play in this series and Moin Khan captained the side in the only Test while sitting out the ODIs.

December 1994/January 1995, Mandela Cup (SA, NZ, PAK, SL)

Contrary to the connotations of the tournament's name, the Mandela Cup gave rise to rumour and rancour within the Pakistani team. This competition also received attention in the King Commission, where Hansie Cronjé testified to what he claimed was his first approach – from match-fixer, 'John'.

Going into the two-legged finals, Pakistan had won five of their six qualifying matches, only to lose the finals in questionable circumstances. Former cricket player and bookie Saleem Pervez maintained that Pakistan deliberately lost the Mandela Trophy to South Africa. Vice captain on this tour, wicketkeeper/batsman Rashid Latif, was one of the loudest voices crying foul during this series, along with team-mate Basit Ali. Javed Burki, Chairman of the Ad Hoc Committee governing cricket in 1994, recalled Latif accusing Malik of fixing matches during Pakistan's tour of South Africa. Wicketkeeper Latif told Burki, while he was on the next leg of the Africa tour in Harare, that Malik and other unnamed players were involved in match-fixing. Lending credence to Latif's claims, Pakistan team manager Intikhab Alam told Qayyum that he had heard rumours that the Pakistani team were going to lose a match. He related that he had received a call during the Mandela Trophy finals in South Africa in which an anonymous informant alleged that eight Pakistani players had been bought, including: Salim Malik, Wasim Akram, Inzamam-ul-Haq, Basit Ali, Ijaz Ahmad, Mushtaq Ahmad, Moin Khan and Waqar Younis.

Pakistani batsman Basit Ali mentioned seeing Hanif Cadbury, a well-known Pakistani bookie, frequenting the South African hotel rooms of several players. Team-mate Aaqib Javed had a similar tale to tell Qayyum. According to Basit Ali, when Aaqib Javed protested to Intikhab Alam, Salim Malik's brother-in-law Ijaz Ahmed insisted that he couldn't be asked not to see old friends. For his part, Ijaz Ahmed denied knowing Hanif Cadbury or Khalid Gitti and claimed that he had never heard of match-fixing and betting. However, he later acknowledged that Rashid Latif and Basit Ali's resignations during the Southern African tour were due to allegations of match-fixing and he confirmed that the team was called upon to swear upon the Quran. Latif alleged that Malik, however, had refused to take the oath. Aaqib Javed recalled the team's oath on the Quran, although there seems to have been more than one on this contentious tour. According to him, Akram and Malik were the main culprits. In his statement to Qayyum, Javed confirmed sports writer Gati-Aslam's story that he was offered PKRs50 lacs (US$82 000) and a Pajero (a 4x4 vehicle) by Saleem Pervez of National Bank of Pakistan to ensure his place on the payroll and on the team. He refused and was never again included in the team while Akram was captain.

Both the finals were day/night games, which meant that the team batting second would be at somewhat of a disadvantage, playing under lights. Apparently, Latif and Malik had an 'open dispute' about who should bat first. On both occasions, Malik won the toss and put the South Africans in to bat. Pakistan lost both finals. However, Qayyum could not confirm that the Mandela Cup finals had been fixed.

First final – SA v PAK, Cape Town, 10 January 1995

It was before this match that Hansie Cronjé claimed to have had his first encounter with the bookmaker known as 'John'. Pakistan won the toss and put South Africa in to bat. The home team were all out for 215 in 49.3 overs, having lost 3 wickets through 'needless run-outs' and a further 3 tail-enders to the bowling of Waqar Younis. Said the match report: 'Cullinan was responsible for the loss of Dave Richardson's and his own wickets, and Rindel fell asleep at the non-striker's end and so didn't make it.' It seems that the South African total might have been less had it not been for some help from the opposition, who let '…several balls through and threw poorly to allow extra runs'.[552] The match report goes on to detail how, in reply, Pakistan seemed set for victory at 101/2 but once again, 3 'unnecessary' run-outs in the Pakistani innings changed the course of the game. Qayyum described these run-outs in his report. Malik's run-out began the collapse, followed by top-scorer Aamer Sohail, who racked up a blistering 71 from 74 balls before being run out while batting with Ijaz Ahmed. Rashid Latif, batting with Wasim Akram, was the next to be run out and the match was all over in the forty-second over as the visitors fell 37 runs short of the target.

Second final – SA v PAK, Johannesburg, 12 January 1995

Once again Pakistan won the toss and sent South Africa in to bat. Chasing a South African total of 266/5, the Pakistanis were all out for 109 in 32.3 overs. Aamer Sohail, Rashid Latif and Akram Raza all failed to get off the mark,

Saeed Anwar managed 3 and Ijaz Ahmed went one better with 4 followed by Younis (6) Malik (12) ul-Haq (19) and Wasim Akram (26). Basit Ali did not play. The tournament favourites lost the final and the tournament by a massive 157 runs.

January/February 1995, PAK in ZIM

Pakistan travelled from South Africa to Zimbabwe on the next leg of their Southern African tour, which comprised three Tests and a three-match ODI series. Rashid Latif told Qayyum that 'things had gotten so bad' that he had called Arif Abbasi of the Pakistan Cricket Board's Ad-hoc Committee and asked him to come out and investigate. However, Mr Saleem Altaf was sent and, according to Abbasi, returned with 'nothing to report'. Latif, however, claimed that he had been told to 'forget everything'. It was during the ODI series that Rashid Latif and Basit Ali suddenly announced their retirement from international cricket, saying that they no longer enjoyed playing.[553] Later, Latif claimed that he had done so because of match-fixing within the Pakistani team.

First Test, Harare, 31 January–4 February 1995

While this Test is not specifically mentioned in Qayyum's report it is noteworthy. In 11 previous Test outings since admission to the ranks of international Test-playing nations, this was the first Test ever to be won by Zimbabwe and emphatically at that, leaving Pakistan an innings and 64 runs in arrears.

February/March 1996, World Cup in IND, PAK and SL

While Qayyum concentrated on testimony regarding the second quarter-final between India and Pakistan, the Ehtesaab Bureau had done some investigation of their own into this World Cup, at the request of the Chairman of the Ad-hoc Committee. With only two days and hearsay evidence at their disposal, the Accountability Bureau's report concluded that the allegations about the World Cup were possibly '... the outcome of an emotional trauma that the nation has gone through during the World Cup'.

Second quarter-final – PAK v IND, Bangalore, 9 March 1996

With Pakistan confronting India on Indian soil for the first time since 1989, this match aroused as much excitement as if it were the final. According to one Pakistani reporter writing for *Dawn,* the subcontinent's unofficial betting total on this game amounted to almost US$80 million. He remarked upon the fact that although Pakistan was the favourite to win, the bookies were giving odds on a Pakistani victory so generous as to be unprecedented.

> The professional bookies in London … are convinced that the betting premiums point to an increasingly susceptible pattern of a fixed match … The unanswered question as to why betting cartels were ready to pay an exorbitantly high premium for taking bets favouring Pakistan right at the start of the match is unique. The odds for hot favourites have never been so high in the history of the subcontinent cricket betting. Someone out there knew that there was only going to be one winner![554]

Pakistani bookie Saleem Pervez told Qayyum that he suspected that Ijaz Ahmed had been involved in fixing the quarter-final.

In a surprise development, captain Wasim Akram did not play due to injury and was replaced by Aamer Sohail '… five minutes before the toss'. The match report in the *Dawn* newspaper admitted that '… there was some whispering going on at the media centre about Wasim not playing'.[555] According to Sohail, the night before the match Akram went to a night club. Akram had told Sohail he would be playing but '… at the last instant on the day of the match, he said he could not play'. Sports writer Fareshteh Gati-Aslam echoed Sohail's allegations, claiming that Dan Keisel, the team's physiotherapist, had told her that Akram had been faking his shoulder injury. Keisel confirmed that Akram's injury was minor. Nonetheless, Qayyum cleared Akram of faking injury.

India won the toss and took to the crease. Pakistan managed to contain the Indian run rate until the last 10 overs, when match reports agree that the Pakistani fielding disintegrated, allowing India to score a whopping 57 runs in the final 4 overs, 22 of those off the forty-eighth over, mis-bowled by Waqar Younis. Pakistan was fined for a slow over rate. After a decent start by acting captain Aamer Sohail and opening partner Saeed Anwar, Anwar exited with Pakistan on 84/1. They then proceeded to lose the remainder of their top 4 batsmen for less than 50 runs; Ijaz Ahmed and Inzamam-ul-Haq 'lost their wickets in sheer hurry'[556] both managing only 12 apiece. In one of the major upsets of the tournament, a shortfall of 39 runs dispatched World Cup holders Pakistan from the competition. They had not been defeated by India since the World Cup of 1992.

A year after the events, Sarfraz Nawaz, government sports advisor and former cricketer, addressed his concerns about two World Cup games involving Pakistan in a letter to the then President of Pakistan, Farooq Leghari. [557] The Bangalore match is one, while a second match involving South Africa is introduced – the Group B match between Pakistan and South Africa in Karachi on 29 February 1996. This match is not mentioned in the Qayyum Report, but the circumstances are eerily familiar. Pakistan's Javed Miandad was left out of this game, ostensibly because of a back injury. However, he had been seen at a street rally late on the night before the encounter. An added spin was the abrupt switch of umpires, with organiser Jagmohan Dalmiya informing Zimbabwean umpire Ian Robinson that his West Indian counterpart, Steve Bucknor, would be replacing him for the PAK/SA game.[558]

July 1997, Pepsi Asia Cup, Sri Lanka (SL, PAK, IND, BDESH)

First ODI – PAK v SL, Colombo, 14 July 1997

Haroon Rasheed, one-time Pakistani player and coach, claimed this match was fixed. Sri Lanka won by 15 runs.

September/October 1997, IND in PAK

Second ODI – PAK v IND, Karachi, 30 September 1997

Haroon Rasheed pointed a finger at Saqlain Mushtaq, who, he claimed, gave away 17 runs in the last over of this match, his first ball being hit for 6. Mushtaq rebutted Rasheed's claims, explaining that he had conceded 15 runs in the last over because he had been asked to bowl with a new ball because of poor visibility and no suitable old ball was found. India won by 4 wickets.

October/November 1997, SA in PAK

Third Test, Faisalabad, 24–28 October 1997

Haroon Rasheed was of the opinion that the Test match played at Faisalabad against South Africa was also fixed, when Pakistan were all out for 116 chasing a target of 144 runs in the second innings. In fact, Pakistan were chasing a target of 146 runs and were all out for 92 in 37.3 overs. South Africa won by 53 runs.

November 1997, Wills Quadrangular, Pakistan (WI, SL, PAK, SA)

Wasim Akram captained Pakistan during this orgy of cricket celebrating the Golden Jubilee of Pakistan's independence, in which four teams played seven matches in eight days. Former Pakistani captain and erstwhile CEO of the Pakistan Cricket Board Majid Khan described the Pakistani team's performance in this competition as 'disappointing'. So disappointing, in fact, that he complained to the coach of the day, Haroon Rasheed, who allegedly retorted that he couldn't be blamed if Akram wasn't interested in winning. Majid Khan pursued the issue and presented detailed charts of Akram manipulating the batting order during this series, promoting himself ahead of Moin Khan and Azhar Mahmood, breaking the game's momentum and ensuring Pakistan's loss. Khan confronted Akram with these stats at the time and Akram confessed himself unaware of who the in-form and out-of-form batsmen were and he promised to rectify this. Yet in Sharjah, Khan claimed, he repeated the same mistake. Coach Rasheed subsequently corroborated Khan's viewpoint, accusing

Akram of promoting himself in the batting order and slowing down the game and putting the target out of reach. However, Qayyum gave Wasim Akram the 'benefit of the doubt'.

April 1999, Coca-Cola Cup, Sharjah (ENG, IND, PAK)

It was during this series that D-Company reportedly lost Rs17 crore (US$4 million) on a Pakistan/England game because the Pakistanis had been paid to lose by the Mumbai syndicate. The bookies were told to cancel all bets. However, Mumbai bookie Shobhan Mehta refused and this led to a long-standing rivalry between Mehta and Dawood Ibrahim's D-Company.[559]

Fifth ODI – PAK v ENG, 12 April 1999

Javed Miandad, previous Pakistani captain and coach, appeared before the Commission twice. The second time he was called back to explain his unexpected resignation as coach after an ODI tournament in Sharjah in 1999. Reluctantly, Miandad related receiving a call during Pakistan's encounter with England from a reliable but unnamed source, who claimed that Shahid Afridi, Moin Khan, Azhar Mahmood, Salim Malik and Inzamam-ul-Haq had conspired to fix the match. All these players were called before Qayyum on 3 September 1999. All denied any involvement. Miandad claimed to have called Wasim Akram to speak with the informant. When Akram was asked about this match, he admitted to speaking to a certain Dawood Ibrahim on the phone. This is a name that has come up often in media reports linking Ibrahim to the elite of Dubai's match-fixing underworld. Apparently, Dawood told Akram that the match was fixed and asked him to make the boys take an oath on the Quran. This didn't happen, as Akram explained there was no Quran available at the ground at that time. Chasing a total of 207, Pakistan was all out in the fortieth over for 144 runs.

May/June 1999, World Cup in ENG

Justice Qayyum was authorised to investigate two World Cup matches involving Pakistan, but subsequently orders came from the presidential office to halt that particular line of inquiry. Qayyum did not, therefore, investigate the 1999 World Cup, although he does explain why in his report: 'It is of great regret that the Commission was prevented from inquiry into the World Cup through a notification dated 18 August 1999 after having initially been given the green light through a notification on 16 August 1999. Questions about the team's performance in the final and against Bangladesh still linger and looking into that matter would have only helped clear up the air.'

Twenty-ninth match – PAK v BDESH, Northampton, 31 May 1999

Underworld sources told *India Today* that the only match fixed during the World Cup was the Bangladesh/Pakistan game, because '… Akram's brother had bet a heavy sum at Ladbroke's on Bangladesh'. [560] Incidentally, Sarfraz Nawaz told Qayyum that the brothers of Salim Malik and Wasim Akram were bookies. Newcomer to the test-cricket ranks Bangladesh beat giants Pakistan by 62 runs in an unimportant Group B match. Chasing 224 for victory, Pakistan slumped to 161 all out in 44.3 overs.

Super Six match** – PAK v IND, **Manchester, 8 June 1999

Ali Bacher told the King Commission that he had heard that this match, played at Old Trafford, was suspect. The ICC's Anti-Corruption Unit investigated claims that this match had been fixed by New Delhi punter and restaurant owner, Ratan Mehta. Pakistan, chasing an Indian total of 227, crumbled and were all out in the forty-fifth over for 180.

World Cup final** – PAK v AUS, **20 June 1999

Pakistan won the toss and opened the batting, but in a spectacular collapse they managed a total of 132 all out in 39 overs. Australia cruised to victory in 20.1 overs and the 1999 World Cup closed with a whimper.

19

Australian Cricket Board (ACB) Player Conduct Inquiry Report

Australian matches under suspicion: 1992–1998

August/September 1992, AUS in SL

First Test, Colombo, 17–22 August 1992

Australia played three Tests in Sri Lanka in August/September 1992. Sri Lanka were heading for their first Test victory over Australia when an unexpected batting collapse saw them lose 8 wickets for 37 runs and with that, the match. Australia won by a scant 16 runs. This was the first Test in a series that would give rise to sensational stories of bookies, bribery and biscuit tins.

Shane Warne and Mark Waugh, Australia's key slow bowler and batsman respectively, were not the first Australian players to reveal publicly that they had been approached by a bookie. Back in February 1995, Australian batsman Dean Jones had told the *Sydney Morning Herald* that a bookmaker had offered him US$50 000 for providing information on the Australian team during their 1992 tour of Sri Lanka. Both Warne and Waugh were also on this tour.

According to Jones's statement to the O'Regan Commission, a retired Indian cricketer had approached him in his hotel room at the Taj Samudra Hotel in Colombo with a business proposition. Jones accompanied the cricketer to the foyer of the hotel where he was introduced to an Indian bookmaker who claimed to have a 'nark' in every Test and one-day team in the world providing him with insider information. While neither of these men was named in the O'Regan Report, evidence presented in the CBI Report of 2000 indicates that the men were none other than Manoj Prabhakar and MK Gupta.

The bookie maintained that he had at least five international cricketers on his payroll. The bookmaker explained that, as someone who bets on cricket matches, he was prepared to pay Jones for insider information on the team's strategy, batting order, injuries, even who the twelfth man was going to be. The bookie produced a mobile phone on which Jones should contact him and a cake tin full of money – some US$50 000 – to underline the seriousness of his offer. Despite the 'sweetener', Jones maintained that he turned down the offer and informed team management. This was confirmed by the then team manager Dr Cameron Battersby, the coach Bob Simpson, the Australian captain Allan Border and top-order batsman David Boon. However, this incident did not appear in the tour manager's report at the end of the tour. By all accounts the incident became something of a team joke. Although Jones was considered to be one of the best one-day batsmen in the world at that time and averaged 55 for the 3 Tests against Sri Lanka, he was dropped from the Test side after this series. He retired from international cricket in 1994.

Greg Matthews, Australia's key off-spinner, also testified to a dubious encounter with a man from the subcontinent in a Sri Lankan bar during this tour. Matthews apparently fobbed him off and didn't take the matter any further with anyone from management.

The opposition too was apparently being targeted by bookies with three Sri Lankan players, Roshan Mahanama, Sanath Jayasuriya and Asanka Gurusinha reputed to have been sounded out for 'information'. While the Board for Control of Cricket in Sri Lanka (BCCSL) apparently knew of the approaches at the time, the incident became public knowledge only when the story was published nearly eight years later, in the UK *Sunday Times* on 30 April 2000.[561]

September/October 1992, World XI v IND XI

The Test series was followed by a three-match, one-day festival series between a World XI and an Indian XI sometime in September or early October of that year. The Australian Cricket Board-appointed inquiry heard allegations from 'various and unrelated sources' that the second game of this series was fixed (and duly lost) by the World XI. Matters went according to plan and the money was paid. The ubiquitous 'John', aka MK Gupta, was once again present, but was not identified as the cashier. The Australians denied any involvement. The ACB Report went on to discuss this evidence and the two Australian players involved in the event in a confidential chapter, which has never been made public. Anecdotal evidence recounted in the O'Regan Report speaks of one player who was batting so well that a fellow player told him that he'd better change down a gear or two as the team were supposed to lose.

April–August 1993, AUS in ENG

Fifth Test, Birmingham, 5–9 August 1993

Australian captain Allan Border told the O'Regan Inquiry that he was approached in the dressing room by a former Pakistani cricketer during the fifth Test of this Ashes series. According to Border, the man told him that some people wanted to put £500 000 on England to win the sixth and final Test at the Oval. The Australian players would be well looked after, he promised, if they could help assure a winning bet. While the public version of the O'Regan Report does not name the cricketer, it was former Pakistani captain Mushtaq Mohammad. Mohammad was Pakistan's coach when his team reached the final of the 1999 World Cup, which was dogged by rumours of Pakistani match-fixing. Mohammad denied Border's claims in his 2006 autobiography, *Inside Out*, saying he merely wanted Border's autograph for his two sons. True to form, no details of this encounter were found in the team manager's tour report. When the issue came up during the O'Regan Inquiry, manager Des Rundle professed astonishment, 'It is absolute news to me'. However, it was obviously common knowledge to a number of Border's team-mates, who corroborated his story.

September 1994, Singer World Series, Sri Lanka (SL, IND, AUS, PAK)

At the beginning of September, in Colombo, Mark Waugh entered into an arrangement to supply Indian bookie 'John', aka MK Gupta, with 'information' on 'the state of the pitch and weather conditions' for the current tour and summer season. The Australian cricketer claimed to have received US$4 000 for these efforts over the next five months. He also introduced MK to Shane Warne – at no extra charge, it seems. Warne pocketed US$5 000 merely for meeting with John, although he did provide the bookie with a handful of pitch reports and information on the make-up of the team in the ensuing months.

When the media got wind of this tale, the players were questioned by team management and subsequently fined by the ACB. The ICC was informed of the actions taken by the Australian Cricket Board and the matter was deemed dead and buried until 1998, when the media again precipitated public disclosure.

Another Australian cricketer and by reputation another keen gambler, middle-order batsman Ricky Ponting, made public a similar approach he had received around the same time as Warne and Waugh. In an exclusive interview with India's *News Today* online on 4 July 2000, Ponting returned to that encounter. While sketchy on the details of where and when the incident happened, who it involved and what it entailed, he did reveal that the bookie concerned was not from the subcontinent. According to Ponting, he informed management of the offer immediately, but said of their reaction, 'They said everyone was being approached by bookies. And that was all'.[562]

September–November 1994, AUS in PAK

First Test, Karachi, 28 September–2 October 1994

On the night before the final day's play, according to Shane Warne, Pakistan's captain Salim Malik proposed that Warne solicit the help of fellow bowler Tim May to manipulate this match to the tune of US$200 000 by bowling poorly the next day. Colin Egar, the team manager at the time, reportedly knew about the

Karachi approach but not the subsequent Rawalpindi offer. Sir Clyde Walcott, the then Chairman of the ICC, was in India at the time and was informed of Malik's Karachi offer, but yet again the incident did not make it into any official tour reports.

October 1994, Wills Triangular Series (AUS, PAK, SA)

Sixth ODI – PAK v AUS, Rawalpindi, 22 October 1994

Mark Waugh claimed to have received a US$200 000 offer from Malik to influence the outcome of this one-day international with the aid of four to five other Australian players. Shane Warne was aware of the approach and Tim May said that he had received a similar proposition from Malik in a separate incident. Despite their insistence that they had told captain Mark Taylor of the encounters and that he had then informed team manager Colin Egar and coach Bob Simpson, there is once again no official record to confirm this. Pakistan scored 81 runs off the first 10 overs and went on to win the match by 9 wickets. The Australians' first public airing of these accusations against Malik came five months after the fact, at the same time as Shane Warne and Mark Waugh's dablings with 'John' came to light.

Mark Waugh, on the tour of Pakistan in 1998, made a personal appearance with his captain Mark Taylor before the Qayyum Commission of Inquiry in Lahore and repeated the allegations against Malik. Taylor and Waugh were also cross-examined. Once Warne and Waugh's cover had been blown by the Australian media, they found themselves testifying once more in the Qayyum investigations, this time revealing their own complicity in the Singer series.

December 1997, Australia

One day in December 1997, according to Ricky Ponting, he accompanied a New South Wales greyhound trainer to a greyhound meet in Sydney. One of the bookies at the ground got into a conversation with Ponting and, in the presence of his acquaintance, offered the Australian player a couple of thousand dollars for information about each upcoming one-day game. Payment would go into a betting account with the bookmaker concerned, whose name Ponting didn't know. Ponting rejected the offer, but the dog trainer called a couple of days later to urge him to take it up. Ponting was not interested and the trainer subsequently denied any connection with the events outlined above. By December 1998, this approach too had been made public by the media.

September–November 1998, AUS in PAK

First Test, Rawalpindi, 1–5 October 1998

Mark Taylor claimed to have received a phone call while on tour in Rawalpindi.

The caller said that he had sent a letter to the player expressing the wish that Australia would beat Pakistan in the series. The conversation turned to information about the weather and the pitch and Taylor cut it short although he didn't know if the man did indeed have betting interests. He hadn't kept the letter in question but recalled that it had come from Karachi. When in Karachi during that tour he was phoned once again by the same man. Again, the conversation was terminated and Taylor said no further calls were received.

20

After Hansiegate

International matches under suspicion: 2000–2007

Despite the glare of public attention that Hansie's confession focused on cricket corruption and the much-publicised establishment of the ICC's Anti-Corruption Unit, rumours of match-fixing did not subside. Other match-fixing scandals would surface throughout the 2000s but only one would result in any concrete action by the cricketing authorities – the life ban on Kenyan Maurice Odumbe, in 2004, who joined a select group of fellow outcasts that included Hansie Cronjé, Mohammad Azharuddin and Salim Malik. The ICC's President in 2003, Malcom Gray, admitted that the organisation was aware of corruption allegations against Brian Lara and Asif Iqbal and an unidentified Sharjah tournament but, of course, the reports remained confidential and Gray indicated that no action would be taken: '… we have been advised that it would not be profitable to pursue any further investigations'. However, Gray insisted that the game was now corruption-free.[563] In India, an unpublicised CBI Report in 2003 warned of the growing influence of mafia syndicates on cricket but to no effect. The BCCI didn't implement any of the CBI's recommendations nor did the government introduce any legislation to counter the threat.[564]

October 2000, ICC Knockout Trophy, Kenya
(AUS, BDESH, ENG, IND, KEN, NZ, PAK, SA, SL, WI, ZIM)

Lord Condon, in his one and only public report, in April 2001, referred to allegations his unit had received about matches other than those covered in the various international inquiries up to 2000. These included the ICC Knockout Trophy in Kenya in October 2000 and Pakistan's tour of New Zealand in early 2001. Nothing came of these allegations.

February/March 2001, PAK in NZ

The ICC's Anti-Corruption Unit added this tour to its investigations following allegations made by sacked Pakistani coach Javed Miandad in April 2001. He had failed to inform the match referee of these concerns at the time, but back home, after losing his coaching position, he asked the Pakistan Cricket Board to institute an inquiry into Pakistan's unexpected loss in the one-day series and comprehensive loss in the final Test against New Zealand.[565] Practically half the team dropped out due to injuries during the New Zealand tour, including Wasim Akram.[566] The controversy resulted in a new coach and a new captain for Pakistan with an injured Moin Khan being replaced by Waqar Younis for the Sharjah tournament that followed.

Fifth ODI, Dunedin, 28 February 2001

With the ODI series at 2-2, the home side sewed things up by 4 wickets despite Pakistan's seemingly match-winning total of 285. Pakistan was fined 35% of their match fee for their slow bowling rate.

Third Test, Hamilton, 27–31 March 2001

Pakistan failed to score more than 120 in either of their innings and crashed to one of their worst defeats ever when New Zealand won the Test by an innings and 185 runs to draw the series. It was the home side's most comprehensive victory in 288 Test matches.

February/March 2001, AUS in IND

Third Test, Chennai, 18–22 March 2001

Australia was on tour in India when on the fifth day of the third Test, two Australian players, Adam Gilchrist and Colin Miller, as well as coach John Buchanan, received phone calls from an Indian man/men inquiring about the state of the pitch, the current state of play and possible outcome. According to Malcom Speed, all those contacted quickly ended the conversation and reported the incidents to team manager Steve Bernard who informed the ACB. They, in turn, claimed to have enlightened the Indian Cricket Board as a 'matter of courtesy' but BCCI Secretary Jaywant Lele denied all knowledge of the approach. India won the Test by 2 wickets and the series 2–1. The incident was made public two months later on 8 May, the delay, as explained by Speed, affording the ICC time to investigate. Thus far, Condon's Anti-Corruption and Security Unit have not made public any findings.

May/June 2001, PAK in ENG

In an exclusive interview with the British tabloid *News of the World* on 3 June 2001, Sir Paul Condon of the ICC's Anti-Corruption Unit admitted to having pre-warned the ECB and the PCB that the first Test of this series was the subject of match-fixing intentions. Apparently, it was Pakistani veteran Sarfraz Nawaz who had alerted ICC investigators.

First Test, London, 17–20 May 2001

With the first day's play washed out by rain, England wrapped up the first Test in 3 days by an innings and 9 runs.

July/August 2001, Coca-Cola Cup, Sri Lanka (SL, IND, NZ)

Fourth ODI, NZ v SL, Colombo, 25 July 2001

Media accounts allege that Dawood Ibrahim's syndicate lost a fortune on this game, with the don himself reportedly losing more than Rs 2,5 crore (US$ 600 000) of his own money. Suspecting that the match had been fixed, Dawood is said to have ordered his bookies in Mumbai not to pay up.[567] New Zealand was looking good after having posted the highest score of the tournament thus far – 236. The Kiwis went on to reduce the Sri Lankan batting order to 27 for 4 by the ninth over before Marvan Atapattu and Russel Arnold staged a come-back to help the Sri Lankans to a 5-wicket victory.

August/September 2002

Three one-day tournaments in 2002 involving Pakistan came under suspicion but the allegations were only made public on 2 February 2004 when a Pakistani daily newspaper, *The News*, reportedly managed to get sight of confidential correspondence from Lord Condon to the PCB Chairman at the time, General Tauqir Zir. In two letters dated 29 September 2002 and 22 March 2003, Condon claimed that his Anti-Corruption Unit had received '... a worrying amount of information from different sources in different countries ...' that the Pakistani team had deliberately under-performed in two ODI tournaments in Kenya and Morocco in 2002 'for betting purposes'. These under-performances were said to have been orchestrated by Delhi punter Ratan Mehta. Condon also raised concerns about the company senior Pakistani players were keeping during the ICC Champions Trophy in Sri Lanka. When the letters were made public in 2004, the incumbent Pakistan Cricket Board Chairman Shaharyar Khan responded:

> In both letters there is a clear indication that the letters were based on information that needed to be confirmed before action was to be taken. Since then, no further correspondence is available with us on this issue and, to the best of my knowledge, the issue did not feature at the ICC meetings ... Accordingly, since the matter has not been raised since March 2003, the PCB will not be taking any action on this issue. There will be no further comment from the PCB on this matter.[568]

August 2002, Morocco Cup (SL, PAK, SA)

Pakistan lost three out of four matches in this tournament, won by Sri Lanka.

August/September 2002, PSO Tri-Nation Tournament, Kenya
(AUS, KEN, PAK)

Pakistan was beaten twice by Australia in the Kenyan ODI tournament – by 224 runs in their first encounter and by 9 wickets in their second. Pakistan looked set to lose to the Aussies a third time, in the final, but rain prevented a result and the two teams shared the trophy. During this same period, Kenyan batsman Maurice Odumbe was regularly enjoying the hospitality of bookie Jagdish Sodha in India. Odumbe's performance in this series was erratic. In 4 appearances he scored a duck and a 10 against Pakistan and a duck and 55 against Australia.

September 2002, ICC Champions Trophy, Sri Lanka
(AUS, BDESH, ENG, IND, KEN, NETH, NZ, PAK, SA, SL, WI, ZIM)

In the leaked letter to the PCB, Condon claimed that two senior Pakistani players were frequently with a suspected Sri Lankan criminal during this tournament.

November/December 2003, ENG in SL
Second Test, Kandy, 10-14 December 2003

Media reports claimed that a staff member of the Pearl Regency Hotel found US$11 500 in local currency in Sri Lankan batsman Marvan Atapattu's hotel room after the team checked out following the second Test against India in Kandy. While Atapattu claimed that the money belonged to some other guest who may have stayed in the room the money was not claimed by anyone and the ICC's Anti-Corruption Unit reportedly mentioned Jagdish Sodha's name in connection with this incident.[569] Like Maurice Odumbe it seems that Sodha treated Atapattu to hotel stays too at the luxurious Sun-'n-Sand in Mumbai[570] although this was subsequently denied by the Indian police officer that reportedly made the allegation.[571] Atapattu continued to play for Sri Lanka.

September 2004, ICC Champions Trophy, England
(ENG, ZIM, NZ, USA, IND, KEN, BDESH, SA, AUS, SL, WI, PAK)

Jagdish Sodha made a guest appearance in the papers once again. Mumbai police reportedly accused Sodha of paying an Rs8 lakh (US$20 000) inducement to a Sri Lankan spinner to help fix matches in this tournament.[572]

July/August 2005, Indian Oil Cup, Sri Lanka (IND, WI, SL)
Final ODI, IND v SL, Colombo, 9 August 2005

ICC investigators explored links between Sri Lankan cricketers and a millionaire Mumbai dancing girl and alleged cricket bookie called Tarannum Khan who reportedly lost Rs1,5 crore (US$37 000) on this game, believing that matters had been arranged so that India would win.[573] In a tight finish, Sri Lanka won the final by 18 runs. A tax raid on Khan's home unearthed Rs22 lakh (US$50 000) in cash,[574] which it is thought she was keeping for a Sri Lankan cricketer.[575] This is apparently the same cricketer that was allegedly on Jagdish Sodha's payroll during the ICC Champions Trophy in England in 2004.[576] Tarannum's cellphone records reportedly revealed the numbers of bookies and Sri Lankan cricketers and she has been linked in media reports to Mumbai bookie Shobhan Mehta[577] and Sri Lankan bowler Muttiah Muralitharan. The Anti-Corruption Unit reportedly believe that Muttiah Muralitharan and two unnamed cricketing friends used Tarannum to transfer money to Sri Lanka.[578]

August/September 2005, Videocon Triangular Series, Zimbabwe (ZIM, IND, NZ)

The Indian media reported that two AC&SU investigators travelled to New Delhi on 12 September 2005 to probe allegations of match-fixing during this triangular series in Zimbabwe, which was won by New Zealand. The Indian Cricket Board denied any knowledge of the visit as did the police. While ICC officials admitted that their staff had been in India, CEO Malcom Speed denied that that Videocon tournament was under investigation.

November 2005, SA in IND

Some sixteen months after the event, the South African team manager Goolam Rajah revealed that an unidentified South African player on tour in India in 2005 was phoned by a bookmaker seeking information. Rajah claimed that the ICC's Anti-Corruption Unit was informed of the approach. And this was the first and last that was heard of the matter.[579]

January 2007, WI in IND

First ODI, Nagpur, 21 January 2007

Nagpur police announced that they have taped conversations between West Indian cricketer Marlon Samuels and an alleged bookie named Mukesh Kochchar who, the police said, was an associate of Dawood Ibrahim. Nagpur police claimed that Kochchar was a 'well-known international bookie' who was betting on the game.[580] The police sent a letter outlining their claims to the Indian Cricket Board. In four separate conversations, the two men apparently discussed the West Indies batting line-up and bowling order as well as the debut of Dwayne Bravo and other confidential team information. The West Indies won the toss and sent India in to bat. The home team went on to make the highest score ever in an ODI in India – 338/3. The West Indies gave chase with Samuels putting on 40 but the visitors fell 14 runs short. The ICC's

Anti- Corruption unit investigated but as the probe was ongoing Samuels was selected for the World Cup in the Caribbean in March 2007.

March/April 2007, World Cup in the WI

First match – WI v PAK, Kingston, 13 March 2007

In the opening match of the 2007 World Cup tournament, Pakistan lost to the home side, the West Indies, in the forty-seventh over, making 187 all out in reply to the West Indies 241/9. After Bob Woolmer's death, a number of media sources reported allegations by former Pakistani fast bowler Sarfraz Nawaz that this match was fixed.

Eighth match – BDESH v IND, Port of Spain, 17 March 2007

In the wake of Bob Woolmer's sudden death in Jamaica, newspaper reports carried allegations that this match was fixed along with the Pakistan/Ireland game played on the same day. An Indian-based bookie told India's DNA newspaper that 'It is no coincidence that both teams lost their matches the same day.'[581] According to various media reports, Pakistani and Indian bookies were in the Caribbean in full force for the World Cup, among them Dawood Ibrahim's brother Anees and lieutenant Chhota Shakeel who were reportedly keeping tabs on the two matches. After winning the toss and going in to bat, India managed to put on only 191 against Bangladesh after the Indian top order failed and the bottom order delivered three ducks. The country cousins took the match, beating India by 5 wickets with 9 balls in hand.

Ninth match – IRE v PAK, Kingston, 17 March 2007

Bob Woolmer's death the day after this match imbued this game with ominous significance and it was investigated by the ICC's Anti-Corruption Unit. However, the Jamaican police would later claim that no evidence of match-fixing was found. Ireland, playing in their first World Cup, won the toss and sent Pakistan in to bat. The first wicket fell in the first over, signalling the beginning of an early batting collapse that took the team to 72 for 6 by the twentieth over. By the forty-fifth over, it *was* all over. The entire Pakistani batting line-up succumbed on 132 with 7 of the Pakistani batsmen managing only single-figure scores. The Pakistani bowlers gave away 14 extras and the team was fined for a slow over rate as the Irish reached the required total with 3 wickets in hand. In this fashion, Pakistan was dispatched from the tournament.

World Cup final – AUS v SL, Bridgetown, 28 April 2007

The World Cup final between Australia and Sri Lanka ended in circumstances eerily similar to the controversial Wills Trophy match played between Pakistan and India in Sharjah on 23 October 1991 in which match officials insisted that the Indian players bat on despite bad light. The start of the match was delayed by rain. However, play finally got underway around noon with the match reduced to 38 overs a side. Australia won the toss and chose to bat first with vice captain and wicketkeeper Adam Gilchrist opening the Australian innings with Matthew Hayden. Gilchrist put on 149 runs – the highest score ever in a World Cup final and Australia posted a final total of 281/4 at a cracking clip of more than 7 runs an over. The Sri Lankans gave chase but, as evening and rain clouds drew in, they found themselves at 206/7 at the end of the thirty-second over, needing 63 runs to win off just 18 balls, an impossible run rate of 21 an over. It seemed as though the Sri Lankans had conceded because of bad light and the Australian team had already launched into victory celebrations on the pitch when the Pakistani umpire, Aleem Dar, stepped in to break up the party and break the news, much to the players' (and commentators') incredulity. The match was not yet over and 3 more overs needed to be played.

It was 6:17 pm, 'traditionally known as night', as the commentators remarked.

The Duckworth-Lewis system of calculation is used where the allotted period of play is reduced by bad light or poor weather. Under this system, once the team chasing has completed 20 overs a result can be declared. Although Sri Lanka had played 32 overs, 3 more overs were duly played in 'pitch black' conditions until, finally, the Australians could get back to their celebrations as they won their third World Cup in a row – by 53 runs.

The farce of this match inevitably resulted in fall-out as questions were asked of the match officials. As befits a World Cup final, the calibre of the presiding officials was first-class. West Indies umpire Steve Bucknor and Pakistan's Aleem Dar were the on-field umpires for the game. South Africa's Rudi Koertzen was the third umpire while the reserve umpire was New Zealand's Billy Bowden. Jeff Crowe, a former Test captain for New Zealand, was the match referee. The umpires all belong to the small and select group of the ICC's elite panel of umpires, which comprises the best umpires in the world and Jeff Crowe, the match referee, is a member of the ICC's elite panel of referees. West Indian Steve Bucknor was umpiring his fifth successive World Cup final, having officiated at 117 Test matches while Rudi Koertzen has umpired more ODIs than Bucknor has Tests – 172. So how could this vastly experienced team of ICC officials have got it so wrong? But no answers were forthcoming. The man in charge of the elite officials was ICC's general manager and former South African wicketkeeper Dave Richardson. Speaking for the umpires he said, 'They are at a loss to try to explain.'[582] While commentators suggested that 'heads should roll for this' the ICC simply banned the officials concerned from presiding over the 20/20 Cricket World Cup in South Africa in September 2007.

Appendix to Chapter 15: the death of Bob Woolmer

Timeline of events

Tuesday 13 March 2007

- In the opening match of the 2007 World Cup tournament, Pakistan loses to the home side, the West Indies. Allegations of match-fixing taint the game.
- Media reports allege that Pakistan's captain Inzamam ul-Haq '... gave some of his players a bashing...' after this loss.[583]

Thursday 15 March 2007

- Two days before the game against Ireland, assistant Pakistani coach Mushtaq Ahmed breaks his nose fielding during practice at the Kensington Oval.

Friday 16 March 2007

- Amid rumours that Inzamam ul-Haq slapped Pakistan's media manager Pervez (PJ) Mir in an argument, and that ul-Haq and Bob Woolmer were having differences, both Mir and ul-Haq deny widespread reports that there is a 'growing rift' in the Pakistani team.[584]
- Later media reports allege that Mushtaq Ahmed and Inzamam ul-Haq had an altercation with Woolmer during the team's practice session on this Friday.[585]

Saturday 17 March 2007

- Pakistan is eliminated from the World Cup by Ireland in the biggest upset in the tournament's history. On the same day, in Trinidad, India loses to Bangladesh. Both these matches will attract accusations of match-fixing.
- Subsequent reports emerge of a furious argument between coach and players in the dressing room after the match and/or on the bus after the game, allegations that are denied by the team's media manager Pervez Mir and the Chairman of the Pakistan Cricket Board Nasim Ashraf as well as the Jamaican police.
- Unwittingly, Bob Woolmer makes his last public appearance at the post-match press conference at Sabina Park after the Irish game.

- 6:30 pm: Woolmer steps off the team bus at the five-star Jamaica Pegasus Hotel.
- 7:00–8:30 pm: Later, media reports will differ over what time Bob went up to his room but the police say 8:30 pm.[586]
- Sometime between 8 pm and 9 pm, Pakistan's coach orders a lasagne from room service.[587]
- Around this time he also sends an e-mail to his wife according to the Jamaican police, which she receives in Cape Town at 3:12 am in the morning.[588]
- The *Sunday Mirror* later reports that a member of the hotel staff saw Woolmer alive at 8:45 pm.[589]
- Pakistan's captain Inzamam ul-Haq apparently changes hotel rooms 'shortly before' Woolmer dies, moving from the twelfth floor to the fifth floor. When questioned by police later, he explains that it was because he wanted to be closer to the other Pakistani players.[590]
- Later, two Pakistani cricketers will reportedly tell police that sometime during this last evening, Woolmer had an argument with a bookie and threw him out of his hotel room.

Sunday 18 March 2007

- 6:00 am: A resignation e-mail is allegedly sent by Bob to Nasim Ashraf, Chairman of the Pakistan Cricket Board. This e-mail is first mentioned by Ashraf himself four days after Woolmer's death, which is when he says he first saw it, as he had been away. However, the e-mail is never made public.
- 10:45 am: Woolmer is found in his hotel room by a chambermaid. The *Jamaica Gleaner*, however, says that Woolmer was discovered earlier – at 8 am.[591]
- 11:45 am: Woolmer is taken to the Accident and Emergency section of the Kingston University of the West Indies Hospital, reportedly in a diplomatic vehicle with police escort.[592]
- 12:14 pm: Bob Woolmer is pronounced dead at the Kingston University of the West Indies Hospital.[593]
- 1:04 pm: A date-stamped *Reuters* report (6:04 pm GMT) carries an announcement by the Pakistani team's spokesperson Pervez Mir that Bob Woolmer is seriously ill in hospital after having being found unconscious in his hotel room.[594]
- 1:45 pm: Mir confirms Woolmer's death and announces that, in line with Jamaican law, an autopsy and coroner's inquest will be held.
- Later, Mir reveals that Woolmer went to his room just after 7 pm the previous evening. He also describes the coach's condition when he was found. 'Hotel staff found him about 10:45. He had blood on him and there was vomit on the walls.' He also says there were signs of diarrhoea.[595]

- The Major Investigation Team Task Force led by Jamaica's Deputy Commissioner of Police (DCP), and former Scotland Yard detective Mark Shields is called in to investigate. Assistant Superintendent of Police Colin Pinnock is put in charge of the investigation.[596]
- Pakistan's team manager Talat Ali moves from his hotel room on the twelfth floor up to the seventeenth floor under the assumed name of Newman. When asked why by the police, he allegedly says, 'We were all scared'.
- The Pakistani team's physiotherapist Darren Lifsun, fitness trainer Murray Stevenson, Pakistani player Danish Kaneria, West Indies team manager Clive Lloyd and captain Brian Lara are also said to have changed rooms 'soon after the incident'.[597]
- Hours after Woolmer is found in his hotel room, Pakistani captain Inzamam ul-Haq announces his retirement from one-day cricket.
- Assistant coach Mushtaq Ahmed is made caretaker coach for the remainder of the World Cup.

Monday 19 March 2007

- The Woolmer family authorises a postmortem but won't be coming to Jamaica. Team trainer and close family friend Murray Stevenson will act on their behalf.
- Jamaican police announce that the postmortem will take place the next day at the Kingston Public Hospital's morgue.[598]
- Bob Woolmer's son Russell tells South African radio station *702* that 'We've been speaking to the doctors and they think it is either stress or a heart attack'.[599]
- A photograph taken a day after Woolmer's death shows the body in the Kingston morgue wrapped in a blue sheet inside a yellow body bag. There is a cut on Bob's nose and abrasions across his right cheek and on the left side of his forehead above his eye.
- Chairman of the Pakistan Cricket Board Nasim Ashraf and the national selection committee resigns.
- Patron of the PCB Pakistan President Musharraf declines to accept Ashraf's resignation. An editorial in Pakistan's *Dawn* newspaper calls Ashraf's resignation, 'a charade'.[600]
- Former Pakistani fast bowler Sarfraz Nawaz tells reporters in Islamabad that certain Pakistani players were involved in fixing Pakistan's matches against the West Indies and Ireland and that Woolmer may have been silenced on the issue of match-fixing.[601]
- An anonymous PCB official speculates that a book Woolmer was writing may have been going to expose match-fixing.[602]

- The British tabloid *The Mirror* speculates that Woolmer died of an accidental drug and alcohol overdose. This is denied by PJ Mir and the Woolmer family.[603]

Tuesday 20 March 2007

- Pakistani team officials are quoted in media reports saying that they think Bob died of a heart attack and that his sugar-testing kit was found near him on the bathroom floor.[604]
- A Pakistani team official says that several unnamed Pakistani players who had rooms on the twelfth floor changed hotel rooms because of the stress of Woolmer's death.[605]
- The Pakistani team had been scheduled to fly from Kingston to Montego Bay on Thursday but reports indicate that the team will not be allowed to leave Jamaica until the cause of death has been determined.[606]
- 9:35 am–12 am: A postmortem is performed by government pathologist Dr Ere Sheshiah.
- 12:35 pm: Gill Woolmer receives official word of the results of the autopsy.
- 3:00 pm: At a press conference, the autopsy results are labelled inconclusive.
- Blood and tissue samples are sent for toxicology and histology analysis. The tests are to be fast-tracked.
- A report broadcast on Indian *Zee TV* claims that both of Pakistan's matches (against West Indies and Ireland) were fixed and that Woolmer was killed to silence him.[607]
- 9:30 pm: That night, in a second impromptu press conference, Shields tells the media: 'Having met with the pathologist, other medical personnel and investigators, there is now sufficient information to continue a full investigation into the circumstances surrounding the death of Mr. Woolmer, which we are now treating as suspicious.'[608]

Wednesday 21 March 2007

- Ten forensic officers search Woolmer's room for evidence.
- Police interview members of the hotel staff and Pakistani cricket team.
- Police go through close-circuit camera tapes.
- There are media reports of 'scratches' on Woolmer's neck, 'blood on his cheek and eyes' and 'traces of poison' on the floor of his hotel room.[609] Police refuse to confirm or deny these reports.
- A *Radio Jamaica* reporter Rohan Powell claims that police will soon confirm that Woolmer was strangled and that strangulation marks were found on Woolmer's neck.[610]
- The results of toxicology tests are apparently due late tonight or early tomorrow.[611]

- Diverse media reports claim an American pathologist is being flown in to perform a second postmortem.
- Late in the evening, the Jamaican police release a statement saying that they are getting the opinion of a second pathologist.[612]
- This is the only official statement from police this day and there is no announcement of any press conferences the following day.[613]
- Pakistan play their last and win their first match in the 2007 World Cup, beating Zimbabwe at Sabina Park, Kingston. Captain ul-Haq dedicates the game to the team's late coach.
- Former Pakistani cricketer Sarfraz Nawaz tells reporters that 'Woolmer's death has some connection with the match-fixing mafia. Woolmer's death is not natural, it's a murder'.[614]
- Former Pakistani captain Abdul Qadir urges the authorities to investigate Nawaz's claims and points out that before the World Cup started, Nawaz had predicted that Pakistan could lose to the West Indies and Ireland.[615]
- Gill Woolmer dismisses overdose rumours, saying that her husband was 'perfectly fit'.[616]

Thursday 22 March 2007

- The Pakistani team is interviewed and fingerprinted by police.[617]
- Reports in the *Jamaica Gleaner*[618] and the *Jamaica Observer*[619] indicate that evidence of murder by strangulation has been found on Woolmer's body.
- *The Australian* reports that there were 'two marks on Woolmer's throat'.[620]
- Multiple media reports continue to allude to an unidentified American pathologist and a second report, the results of which are expected imminently.
- Jamaican police later deny that this pathologist's report ever took place despite media reports that it did.
- At an early evening press conference, Jamaican police confirm that they are treating Woolmer's death as murder.
- Referring to the government pathologist's report, Deputy Commissioner Mark Shields tells reporters at a later press conference that 'We are confident in the result'.[621]
- No pathologists' reports are ever officially released.
- Alleged Indian mafia don and one-time associate of Dawood Ibrahim, Babloo Srivastava speculates on Indian TV that Ibrahim's D-Company may have had a lot of money riding on the Pakistan/Ireland game and Woolmer may have found out that the match had been fixed and thus was killed.[622]
- Chairman of the PCB Nasim Ashraf tells a news conference in Islamabad that he had received a resignation e-mail from Bob Woolmer sent at 6 am on the morning of his death.[623]

- The Pakistani team leave Kingston fly to Montego Bay.
- A senior Scotland Yard detective is reportedly '... already in the Caribbean to liase with the Jamaican police.'[624]
- Pakistan announce that they will be sending '... a senior official from our Washington mission to interact with the Caribbean authorities.'[625]
- Pakistan's President Pervez Musharraf awards Bob Woolmer the Sitara-i-Imtiaz (Star of Excellence), one of the highest civilian honours in Pakistan.

Friday 23 March 2007

- In Montego Bay, DNA samples are taken from all the Pakistani players.
- Team manager Talat Ali tells *Reuters*: 'We want to get back to Pakistan as soon as possible and we would like to catch the first available flight but we are waiting on clearance from the police.' [626]
- After a meeting between police and the Jamaican coroner Patrick Murphy, an official statement announces that a coroner's inquest with a jury will be held '... as soon as practical.' The coroner orders that Bob Woolmer's body remain in Jamaica until the inquest is held.[627]
- TV *Jamaica* reports that two unnamed Pakistani players have been asked to remain in Jamaica while the inquest into Bob's death takes place.[628] This is denied by Pakistan's spokesperson PJ Mir.
- *Geo TV* in Pakistan reports that Inzamam ul-Haq and Mushtaq Ahmed have been subjected to lengthy questioning by the Jamaican police.[629]
- *Geo TV* claims that Jamaican police have arrested a suspect who is not from Jamaica. Apparently, the man had been in touch with members of the Pakistan, Sri Lankan and Indian teams. The TV channel is confident that his name will be released within the next eight to ten hours. This does not happen.[630]
- *New Delhi TV* (NDTV) in India also reports that a non-Jamaican national has been held and that Jamaican police have confiscated his telephone.
- *Geo TV's* Chief Executive Officer Hamid Mir tells *NDTV* that the man had been a regular visitor to Bob Woolmer and was '... in contact with many members of the Pakistani team.'[631]
- Media reports suggest that a Pakistani batsman has been arrested but this is denied by Assistant Commissioner of Police Les Green. [632]
- Hamid Mir also reveals that ul-Haq and Ahmed had an argument with Woolmer the day before the Irish game.[633]
- In an interview on BBC's *Radio Five Live*, Shields denies that there is any truth in the reports.
- Shields says Woolmer went to his room at 8:30 pm and was found by a chambermaid at 10:45 am the next morning. He puts the time of death '... closer towards the time he was found.'[634]

- Explaining the delay in announcing strangulation as the cause of death, Shields tells BBC radio that 'There were no visible signs in this particular case and we had to make sure.'[635]
- Histology and toxicology reports are still awaited. Police spokesman Karl Angell says, 'We have still not received the results of the tests. We cannot at this stage tell you when the results will become available, but as soon as they are, we will pass them on to the media.'[636]
- No toxicology or histology reports are ever made public.
- Police say that Woolmer probably knew his attacker or attackers as his room showed no signs of forced entry.[637]
- *DNA India* reports that Woolmer had made recommendations to the previous head of the PCB, Shahryar Khan, to combat match-fixing. These recommendations were not taken up.[638]
- Media manager PJ Mir says Woolmer had told him that he'd lost the proofs of a book he was writing.[639]

Saturday 24 March 2007

- An India media report quotes a 'leading bookie' who alleges that both the Pakistan/Ireland game and the India/Bangladesh match were fixed.[640]
- Sarfraz Nawaz accuses PCB players and officials as well as ICC officials of links to the betting mafia.[641]
- Former South African batsman Barry Richards says that 'There is a strong feeling around that Bob was going to expose something … People are asking that question and I must admit it is one I am asking myself. Why else would this happen? It may have been a fight gone wrong.'[642]
- Jamaican police believe that Bob's room service meal might have been poisoned.[643]
- Police take a DNA sample from Brian Lara.
- PJ Mir denies reports that he was the last person to see Bob Woolmer on Saturday night.[644]
- PJ Mir says that Talat Ali was the first to see Woolmer's inert body in his hotel room.[645]
- The *Daily Telegraph* reports that Woolmer had sent an e-mail to a Pakistani journalist requesting his help in a book he was planning to write about his time in Pakistan.[646]
- Reports that Woolmer was going to reveal match-fixing details are scotched by members of his family, friends and publishers.
- In Montego Bay, police question Inzamam ul-Haq, assistant coach Mushtaq Ahmed and team manager Talat Ali again.
- The three men fly to London with the rest of the team this evening.

- Assistant manager Asad Mustafa and physical trainer Murray Stevenson stay behind in Jamaica.[647]
- Two Pakistani diplomats, First Secretary Zahid Chaudhri and Counsellor Shahid Ahmed, arrive in Jamaica.[648]

Sunday 25 March 2007

- The *Sunday Mirror* reports that Woolmer's key card, which allowed him to enter his hotel room, was stolen hours before he died. Shields, however, refuses to comment on this report.[649]
- The same *Mirror* article claims that detectives were investigating whether two security guards posted to the twelfth floor had left their posts on the night in question.
- Former Chairman of the PCB Shahryar Khan tells the BBC that 'I think "spot-fixing" is very much prevalent and really something you cannot prevent'.[650]
- The ECB's David Morgan says that the England and Wales Cricket Board is not aware of spot-fixing.[651]
- Former South African cricket captain Clive Rice tells *News of the World* that he believes Woolmer was killed on the instructions of a match-fixing syndicate as was Hansie Cronjé.[652]
- The Pakistani team arrives in London.
- DCP Shields tells the *Sunday Observer*: 'There is no extradition treaty between Jamaica and Pakistan, but we trust that the Pakistan government will co-operate on this issue.'[653]
- PJ Mir denies reports of an argument between players and Woolmer in the dressing room or on the team bus.[654]
- Pakistani diplomats visit the crime scene.[655]

Monday 26 March 2007

- Woolmer's personal effects are released to his family except for his cellphone and laptop computer.[656]
- *The Guardian* reports that Pakistan wants to send its own detective to Jamaica to investigate links that it claims exist between an Indian bookmaker and the murder.[657]
- A senior Pakistani government official tells *The Guardian* that three Indian bookies checked into the Pegasus Hotel before the World Cup began and Woolmer threw one of the bookies out of his room on the night of his death after a 'blazing argument'. This is discounted by Jamaican police and denied by the Indian Cricket Board.[658]
- *AFP* publishes claims by a Pakistan-based bookie that Pakistan's loss to the West Indies and India's loss to Bangladesh were both arranged.[659]

- Nasim Ashraf, Chairman of the Pakistan Cricket Board, denies that the Pakistani team is involved in match-fixing or corruption.[660]
- Pakistani players Younis Khan and Mohammed Yousuf arrive in Karachi.[661]

Tuesday 27 March 2007

- The rest of the Pakistani cricket team flies out of London on different flights at different times.
- Mark Shields says he has approached Kent Pantry, the Director of Public Prosecutions, for his help with the case.

Wednesday 28 March 2007

- The police report of the investigation reaches the coroner's office and marks the beginning of inquest proceedings.[662]
- Shields tells reporters that he believes Woolmer was killed early on Sunday morning.[663]
- Shields says that police are concentrating on the people '… we know were close to Bob Woolmer, were associates of Bob Woolmer, people who were on the same floor or close to him, from the time he returned to the hotel until the time he was murdered'.[664]
- Shields admits that the match-fixing theory is a '… clear line of inquiry, but it is not the only one'.[665]
- According to Shields, police are looking at CCTV footage but because of the cameras' position they won't show people entering or leaving Woolmer's room.[666]
- The Indian media reports that 'highly-placed sources close to the Jamaican police' are saying that CCTV footage reveals two men going into, but not coming out of, Woolmer's room 'some hours' before the coach was found on that Sunday morning.[667]
- The same media source reports that Woolmer had an argument with two senior members of the Pakistani squad after they lost to the West Indies.[668]
- Shields dismisses any suggestion that he is under pressure to slow down the investigation.[669]
- Media reports in Britain begin to discredit the Jamaican investigation and suggest that a second autopsy will be performed on Bob Woolmer.[670]
- *The Guardian* quotes an unnamed senior Pakistan Cricket Board official as saying that the Jamaican police are considering having a second autopsy because of possible errors in the first postmortem.[671]
- Shields refutes all these allegations in a press conference at the Jamaica Pegasus Hotel. He says he is '100% certain' of Dr Seshaiah's postmortem findings and insists that 'There is very clear evidence of murder'[672] and that there won't be

a second postmortem on Woolmer's body.[673]

- Pathologist Ere Seshiah stands by his cause of death verdict on NDTV.[674]
- Apparently, pathology and toxicology reports are still being carried out.[675]

Thursday 29 March 2007

- According to the Indian daily newspaper the *Asian Age*, Jamaican police want to question a bookmaker named Mr Chadda who was in the Jamaica Pegasus Hotel on 18 March.[676]

Friday 30 March 2007

- Jamaican newspapers report that a blood-soaked pillow is being examined as an important piece of evidence.[677]
- Shields announces that a team of Scotland Yard detectives will be joining the Jamaican investigation at his request.[678]
- Pakistan offers to send their own team of investigators to 'observe' the Jamaican investigation – Zubair Mahmood, who investigated the beheading of US reporter Daniel Pearl, and Mr Kaleem Imam of the Federal Investigation Agency.[679]
- Shields says he has not yet received the toxicology or histology results.[680]
- PCB sources explain that Talat Ali moved to a new room in the Jamaica Pegasus hotel under an assumed name because the ICC and hotel management advised him to.[681]
- The Pakistan Cricket Board says no player will be allowed to speak to Jamaican police again without a lawyer present.[682]

Sunday 1 April 2007

- Jamaican police reportedly confirm that they are taking seriously a telephone tip-off that aconite was used to poison Bob Woolmer and say that they have received information that Woolmer was poisoned from a 'number of sources'.[683]
- Lord Condon's Anti-Corruption and Security Unit is reportedly investigating three elite ICC umpires and their offshore banking accounts, believed to be connected to match-fixers.[684]
- Two hundred people attend a memorial service for Woolmer held at the Sacred Heart Cathedral in Lahore.

Monday 2 April 2007

- Four Scotland Yard detectives from the Specialist Crime Directorate, as well as two Interpol forensic experts, arrive to help with the investigation at the reported request of the Jamaican government.

Wednesday 4 April 2007

- A South African memorial service is held for Bob Woolmer at Wynberg Boys High in Cape Town.

Friday 6 April 2007

- Sarfraz Nawaz tells *The Sun* that five Pakistani bookies were in the West Indies for the World Cup and offers to trace them.[685]

Monday 9 April 2007

- *The Australian* reports that Jamaican police will be travelling to Pakistan to take further statements. The paper quotes Mark Shields as saying, 'Having reviewed the witness statements, it is probable that we will need to clear up further ambiguities'.[686]

Tuesday 10 April 2007

- Police spokesperson Karl Angell says no breakthroughs have been made yet and police are waiting for the results of a toxicology test.
- The Pakistan team's manager has left but one Pakistani diplomat remains behind to keep an eye on the investigation.[687]
- The West Indies bow out of the World Cup after losing to South Africa in a Super Eights match.

Wednesday 11 April 2007

- Brian Lara announces that he will retire from one-day cricket at the end of the World Cup.[688]

Thursday 12 April 2007

- The press reports that the Woolmer murder inquest will begin on 23 April.[689]

Friday 13 April 2007

- Jamaican police receive a toxicology report and a report 'containing recommendations' from the Scotland Yard detectives. Apparently, one of the recommendations of the Metropolitan Police Service's review team is to get the views of a second pathologist – Dr Nat Carey.[690]
- Meetings are held by Mr Shields, Patrick Murphy the coroner and Kent Pantry QC, the Director of Public Prosecutions.[691]
- Two of the four Scotland Yard detectives, Dean Lawrence and Joe Marchesi, return to London.[692]
- The two Pakistani investigators remain in Jamaica.[693]

Saturday 14 April 2007

- At the first press briefing in two weeks, Jamaican police confirm that they have received the results of toxicology reports but decline to publicise them. Shields says that the tests, which he describes as 'encouraging'[694] '... require further analysis and investigation'.[695]
- The tests also reportedly show that Woolmer was not drunk.[696]
- Police are now '100% certain' that Woolmer's death was not accidental and that they have a motive for the murder.[697]
- No toxicology report is ever made public.

Sunday 15 April 2007

- The British *Sunday Times* quotes Jamaican police sources as saying they believe that poison was used to weaken Woolmer. They deny the poison was aconite.[698]

Monday 16 April 2007

- The remaining Scotland Yard detectives leave Jamaica taking samples of the toxicology tests with them.[699]
- *The Guardian* reports that Jamaican police want to re-interview some members of the Pakistan cricket team to clear up 'ambiguities' in their earlier statements.[700] Inzamam ul-Haq and Younis Khan's names are mentioned.[701]
- *The Times* quotes Shields as saying '... officers will be travelling abroad in order to conduct further enquiries'.[702]

Tuesday 17 April 2007

- The *Jamaica Gleaner* is informed by a 'well-placed government official' that toxicology results confirm a foreign chemical substance in Woolmer's stomach contents, urine and blood.[703]

Wednesday 18 April 2007

- A Ministry of Justice press briefing informs journalists of correct procedures and restrictions during the inquest due to start at 10 am on 23 April 2007.[704]
- Pakistan appoints Shoaib Malik as their new national cricket captain.

Thursday 19 April 2007

- Indian media reports claim that the Jamaican coroner Patrick Murphy has summonsed Inzamam ul-Haq, Younis Khan and Mushtaq Ahmed to attend the inquest. The PCB denies receiving any such letter.[705]
- Jamaican police take statements, fingerprints and DNA samples from the Irish team.[706]

- The Ministry of Justice in Jamaica announces that Woolmer's inquest is to be postponed indefinitely because of 'new and material developments' in the investigation.[707] These developments are never revealed.

Friday 20 April 2007

- The *Sun* reports that a senior police source has confirmed that the toxicology results show 'significant traces of aconite'.[708]
- In a closed, internal inquiry, the PCB finds '... no evidence of any targeted match-fixing'. No report is ever publicised.[709]
- Talat Ali is appointed interim Pakistan coach by the PCB.[710]

Saturday 21 April 2007

- Unconfirmed media reports from Britian claim a suspect has been identified from the CCTV footage.[711]

Monday 23 April 2007

- West Indies coach Bennet King resigns.[712]

Tuesday 24 April 2007

- Jamaica's National Security Ministry announces that Woolmer's body is to be released by the coroner but gives no reasons.[713]

Wednesday 25 April 2007

- Police spokesperson Karl Angell tells *Associated Press* that DCP Mark Shields and other investigators will return the coach's body to Woolmer's family in Cape Town.[714]

Thursday 26 April 2007

- Late Thursday night, Woolmer's body leaves Jamaica for Cape Town.[715]

Sunday 29 April 2007

- Woolmer's body arrives in South Africa.

Monday 30 April 2007

- The BBC, in their *Panorama* programme, claims that toxicology reports will prove that Woolmer was poisoned before being strangled. The drug used is not identified. Shields denies that poison has been confirmed.[716]

Friday 4 May 2007

- Woolmer is cremated after a private ceremony in Observatory, Cape Town.

Saturday 5 May 2007

- Two Pakistani detectives submit their report to the Pakistani Interior Ministry. They conclude that there is no evidence that Woolmer was strangled.[717]

Sunday 6 May 2007

- The British *Sunday Times* quotes a source close to the Jamaican police who says that an unusual herbicide found in Woolmer's stomach and on a champagne glass used by him '... was enough to kill him'.[718]

Monday 7 May 2007

- Shields leaves this week for South Africa via London to interview Woolmer's family and friends and update South African police.

Thursday 10 May 2007

- Team spokesperson Pervez Mir tells the Pakistani TV channel *ARY* that Talat Ali, the Pakistan manager, saw Mushtaq Ahmed pass two champagne bottles on to Woolmer in the team hotel in Jamaica.[719]

Sunday 13 May 2007

- The *Sunday Gleaner* claims a Scotland Yard pathology report has concluded that Woolmer died of heart failure and there is no evidence to suggest foul play.[720]

Tuesday 15 May 2007

- *The Times* in the UK reports that Nat Carey, a senior British Home Office pathologist, has concluded that Woolmer was not strangled.[721]
- A *Jamaican Gleaner* editorial calls for the publication of the pathology reports and a reason for the postponement of the coroner's inquest. Neither are forthcoming.[722]

Friday 18 May 2007

- A report in the *Cape Argus* quotes Mark Shields at the end of his visit to South Africa: 'I get the impression that Bob Woolmer didn't have enemies.'[723]

Sunday 20 May 2007

- The UK *Sunday Times* reports that the 'bungling' detectives based their investigation on a flawed autopsy by Dr Seshaiah.[724]

Saturday 2 June 2007

- The *Daily Mail* reports that police will announce next week that Woolmer was not murdered, the weedkiller was found in small quantities and was a common herbicide used on cricket pitches and that Woolmer was 'desperately ill' and died of 'chronic ill health' while chipping a neck bone in a fall.[725]

Sunday 3 June 2007

- The *Sunday Times* (UK) reports that a review by a Canadian pathologist has reached the same conclusions as the British pathologist – that Woolmer died of natural causes. Seshaiah reportedly says, 'I can't comment. I didn't get any report.'[726]
- The *Jamaica Gleaner* quotes police spokesperson Karl Angell as saying that no Scotland Yard report has been received and no press conference is scheduled.[727]

Monday 4 June 2007

- The *Jamaica Gleaner* quotes an anonymous senior local police officer as saying that Woolmer was not murdered.[728]

Thursday 7 June 2007

- Pakistan team spokesperson PJ Mir demands a 'public apology' from the Jamaican police and says that he will recommend that the PCB take legal action.[729]

Sunday 10 June 2007

- Former South African skipper Clive Rice tells *Times Now* that he is '…afraid this is a cover-up again.'[730]

Tuesday 12 June 2007

- At a news conference in Kingston, Lucius Thomas, Commissioner of Jamaican Police, announces that the Jamaican police accept the findings of three pathologists, Dr Nat Carey from Britain, Professor Lorna Martin from South Africa and Dr Michael Pollanen from Canada, that Woolmer died of natural causes and thus the JCF closes its investigation into Bob Woolmer's death.[731]
- Former Pakistani captain Inzamam ul-Haq advises against taking legal action against the Jamaican police.[732]

Wednesday 13 June 2007

- Pathologist Ere Seshaiah sticks by his findings.[733]
- Jamaica's National Security Minister announces in Parliament that he has ordered an official review of the Woolmer investigation.

- The Pakistan Cricket Board announces that it won't be taking legal action against the Jamaican police.[734]

Thursday 14 June 2007

- *AFP* reports that West Indies legend Brian Lara may return to cricket.[735]

Endnotes

CHAPTER 1 **Too close to the sun**

1 Online Letters: *Mail and Guardian*, 17 April 2000.

2 United Cricket Board of South Africa media release on match-fixing allegations – *UCBSA*, 8 April 2000.

3 'Cronjé denies match-fixing charges' – *AFP*, 7 April 2000.

4 United Cricket Board of South Africa media release on match-fixing allegations – *UCBSA*, 8 April 2000.

5 Reuters: 'Cronjé proclaims innocence' – *The Tribune* (Chandigarh), 11 April 2000.

6 Trevor Chesterfield: 'Indian police failed to follow diplomatic protocols' – *cricinfo.com*, 9 April 2000.

7 '"It's absurd" says Indian skipper' – *Sunday Times (RSA) Cricket Online*, 9 April 2000.

8 AFP: 'ICC to hold emergency match-fixing meeting' – *Mail and Guardian* online *ZA Sports*, 17 April 2000.

9 Partab Ramchand: 'How the match-fixing drama unfolded' – *cricinfo.com*, 11 April 2000.

10 Deon Gouws: *And Nothing But the Truth?* Zebra Press 2000, p114.

11 Extract from Cronjé's confession.

12 Quoted in Jennifer Crwys-Williams (ed): *Dictionary of South African Quotations*, (2nd edition), Penguin, 1999.

13 Quoted in Jennifer Crwys-Williams (ed): *Dictionary of South African Quotations*, (2nd edition), Penguin, 1999.

14 Owen Slot: 'Revealed: The bribe that split Cronjé's team' – *Electronic Telegraph* (UK), 16 April 2000.

15 Edwin Naidu: 'A state of shock' – *India Today*, 24 April 2000.

16 Kevin Mitchell: 'Cronjé tape may be a hoax' – *The Observer* (UK), 9 April 2000.

17 Michael Henderson: 'Cronjé an unlikely target' – *Electronic Telegraph* (UK), 8 April 2000.

18 Michael Henderson: 'Affair does not stop with Cronjé' – *Electronic Telegraph* (UK), 12 April 2000.

19 'Let's not cast the sinner adrift' – *ThePavilion.com*, 2 May 2000.

20 Zapiro cartoon: *Mail and Guardian*, 23–29 June 2000.

21 AFP: 'Mugabe says he feels sorry for Cronjé' – *ThePavilion.com*, 14 June 2000.

22 Ramesh Venkat: 'Cut from the same cloth' – *rediff.com*, 21 August 2000.

CHAPTER 2 **Passage to India**

23 Imtiaz Patel, Quoted by Deon Gouws: *And Nothing But the Truth?* Zebra Press 2000, pp117–118.

24 Andre Odendaal: 'Some forgotten South African cricket history' – 1997 Brochure celebrating Langa Cricket Club's twenty-first birthday.

25 John Young: 'Cricket at Langa – 21 years and much more' – Brochure celebrating Langa Cricket Club's twenty-first birthday.

26 Edward Griffiths: *Kepler: The Biography* Pelham Books 1994.

27 Deon Gouws: *And Nothing But the Truth?* Zebra Press 2000, p69.

28 Mike Haysman interviewing Cronjé on *Hansie: The Fallen Idol* – M-Net Supersport, 24-26 August 2000.

29 Mike Haysman interviewing Cronjé on *Hansie: The Fallen Idol* – M-Net Supersport, 24-26 August 2000.

30 'Cronjé's five years of hell' – *Mail and Guardian*, 15 June 2000.

31 Owen Slot: 'South Africa go soft on Cronjé' – *Electronic Telegraph* (UK), 18 February 2001.

32 'Donald says he wanted to celebrate 300th test wicket with Hansie Cronjé' – *AFP*, 20 November 2000.

33 Qamar Ahmed: 'Bad day for Pakistan and South Africa' – *Dawn* (PAK), 14 March 1996.

34 Rodney Hartman: *Hansie and the Boys* Zebra Press 1997, p109.

CHAPTER 3 **A shining light?**

35 Trevor Chesterfield: 'UCB development: Fact or fallacy' – *Pretoria News*, Reproduced on *cricinfo.com*, 10 January 1998.

36 Trevor Chesterfield : 'UCB development: Fact or fallacy' – *Pretoria News*, Reproduced on *cricinfo.com*, 10 January 1998.

37 Liz Hannan: 'Gillespie helps ACB right the wrongs' – *ThePavilion.com*, 15 April 2001.

38 AAP: 'Coach blasts cricket's elitist culture' – *ThePavilion.com*, 20 April 2001.

39 Trevor Chesterfield: 'How Mpitsang has overtaken Ntini' – *cricinfo.com*, 18 November 1999.

40 Peter Robinson: 'Peterson joins SA squad' – *cricinfo.com*, 15 July 2000.
41 Ken Borland: 'Arthur backs questioned trio' – *cricinfo.com*, February 16, 2007.
42 Stuart Hess: 'SA's world cup report card' – *Weekend Argus*, 28 April 2007.
43 Interview with Desmond Haynes: 'Cricket at Langa – 21 years and much more' – Brochure celebrating Langa Cricket Club's twenty-first birthday.
44 Mike Haysman interviewing Cronjé on *Hansie: The Fallen Idol* – M-Net Supersport, 24-26 August 2000.
45 'Woolmer claims Cronjé tried to sack him' – *ThePavilion.com*, 6 June 2000.
46 Peter Robinson: 'No such thing as a free *stuk* of *biltong*' – *Mail and Guardian*, 23–29 June 2000.
47 Martin Gillingham: *Cape Talk*, 6 February 2001.
48 Qayyum Report: p28.
49 Aniruddha Bahal: 'Interview with Rashid Latif' – *Outlook*, 19 July 2000.
50 Paddy Harper: 'Colour coded' – *Outlook*, 24 April 2000.

CHAPTER 4 **Cronjé and his cronies**

51 AFP: 'Round one of King Inquiry ends' – *Total-Cricket.com*, 26 June 2000.
52 Prem Panicker: ' India go down 1-0' – *rediff.com*, 26 February 2007.
53 Prem Panicker: 'Ganguly ton takes India to 2-0' – *rediff.com*, 12 March 2000.
54 Michael Henderson: 'Affair does not stop with Cronjé' – *Electronic Telegraph* (UK), 12 April 2000.
55 Prem Panicker: 'Ganguly ton takes India to 2-0' – *rediff.com*, 12 March 2000.
56 Prem Panicker: 'India pull it off with one ball to spare' – *rediff.com*, 17 March 2000.
57 Rohit Brijnath: 'Shame on the game' – *India Today*, 24 April 2000.
58 Partab Ramchand: 'How the match-fixing drama unfolded' – *cricinfo.com*, 11 April 2000.
59 'Klusener denies fingering Cronjé' – *Mail and Guardian* online, *ZASports*, 13 April 2000.
60 Peter Robinson: 'Scandal that sent South Africa into denial' – *Electronic Telegraph* (UK), 15 April 2000.
61 M Subramoney: 'Cronjé fans beat up SA official of Indian origin' – *Indian Express*, 16 April 2000.
62 Sports Quotes: *Mail and Guardian* online, *ZA Sports*, 14 April 2000.
63 Press conference, Johannesburg, 28 August 2000.
64 Archie Henderson Says: 'Gibbs still batting on sticky wicket' – *Cape Argus*, 4 January 2001.
65 Michael Doman Says: 'Gibbs still batting on sticky wicket' – *Cape Argus*, 4 January 2001.
66 Special Correspondent: 'I accepted Cronjé's offer, says Gibbs' – *The Telegraph* (Calcutta), 13 October 2006.
67 Stuart Hess and SAPA-AFP: 'Crookes declares his innocence in cricket scandal' – *Cape Times*, 13 October 2006.
68 '"Boje is innocent," says Bacher' – *The Hindu*, 31 May 2006.
69 Peter Robinson: 'Faint light at the end of the tunnel for Cronjé?' – *cricinfo.com*, 2 November 2000.
70 Peter Robinson: 'Sonn on his own on lifting of Cronjé ban' – *cricinfo.com*, 4 January 2002.
71 Jermaine Craig and Willem Steenkamp: 'Hansie's fatal decision' – *Sunday Independent* (RSA), 2 June 2002.
72 Daniel Murt, Marcus Prior and Telford Vice: 'Was Hansie Cronjé murdered?' – *The Observer* (UK), 3 August 2003.
73 Interview with Aden Thomas on the Morning Show: *Cape Talk*, 26 March and 23 March 2007.
74 Michael Owen-Smith: 'The greatest captain would have returned' – *Cape Times*, 3 June 2002.
75 'Tributes pour in: The team would have walked off Table Mountain for him.' – *Cape Times*, 3 June 2002.

CHAPTER 5 **The whole truth and nothing but the truth**

76 Patrick Symcox: 'Whom do we trust?' – *India Today*, 24 April 2000.
77 Qamar Ahmed: 'Bogus journalists and shady agents' – *The Independent* (UK), 14 February 1996.
78 Aniruddha Bahal and Krishna Prasad: 'Cricket's dirty games' – *Outlook*, 11 June 1997.
79 IS Bindra statement in the CBI Report.
80 Murali Krishnan, Sujata Anandan and Manu Joseph: 'Any more bets?' – *Outlook*, 24 April 2000.
81 Aniruddha Bahal and Krishna Prasad: 'Cricket's dirty games' – *Outlook*, 11 June 1997.

82 Pradeep Magazine: *Not Quite Cricket* Penguin 2000, p14.
83 Pradeep Magazine: *Not Quite Cricket* Penguin 2000, p22.
84 Manu Joseph: Interview with Sachin Tendulkar, 'I'm clean … I don't have anything to say in my defence' – *Outlook*, 24 July 2000.
85 PTI: 'Bookie Mehta had links with prominent players' – *The News* (Pakistan), 12 June 2005.
86 Nawaal Deane: 'Banjo cashes in on Hansie biltong' – *Mail and Guardian*, 30 June–6 July 2000.
87 Mzilikazi Wa Afrika, Jessica Bezuidenhout and André Jurgens: 'Tony Yengeni, the 4x4 and the R43bn arms probe' – *Sunday Times* (RSA), 25 March 2001.
88 Sayantan Chakravarty: 'The murky world of Mr Dalmiya' – *India Today*, 15 May 2000.
89 Readers Poll Results – *The Star* (RSA), 13 April 2000.

CHAPTER 6 **The fix**

90 Centre for Gambling Research, Australian National University, Factsheets 2005, Sports Betting: Summary 2005.
91 Siddharth Srivastava: 'Indians love cricket, you bet' – *Asia Times*, 15 March 2007.
92 Mazher Mahmood: 'Caught at last – The man fixing test matches' – *News of the World* (UK), 21 May 2000.
93 Ian MacKinnon: 'Cricket: Seedy world of the Indian bookies' – *The Independent* (UK), 12 April 2000.
94 Raju Parulekar and Anupam Dasgupta: 'City bookies had no role in Woolmer murder' – *dnaindia.com*, 7 April 2007.
95 Reuters: 'Former captain suspects betting ring in Woolmer murder' – *www.stuff.co.nz*, 24 March 2007.
96 SAPA-AFP, Daily Mail: 'Woolmer: fixing probe' – *Cape Argus*, 26 March 2007
97 'ECB Chairman: "We're not aware of spot fixing"' – *The Mail on Sunday* (UK), 25 March 2007.
98 'Fresh bribery allegations surface' –*ThePavilion.com*, 12 February 2001.
99 Mazher Mahmood: 'Caught at last – The man fixing test matches' – *News of the World* (UK), 21 May 2000.
100 Aniruddha Bahal: 'Azhar, Jaddu used to call me' – *Outlook*, 30 July 1997.
101 Aniruddha Bahal and Krishna Prasad: Cricket's dirty games' – *Outlook*, 11 June 1997.
102 Hansie Cronjé: 'The cup runneth empty' – *rediff.com*, 18 March 2000.
103 Aniruddha Bahal and Krishna Prasad: 'Cricket's dirty games' – *Outlook*, 11 June 1997.
104 Murali Krishnan, Sujata Anandan, Ajith Pillai: 'Caught out' – *Outlook*, 5 June 2000.
105 PTI: 'It's umpires' turn to reveal' – *The Hindu*, 21 April 2000.
106 CBI Report on Cricket Match-fixing and ICC Report on Corruption in International Cricket.
107 'Fresh bribery allegations surface' –*ThePavilion.com*, 12 February 2001.
108 Mazher Mahmood: 'Caught at last – The man fixing test matches' – *News of the World* (UK), 21 May 2000.
109 'Cricket World Cup set to deliver $239m profit' – *sportbusiness.com*, 15 March 2007.
110 The Inderjit Singh Bindra Chat: *rediff.com*, 15 April 2000.
111 Jon Swift: Quoted in Jennifer Crwys-Williams (ed): *Dictionary of South African Quotations* (2nd edition), Penguin, 1999.

CHAPTER 7 **One for all and all for one**

112 According to underworld sources quoted by Sayantan Chakravarty: 'Dirty talk' – *India Today*, 24 April 2000
113 Prem Panicker: 'India down and almost out of Titan Cup' – *rediff.com*, 29 October 1996.
114 Prem Panicker: 'India down and almost out of Titan Cup' – *rediff.com*, 29 October 1996.
115 Prem Panicker: 'India down and almost out of Titan Cup' – *rediff.com*, 29 October 1996.
116 Prem Panicker: 'India down and almost out of Titan Cup' – *rediff.com*, 29 October 1996.
117 Harsha Bhogle: 'Third Test: South Africa v India, match report' – *Electronic Telegraph* (UK), 8–12 December 1996.
118 Prem Panicker: 'India win toss, South Africa take the advantage' – *rediff.com*, 8 December 1996.
119 Peter Robinson: 'Day 3 report' – *The Star* (RSA), 10 December 1996.
120 R. Mohan: 'Raman and Adams share day's honours' – *The Hindu*, 9 December 1996.
121 Prem Panicker: 'Day 2 report' – *rediff.com*, 9 December 1996.
122 R. Mohan: 'Raman and Adams share day's honours' – *The Hindu*, 9 December 1996.

123 R. Mohan: 'Raman and Adams share day's honours' – *The Hindu*, 9 December 1996.
124 'UCB to probe 1996 Mumbai meeting' – *AFP*, 18 April 2000.
125 Judith Soal: 'King report 'doubts' Hansie's testimony' – *Cape Times*, 10 August 2000.
126 G Viswanath: 'Blanket ban on Cronjé absurd, says Woolmer' – *The Hindu*, 16 October 2001.
127 Rohit Brijnath: 'Shame on the game' - *India Today*, 24 April 2000
128 Greg Baum: 'Woolmer claims Cronjé tried to sack him' – *ThePavilion.com*, 6 June 2000.
129 Staff Reporter: '"Bacher knew of fixing offer" – White' – *Cape Argus*, 29 June 2000.

CHAPTER 8 **A fix for the history books**

130 Nasser Hussain: 'Why I'm sure Centurion was no fix' – *Electronic Telegraph* (UK), 16 April 2000.
131 Trevor Chesterfield: 'Cronjé slams ICC over negative whispers on declaration' – *cricinfo.com*, 18 January 2000.
132 Trevor Chesterfield: 'South Africa v England at Centurion' – *cricinfo.com*, 14–18 January 2000.
133 Michael Henderson: 'Rain means only spin is off the field' – *Electronic Telegraph* (UK), 18 January 2000.
134 Donald McRae: 'Dazzler waltzes in to revive Yorkshire fortunes' – *The Guardian* (UK), 10 April 2007.
135 Online Chat: IS Bindra – *rediff.com*, 15 April 2000.
136 Trevor Chesterfield: 'Cronjé slams ICC over negative whispers on declaration' – *cricinfo.com*, 18 January 2000.
137 AFP: 'England win after deal between captains' – *cricinfo.com*, 18 January 2001.
138 Trevor Chesterfield: 'Cronjé slams ICC over negative whispers on declaration' – *cricinfo.com*, 18 January 2000.
139 Michael Henderson: 'England win with perfect timing' – *Electronic Telegraph* (UK), 19 January 2000.
140 Trevor Chesterfield: 'Cronjé slams ICC over negative whispers on declaration' – *cricinfo.com*, 18 January 2000.
141 Nasser Hussain: 'Why I'm sure Centurion was no fix' – *Electronic Telegraph* (UK), 16 April 2000.
142 Reuters: 'Atherton retirement hint as he reveals Cronjé doubts' – *ya.co.za*, 31 August 2000.

CHAPTER 9 **Long live cricket?**

143 Amberish K Diwanji: 'Officials in Delhi pleased with Cronjé's suspension' – *rediff.com*, 11 April 2000.
144 Tim Mitchell: 'He's been punished enough already' – *Sunday Argus*, 24/25 June 2000.
145 Partab Ramchand: 'How the match-fixing drama unfolded' – *cricinfo.com*, 11 April 2000.
146 Partab Ramchand: 'How the match-fixing drama unfolded: Part 2' – *cricinfo.com*, 2 May 2000.
147 'Speed up Hansie inquiry says ICC' – *Mail and Guardian* online, *ZASports*, 12 April 2000.
148 Partab Ramchand: 'How the match-fixing drama unfolded' – *cricinfo.com*, 11 April 2000.
149 AFP: 'Cronjé inquiry seeks truth not criminals' – *rediff.com*, 8 May 2000.
150 'CBI moves Interpol for Cronjé's voice samples' - *Indian Express*, 18 April 2001.
151 AFP: 'Indian police fume as Cronjé trial set to be delayed' – *ThePavilion.com*, 8 June 2000.
152 '"Nothing much" in report on Cronjé scandal' - *rediff.com*, 24 August 2000.
153 AFP:'South African prosecutor asks India to authenticate Cronjé tapes' – *cricinfo.com*, 20 September 2000.
154 Dinesh Chopra: 'Second phase of the King probe to resume in November' – *Total-Cricket.com*, 4 October 2000.
155 Neil Manthorp: 'South African corruption hearings resume in January' – *Electronic Telegraph* (UK), 12 November 2000.
156 Mihir Bose: 'King Commission: Judge told to cut short inquiry' – *Electronic Telegraph* (UK), 16 November 2000.
157 'Cronjé forces delay in resumption of King Commission' – *rediff.com*, 23 December 2000.
158 'World cup loss, Cronjé episode most disappointing' - *India Times*, 28 December 2000.
159 Exclusive interview with Gerald Majola – *rediff.com* and *Sport Africa Broadcasting*, 26 December 2000.
160 SAPA:'"Corruption governs SA" – Heath' – *woza.co.za*, 4 April 2001.
161 Johan Schronen and Jeanne van der Merwe: 'White-collar crime cleans up R40bn a year' – *Cape Argus*, 19 March 2001.
162 Paddy Harper: 'Colour coded' – *Outlook*, 24 April 2000.

163 Kevin Mitchell and Luke Harding: 'Hansie Cronjé, mystery man' – *Mail and Guardian*, 17 April 2000.

164 PTI: 'King Commission's fate hangs in jeopardy' – *Total-Cricket.com*, 21 February 2001.

165 'House of Lords Debates – Corruption Bill' – *TheyWorkForYou.com*, 16 March 2007.

CHAPTER 10 **Match-fixing on the Orient Express**

166 Manoj Prabhakar to *The Statesman*, 10 June 1997 – Quoted in the Chandrachud Report.

167 Partab Ramchand: 'ICC should act swiftly to eradicate match-fixing menace' – *cricinfo.com*, 10 April 2000.

168 Sayantan Chakravarty: 'Dirty talk' – *India Today*, 24 April 2000.

169 Online chat: Atul Wassan – *India Today*, 15 June 2000.

170 Prabhu Chawla and Sayantan Chakravarty: 'Junior Cricketers are Worth Rs10 Crore; For Seniors it is Rs200 Crore' – *India Today*, 8 July 2000.

171 Neena Chaudhary: 'Senior cricketers have assets worth Rs2 billion, says Dhindsa' – *rediff.com*, 9 July 2000.

172 'Cricket in India: It's big business but not businesslike' – *Knowledge@Wharton*, University of Pennsylvania, 5 April 2007.

173 'Cricket: South Africa win ODI Championship, $175 000' – *Telugaportal.net*, 2 April 2007.

174 'Prize money at Cricket World Cup 2007' – *StickieWicket.com*, 30 April 2007.

175 S Ram Mahesh: 'The cult of the superstar' – *Sportstar Weekly Vol 29 No 41*, 14 October 2006.

176 'Cricket in India: It's big business but not businesslike' – *Knowledge@Wharton*, University of Pennsylvania, 5 April 2007.

177 Ishan Joshi: 'Kapil's Devils' – *Outlook*, 22 May 2000.

178 Online chat: Atul Wassan – *India Today*, 15 June 2000.

179 Scyld Berry: 'Cronjé's illegal cash stash found' – *The Sunday Telegraph* (UK) on *theage.com.au*, 17 March 2003.

180 Partab Ramchand: 'BCCI takes cautious line on match-fixing scam' – *cricinfo.com*, 10 April 2000.

181 Online chat: Arun Aggarwal: 'The big fish in the TV scam is Dalmiya' – *rediff.com*, 16 November 2000.

182 Anand Vasu: 'Borde: Who would have thought Cronjé could have done it' – *cricinfo.com*, 11 April 2000.

183 Partab Ramchand: 'BCCI takes cautious line on match-fixing scam' – *cricinfo.com*, 10 April 2000.

184 Partab Ramchand: 'How the match-fixing drama unfolded' – *cricinfo.com*, 11 April 2000.

185 Online interview: SS Dhindsa – *India Today*, 8 July 2000.

186 'Chandrachud Committee to probe betting scam' – *rediff.com*, 21 June 1997.

187 Siddharth Srivastava: 'Indians love cricket, you bet' – *Asia Times*, 15 March 2007.

188 Prem Panicker: 'The four monkeys' – *rediff.com*, 22 April 2000.

189 NDTV Release – New Delhi, 14 December 1997.

190 Interview to Zee TV, 15 June 1997.

191 'Indian prosecutor in Hansiegate receives death threat' – *India Today*, 14 July 2000.

192 Manoj Prabhakar: 'I was offered Rs25 lakh by a team-mate to sabotage a match in Pakistan's favour' – *Outlook*, 11 June 1997.

193 Murali Krishnan with Sujata Anandan and Ajith Pillai: 'Caught out' – *Outlook*, 5 June 2000.

194 Peter Roebuck: 'Big-time crooks prey on the game' – *ThePavilion.com*, 2 November 2000.

195 Pradeep Magazine: *Not Quite Cricket* (Revised edition), Penguin 2000, p96.

196 Bob Woolmer: 'Earpieces were not for betting' – *cricinfo.com*, 23 October 2006.

197 Greg Baum: 'Good wicket gets sticky for Dalmiya' – *ThePavilion.com*, 15 November 2000.

198 Pradeep Magazine: 'The power of the pitch' – *Indian Express*, 11 April 1999.

199 'Cricket in India: It's big business but not businesslike' – *Knowledge@Wharton*, University of Pennsylvania, 5 April 2007.

200 Vivek Chaudhar: 'Who is Jagmohan Dalmiya and how did he come to power?' – *ThePavilion.com*, 3 May 2000.

201 Prem Panicker: 'Did Dalmiya bribe his way to the ICC chairmanship?' – *rediff.com*, 13 May 2000.

202 Prem Panicker: 'Did Dalmiya bribe his way to the ICC chairmanship?' – *rediff.com*, 13 May 2000.

203 Prem Panicker: 'Did Dalmiya bribe his way to the ICC chairmanship?' – *rediff.com*, 13 May 2000.

204 S. Santhanam: ' Bindra flays ICC chief Dalmiya' – *Indian Express*, 21 August 1998.
205 'The Inderjit Singh Bindra chat' – *rediff.com*, 15 April 2000.
206 UNI: 'Dalmiya in grip of Mafia says Bindra' – *ThatsCricket.com*, 19 April 2000.
207 Partab Ramchand: 'How the match-fixing drama unfolded' – *cricinfo.com*, 11 April 2000.
208 Partab Ramchand: 'How the match-fixing drama unfolded: Part 2' – *cricinfo.com*, 2 May 2000.
209 AFP: 'ICC clear Dalmiya of malpractice' – *cricinfo.com*, 2 May 2000.
210 Pradeep Magazine: *Not Quite Cricket* (Revised edition), Penguin 2000, pp152-153.
211 Prem Panicker: 'It's just not cricket' – *rediff.com*, 23 September 1997.
212 *The Sunday Times* (UK) and Sapa-AFP: 'Match-fix probe focuses on Azhar' – *Cape Argus*, 26 July 2000.
213 Liz Jackson: 'Fixing Cricket' on 'Four Corners' - Australian Broadcasting Corporation, 24 July 2000
214 Sayantan Chakravarty: 'A friend indeed?' – Web Exclusive Interview, *India Today*, 20 June 2000.
215 Murali Krishnan and Manu Joseph: 'Gentlemen, game's up!' – *Outlook*, 31 July 2000.
216 Scyld Berry: 'Match-fixing remains fact of cricketing life' – *Sunday Telegraph* (UK), 25 March 2007.
217 AFP: 'Azhar, Kapil among top tax defaulters' – *ThePavilion.com*, 8 December 2000.
218 Pradeep Magazine: *Not Quite Cricket* (Revised edition) Penguin 2000, p74.

CHAPTER 11 **The bookies and the dons**

219 Sayantan Chakravarty: 'Dirty talk' – *India Today*, 24 April 2000.
220 Somnath Batabyal: 'Gotcha!' – *The Week*, 23 April 2000.
221 Sayantan Chakravarty: ' Dirty talk' – *India Today*, 24 April 2000.
222 Brajesh Upadhyay and Vinay Tewari: 'Kishan Kumar being questioned over match-fixing' – *indiatimes.com*, 9 April 2000.
223 Iqbal Khan: 'Hansie's confession just "the tip of the iceberg"' – *Cape Times*, 17 April 2000.
224 Scyld Berry: 'Cronjé's last act of defiance' – *The Telegraph* (UK), 1 June 2002.
225 Syed Ali Mujtaba: 'World Cup: Punters, bookies and betting' – *indolink.com*, 27 May 2007.
226 'Odds and ends' – *The Telegraph* (Calcutta), 28 August 2004 and Murali Krishnan: 'Mehta was active in Indo-Pak series' – *The Tribune* (Chandigarh), 19 May 2005.
227 Ramola Talwar Badam: ' Police question Azhar, Sanjay Dutt' – *The Times of India*, 29 April 2000.
228 Ajith Pillai, Rajesh Joshi and Sujata Anandan: 'Guilty and afraid' – *Outlook*, 1 May 2000.
229 'Sharad Shetty killed by two Rajan hitmen' – *The Times of India*, 20 January 2003
230 USA Office of Public Affairs: 'US designates Dawood Ibrahim as terrorist supporter' – js909, 16 October 2003.
231 'Wanted, Dawood Ibrahim' – *Noseweek*, Issue No. 90, April 2007.
232 Rajeev Sharma:'Why Dawood was named global terrorist' – *Tribune News Service*, 19 October 2003.
233 IANS: 'D-wedding, underworld and Pak cricket' – *The Times of India*, 4 July 2005.
234 'Profile: India's fugitive gangster' – *BBC News*, 12 September 2006.
235 Murali Krishnan, Sujata Anandan and Manu Joseph: 'Any more bets?' – *Outlook*, 24 April 2000.
236 Prem Panicker: 'A horse to water' – *rediff.com*, 27 April 2000.
237 NDTV Correspondent, 'Dawood offered Team India gifts: Lele' – *New Delhi Television Limited*, 17 May 2005.
238 Amrit Mathur: 'Calcutta has a different flavour' – *The Hindu*, Volume 22, No. 10, 6–12 March 1999.
239 Luke Alfred: 'Young cricketers taught to beware strangers bearing gifts' – *Sunday Independent* (RSA), 2 July 2000.
240 Telegraph Bureau: 'Bookie spills more' – *The Telegraph* (Calcutta), 13 June 2005.
241 Murali Krishnan, Sujata Anandan and Manu Joseph: 'Any more bets?' – *Outlook*, 24 April 2000.
242 Aniruddha Bahal and Krishna Prasad: 'Cricket's dirty games' – *Outlook*, 11 June 1997.
243 Sayantan Chakravarty: 'Dirty talk' – *India Today*, 24 April 2000.
244 Murali Krishnan and Manu Joseph: 'Gentlemen, game's up!' – *Outlook*, 31 July 2000.

245 Manu Joseph: 'I'm clean … I don't have anything to say in my defence' – Interview with Sachin Tendulkar – *Outlook*, 24 July 2000.
246 Sheela Raval: 'Carving up Mumbai, – *India Today*, 29 May 2000.
247 'Wanted: Dawood Ibrahim' – *Noseweek*, Issue No. 90, April 2007.

CHAPTER 12 **Dirty laundry**

248 'Bacher claims match-fixing is common practice but denies naming teams' – *cricinfo.com*, 20 April 2000.
249 Aniruddha Bahal: 'I took 10 lakhs' – *Outlook*, 18 April 2005.
250 Murali Krishnan: 'Plumb in the middle' – *Outlook*, 16 February 2004.
251 Scyld Berry: 'Two World Cup games "fixed"' – *The Telegraph* (UK), 14 February 2004.
252 Tony Cozier: 'Final: Australia v Pakistan – No contest' – *cricinfo.com*, 20 June 1999.
253 *The Barbados Nation*: 'Pakistan media blasted for match-fixing claims' – *cricinfo.com*, 25 June 1999.
254 James Millbank: 'Gang wanted Stewart to drop vital catches and Mullally to bowl wide' – *News of the World* (UK), 12 September 1999.
255 Owen Slot: 'Pakistan president halted fixing probe' – *Sunday Telegraph* (UK), 23 April 2000.
256 AFP: 'Pakistan to probe '99 World Cup defeats' – *Total-Cricket.com*, 22 May 2001.
257 BBC Sport Online Correspondent: 'Wasim called by fixing inquiry' – *BBC Sport*, 17 November 2001.
258 Ivo Tennant: 'Woolmer struggled to cope with snake pit that is Pakistan game' – *The Times*, (UK) 26 March 2007.
259 Mazher Mahmood: 'Caught at last – The man fxing test matches' – *News of the World* (UK), 21 May 2000.
260 Mazher Mahmood: 'Caught at last … the man fixing test matches' – *News of the World* (UK), 21 May 2000.
261 'Cricket's molotov mixture' – *Icricketer.com*, 15 November 2000.
262 Raymond Joseph: 'Probe into cricket bookie's death given new spin by fresh info' – *Big Issue*, July 2001.
263 Pradeep Magazine: *Not Quite Cricket* (Revised edition) Penguin 2000, p14.
264 Sharda Ugra: 'Outlaw' – *India Today*, 26 June 2000 and Ali Bacher's counsel, Jeremy Gauntlett, during the King Commission.
265 Sheela Raval: 'Carving up Mumbai' – *India Today*, 29 May 2000.
266 Peter Deeley: 'Illegal betting casts dark cloud over cricket' – *Electronic Telegraph* (UK), 16 February 1996.
267 Khalid Mahmood, Chairman of Pakistan Cricket Board to Qayyum Commission.
268 Michael Parkinson: 'Time for ICC to take real action' – *Electronic Telegraph* (UK), 17 April 2000.
269 Mihir Bose: 'The fix' – *SA Sports Illustrated*, July 2000.

CHAPTER 13 **Kangaroo court**

270 Introduction to the O'Regan Report.
271 Excerpt from Mark Waugh's statement to Qayyum Commission in Australia – *cricinfo.com*, 8 January 1999.
272 Excerpt from Shane Warne's statement to Qayyum in Australia – *cricinfo.com*, 8 January 1999.
273 Mark Fuller and Mark Ray: 'Waugh fends off new bookie cash allegation' – *ThePavilion.com*, 3 November 2000.
274 AFP: 'Punishing Mark Waugh could have legal implications' – *rediff.com*, 22 November 2000.
275 ACB/ICC investigations update – *cricinfo.com*, 16 January 2000.
276 AAP: Text of ACB letter to Mark Waugh –*ThePavilion.com*, 24 January 2001.
277 'The Inderjit Singh Bindra chat' – *rediff.com*, 15 April 2000.
278 The ACB Report – Reproduced on *rediff.com* on 9 May 2000 from Melbourne newspaper *The Age*, 25 February 1999.

CHAPTER 14 **The green fields of home**

279 'MCC history' on *lords.org.*
280 'Cronjé loses lucrative sponsorships' – *Indian Express*, 13 April 2000.
281 Derek Birley: *A Social History of English Cricket* Aurum Press 2000, p29.
282 Derek Birley: *A Social History of English Cricket* Aurum Press 2000, p39.
283 Derek Birley: *A Social History of English Cricket* Aurum Press 2000, p44.
284 Derek Birley: *A Social History of English Cricket* Aurum Press 2000, p60.
285 Derek Birley: *A Social History of English Cricket* Aurum Press 2000, p38.
286 Derek Birley: *A Social History of English Cricket* Aurum Press 2000, p63.
287 Derek Birley: *A Social History of English Cricket* Aurum Press 2000, p68.

288 'MCC history' on *lords.org.*
289 Derek Birley: *A Social History of English Cricket* Aurum Press 2000, p72.
290 Quoted by Bob Woolmer in article by Rohit Brijnath: 'Shame on the game' – *India Today*, 24 April 2000.
291 Derek Birley: *A Social History of English Cricket* Aurum Press 2000, p164.
292 Derek Birley: *A Social History of English Cricket* Aurum Press 2000, p94.
293 Derek Birley: *A Social History of English Cricket* Aurum Press 2000, p95.
294 Derek Birley: *A Social History of English Cricket* Aurum Press 2000, p96.
295 Ted Smart: *Bloomsbury Dictionary of Quotations*: WG Grace: Bloomsbury 1991, p166.
296 Scyld Berry: 'Cronjé takes cover from the fire' - *Electronic Telegraph* (UK), 9 April 2000.
297 Nasser Hussain: 'Why I'm sure Centurion was no fix' – *Electronic Telegraph* (UK), 16 April 2000.
298 Matthew Engel: 'After the cover-ups time for the whole truth' – *The Guardian* (UK), 3 November 2000.
299 'Hollioake reveals bookies' offer' – *BBC News*, 13 December 1998.
300 Mazher Mahmood, 'Caught at last … the man fixing test matches' – *News of the World* (UK), 21 May 2000.
301 James Millbank: 'Gang wanted Stewart to drop vital catches and Mullally to bowl wide' – *News of the World* (UK), 12 September 1999.
302 'Lewis hits out' – *The Northern Echo*, 20 April 2000.
303 VK Santosh Kumar: 'The big fix' – *India Today*, 18 October 1999.
304 James Millbank: 'Gang wanted Stewart to drop vital catches and Mullally to bowl wide' – *News of the World* (UK), 12 September 1999.
305 Michael Henderson: '4th Test: England v New Zealand – Day 1: England start to look the part' – *The Electronic Telegraph* (UK), 19–23 August 1999.
306 'England flops are "beyond belief"' – *BBC News*, 23 August 1999.
307 'England cricketers "offered £1m bribe"' – *BBC News*, 12 September 1999.
308 Jim Holden: 'Lewis hurls down another bouncer' – *International Express*, 25 April 2000.
309 'Mr Big told me 3 of my England mates were on the take' – *News of the World* (UK), 16 April 2000.
310 Sayantan Chakravarty: 'Man in a fix' – *India Today*, 22 May 2000.
311 Pradeep Magazine: *Not Quite Cricket* – (Revised edition), Penguin 2000, p154.
312 Simon Wilde: 'ICC president linked to Lewis affair' – *The Sunday Times* (UK), 21 May 2000.
313 NZPA: 'Fleming tells of approach by fixer' – *Sydney Morning Herald*, 8 November 2004.
314 P. Subramanyam: 'Fleming claims he was approached by Indian bookie' – *The Hindu*, 8 November 2004.
315 House of Lords Debate on Corruption Bill, 16 March 2007.
316 Sayantan Chakravarty: 'Man in a fix' – *India Today*, 22 May 2000.
317 'Mr Big told me 3 of my England mates were on the take' – *News of the World* (UK), 16 April 2000.
318 '"Name names", cricket star told' – *BBC News*, 17 April 2000.
319 ECB Statement on match-fixing and betting allegations – 27 April 2000.
320 '3 England tests fixed' – *News of the World* (UK), 16 April 2000.
321 'England's sorry farewell allows India to party on' – *Electronic Telegraph* (UK), 30 May 1999.
322 John Polack and Duane Pettet: 'A definitive overview of cricket match-fixing, betting and corruption allegations' – *cricinfo.com*, 10 May 2000.
323 'Stewart cleared of corruption charges' – ECB media release, 11 July 2001.
324 Derek Birley: *A Social History of English Cricket* Aurum Press 2000, p272.
325 History of the ICC: 1989–Present – International Cricket Council on the ICC's official website.
326 'In London, it's the same old story for the ICC' – *The Pavilion.com*, 4 May 2000.
327 *Guardian* staff and agencies: 'Lawrences insist nothing has changed as Condon admits shame' – *The Guardian* (UK), 24 February 1999.
328 Reuters: 'Fixing's big says Botham' – *rediff.com*, 21 May 2001.
329 'CWC to make $239m profit' – Sport Industry Group, 15 March 2007.
330 'Condon will call on ICC to get tough over match-fixing' – *cricinfo.com*, 6 April 2001.

331 Murali Krishnan: 'I met Warne at five-star parties' – Interview with Ratan Mehta, *Outlook*, 12 July 2004.

332 'ICC announces code of conduct hearing into allegations against Maurice Odumbe' – ICC Media Release, 12 March 2004.

CHAPTER 15 **Pulling the wool**

333 Simon Robinson: 'Woolmer death highlights cricket's dangerous game' – *Time.com*, 29 May 2007.

334 Dudley Moore: 'Cricketer of the Year 1976 – Bob Woolmer' – *Wisden Almanack* on *cricinfo.com*.

335 'Bacher fixed match, inquiry told' – *ThePavilion.com*, 15 June 2000.

336 G Viswanath: 'Blanket ban on Cronjé absurd, says Woolmer' – *The Hindu*, 16 October 2001.

337 Reuters, Sapa-AP, AFP: 'Woolmer was a coach driven by desire' – *Mail and Guardian*, 18 March 2007.

338 John Polack: 'India v South Africa' – *cricinfo.com*, 15 May 1999.

339 'Tauqir demands ICC to probe into World Cup upsets' – *The News International*, 20 February 2001.

340 AFP: 'Delhi police probe match-fixing In England World Cup' – *cricinfo.com*, 22 October 2006.

341 The Times News Service, London: 'Focus turns to UK World Cup in Cronjé saga' – *Sunday Times* (RSA), 22 October 2006.

342 AFP: 'Delhi police probe match-fixing in England World Cup' – *cricinfo.com*, 22 October 2006.

343 Vedam Jaishankar: 'Ali Bacher lashes out at Bob Woolmer for not heeding advice' – *Indian Express*, 17 May 1999.

344 Bob Woolmer: 'Earpieces were not for betting' – *cricinfo.com*, 23 October 2006.

345 Bob Woolmer: 'Earpieces were not for betting' – *cricinfo.com*, 23 October 2006.

346 AFP 'Delhi police probe match-fixing in England World Cup' – *cricinfo.com*, 22 October 2006.

347 Tom Eaton: 'The death of a legacy' – *Mail & Guardian*, 23–29 March 2007.

348 Bob Woolmer: 'Earpieces were not for betting' – *cricinfo.com*, 23 October 2006.

349 Sa'adi Thawfeeq: 9th Super Six Match: Australia v South Africa – 'Gibbs ton sees South Africa to 271 for 7'– *cricinfo.com*, 13 June 1999.

350 Tony Cozier: 'Waugh beats the odds' – *cricinfo.com*, 13 June 1999.

351 Michael Henderson: 'Waugh's masterful display'– *cricinfo.com*, 13 June 1999.

352 Keith Lane: 'First blood to Australia' – *cricinfo.com*, 13 June 1999.

353 Neil Manthorp: *Gazza* (2nd impression) Don Nelson Publishers 2005, pp90-91.

354 Neil Manthorp: *Gazza* (2nd impression) Don Nelson Publishers 2005, pp90-91.

355 Luke Alfred: 'When Bob wanted to bat, Hansie decided to bowl' – *Sunday Times* (RSA), 25 March 2007.

356 Rodney Harman: 'Betting mafia behind deaths of Woolmer and Hansie, says Rice' – *Weekend Argus*, 24 March 2007.

357 Agencies: 'Now a second autopsy likely to be ordered' – *Indian Express*, 28 March 2007.

358 Rodney Harman: 'Betting mafia behind deaths of Woolmer and Hansie, says Rice' – *Weekend Argus*, 24 March 2007.

359 *Cape Talk Radio*, 23 March 2007.

360 G. Viswanath: 'Blanket ban on Cronjé absurd, says Woolmer' – *The Hindu*, 16 October 2001.

361 Boria Majumdar and Shantanu Guha Ray: 'Cricket, infamy has become thy name' – *tehelka.com*, 7 April 2007.

362 Shaharyar Khan: 'A gentle man, a superb coach' – *cricinfo.com*, 25 March 2007.

363 Ivo Tennant: 'Cricket is my religion' – *Sunday Times* (RSA), 25 March 2007.

364 'Woolmer wants Shoaib to cut his run-up' – *cricinfo.com*, 20 December 2004.

365 AFP: 'Pakistan crash to defeat in first match of Australian tour' – *Daily Times* (PAK), 4 December 2004.

366 Nick Parker, Neil Syson: 'Misson of murdered coach Bob' – *The Sun* (UK), 26 March 2007.

367 'Aspects of cricket games fixed' – *BBC Sport*, 25 March 2007.

368 Lawrence Booth: 'Excluded Woolmer never had full control of the team' – *The Observer* (UK), 26 March 2007.

369 Reuters: 'Inzy was a dictator – Akram' – *Jamaica Gleaner*, 15 April 2007.

370 Susan Sachs: 'Muslim missionary group draws new scrutiny in US' – *The New York Times*, 14 July 2003.

371 Nicholas Howenstein: 'The case of Tablighi Jamaat' – *United States Institute of Peace*, USI Peace Briefing, October 2006.

372 Alex Alexiev: 'Tablighi Jamaat: Jihad's stealthy legions – *Middle East Quarterly*, Winter 2005.

373 Alex Alexiev: 'Tablighi Jamaat: Jihad's

stealthy legions – *Middle East Quarterly*, Winter 2005.

374 Amir Mir: 'A catch in the deep' – *Outlook*, 12 March 2007.

375 Bruce Loudon: 'Religion blamed for Pakistan's Cup failure' – *The Australian*, 9 April 2007.

376 Ed Pilkington, Declan Walsh and Hugh Muir: 'Yard veteran grapples with mystery of room 374' – *The Guardian* (UK), 24 March 2007.

377 Reuters: 'Pakistan assistant coach suffers nose injury' – *cricketworld.com*, 15 March 2007.

378 Sujay Gupta: 'Match-fixing judge hits out' – *NDTV.com*, 31 March 2007.

379 'Suspect held in Woolmer case: Geo TV' – *rediff.com*, 23 March 2007.

380 Melissa Leong: 'Death of Pakistan's coach stuns cricket world' – *National Post* (CAN), 18 March 2007.

381 John Peters: 'The cancer in cricket' – *You Magazine*, 5 April 2007.

382 Michelle McDonald: 'Why does anything happen?' – *caribbeancricket.com*, 18 March 2007.

383 Dileep Premachandran: 'Woolmer apologises on Inzamam's worst day' – *cricinfo.com*, 17 March 2007.

384 Sharon Churcher and Dennis Rice: 'Cricket murder: Woolmer case police in dramatic swoop on Pakistan team hotel' – *The Mail on Sunday* (UK), 25 March 2007.

385 'CCTV pics boost to probe' – *Sky News*, 25 March 2007.

386 Stephen Brenkley: 'Police optimistic CCTV footage will help identify Woolmer's killer' – *The Independent* (UK), 26 March 2007.

387 PTI: 'Speculation rife that Bob's death was an accident' – *indiatimes.com*, 1 April 2007.

388 Steven Swinford and Jonathan Calvert: 'Woolmer was "poisoned and then strangled"' – *The Sunday Times* (UK), 15 April 2007.

389 AP: 'Cricket no longer a gentleman's game: Woolmer's murder points to sleazy side of sport' – *Jamaica Gleaner*, 25 March 2007.

390 Jason Benneto, Stephen Brenkley: 'How a shock cricket result turned into a murder investigation' – *The Independent* (UK), 24 March 2007.

391 'Woolmer murder mystery deepens' – *TimesNow.tv*, 24 March 2007.

392 Petrina Francis: 'Suspicious – New evidence uncovered in Woolmer's death' – *Jamaica Gleaner*, 21 March 2007.

393 'Pakistan coach Bob Woolmer dies' – *BBC News*, 18 March 2007.

394 AP: 'Cricket no longer a gentleman's game: Woolmer's murder points to sleazy side of sport' – *Jamaica Gleaner*, 25 March 2007.

395 Barbara Gayle: 'The role of the coroner' – *Jamaica Gleaner*, 26 March 2007.

396 Associated Press, Howard Campbell, Rizwan Ali: 'Pakistan coach Bob Woolmer dies during World Cup' – *International Herald Tribune*, 18 March 2007.

397 'Stress may have killed Woolmer – son' – *The Age* (AUS), 19 March 2007.

398 AP: 'Cricket no longer a gentleman's game: Woolmer's murder points to sleazy side of sport' – *Jamaica Gleaner*, 25 March 2007.

399 D.Anthony Luton: 'Pakistan cricket coach dies' – *Jamaica Gleaner*, 19 March 2007.

400 'Woolmer murder mystery deepens' – *TimesNow.tv*, 24 March 2007.

401 Bureau Report: 'Pak manager claims he shifted floors on hotel security's advice' – *zeenews.com*, 30 March 2007.

402 Online Reporter: Fury over Woolmer claims, *The Sun* (UK), 7 June 2007.

403 Jonathan Clavert and Steven Swinford: 'Experts doubtful Woolmer was strangled' – *The Sunday Times* (UK), 1 April 2007.

404 Inzamam ul-Haq: 'Bob was a super human being' – *bigstarcricket.com*, 18 March 2007.

405 Ed Pilkington, Declan Walsh and Hugh Muir: 'Yard veteran grapples with mystery of room 374' – *The Guardian* (UK), 24 March 2007.

406 Tim Reid: 'Scotland Yard called in as cricket murder police struggle to cope' – *The Times* (UK), 31 March 2007.

407 Lawrence Booth: 'Jamaican police detail the last moments of Woolmer as Inzamam mourns Pakistan's loss' – *The Guardian* (UK), 20 March 2007.

408 Lawrence Booth: 'Jamaican police detail the last moments of Woolmer as Inzamam mourns Pakistan's loss' – *The Guardian* (UK), 20 March 2007.

409 Woolmer's postmortem inconclusive – *cricinfo.com*, 20 March 2007.

410 PTI: 'Speculation rife that Bob's death was an accident' – *indiatimes.com*, 1 April 2007.

411 'Woolmer's body was blocking hotel door' – *Jamaica Observer*, 6 June 2007.

412 Ed Pilkington, Declan Walsh and Hugh Muir: 'Yard veteran grapples with mystery of room 374' – *The Guardian* (UK), 24 March 2007.
413 Ed Pilkington, Andrew Culf, Declan Walsh: 'A suspicious death, say police, as the rumours of murder or accident abound' – *The Guardian* (UK), 22 March 2007.
414 D. Anthony Luton: 'Pakistan cricket coach dies' – *Jamaica Gleaner*, 19 March 2007.
415 Andy Gardner, Grant Hodgson: 'Bob was poisoned' – *Sunday Mirror* (UK), 1 April 2007.
416 Qmar Ahmed interviewed on *Sky News* before Jamaican police press conference, 12 June 2007.
417 Ed Pilkington, Declan Walsh and Hugh Muir: 'Yard veteran grapples with mystery of room 374' – *The Guardian* (UK), 24 March 2007.
418 Ed Pilkington, Declan Walsh and Hugh Muir: 'Yard veteran grapples with mystery of room 374' – *The Guardian* (UK), 24 March 2007.
419 PTI: 'Woolmer's family not to travel to Jamaica' – *dnaindia.com*, 20 March 2007.
420 Patrick Hruby: 'Murder by cricket' – E-Ticket, *ESPN.com*
421 Marc Lacey and Salman Masood: 'Jamaican police seek killer of Pakistan cricket coach' – *International Herald Tribune*, 23 March 2007.
422 'Match-fixing surfaces as Bob's autopsy remains inconclusive' – *The Post* (PAK), 21 March 2007.
423 Associated Press: 'Pakistan shocked by Woolmer's sudden death' – *International Herald Tribune*, 18 March 2007.
424 'Pakistan players being questioned over Woolmer' – *cricinfo.com*, 21 March 2007.
425 Murray Williams: 'Woolmer family dismay at overdose rumours' – *Cape Argus*, 21 March 2007.
426 Carla Calitz and Charlene Rolls: 'Now it's come to murder' – *You Magazine*, 5 April 2007.
427 Carla Calitz and Charlene Rolls: 'Now it's come to murder' – *You Magazine*, 5 April 2007.
428 'Woolmer Strangled – New twist in death of Pakistan's cricket coach' – *Jamaica Gleaner*, 22 March 2007.
429 Karyl Walker: 'Woolmer strangled?' – *The Jamaica Observer*, 22 March 2007.
430 Stewart Tendler: 'Second Woolmer postmortem in doubt' – *The Times* (UK), 4 April 2007.
431 Richard Sydenham: 'PCB says Woolmer postmortem inconclusive – *Reuters*, 21 March 2007.
432 'Woolmer strangled – New twist in death of Pakistan's cricket coach' – *Jamaica Gleaner*, 22 March 2007.
433 Philippe Naughton and agencies: 'US pathologist called in over Woolmer as Pakistan team faces quiz' – *The Times* (UK), 22 March 2007.
434 Toby Harnden and agencies: 'Pakistan team quizzed over Woolmer's death' – *The Telegraph* (UK), 23 March 2007.
435 'US expert sought in Woolmer case' – *rediff.com*, 22 March 2007.
436 'Murder inquiry "imminent" into Woolmer death' – *Channel 4 News*, 22 March 2007.
437 Stewart Tendler: 'Second Woolmer postmortem in doubt' – *The Times* (UK), 4 April 2007.
438 Tim Reid and Pat Gibson: 'More than one killer was involved' – *The Times* (UK), 23 March 2007.
439 Jon Pierik: 'Conflicting claims on Woolmer' – *Adelaide Now*, 30 March 2007.
440 Toby Harnden: 'Woolmer strangled in "evil circumstances"' – *The Telegraph* (UK), 24 March 2007.
441 Jason Benneto, Stephen Brenkley: 'How a shock cricket result turned into a murder investigation' – *The Independent* (UK), 24 March 2007.
442 Jon Pierik: 'Conflicting claims on Woolmer' – *Adelaide Now*, 30 March 2007.
443 Paul Henderson, Michael Duffy, Andy Gardner: 'Skipper is quizzed' – *Sunday Mirror* (UK), 25 March 2007.
444 'Police hunt Woolmer's murderer' – *cricinfo.com*, 23 March 2007.
445 Paul Henderson, Michael Duffy, Andy Gardner: 'Skipper is quizzed' – *Sunday Mirror* (UK), 25 March 2007.
446 Jon Pierik: 'Conflicting claims on Woolmer' – *Adelaide Now*, 30 March 2007.
447 'More questions on Woolmer autopsy' – *Jamaica Gleaner*, 24 March 2007.
448 'More questions on Woolmer autopsy' –*Jamaica Gleaner*, 24 March 2007.
449 'Betting poisons Woolmer' – *Deccan Chronicle*, 21 March 2007.
450 Paul Chapman: 'Sarfraz denies coach murder claim' – *Reuters*, 22 March 2007.

451 'Match-fixing mafia killed Woolmer' – *saharasamay.com*, 21 March 2007.
452 'Match-fixing mafia killed Woolmer' – *saharasamay.com*, 21 March 2007.
453 Agencies: Was Pak match-fixing mafia behind Bob's death' – *indiatimes.com*, 21 March 2007.
454 Amir Mir: 'Woolmer death draws out foul play rumours' – *dnaindia.com*, 20 March 2007.
455 Ruhi Khan: 'Underworld bookies spotted in W Indies' – *ndtv.com*, 31 March 2007.
456 Ruhi Khan: 'Underworld bookies spotted in W Indies' – *ndtv.com*, 31 March 2007.
457 Rashid Razaq: 'Yard officers called in to help solve Woolmer death riddle' – *Evening Standard* (UK), 22 March 2007.
458 Mansoor Khan: 'Arshad Pappu netted' – *The Nation* (PAK), 12 October 2006.
459 'Hunt for missing Pak bookie' – *india-times.com*, 26 March 2007.
460 Sapa-AP and Sapa-AFP: 'Woolmer murder: Man arrested' – *iol.co.za*, 23 March 2007.
461 Deepak Gidwani: 'Babloo Srivastava on Dawood hit list' – *dnaindia.com*, 3 August 2006.
462 Sapa-AP and Sapa-AFP: 'Woolmer murder: Man arrested' – *iol.co.za*, 23 March 2007.
463 Andrew Alderson, Simon Hart and Philip Sherwell: 'Sad end to cricket pioneer's great innings' – *The Sunday Telegraph* (UK) – Reprinted in the *Cape Argus*, 28 March 2007.
464 NDTV Correspondent: 'Woolmer was murdered: Police' – *ndtv.com*, 23 March 2007.
465 Amir Mir: 'Sarfraz indicts betting mafia, blames ICC too' – *dnaindia.com*, 24 March 2007.
466 Aamir Mir: 'Woolmer death draws out foul play rumours' – *dnaindia.com*, 20 March 2007.
467 Pradeep Magazine: 'Cops suspect foul play' – *Hindustan Times*, 21 March 2007.
468 'Woolmer planned book on Pak experi-ence'– *cricinfo.com*, 24 March 2007.
469 Sharon Churcher, Dennis Rice and Sapa-AP-AFP: 'Syndicate "wanted Woolmer dead"'– *iol.co.za*, 26 March 2007.
470 'New twist in Woolmer murder' – *Cape Talk Radio*, 27 March 2007.
471 Rodney Harman: 'Betting mafia behind deaths of Woolmer and Hansie, says Rice' – *Weekend Argus*, 24 March 2007.
472 PTI: 'Was Woolmer going to blow the whistle?' – *dnaindia.com*, 24 March 2007.
473 Reuters: 'Former captain suspects betting ring in Woolmer murder' – *stuff.co.nz*, 24 March 2007.
474 'Betting poisons Woolmer' – *Deccan Chronicle*, 21 March 2007.
475 PTI: 'Police order second postmortem of Woolmer' – *Outlook*, 28 March 2007.
476 'Aspects of cricket games "fixed"' – *BBC Sport*, 25 March 2007.
477 Tim Reid: 'Woolmer police order new postmortem' – *The Times* (UK), 28 March 2007.
478 'Match-fixing returns to hit Windies' cricket' – *TimesNow.tv*, 8 February 2007.
479 NDTV Correspondent: 'Betting scandal: Samuels claims innocence' – *ndtv.com*, 9 February 2007.
480 IANS: 'Dawood back in cricket betting racket: Mumbai police' – *zeenews.com*, 9 February 2007.
481 'I know Marlon Samuels, says Kochchar' – *indiatimes.com*, 9 February 2007.
482 'Jamaican police hunts for a bookie' – *Deccan Chronicle*, 30 March 2007.
483 'Indian bookie linked to Woolmer murder' – *indiatimes.com*, 31 March 2007.
484 IANS: 'Match-fixing: Mumbai police looking for Dawood aide' – *India Gazette*, 8 February 2007.
485 IANS: 'I am a not a bookie: Kochchar' – *dnaindia.com*, 8 February 2007.
486 'Suspect held in Woolmer case: Geo TV' – *rediff.com*, 23 March 2007.
487 'Suspect held in Woolmer case: Geo TV' – *rediff.com*, 23 March 2007.
488 PTI: 'Woolmer case: Arrested man has players' numbers' – *Mid Day News (IND)*, 23 March 2007.
489 'New theory on Talat move' – *The Telegraph* (Calcutta), 30 March 2007.
490 Sharon Churcher and Dennis Rice: 'Cricket murder: Woolmer case police in dramatic swoop on Pakistan team hotel' – *The Mail on Sunday* (UK), 25 March 2007.
491 'Woolmer: fixing probe' – SAPA-AFP and *Daily Mail* (UK), Reprinted in *Cape Argus*, 26 March 2007.
492 Karyl Walker: '3 Pakistanis quizzed a second time' – *The Jamaica Observer*, 25 March 2007.
493 Ed Pilkington, Declan Walsh and Karen McVeigh: 'Murder in room 374: CCTV cameras may hold key to Woolmer

inquiry, say police' – *The Guardian* (UK), 26 March 2007.
494 Nick Parker: 'Al-Qaeda link to Woolmer death' – *The Sun* (UK), 29 March 2007.
495 Patrick Hruby: 'Murder by cricket' – E-Ticket, *ESPN.com*
496 PTI: 'Mystery surrounds Woolmer's murder even after a week' – *Outlook*, 25 March 2007.
497 Syed Saleem Shahzad: 'An invisible hand in Pakistani politics' – *Asia Times*, 19 March 2003.
498 Times News Network and Chandresh Narayan: 'Poison found in Woolmer's room' – *indiatimes.com*, 21 March 2007.
499 'Betting poisons Woolmer' – *Deccan Chronicle*, 21 March 2007.
500 Sharon Churcher, Dennis Rice and Sapa-AP-AFP: 'Syndicate "wanted Woolmer dead"' – *iol.co.za*, 26 March 2007.
501 Andy Gardner and Grant Hodgson: 'Bob was poisoned' – *Sunday Mirror* (UK), 1 April 2007.
502 'Major development in Woolmer case' – *BBC News*, 21 April 2007.
503 PTI: 'Enter a high-profile sleuth' – *The Statesman* (IND), 3 April 2007.
504 Commissioner of Jamaican Police, Lucius Thomas: Statement made at a Press Conference at the Police Officers' Club, Kingston, 12 June 2007.
505 Ross Sheil: 'Woolmer case – Some toxicology results in' – *Jamaica Gleaner*, 15 April 2007.
506 Steven Swinford and Jonathan Calvert: 'Woolmer "was poisoned and then strangled"' – *The Sunday Times* (UK), 15 April 2007.
507 Daraine Luton and Glenroy Sinclair: "Foreign substance' found in Woolmer's system' – *Jamaica Gleaner*, 17 April, 2007.
508 'Cricket coach Woolmer "poisoned"' – *BBC News*, 29 April 2007.
509 Andy Gardner, Grant Hodgson: 'Bob was poisoned' – *Sunday Mirror* (UK), 1 April 2007.
510 Mike Sullivan: 'Potter drug did kill Woolmer' – *The Sun* (UK), 20 April 2007.
511 'Champagne was passed on to Woolmer' – *cricinfo.com*, 10 May 2007.
512 Cahal Milmo: 'Breakthrough as Woolmer suspect is caught on camera' – *The Independent* (UK), 21 April 2007.
513 Catherine Elsworth: 'New doubts cast on Woolmer "murder"' – *The Telegraph* (UK), 10 May 2007.
514 Steven Swinford: 'Pathologist urged to quit after Woolmer blunder' – *The Sunday Times* (UK), 3 June 2007.
515 Deepa Seetharaman and Melanie Peters: 'Cops in big bungle' – *Daily Mail* (UK) and *Sunday Telegraph* (UK), Reprinted in *Cape Argus*, 3 June 2007.
516 'Woolmer Verdict: Doctor under fire' – *The Sunday Times* (UK), Reprinted in *Sunday Times* (SA), 3 June 2007.
517 Steven Swinford: 'Pathologist urged to quit after Woolmer blunder' – *The Sunday Times* (UK), 3 June 2007.
518 Steven Swinford: 'Pathologist urged to quit after Woolmer blunder' – *The Sunday Times* (UK), 3 June 2007.
519 Karyl Walker: 'A vow of silence' – *The Jamaica Observer*, 14 June 2007.
520 Daraine Luton: 'The Woolmer bone of contention' – *Jamaica Gleaner*, 17 June 2007.
521 Commissioner of Jamaican Police, Lucius Thomas: Statement made at a Press Conference at the Police Officers' Club, Kingston, 12 June 2007.
522 Commissioner of Jamaican Police, Lucius Thomas: Statement made at a Press Conference at the Police Officers' Club, Kingston, 12 June 2007.
523 'It wasn't murder!' – Scotland Yard says Woolmer died of heart failure ... No clear evidence to prove Woolmer was murdered ... Local police sticking by their word that Woolmer died of manual strangulation' – *Jamaica Gleaner*, 13 June 2007.
524 Erica Virtue: 'Cop says about-turn in Woolmer case spoils JCF record' – *The Jamaica Observer*, 13 June 2007.
525 BD Venter, Durbanville: Letter in *Cape Argus*, 13 June 2007.
526 Karyl Walker: 'Pathologist insists Woolmer murdered' – *The Jamaica Observer*, 13 June 2007.
527 Woolmer's death a cover-up: *TimesNow.tv*, 10 June 2007.
528 PTI: 'Talat shifted hotel room on ICC instruction' – *indiatimes.com*, 29 March 2007.
529 Karyl Walker: 'Shields gagged' – *The Jamaica Observer*, 15 June 2007.
530 'Pakistan Cricket Board likely to sue Jamaica police' – *indiatimes.com*, 10 June 2007.

CHAPTER 16 **King Commission of Inquiry into Match-fixing and Related Matters**

531 Ivo Tennant: 'Woolmer's enemy within' – *The Times* (UK), 22 April 2000.

532 Excerpt from the unverified transcripts of the Delhi police tapes.

533 AFP: 'Surprising Indian victory marked scandal-tainted series' – *cricinfo.com*, 7 April 2000.

CHAPTER 17 **CBI Report on Cricket Match-fixing and Related Malpractices**

534 Manoj Prabhakar: 'I was offered Rs25 lakh by a team-mate to sabotage a match in Pakistan's favour' – *Outlook*, 11 June 1997.

535 Kuldip Lal: 'Betting scandal leaves cricket's bosses groping in the dark' – AFP on *cricinfo.com*, 8 January 1999.

536 Manoj Prabhakar: 'I was offered Rs25 lakh by a team-mate to sabotage a match in Pakistan's favour' – *Outlook*, 11 June 1997.

537 Report on Corruption in International Cricket, April 2001.

538 Quoted in Justice Chandrachud Committee Report, 22 April 2000. Sources listed as: Interview to *Zee TV* in the *Aap Ki Adalat* programme telecast on 15 June 1997 and also reported in *The Statesman*, 15 June 1997.

539 Murali Krishnan, Sujara Anandan and Manu Joseph: 'Any more bets?' – *Outlook*, 24 April 2000.

540 Murali Krishnan, Sujara Anandan and Manu Joseph: 'Any more bets?' – *Outlook*, 24 April 2000.

541 Prem Panicker: 'India down and almost out of Titan Cup' – *rediff.com*, 29 October 1996.

542 Murali Krishnan, Sujata Anandan and Manu Joseph: 'Any more bets?' – *Outlook*, 24 April 2000.

543 Sayantan Chakravarty: 'Dirty talk' – *India Today*, 24 April 2000.

544 Murali Krishnan, Sujara Anandan and Manu Joseph: 'Any more bets?' – *Outlook*, 24 April 2000.

545 Pradeep Magazine: *Not Quite Cricket* (Revised edition) Penguin 2000.

546 Vijay Singh: 'Who is Shobhan Mehta?' – *rediff.com*, 3 June 2005.

547 John Polack and Duane Pettet: 'A definitive overview of cricket match-fixing, betting and corruption allegations' – *cricinfo.com*, 10 May 2000.

CHAPTER 18 **The Justice Qayyum Report**

548 'Sarfraz and Imran exchange insults as Pakistan row turns hostile' – *Electronic Telegraph* (UK), 27 February 1995.

549 Peter Roebuck: 'Bribery storm hits Pakistan' – *The Sunday Times* (UK), 21 February 1995.

550 John Polack and Duane Pettet: 'A definitive overview of cricket match-fixing, betting and corruption allegations' – *cricinfo.com*, 10 May 2000.

551 John Polack and Duane Pettet: 'A definitive overview of cricket match-fixing, betting and corruption allegations' – *cricinfo.com*, 10 May 2000.

552 'Match report' – *cricinfo.com*, 12 January 1995.

553 John Polack and Duane Pettet: 'A definitive overview of cricket match-fixing, betting and corruption allegations' – *cricinfo.com*, 10 May 2000.

554 Iqbal Latif: 'Bangalore match biggest gamble of the decade' – *Dawn (PAK)*, 16 March 1996.

555 Tanvir Ahmed: 'India v Pakistan, match report: Pakistan disappoints at Bangalore' – *Dawn (PAK)* on *cricinfo.com*, 9 March 1996.

556 Tanvir Ahmed: 'India v Pakistan, match report: Pakistan disappoints at Bangalore' – *Dawn (P AK)* on *cricinfo.com*, 9 March 1996.

557 John Polack and Duane Pettet: 'A definitive overview of cricket match-fixing, betting and corruption allegations' – *cricinfo.com*, 10 May 2000.

558 'World Cup: Pakistan "match-throwing" allegation' – *Electronic Telegraph* (UK), 3 March 1996.

559 Sheela Raval: 'Carving up Mumbai' – *India Today*, 29 May 2000.

560 Sayantan Chakravarty: 'Dirty talk' – *India Today*, 24 April 2000.

CHAPTER 19 **Australian Cricket Board Player Conduct Inquiry Report**

561 'Sri Lankan players approached by bookmakers – Newspaper' – *cricinfo.com*, 30 April 2000.

562 Manish Kumar: Exclusive interview with Ricky Ponting – *India News*, 4 July 2000.

CHAPTER 20 **After Hansiegate**

563 Neil Manthorp and Scyld Berry: ' Law

officers' new twist to Cronjé case' – *The Telegraph* (UK), 22 March 2003.
564 Bhavna Vij-Aurora: 'High stakes bring in the hyenas' – *Outlook*, 9 April 2007.
565 Mihir Bose: 'Miandad opens new controversy' – *Electronic Telegraph* (UK), 9 April 2001.
566 Imran Naeem Ahmad: 'Nur Khan urges PCB boss to accept rot and step down' – *Dawn (PAK)*, 7 April 2001.
567 Sheela Raval: 'Russel, Suresh fightback triggers bookie clash' – *The Newspaper Today* (IND), Reprinted in *The Sunday Times on the Web* (Sri Lanka) 5 August 2001.
568 Scyld Berry: 'Two world cup games fixed' – *The Telegraph* (UK), 14 February 2004
569 'ICC probing into Lankans' links with Mumbai dancer' – *Daily Mail* (PAK), 13 September 2005.
570 Chandresh Narayanan and J Dey: '"I gave Odumbe Rs 25,000, it was for hotel, brother's surgery"' – *Indian Express*, 19 August 2004.
571 'Mumbai police reopen match-fixing probe' – *indiatimes.com*, 20 August 2004.
572 *Mumbai Mirror*: 'Sri Lankan spinner got Rs8 lac in bribe' – *daijiworld.com*, 10 September 2005.
573 Nishant A Bhuse: 'Bar girl loses Rs 1,5 Cr in cricket bet' – *Mid-day.com*, 5 September 2005.
574 G Rajaraman: 'Dance in the dark' – *Outlook*, 26 September 2005.
575 Naveeta D. Singh: 'Mumbai police suspect Sri Lankan spinner's link with dance bar girl' – *Times Group* (India) on *daijiworld.com*, 3 September 2005.
576 *Mumbai Mirror*: 'Sri Lankan spinner got Rs8 lac in bribe' – *daijiworld.com*, 10 September 2005.
577 'Cheating charge against Tarannum Khan dropped' – *Indian Express*, Reprinted on *Yahoo India News*, 11 June 2006.
578 'The Tarannum connection' - *The Sunday Times* (SL), 18 September 2005.
579 SAPA-AFP: 'Bookmakers constantly approach the players' – *Weekend Argus*, 24 March 2007.
580 'What the Indian police said' *GuyanaChronicle.com*, 8 February 2007.
581 Raju Parulekar: '"Dawood gang fixed Pak-Ireland match," says a Mumbai bookie' - *dnaindia.com*, 24 March 2007.
582 Andrew Miller: 'Speed apologises for light chaos' – *cricinfo.com*, 29 April 2007.

APPENDIX TO CHAPTER 15: **the death of Bob Woolmer. Timeline of events**

583 Correspondent: 'Gossipmongers spreading false rumours, says PJ Mir' – *The News* (PAK), 17 March 2007.
584 PTI: 'No rift in Pak camp: Manager' – *The Tribune* (Chandigarh), 18 March 2007.
585 'Suspect held in Woolmer case: Geo TV' – *rediff.com*, 23 March 2007.
586 Jason Benneto, Stephen Brenkley: 'How a shock cricket result turned into a murder investigation' – *The Independent* (UK), 24 March 2007.
587 Steven Swinford and Jonathan Calvert: 'Woolmer was poisoned and strangled' – *The Sunday Times* (UK), 15 April 2007.
588 'Shields: It is "categorically" a murder investigation' – *cricinfo.com*, 30 March 2007.
589 Paul Henderson, Michael Duffy, Andy Gardner: 'Skipper is quizzed' – *Sunday Mirror* (UK), 25 March 2007.
590 Ed Pilkington, Declan Walsh and Karen McVeigh: 'Murder in Room 374: CCTV cameras may hold key to Woolmer inquiry, say police' – *The Guardian* (UK), 26 March 2007.
591 Petrina Francis: 'Suspicious – new evidence uncovered in Woolmer's death' – *Jamaica Gleaner*, 21 March 2007.
592 AP: 'Cricket no longer a gentleman's game: Woolmer's murder points to sleazy side of sport' – *Jamaica Gleaner*, 25 March 2007.
593 Daraine Luton: 'The Woolmer bone of contention' – *Sunday Gleaner*, 17 June 2007.
594 Richard Sydenham: 'Pakistan coach Woolmer "seriously ill"' – *Reuters*, 18 March 2007.
595 AP: 'Cricket no longer a gentleman's game: Woolmer's murder points to sleazy side of sport' – *Jamaica Gleaner*, 25 March 2007.
596 'AP: 'Cricket no longer a gentleman's game: Woolmer's murder points to sleazy side of sport' – *Jamaica Gleaner*, 25 March 2007.
597 PTI: 'Talat shifted hotel room on ICC instruction' – *indiatimes.com*, 29 March 2007.
598 AP: 'Cricket no longer a gentleman's game: Woolmer's murder points to sleazy side of sport' – *Jamaica Gleaner*, 25 March 2007.

599 Richard Sydenham: 'Pakistan coach died "of stress or heart attack" – Son' – *New Zealand Herald on Sunday*, 19 March 2007.
600 Dawn editorial: 'The PCB charade' – *Dawn* (PAK), 1 April 2007.
601 'Betting poisons Woolmer' – *Deccan Chronicle*, 21 March 2007.
602 Aamir Mir: 'Woolmer death draws out foul play rumours' – *dnaindia.com*, 20 March 2007.
603 Graham Brough: 'Bob "dies of drugs and booze overdose"' – *The Mirror*, 19 March 2007.
604 PTI: 'Woolmer's family not to travel to Jamaica' – *dnaindia.com*, 20 March 2007.
605 PTI: 'Woolmer's family not to travel to Jamaica' – *dnaindia.com*, 20 March 2007.
606 Bureau Report: 'Match-fixing clouds over coach's death' – *zeecric.com*, 20 March 2007.
607 'Match-fixing surfaces as Bob autopsy remains inconclusive' – *The Post* (PAK), 21 March 2007.
608 Petrina Francis: 'Suspicious – new evidence uncovered in Woolmer's death' – *Jamaica Gleaner*, 21 March 2007.
609 Times News Network and Chandresh Narayan: 'Poison found in Woolmer's room' – *indiatimes.com*, 21 March 2007.
610 'Bob Woolmer was strangulated: Radio Jamaica' – *netscape.com*, 21 March 2007.
611 Cahal Milmo: 'Cricket courts controversy: Mystery of Bob Woolmer's death' – *The Independent* (UK), 22 March 2007.
612 'Cricket no longer a gentleman's game: Woolmer's murder points to sleazy side of sport' – *Jamaica Gleaner*, 25 March 2007.
613 'Bob Woolmer's death two months later: Two steps forward, several backwards' – *Jamaica Gleaner*, 20 May 2007.
614 Jason Benneto, Stephen Brenkley: 'How a shock cricket result turned into a murder investigation' – *The Independent* (UK), 24 March 2007.
615 Ashish Shukla: 'Bob Woolmer knew it all' – *indiatimes.com*, 21 March 2007.
616 Murray Williams: 'Woolmer family dismay at overdose rumours' – *Cape Argus*, 21 March 2007.
617 Daraine Luton: 'It was murder! - Police confirm Woolmer strangled - Pakistan delegation fingerprinted' – *Jamaica Gleaner*, 23 March 2007.
618 'Woolmer strangled - New twist in death of Pakistan's cricket coach' – *Jamaica Gleaner*, 22 March 2007.
619 'Karyl Walker: Woolmer strangled?' – *The Jamaica Observer*, 22 March 2007.
620 Jon Pierik and Robert Craddock: ' Betting ring "may have murdered Woolmer"' – *The Australian* on *news.com.au*, 22 March 2007.
621 'Bob Woolmer's death two months later: Two steps forward, several backwards' – *Jamaica Gleaner*, 20 May 2007.
622 Raju Parulekar: '"Dawood gang fixed Pak-Ireland match" says a Mumbai bookie' – *dnaindia.com*, 24 March 2007.
623 PTI: 'Team to leave on Saturday evening - PCB Chief' – *cricinfo.com*, 23 March 2007.
624 'Scotland Yard to probe Woolmer case' – *rediff.com*, 22 March 2007.
625 'Police hunt Woolmer's murderer' – *cricinfo.com*, 23 March 2007.
626 'Pakistan team wants to leave Jamaica' – *rediff.com*, 23 March 2007.
627 Ministry of National Security: 'Coroner's inquest ordered' – 23 March 2007.
628 'Two Pakistani players ordered to stay back in Jamaica' – *zeecric.com*, 24 March 2007.
629 'Suspect held in Woolmer case: Geo TV' – *rediff.com*, 23 March 2007.
630 'Suspect held in Woolmer case: Geo TV' – *rediff.com*, 23 March 2007.
631 'Suspect held in Woolmer case: Geo TV' – *rediff.com*, 23 March 2007.
632 Karyl Walker: 'Coroner's inquest ordered in Woolmer's murder' – *The Jamaica Observer*, 24 March 2007.
633 'Suspect held in Woolmer case: Geo TV' – *rediff.com*, 23 March 2007.
634 'Police hunt Woolmer's murderer' – *cricinfo.com*, 23 March 2007.
635 'Police hunt Woolmer's murderer' – *cricinfo.com*, 23 March 2007.
636 'Two Pakistani players ordered to stay back in Jamaica' – *zeecric.com*, 24 March 2007.
637 'Sussex cricket star quizzed over Woolmer's Death' – *The Argus* (UK), 25 March 2007.
638 Amir Mir: 'Woolmer had a plan to fix match-fixing' – *dnaindia.com*, 23 March 2007.
639 Andrew Alderson, Simon Hart, Philip Sherwell: 'Sad end to cricket pioneer's great innings' – *The Sunday Telegraph*

– Reprinted in the *Cape Argus*, 28 March 2007.
640 Raju Parulekar: '"Dawood gang fixed Pak-Ireland match," says a Mumbai bookie' – *dnaindia.com*, 24 March 2007.
641 Amir Mir: 'Sarfraz indicts betting mafia, blames ICC too' – *dnaindia.com*, 24 March 2007.
642 PTI: 'Was Woolmer going to blow the whistle?' – *dnaindia.com*, 24 March 2007.
643 Andrew Pierce, Nick Hoult and Toby Harnden: 'Woolmer "poisoned and strangled"' – *The Telegraph* (UK), 25 March 2007.
644 'Woolmer murder mystery deepens' – *TimesNow.tv*, 24 March 2007.
645 'Woolmer murder mystery deepens' – *TimesNow.tv*, 24 March 2007.
646 Andrew Pierce, Nick Hoult and Toby Harnden: 'Woolmer "poisoned and strangled"' – *The Telegraph* (UK), 25 March 2007.
647 'Pakistan gone: Top brass quizzed again by cops' – *Jamaica Gleaner*, 25 March 2007.
648 Mark Beckford: '"We're closer!" – Police gather vital evidence in Woolmer case – ICC launches probe into match-fixing allegations' – *Jamaica Gleaner*, 26 March 2007.
649 Paul Henderson, Michael Duffy and Andy Gardner: 'Skipper is quizzed' – *Sunday Mirror* (UK), 25 March 2007.
650 Mike Dickson: 'Pakistan Chief hints at corruption in wake of Woolmer murder' –*The Mail on Sunday* (UK), 26 March 2007.
651 'ECB Chairman: "We're not aware of spot fixing"' – *The Mail on Sunday* (UK), 25 March 2007.
652 Ryan Sabey and Ross Hall: 'Bob knew names of the match fix mafia' – *News of the World* (UK), 25 March 2007.
653 Karyl Walker: '3 Pakistanis quizzed a second time' – *The Jamaica Observer*, 25 March 2007.
654 'Pakistan squad deny Woolmer rift' – *BBC News*, 25 March 2007.
655 Ed Pilkington, Declan Walsh and Karen McVeigh: 'Murder in Room 374: CCTV cameras may hold key to Woolmer inquiry, say police' – *The Guardian* (UK), 26 March 2007.
656 Ed Pilkington, Declan Walsh and Karen McVeigh: 'Murder in Room 374: CCTV cameras may hold key to Woolmer inquiry, say police' – *The Guardian* (UK), 26 March 2007.
657 Ed Pilkington, Declan Walsh and Karen McVeigh: 'Murder in Room 374: CCTV cameras may hold key to Woolmer inquiry, say police' – *The Guardian* (UK), 26 March 2007.
658 Ed Pilkington, Declan Walsh and Karen McVeigh: 'Murder in Room 374: CCTV cameras may hold key to Woolmer inquiry, say police' – *The Guardian* (UK), 26 March 2007.
659 AFP: 'Injury after insult: Bookie claims India-Bangladesh tie was fixed' – *Indian Express*, 26 March 2007.
660 Andy Clarke: 'PCB: Woolmer was to retire' – *skysports.com*, 26 March 2007.
661 Bloomberg News: 'Cricket: Police deny report on Woolmer killing suspects' – *International Herald Tribune*, 27 March 2007.
662 PTI: 'Coroner gets report' – *The Telegraph* (Calcutta), 30 March 2007.
663 Tim Reid: 'Breakthrough on Woolmer inquiry images' – *The Times* (UK), 29 March 2007.
664 'Police dismiss speculation about second autopsy' – *cricinfo.com*, 28 March 2007.
665 Tim Reid: 'Breakthrough on Woolmer inquiry images' – *The Times* (UK), 29 March 2007.
666 Jon Pierik: 'Conflicting Claims on Woolmer' – *Adelaide Now*, 30 March 2007.
667 'CCTV catches 2 men entering Bob's room' – *The Pioneer*, 27 March 2007.
668 'CCTV catches 2 men entering Bob's room' – *The Pioneer*, 27 March 2007.
669 Tim Reid: 'Breakthrough on Woolmer inquiry images' – *The Times* (UK), 29 March 2007.
670 Tim Reid: 'Breakthrough on Woolmer inquiry images' – *The Times* (UK), 29 March 2007.
671 Staff and agencies: 'Woolmer may not have been murdered claims PCB official' – *The Guardian* (UK), 28 March 2007.
672 Jon Pierik: 'Conflicting claims on Woolmer' – *Adelaide Now*, 30 March 2007.
673 Daraine Luton: 'Woolmer documents sent to coroner' – *Jamaica Gleaner*, 29 March 2007.
674 Tim Reid: 'Pathologist standing by his

verdict on Woolmer' – *The Times* (UK), 29 March 2007.
675 Jon Pierik: 'Conflicting claims on Woolmer' – *Adelaide Now*, 30 March 2007.
676 'Jamaican police hunt for a bookie' – *Deccan Chronicle*, 30 March 2007.
677 Glenroy Sinclair: 'Scotland Yard called in - Team to review Woolmer investigation - Will work alongside Operation Kingfish' – *Jamaica Gleaner*, 31 March 2007.
678 Tim Reid: 'Scotland Yard called in as cricket murder police struggle to cope' – *The Times* (UK), 31 March 2007.
679 PTI: 'Enter a high-profile sleuth' – *The Statesman* (IND), 3 April 2007.
680 Tim Reid: 'Scotland Yard called in as cricket murder police struggle to cope' – *The Times* (UK), 31 March 2007.
681 'New theory on Talat move' – *The Telegraph* (Calcutta), 30 March 2007.
682 Cole Moreton: 'Pakistani players suspended after Woolmer death' – *The Independent* (UK), 1 April 2007.
683 Andy Gardner, Grant Hodgson: ' Bob was poisoned' – *Sunday Mirror* (UK), 1 April 2007.
684 'Dark side of the coin' – *Jamaica Gleaner*, 1 April 2007.
685 Oliver Harvey: 'Woolmer: Hunt for 5 bookies' – *The Sun* (UK), 6 April 2007.
686 Bruce Loudon: 'Religion blamed for Pakistan's Cup failure' – *The Australian*, 9 April 2007.
687 *News24/AP*: Woolmer: No breakthrough' – *news24.com*, 11 April 2007.
688 Martin Rose and agencies: 'Lara to sign off from one-day game' – *The Guardian* (UK), 11 April 2007.
689 'Woolmer murder inquest starts April 23' – *The Jamaica Observer*, 12 April 2007.
690 Statement by Commissioner of Jamaican Police, Lucius Thomas at Police Officer's Club, Kingston, 12 June 2007.
691 Jacqui Goddard: 'Woolmer tests support poison theory' – *The Times* (UK), 16 April 2007.
692 Jacqui Goddard: 'Woolmer tests support poison theory' – *The Times* (UK), 16 April 2007.
693 Jacqui Goddard: 'Woolmer tests support poison theory' – *The Times* (UK), 16 April 2007.
694 Steven Swinford and Jonathan Calvert: 'Woolmer was poisoned and strangled' – *The Sunday Times* (UK), 15 April 2007.
695 Daraine Luton and Glenroy Sinclair: '"Foreign substance" found in Woolmer's system' – *Jamaica Gleaner*, 17 April 2007.
696 Steven Swinford and Jonathan Calvert: 'Woolmer was poisoned and strangled' – *The Sunday Times* (UK), 15 April 2007.
697 Justin Penrose: 'Woolmer: He was murdered' – *Sunday Mirror* (UK), 15 April 2007.
698 Steven Swinford and Jonathan Calvert: 'Woolmer was poisoned and strangled' – *The Sunday Times* (UK), 15 April 2007.
699 Mark Townsend: 'Met officers fly home as Woolmer inquiry falters' – *The Observer* (UK), 15 April 2007.
700 Mark Townsend: 'Met officers fly home as Woolmer inquiry falters' – *The Observer* (UK), 15 April 2007.
701 Cahal Milmo: 'Breakthrough as Woolmer suspect is caught on camera' – *The Independent* (UK), 21 April 2007.
702 Jacqui Goddard: 'Woolmer tests support poison theory' – *The Times* (UK), 16 April 2007.
703 Daraine Luton and Glenroy Sinclair: '"Foreign substance" found in Woolmer's system' – *Jamaica Gleaner*, 17 April 2007.
704 Ministry of Justice: 'Restrictions announced for coroner's inquest into Woolmer's death' – Jamaican Information Service, 20 April 2007.
705 Agencies: 'Inzamam, Younis, Mushtaq to return to West Indies?: Woolmer death investigations' – *Dawn* (PAK), 20 April 2007.
706 'Irish give DNA to Woolmer police' – *BBC News*, 19 April 2007.
707 Ross Sheil: 'Woolmer's coroner's inquest postponed' – *Jamaica Gleaner*, 20 April 2007.
708 Mike Sullivan: 'Potter drug did kill Woolmer' – *The Sun* (UK), 20 April 2007.
709 *News24/SAPA*: 'No Pakistan match-fixing' - 20 April 2007.
710 Khalid Hussain: 'Talat to act as interim coach' – *cricinfo.com*, 20 April 2007.
711 Cahal Milmo: 'Breakthrough as Woolmer murder suspect is caught on camera' – *The Independent* (UK), 21 April 2007.
712 'Bennet King resigns as West Indies coach' – *cricinfo.com*, 23 April 2007.
713 *AP*: 'Woolmer's body released' – *Herald Sun*, 24 April 2007.
714 *Sapa-AP*: 'Jamaican cops to travel with Woolmer's body' – *iol.co.za*, 26 April 2007.

715 Ross Sheil: 'Woolmer's body to leave for South Africa today' – *Jamaica Gleaner*, 26 April 2007.
716 Andrew Selsky: 'Lead investigator in killing of World Cup coach does not confirm drugging' - *USA Today*, 30 April 2007.
717 Catherine Elsworth: 'New doubts cast on Woolmer "murder"' – *The Telegraph* (UK), 10 May 2007.
718 Steven Swinford and Jonathan Calvert: 'Woolmer was "poisoned by weed killer"' – *The Sunday Times* (UK), 6 May 2007.
719 Agencies: 'Mushtaq gifted champagne bottles to Woolmer: Mir' – *Dawn* (PAK), 10 May 2007.
720 "It wasn't Murder!' Scotland Yard says Bob Woolmer died Of heart failure' – *Jamaica Gleaner*, 13 May 2007.
721 Stewart Tendler: 'Bob Woolmer was not strangled Home Office pathologist decides' – *The Times* (UK), 15 May 2007.
722 'Woolmer case a woolly affair' – *Jamaica Gleaner*, 15 May 2007.
723 Mike Behr: 'Woolmer did not have enemies – Shields' – *Cape Argus*, 18 May 2007.
724 Steven Swinford and Jonathan Calvert: 'Bungles led to Woolmer murder claim' – *The Sunday Times* (UK), 20 May 2007.
725 Deepa Seetharaman and Melanie Peters: Cops in big bungle' – *Daily Mail* and *Sunday Telegraph* (UK), Published in *Cape Argus*, 3 June 2007.
726 Steven Swinford: 'Pathologist urged to quit after Woolmer blunder' – *The Sunday Times* (UK), 3 June 2007.
727 'Bob Woolmer's death probe - No pathology report from Scotland Yard – JCF' – *Jamaica Gleaner*, 3 June 2007.
728 'Local cop confirms Woolmer wasn't slain' – *Jamaica Gleaner*, 4 June 2007.
729 'Pakistan outrage over Woolmer investigation' – *Daily Mail* (UK), 7 June 2007.
730 'Woolmer's death a cover-up' – *TimesNow.tv*, 10 June 2007.
731 Statement by Commissioner of Jamaican Police Lucius Thomas at Police Officers' Club, Kingston, 12 June 2007.
732 Osman Samiuddin: 'PCB says legal action unlikely' – *cricinfo.com*, 12 June 2007.
733 Karyl Walker: 'Pathologist insists Woolmer murdered' – *The Jamaica Observer*, 13 June 2007.
734 'No intentions to take legal action against Jamaican police: Naseem Ashraf' – *Pak Tribune*, 14 June 2007.
735 'Lara set for cricket U-turn' – *The News Today* (BDESH), 14 June 2007.